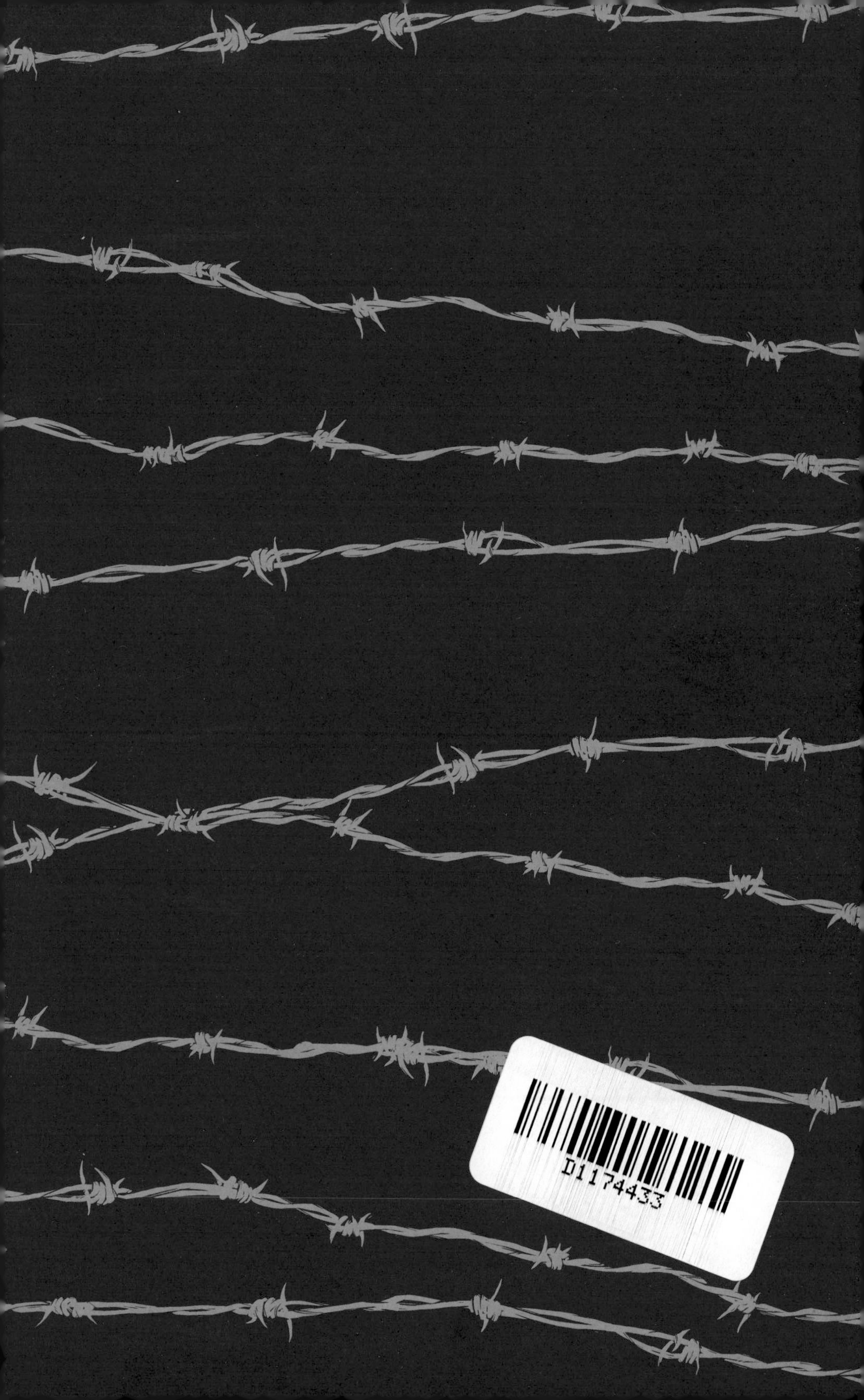

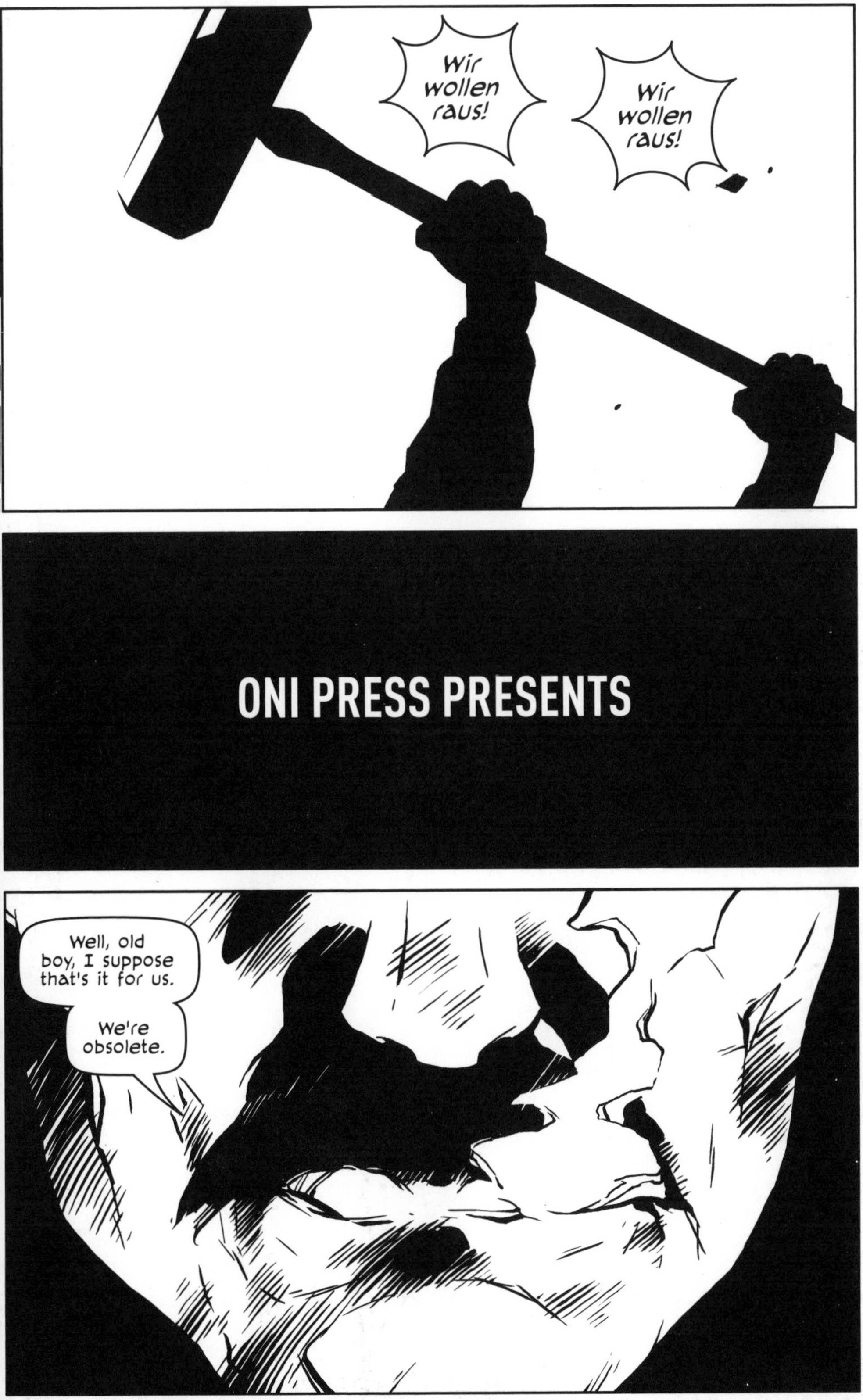
Wir wollen raus!
Wir wollen raus!
ONI PRESS PRESENTS
Well, old boy, I suppose that's it for us.
We're obsolete.

Kommen!
Schnell, schnell!
A GRAPHIC NOVEL
I suppose now I'll have to go home.

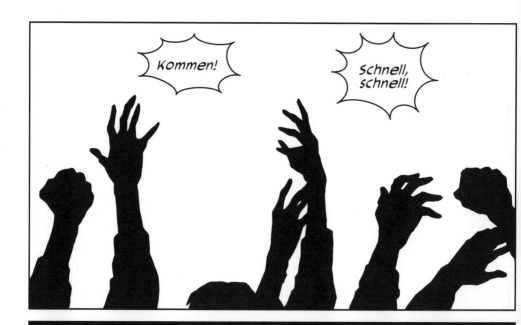

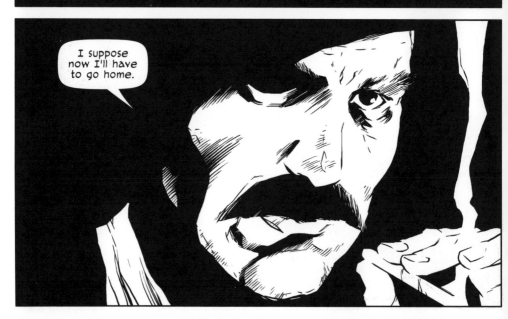

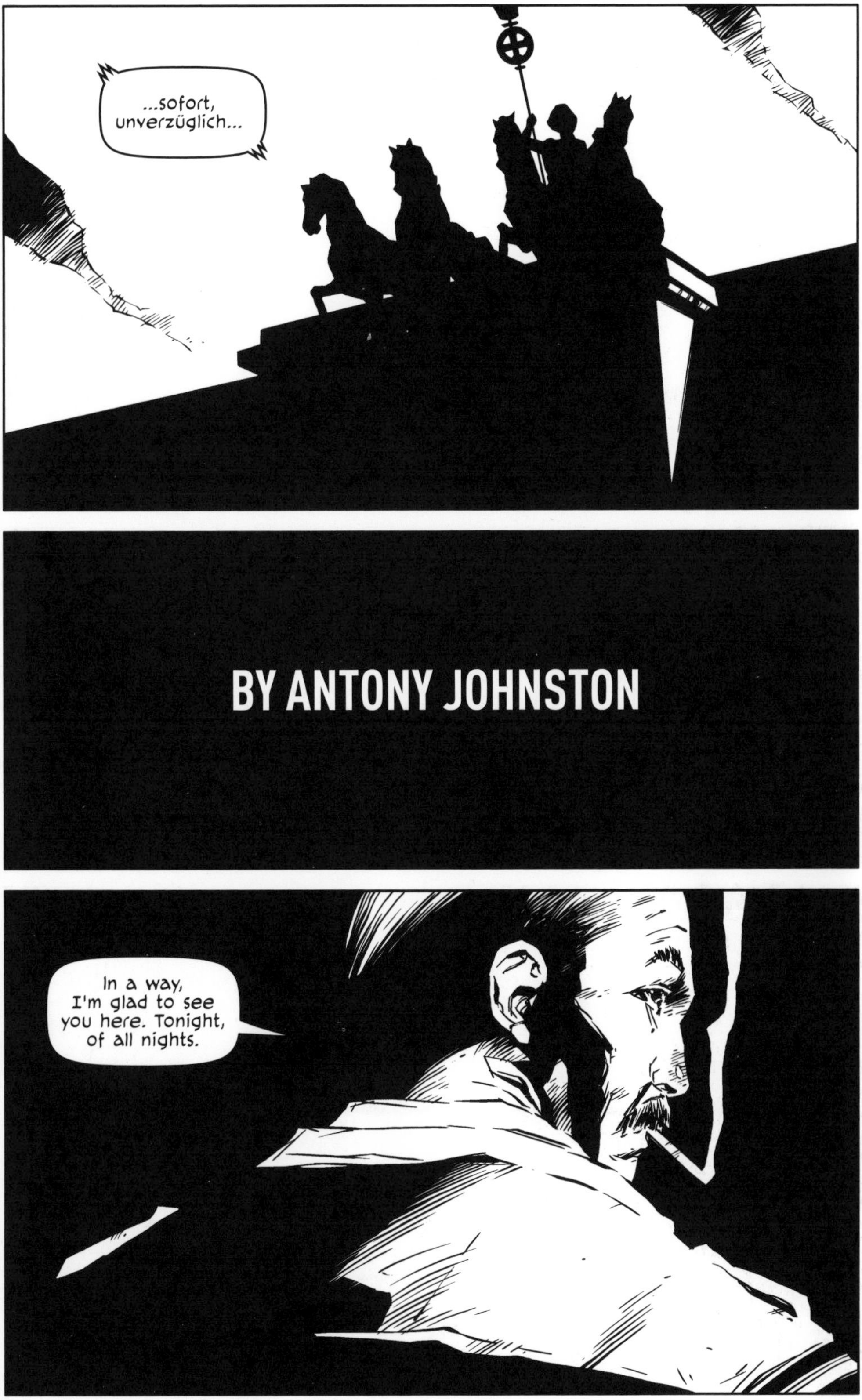
...sofort, unverzüglich...
BY ANTONY JOHNSTON
In a way, I'm glad to see you here. Tonight, of all nights.

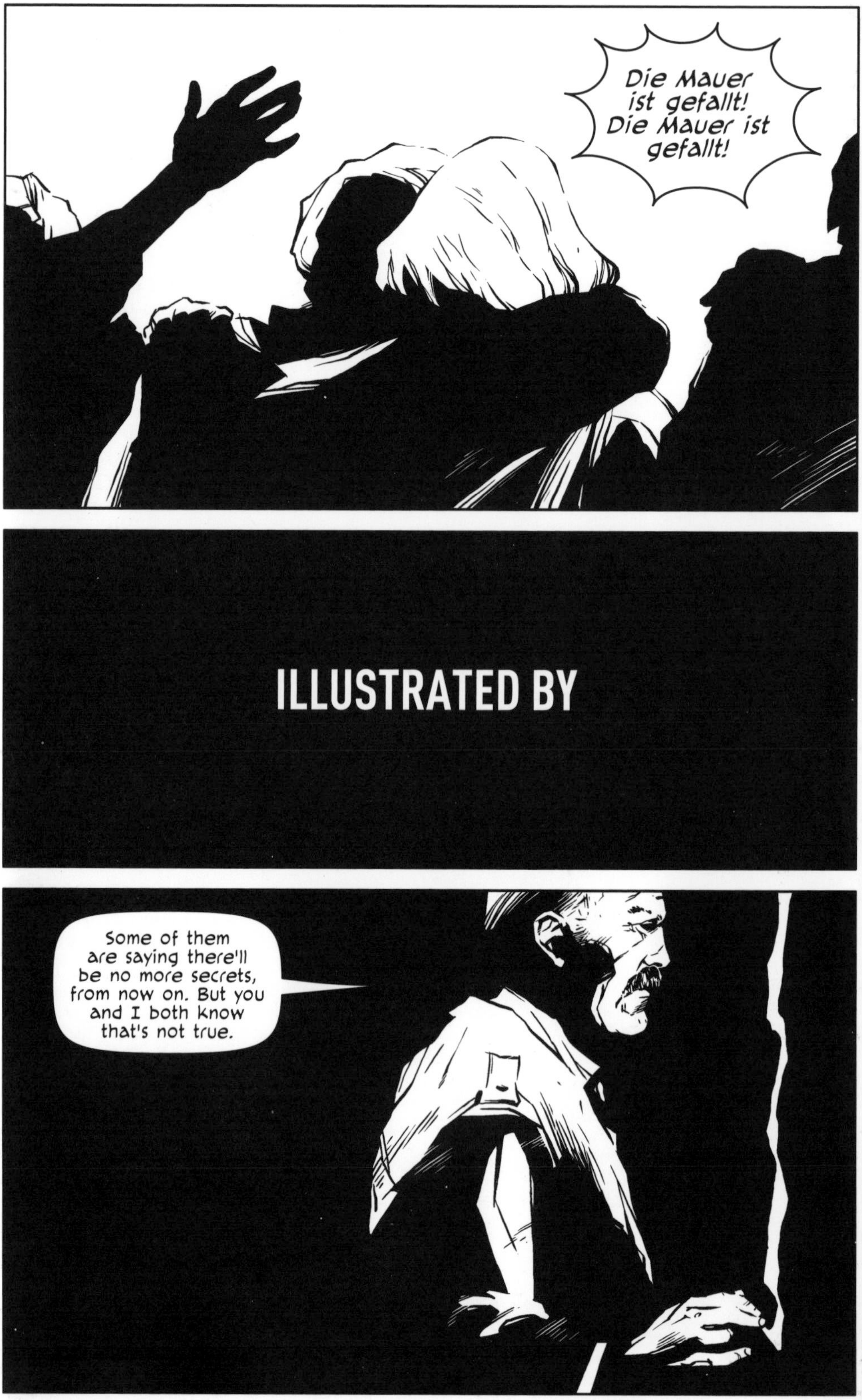
Die Mauer ist gefallt! Die Mauer ist gefallt!
ILLUSTRATED BY
Some of them are saying there'll be no more secrets, from now on. But you and I both know that's not true.

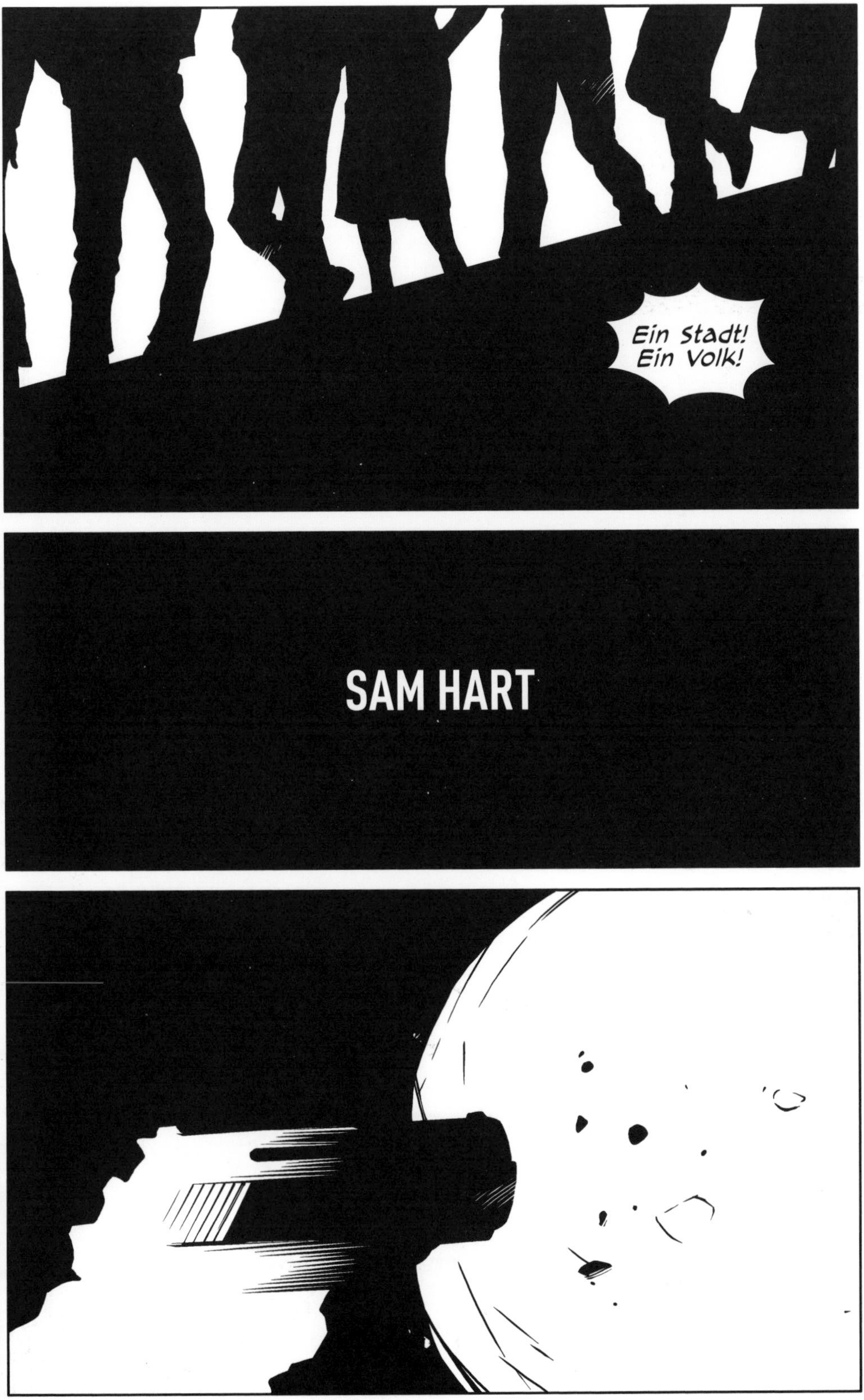
Ein Stadt!
Ein Volk!
SAM HART

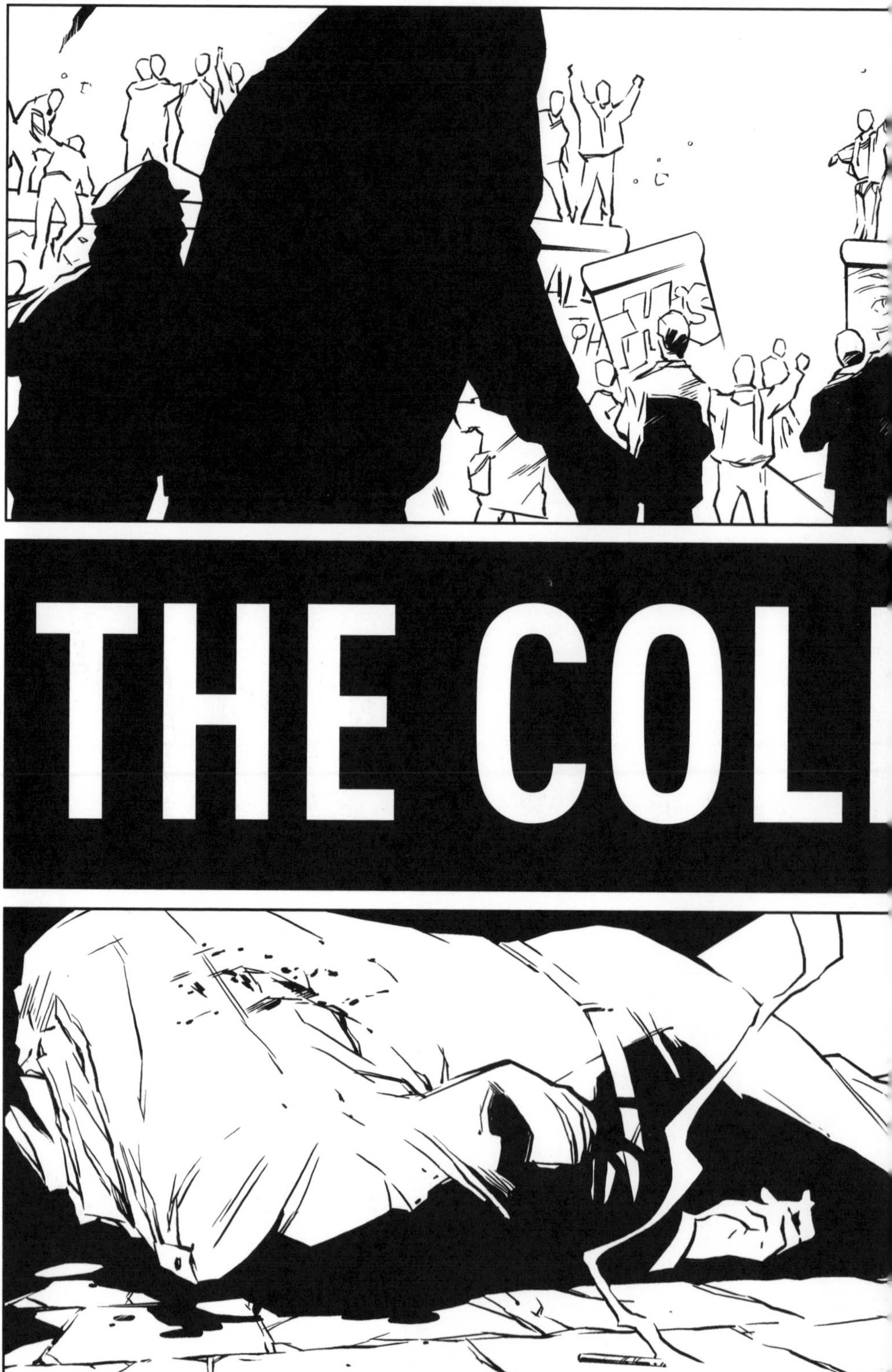
THE COL

EST CITY

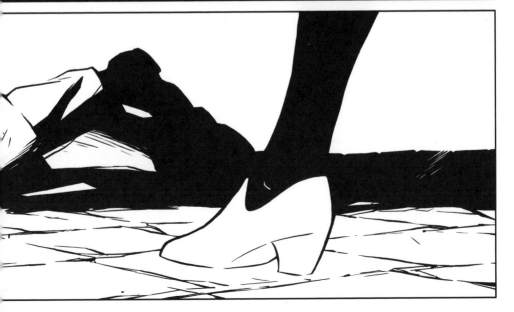

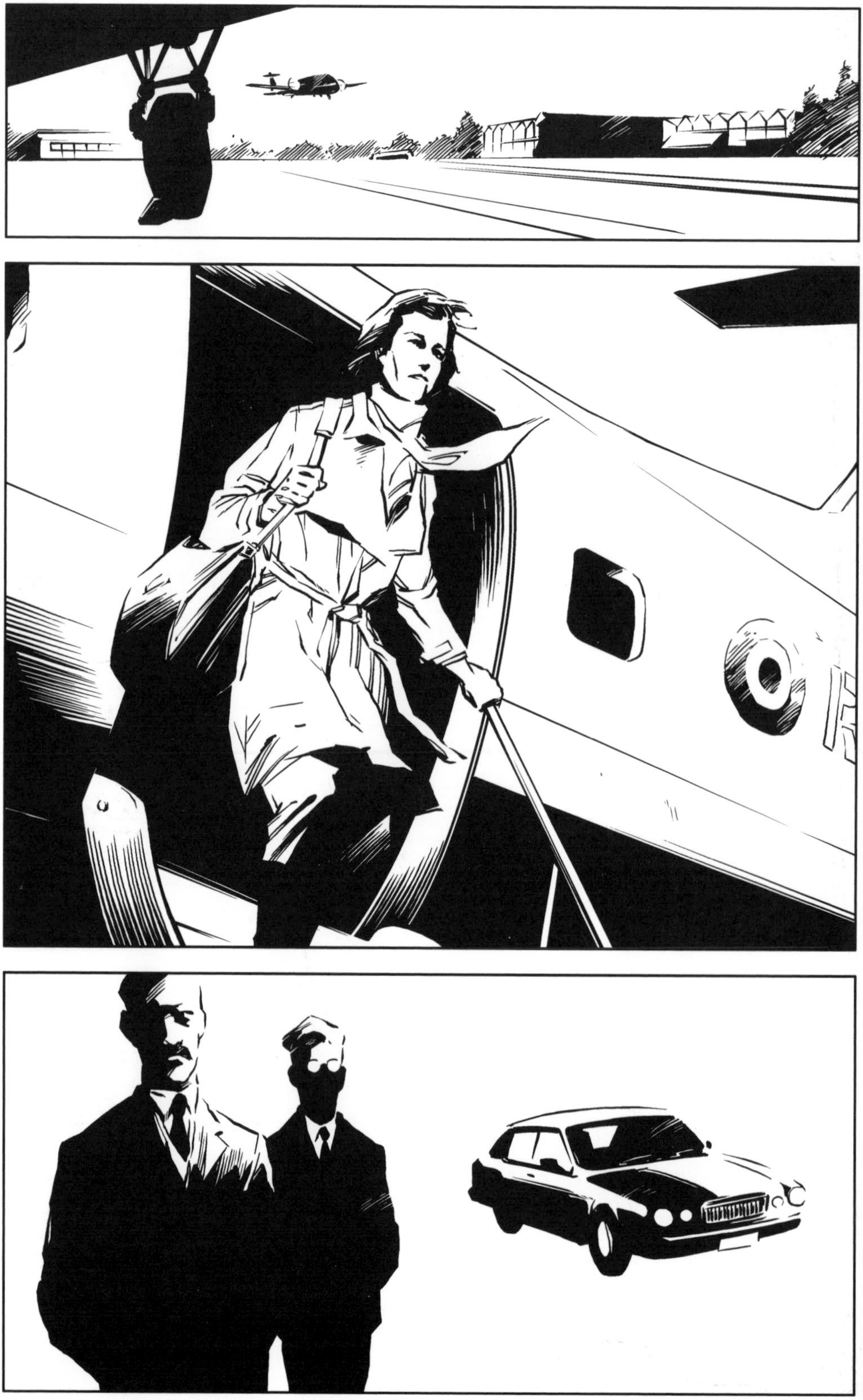

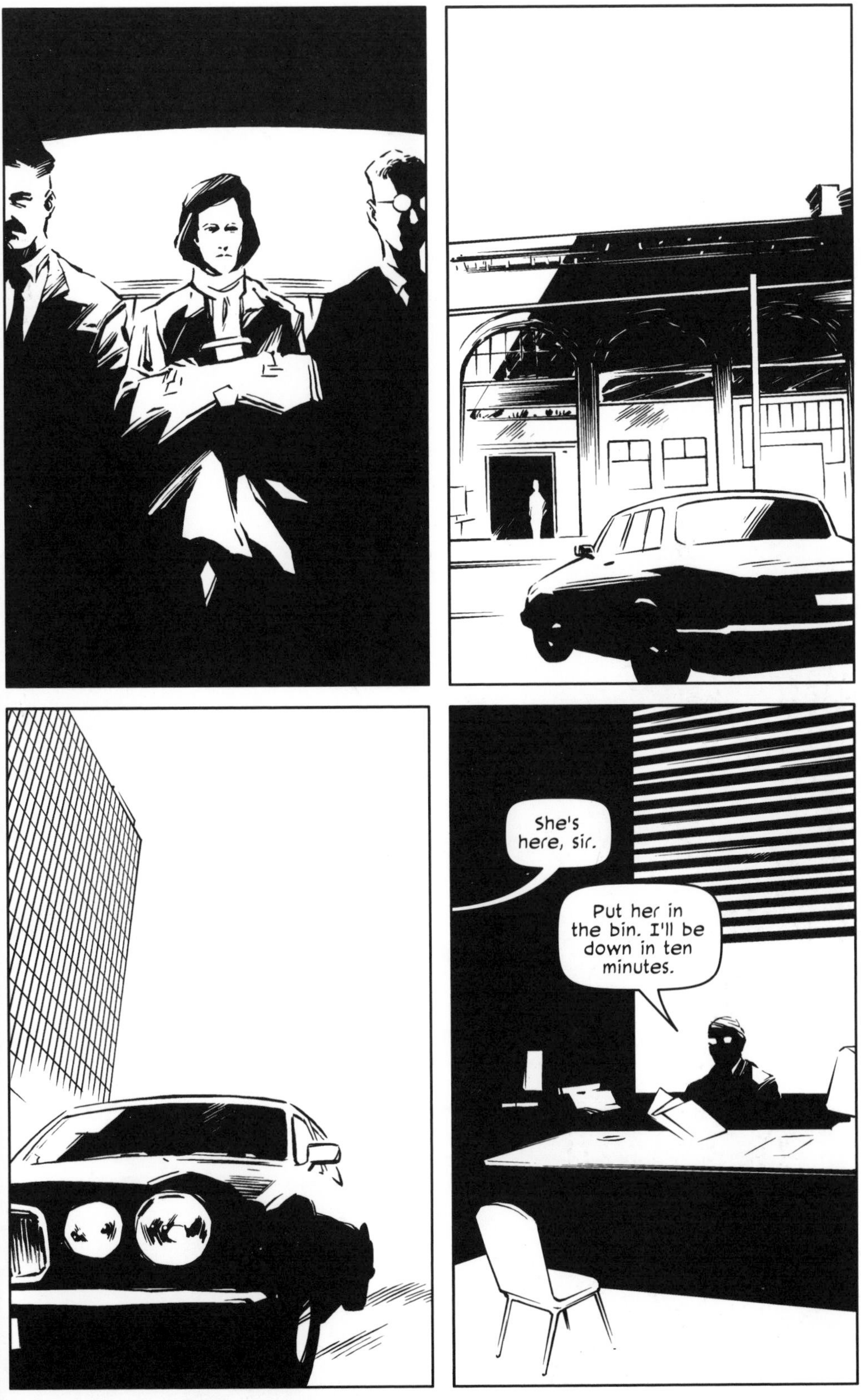
She's here, sir.
Put her in the bin. I'll be down in ten minutes.

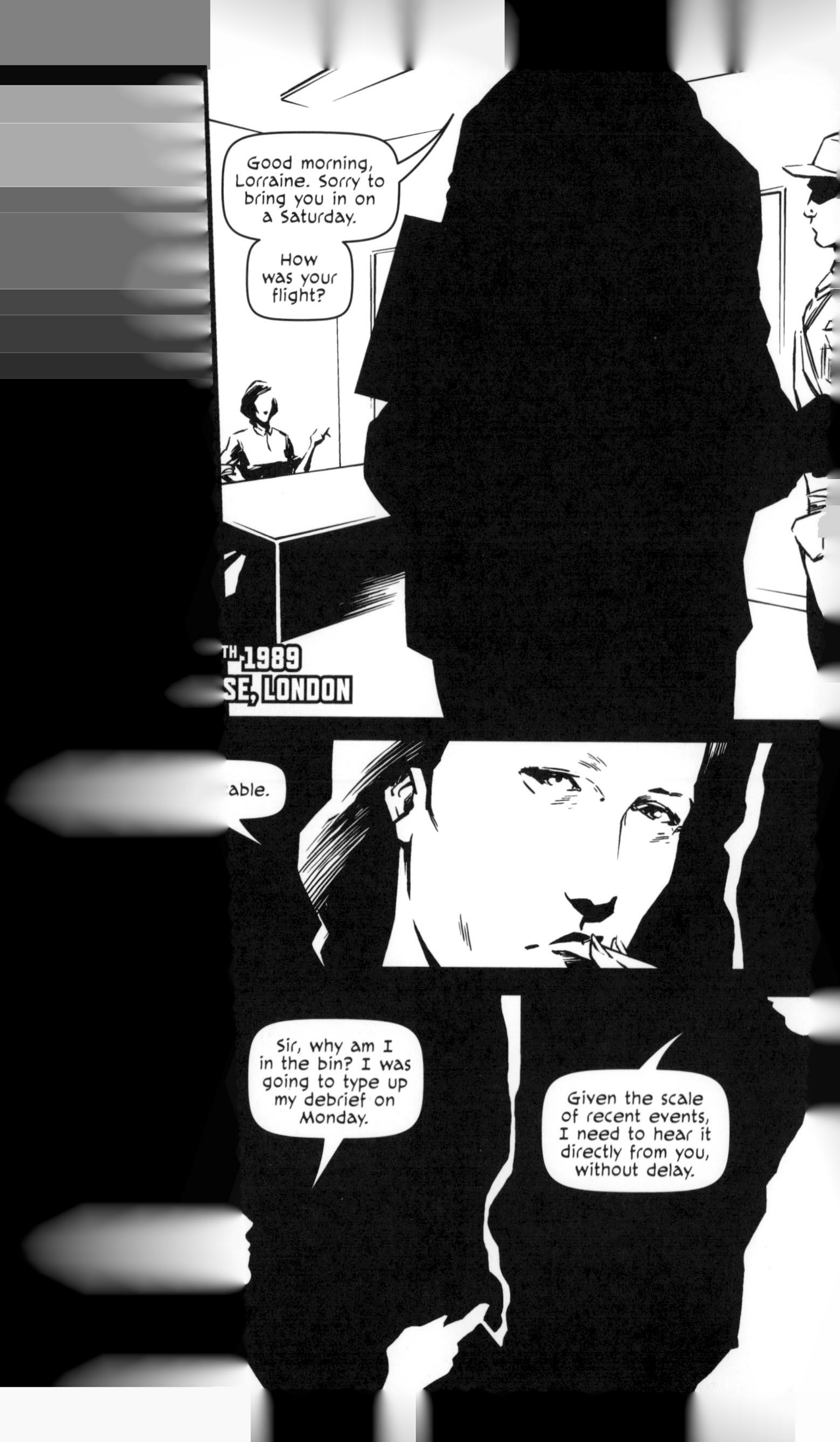

Good morning, Lorraine. Sorry to bring you in on a Saturday.
How was your flight?
Sir, why am I in the bin? I was going to type up my debrief on Monday.
Given the scale of recent events, I need to hear it directly from you, without delay.

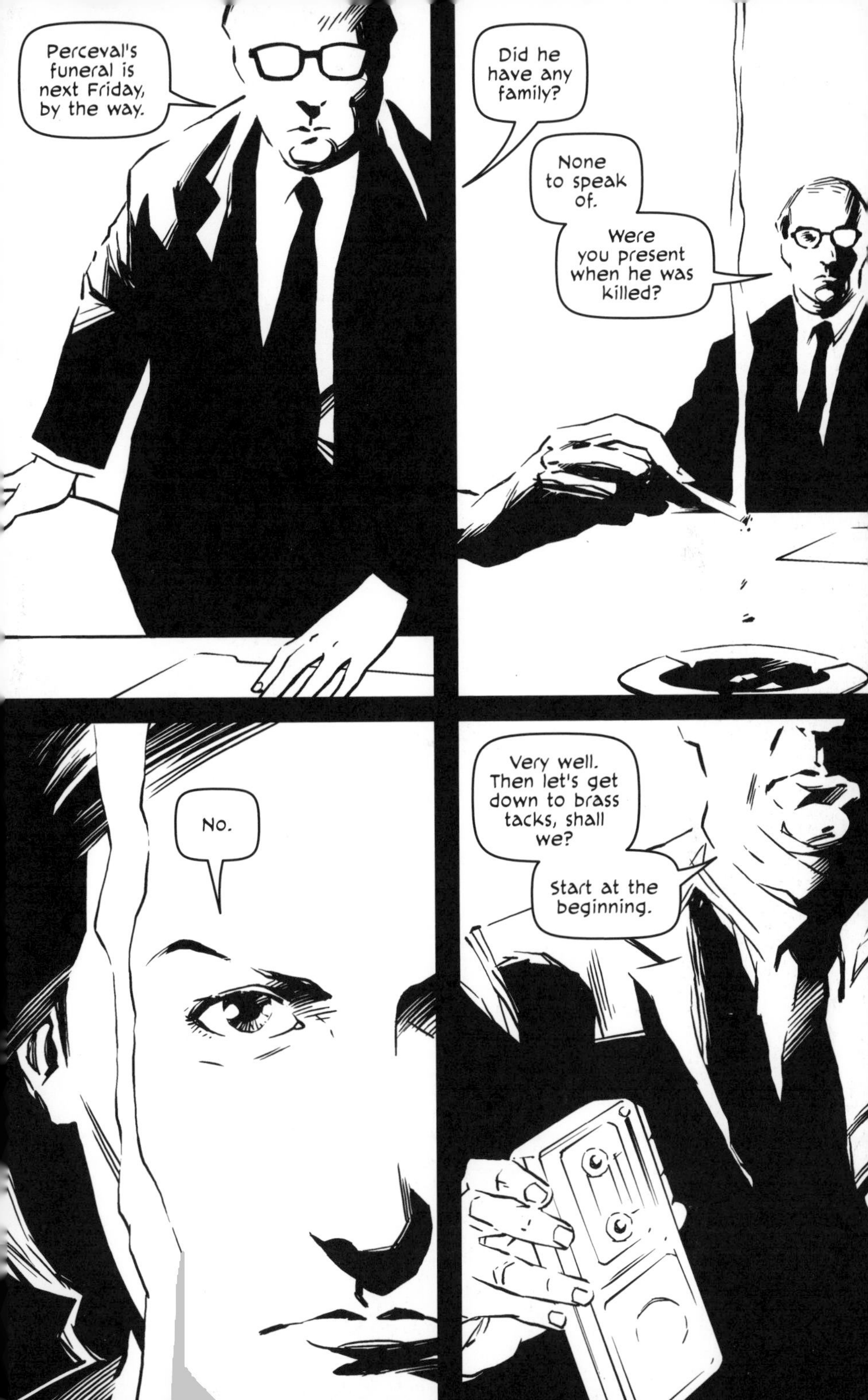
Perceval's funeral is next Friday, by the way.
Did he have any family?
None to speak of.
Were you present when he was killed?
No.
Very well. Then let's get down to brass tacks, shall we?
Start at the beginning.

H/BER will *see* you now.

OCTOBER 28TH 1989
CENTURY HOUSE

Ah, Lorraine. Long time no see, and all that. Sorry to bring you in on a Saturday.

It's fine, sir.

You know C, of course.

Oh. Yes, yes of course.

Sit down, Broughton.

I'll get straight to the point. How well do you know BER-2, James Gascoine?

Not very well. Enough to say hello, but we don't move in the same circles.

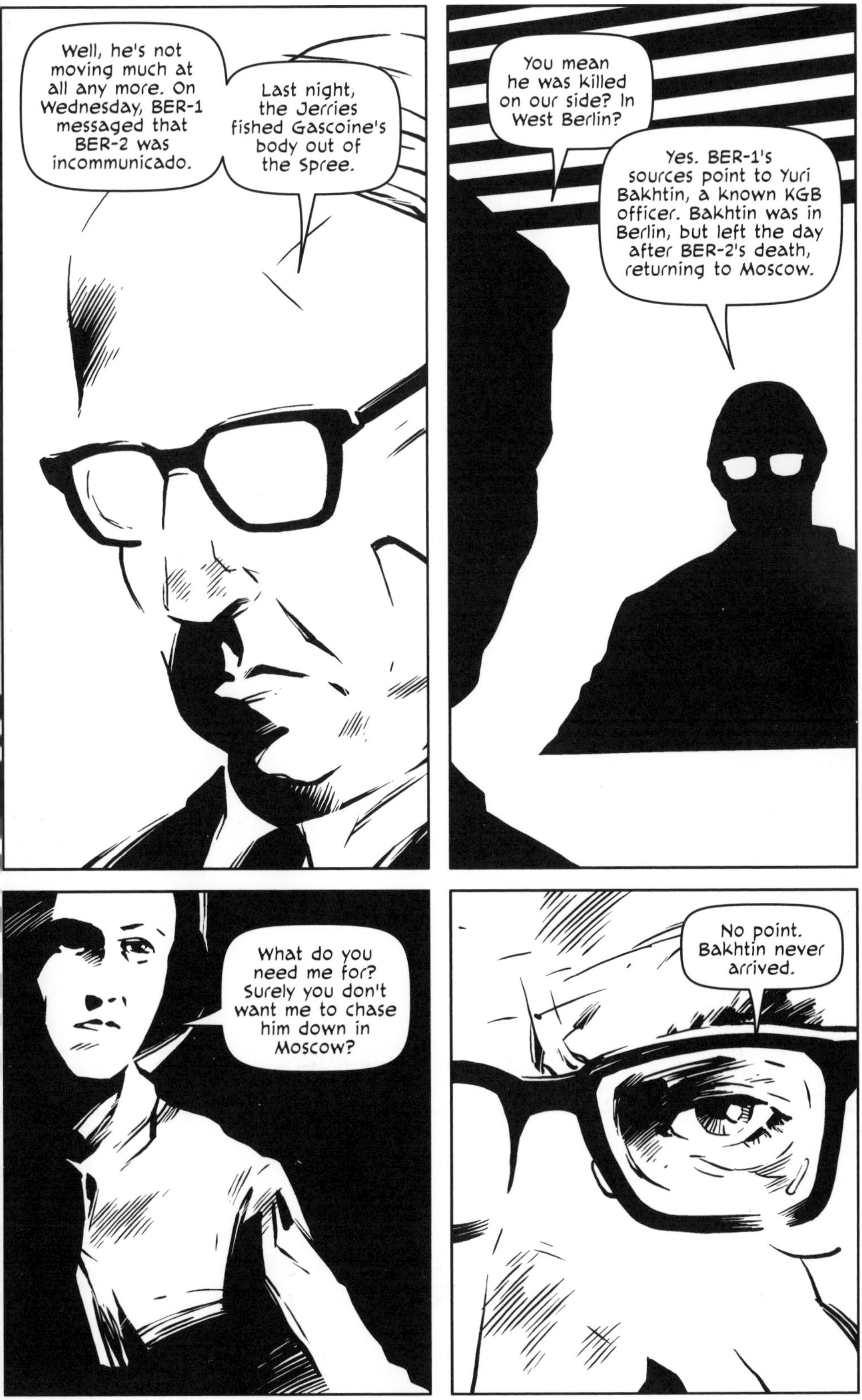
Well, he's not moving much at all any more. On Wednesday, BER-1 messaged that BER-2 was incommunicado.
Last night, the Jerries fished Gascoine's body out of the Spree.
You mean he was killed on our side? In West Berlin?
Yes. BER-1's sources point to Yuri Bakhtin, a known KGB officer. Bakhtin was in Berlin, but left the day after BER-2's death, returning to Moscow.
What do you need me for? Surely you don't want me to chase him down in Moscow?
No point. Bakhtin never arrived.

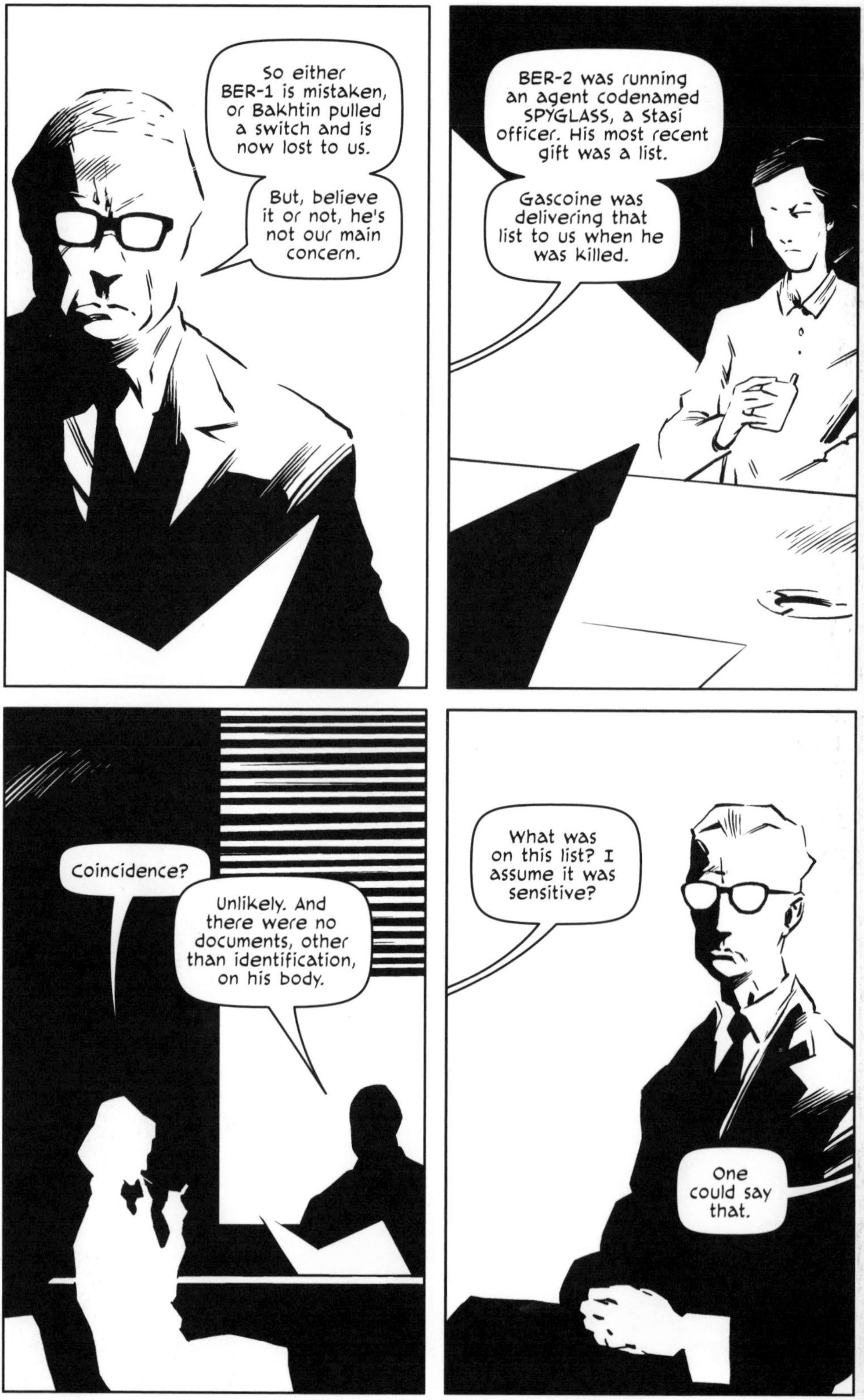
So either BER-1 is mistaken, or Bakhtin pulled a switch and is now lost to us.
But, believe it or not, he's not our main concern.
BER-2 was running an agent codenamed SPYGLASS, a Stasi officer. His most recent gift was a list.
Gascoine was delivering that list to us when he was killed.
Coincidence?
Unlikely. And there were no documents, other than identification, on his body.
What was on this list? I assume it was sensitive?
One could say that.

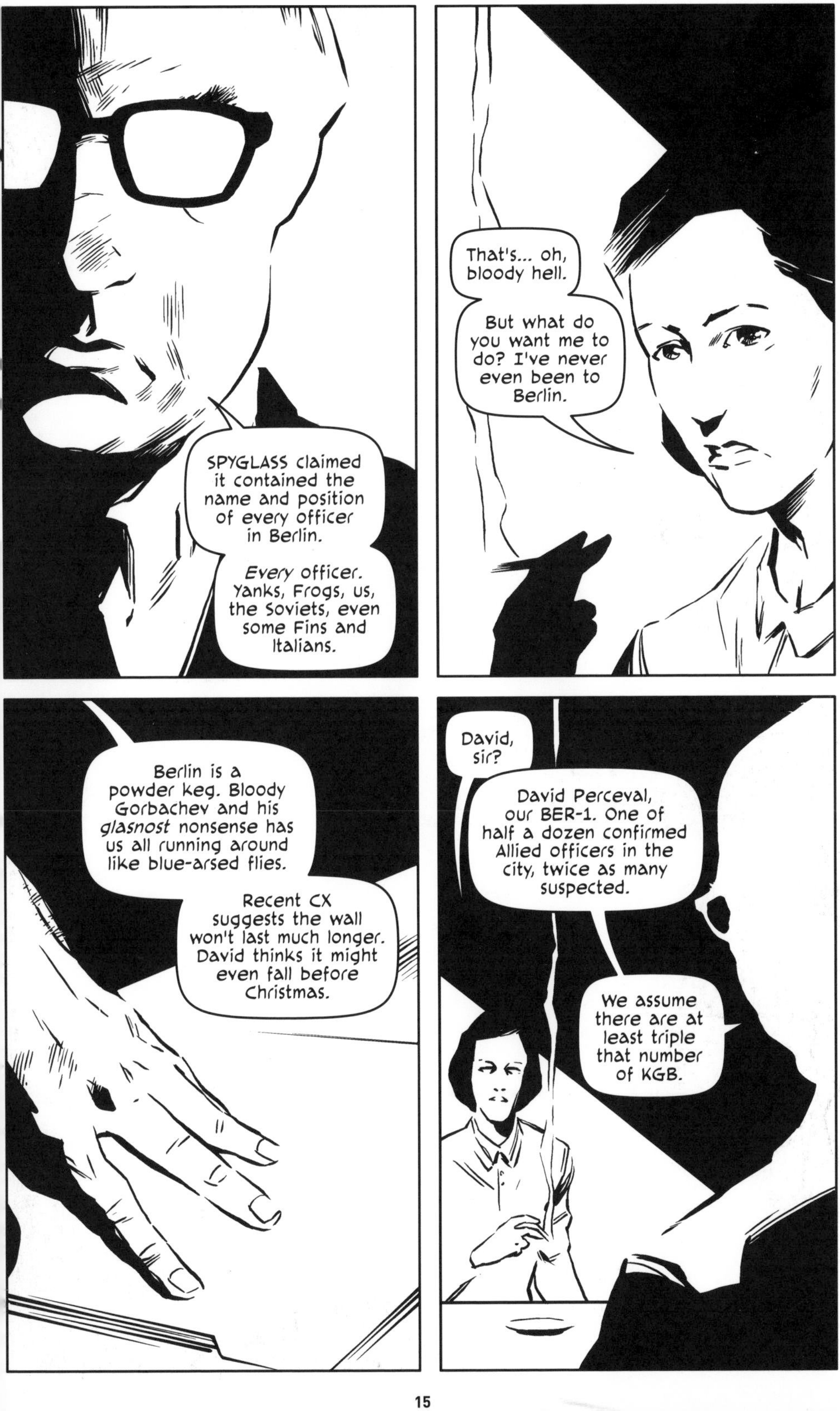
SPYGLASS claimed it contained the name and position of every officer in Berlin.
Every officer. Yanks, Frogs, us, the Soviets, even some Fins and Italians.
That's... oh, bloody hell.
But what do you want me to do? I've never even been to Berlin.
Berlin is a powder keg. Bloody Gorbachev and his *glasnost* nonsense has us all running around like blue-arsed flies.
Recent CX suggests the wall won't last much longer. David thinks it might even fall before Christmas.
David, sir?
David Perceval, our BER-1. One of half a dozen confirmed Allied officers in the city, twice as many suspected.
We assume there are at least triple that number of KGB.

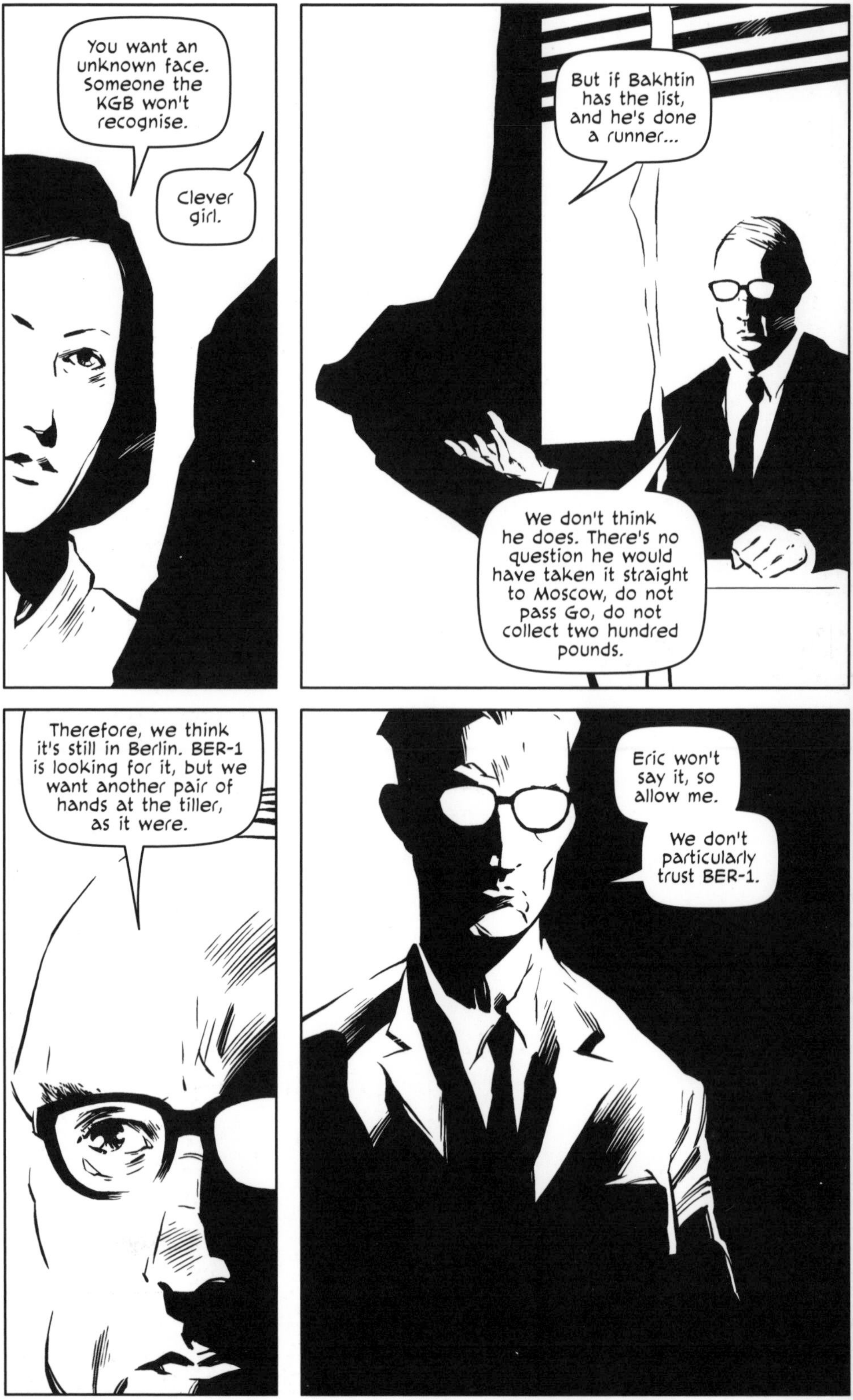
You want an unknown face. Someone the KGB won't recognise.
Clever girl.
But if Bakhtin has the list, and he's done a runner...
We don't think he does. There's no question he would have taken it straight to Moscow, do not pass Go, do not collect two hundred pounds.
Therefore, we think it's still in Berlin. BER-1 is looking for it, but we want another pair of hands at the tiller, as it were.
Eric won't say it, so allow me.
We don't particularly trust BER-1.

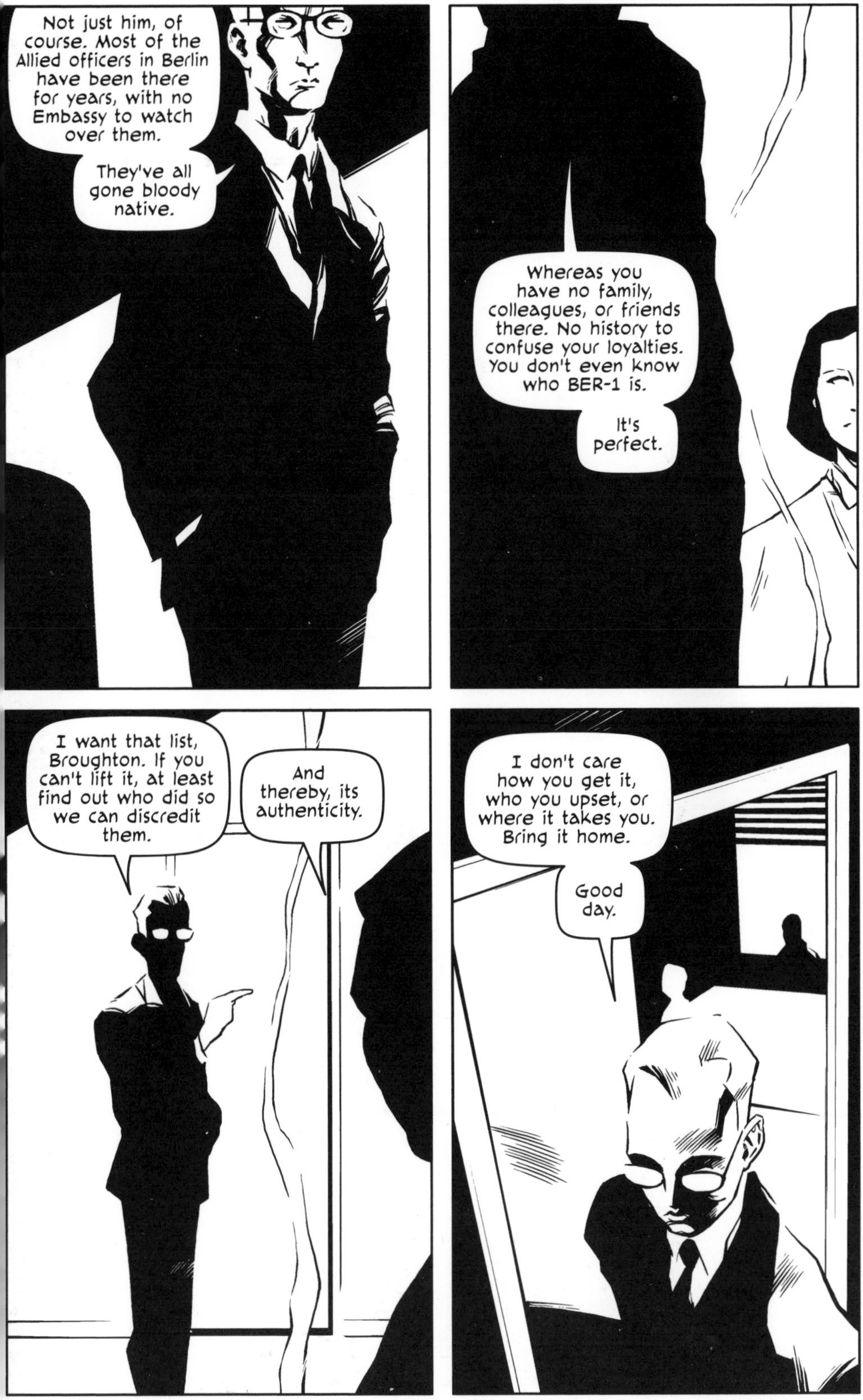
Not just him, of course. Most of the Allied officers in Berlin have been there for years, with no Embassy to watch over them.
They've all gone bloody native.
Whereas you have no family, colleagues, or friends there. No history to confuse your loyalties. You don't even know who BER-1 is.
It's perfect.
I want that list, Broughton. If you can't lift it, at least find out who did so we can discredit them.
And thereby, its authenticity.
I don't care how you get it, who you upset, or where it takes you. Bring it home.
Good day.

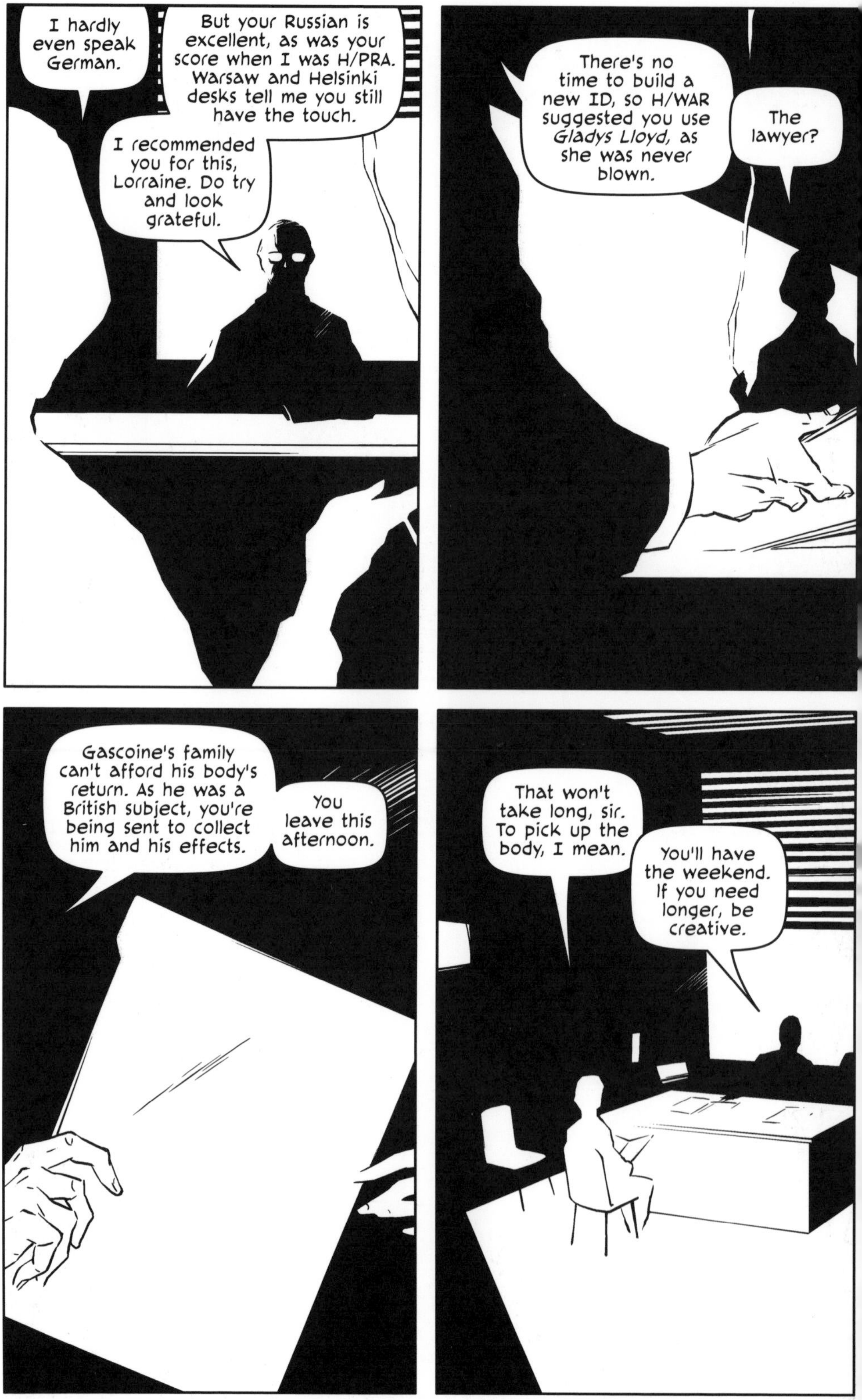
I hardly even speak German.
But your Russian is excellent, as was your score when I was H/PRA. Warsaw and Helsinki desks tell me you still have the touch.
I recommended you for this, Lorraine. Do try and look grateful.
There's no time to build a new ID, so H/WAR suggested you use *Gladys Lloyd,* as she was never blown.
The lawyer?
Gascoine's family can't afford his body's return. As he was a British subject, you're being sent to collect him and his effects.
You leave this afternoon.
That won't take long, sir. To pick up the body, I mean.
You'll have the weekend. If you need longer, be creative.

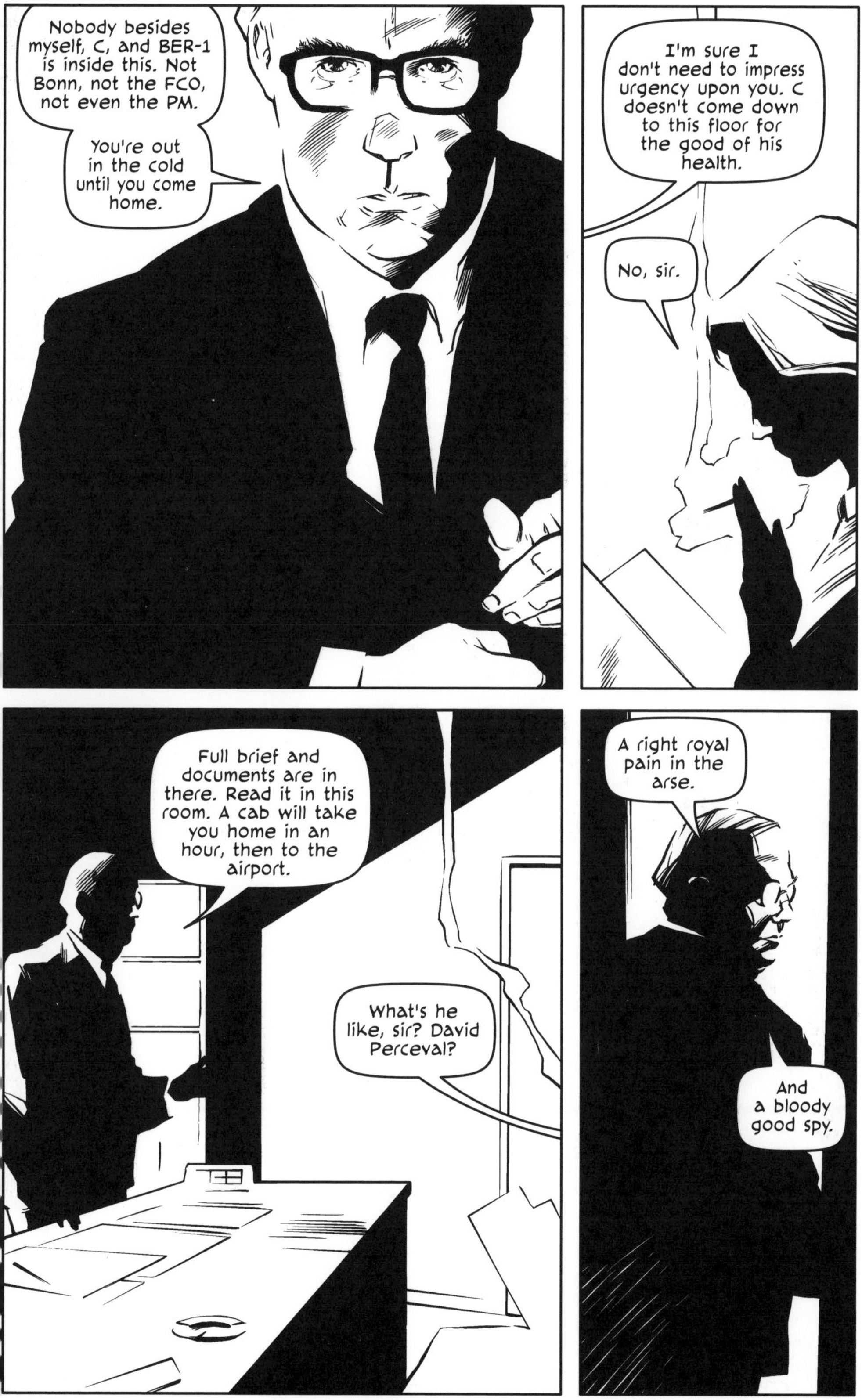
Nobody besides myself, C, and BER-1 is inside this. Not Bonn, not the FCO, not even the PM.
You're out in the cold until you come home.
I'm sure I don't need to impress urgency upon you. C doesn't come down to this floor for the good of his health.
No, sir.
Full brief and documents are in there. Read it in this room. A cab will take you home in an hour, then to the airport.
What's he like, sir? David Perceval?
A right royal pain in the arse.
And a bloody good spy.

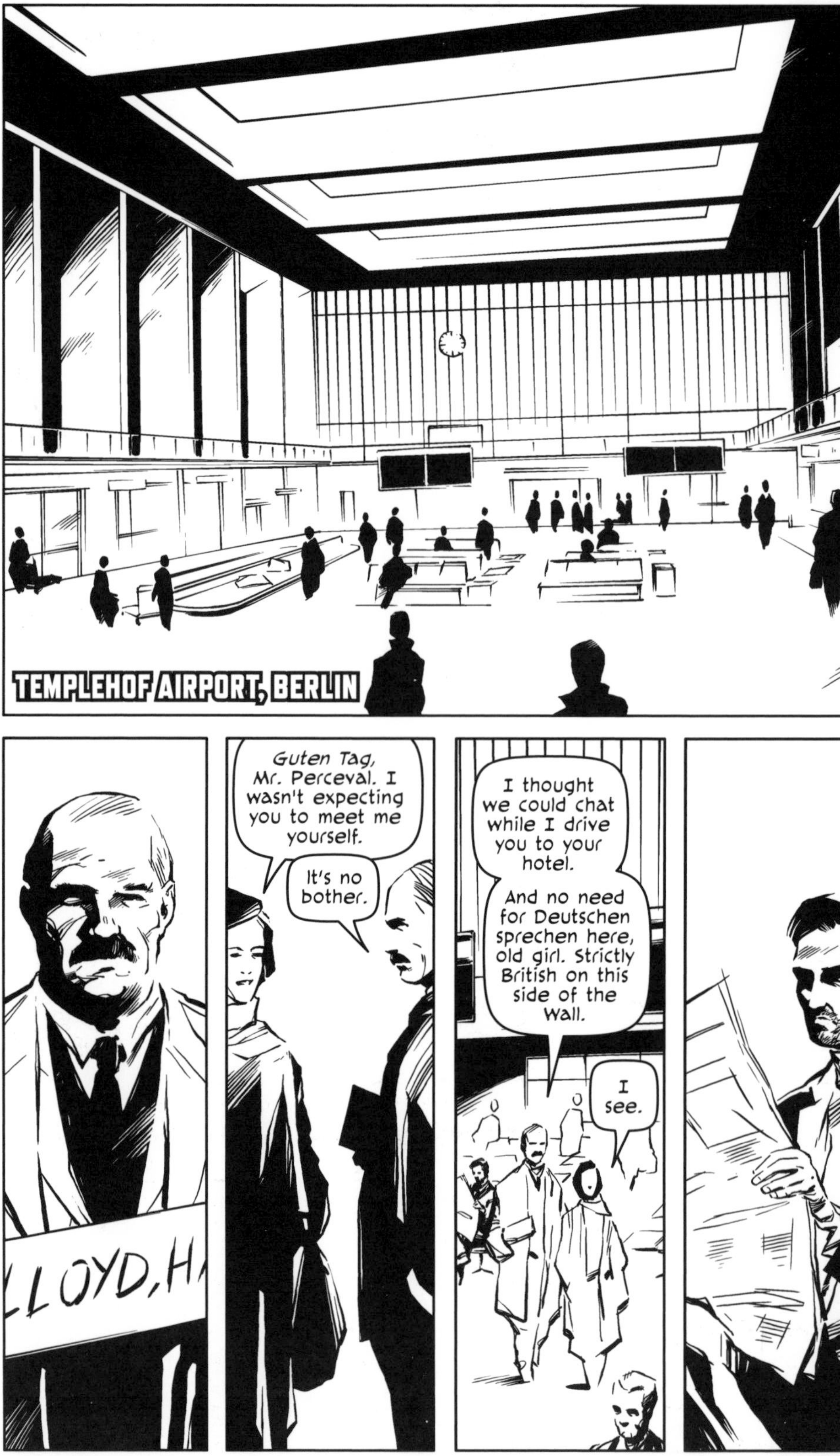

TEMPLEHOF AIRPORT, BERLIN
LLOYD,H
Guten Tag, Mr. Perceval. I wasn't expecting you to meet me yourself.
It's no bother.
I thought we could chat while I drive you to your hotel.
And no need for Deutschen sprechen here, old girl. Strictly British on this side of the Wall.
I see.

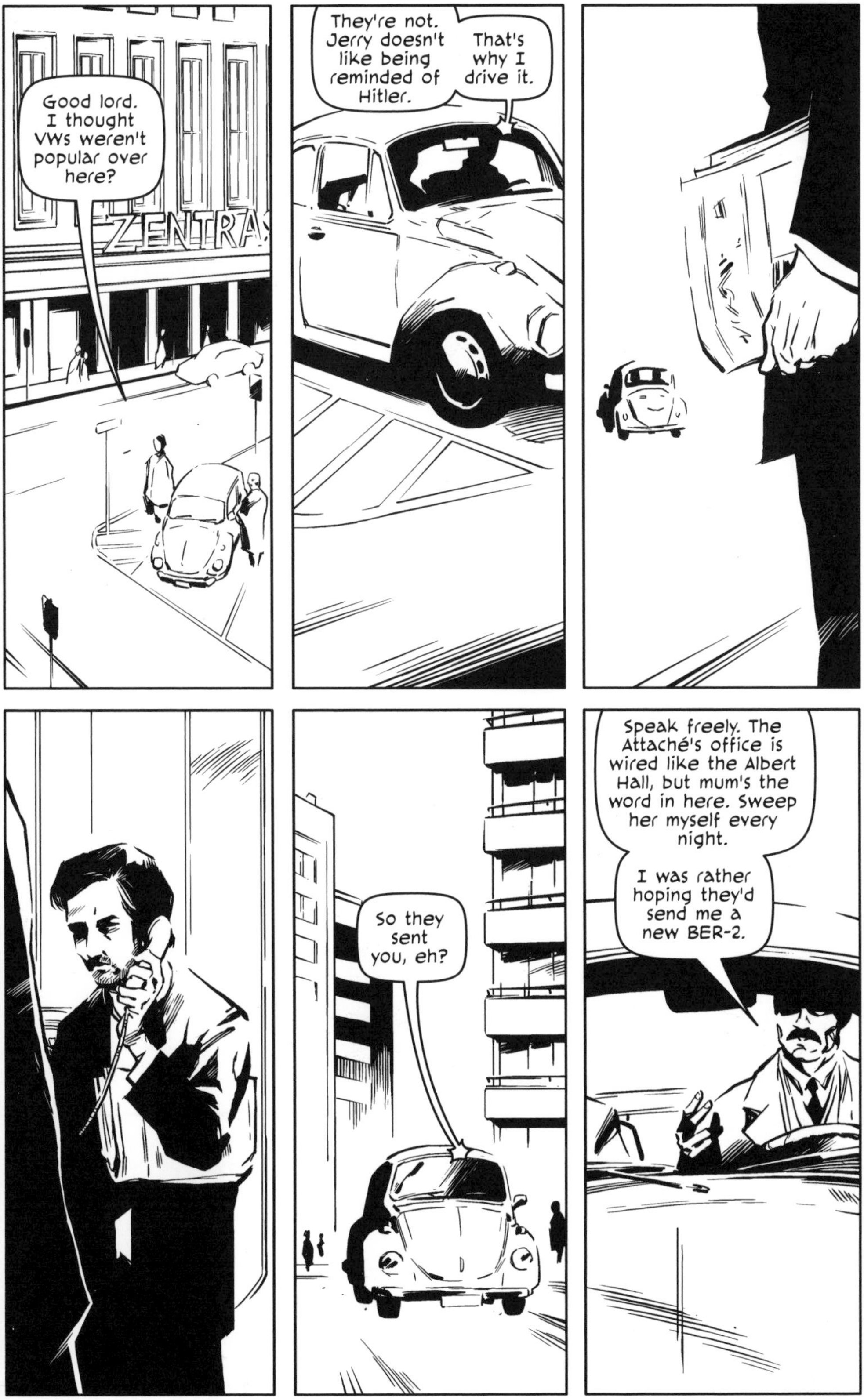
Good lord. I thought VWs weren't popular over here?
ZENTRA
They're not. Jerry doesn't like being reminded of Hitler.
That's why I drive it.
So they sent you, eh?
Speak freely. The Attaché's office is wired like the Albert Hall, but mum's the word in here. Sweep her myself every night.
I was rather hoping they'd send me a new BER-2.

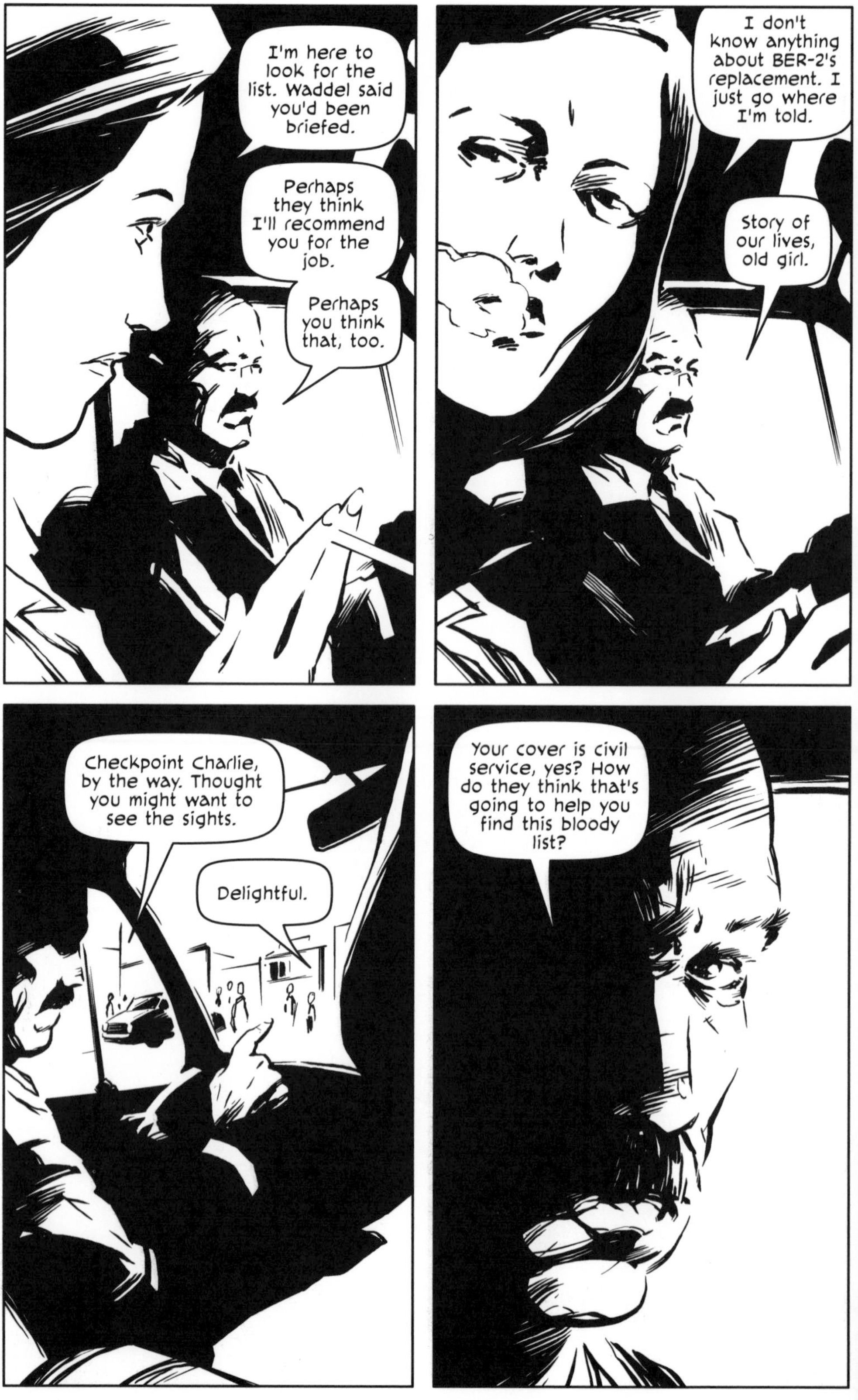
I'm here to look for the list. Waddel said you'd been briefed.
Perhaps they think I'll recommend you for the job.
Perhaps you think that, too.
I don't know anything about BER-2's replacement. I just go where I'm told.
Story of our lives, old girl.
Checkpoint Charlie, by the way. Thought you might want to see the sights.
Delightful.
Your cover is civil service, yes? How do they think that's going to help you find this bloody list?

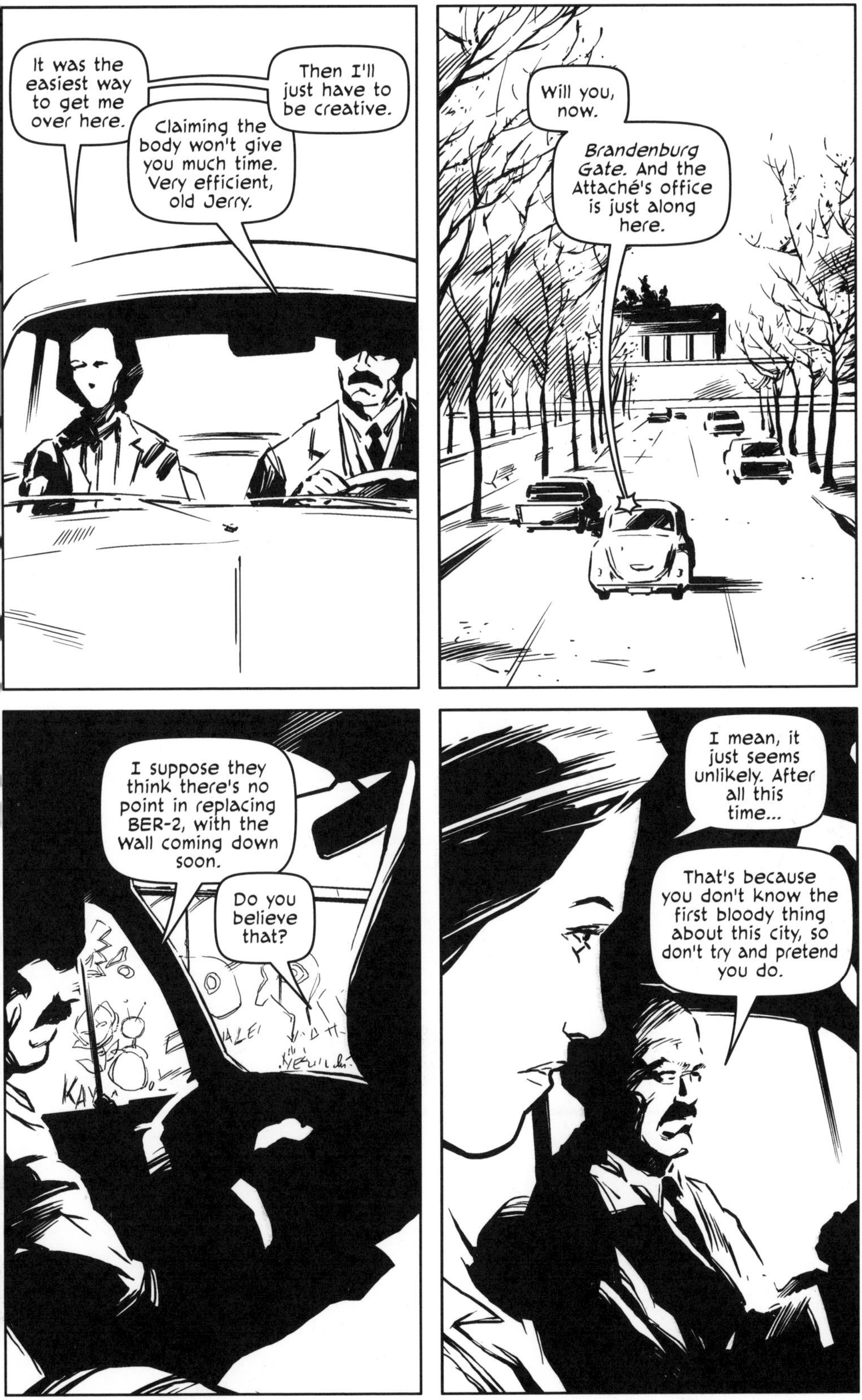
It was the easiest way to get me over here.
Then I'll just have to be creative.
Claiming the body won't give you much time. Very efficient, old Jerry.
Will you, now.
Brandenburg Gate. And the Attaché's office is just along here.
I suppose they think there's no point in replacing BER-2, with the Wall coming down soon.
Do you believe that?
I mean, it just seems unlikely. After all this time...
That's because you don't know the first bloody thing about this city, so don't try and pretend you do.

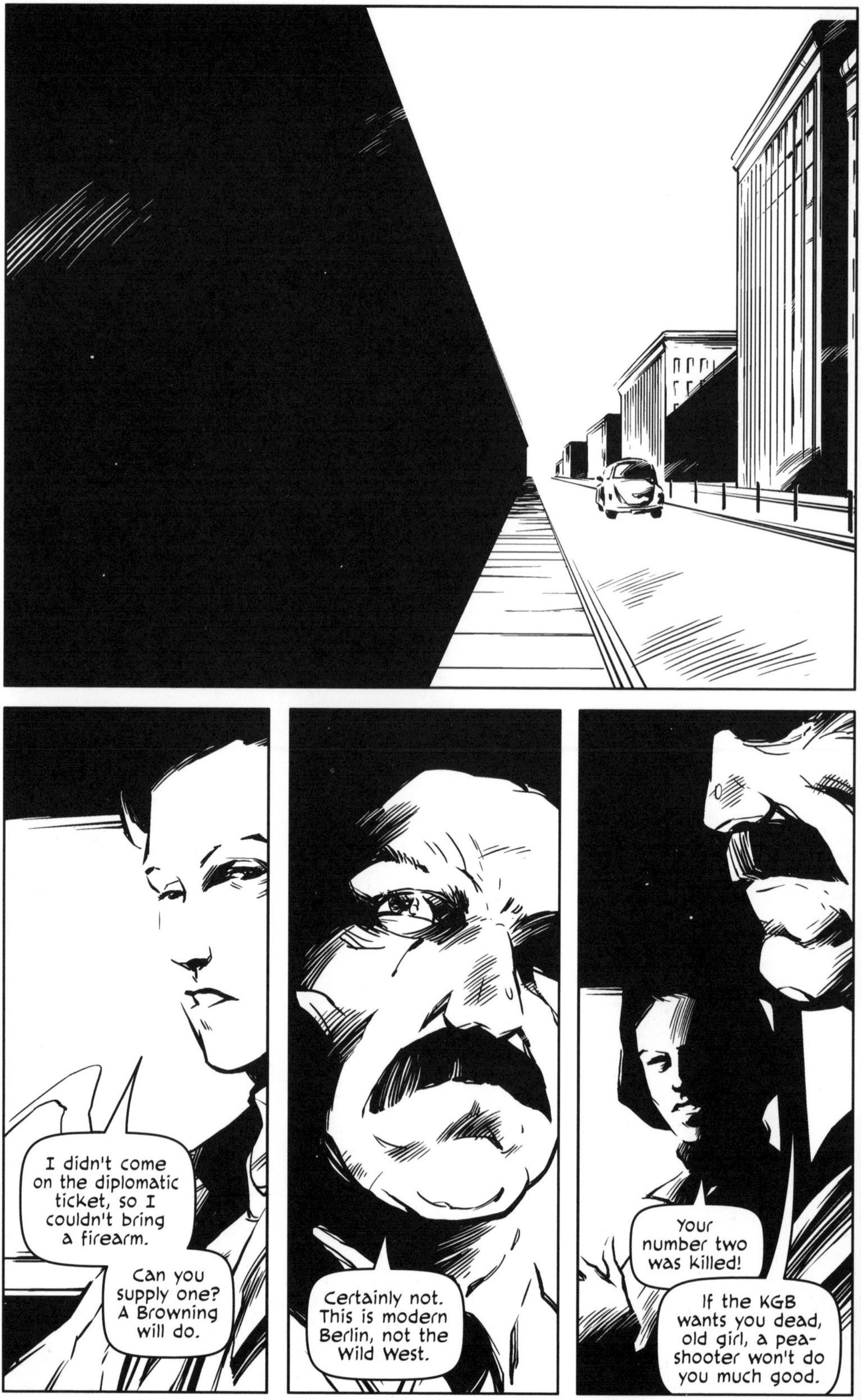
I didn't come on the diplomatic ticket, so I couldn't bring a firearm.
Can you supply one? A Browning will do.
Certainly not. This is modern Berlin, not the Wild West.
Your number two was killed!
If the KGB wants you dead, old girl, a pea-shooter won't do you much good.

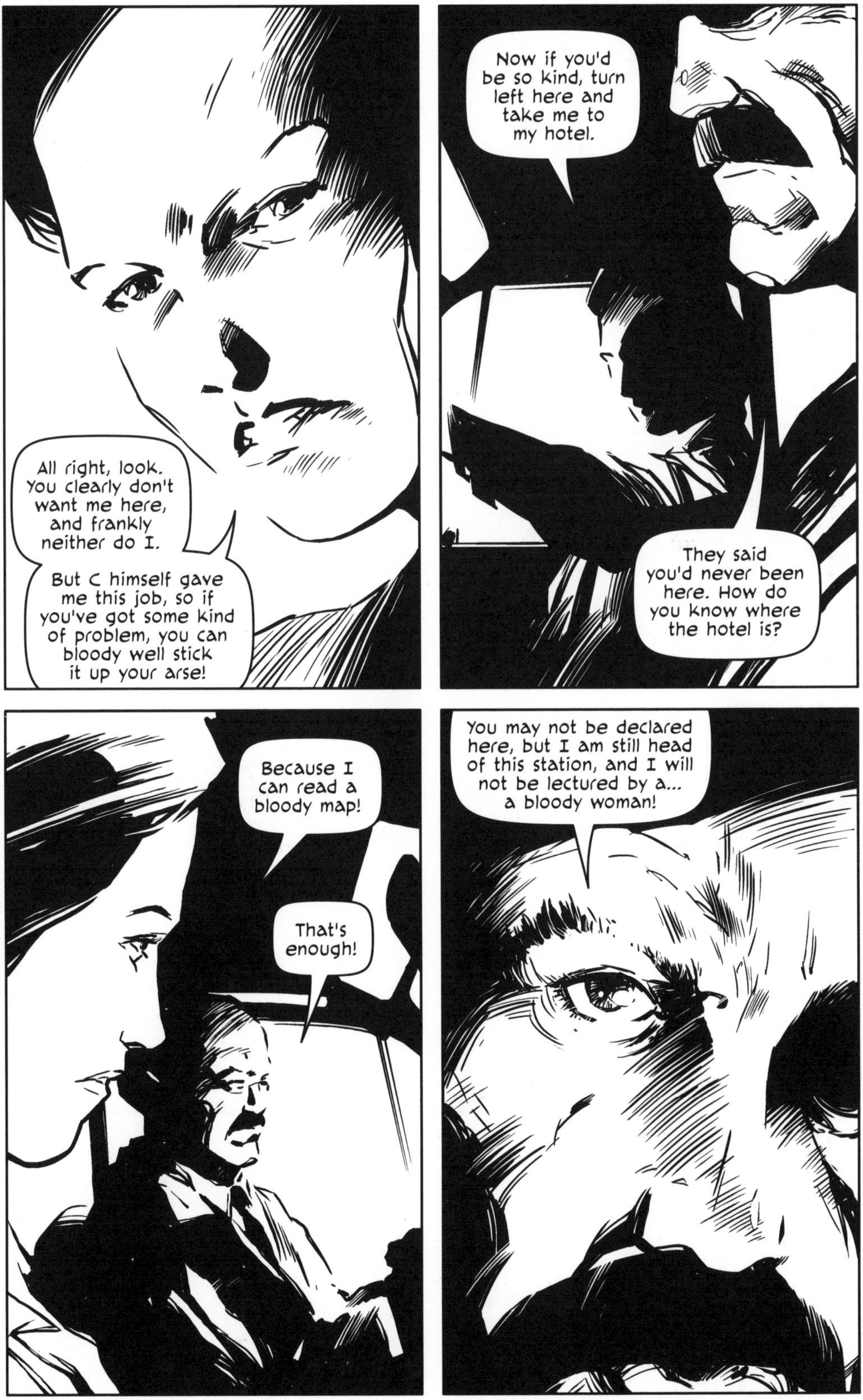
All right, look. You clearly don't want me here, and frankly neither do I.
But C himself gave me this job, so if you've got some kind of problem, you can bloody well stick it up your arse!
Now if you'd be so kind, turn left here and take me to my hotel.
They said you'd never been here. How do you know where the hotel is?
Because I can read a bloody map!
That's enough!
You may not be declared here, but I am still head of this station, and I will not be lectured by a... a bloody woman!

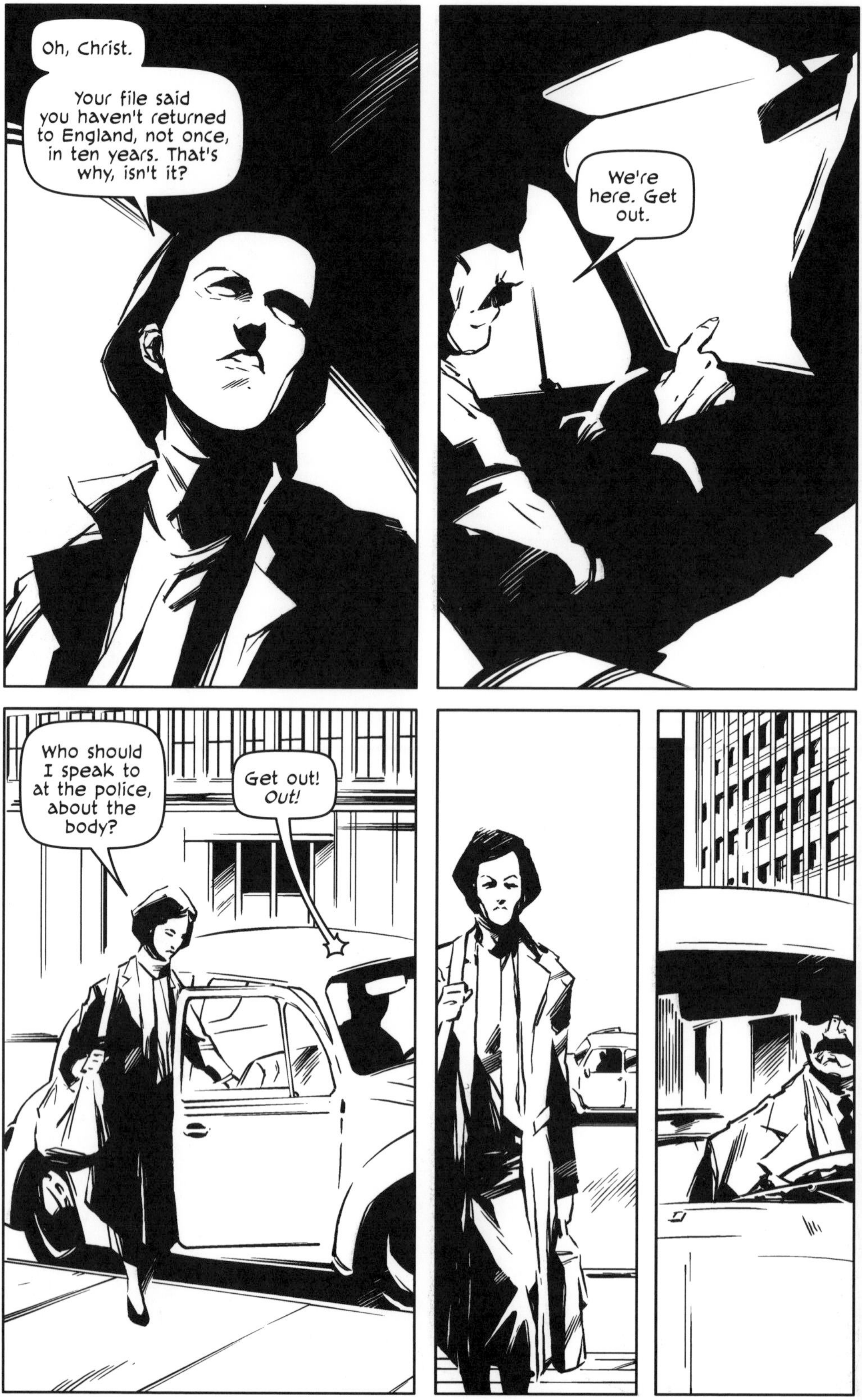
Oh, Christ.
Your file said you haven't returned to England, not once, in ten years. That's why, isn't it?
We're here. Get out.
Who should I speak to at the police, about the body?
Get out! *Out!*

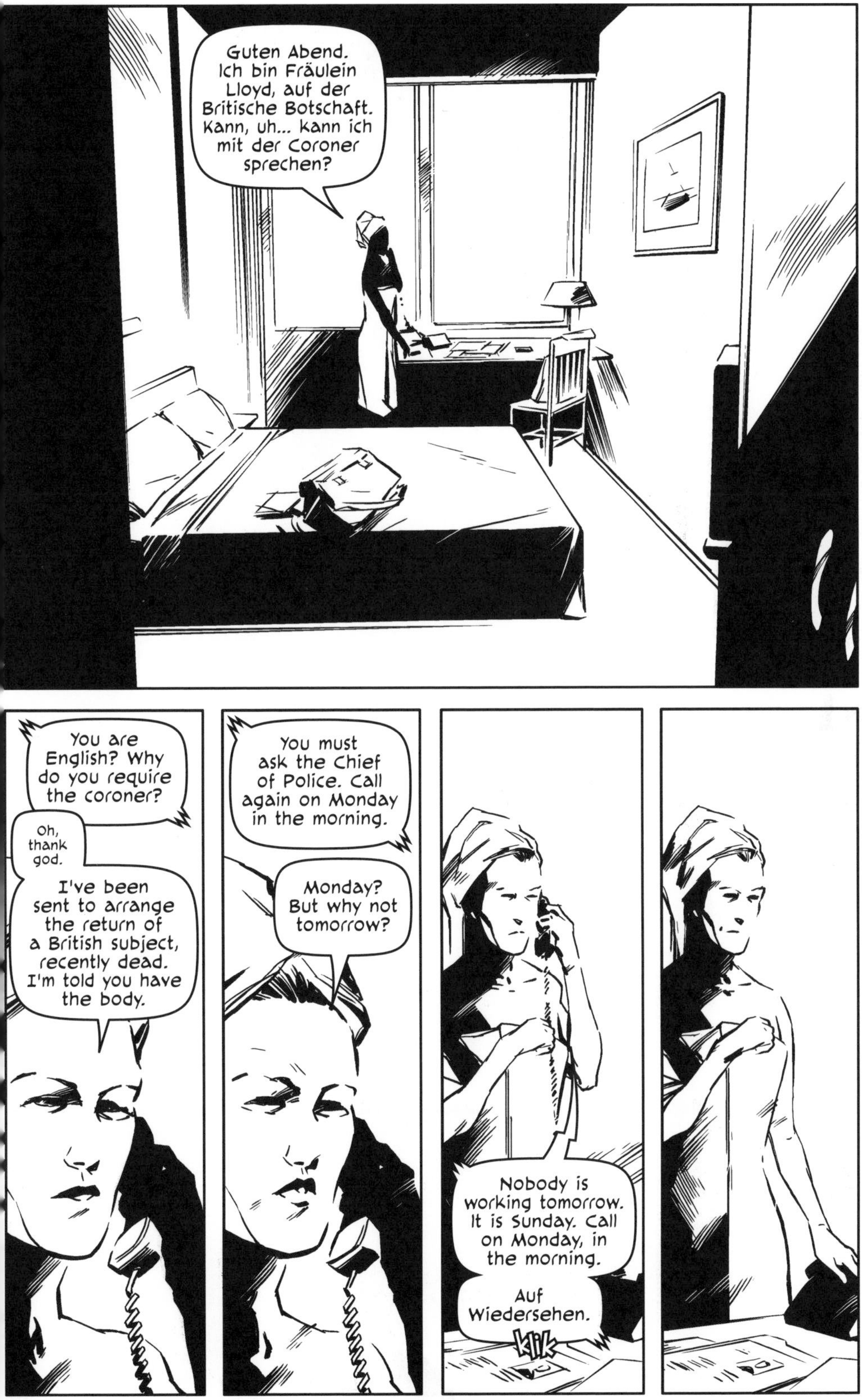
Guten Abend. Ich bin Fräulein Lloyd, auf der Britische Botschaft. Kann, uh... kann ich mit der Coroner sprechen?
You are English? Why do you require the coroner?
Oh, thank god.
I've been sent to arrange the return of a British subject, recently dead. I'm told you have the body.
You must ask the Chief of Police. Call again on Monday in the morning.
Monday? But why not tomorrow?
Nobody is working tomorrow. It is Sunday. Call on Monday, in the morning.
Auf Wiedersehen.
KLIK

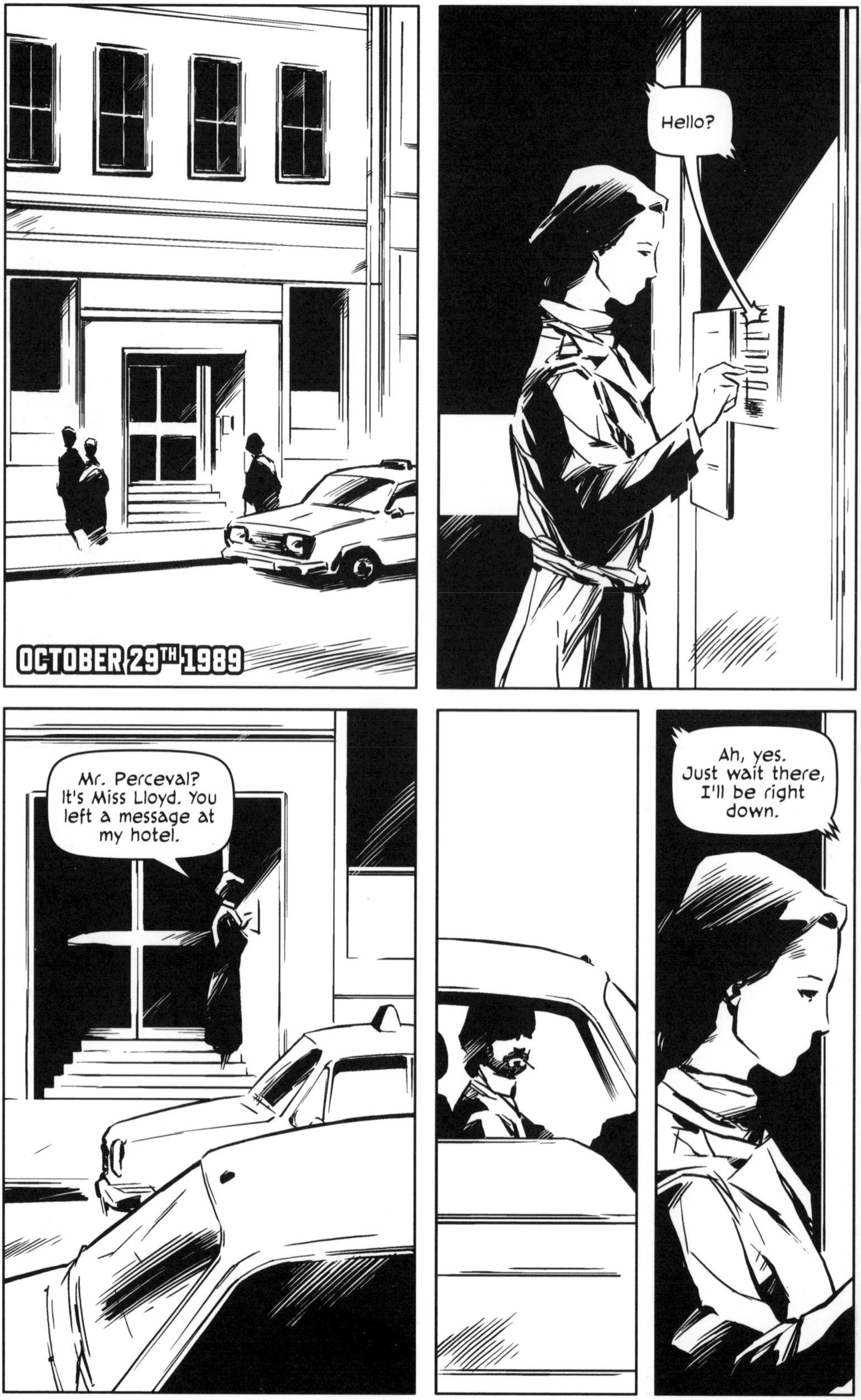
OCTOBER 29TH 1989
Hello?
Mr. Perceval? It's Miss Lloyd. You left a message at my hotel.
Ah, yes. Just wait there, I'll be right down.

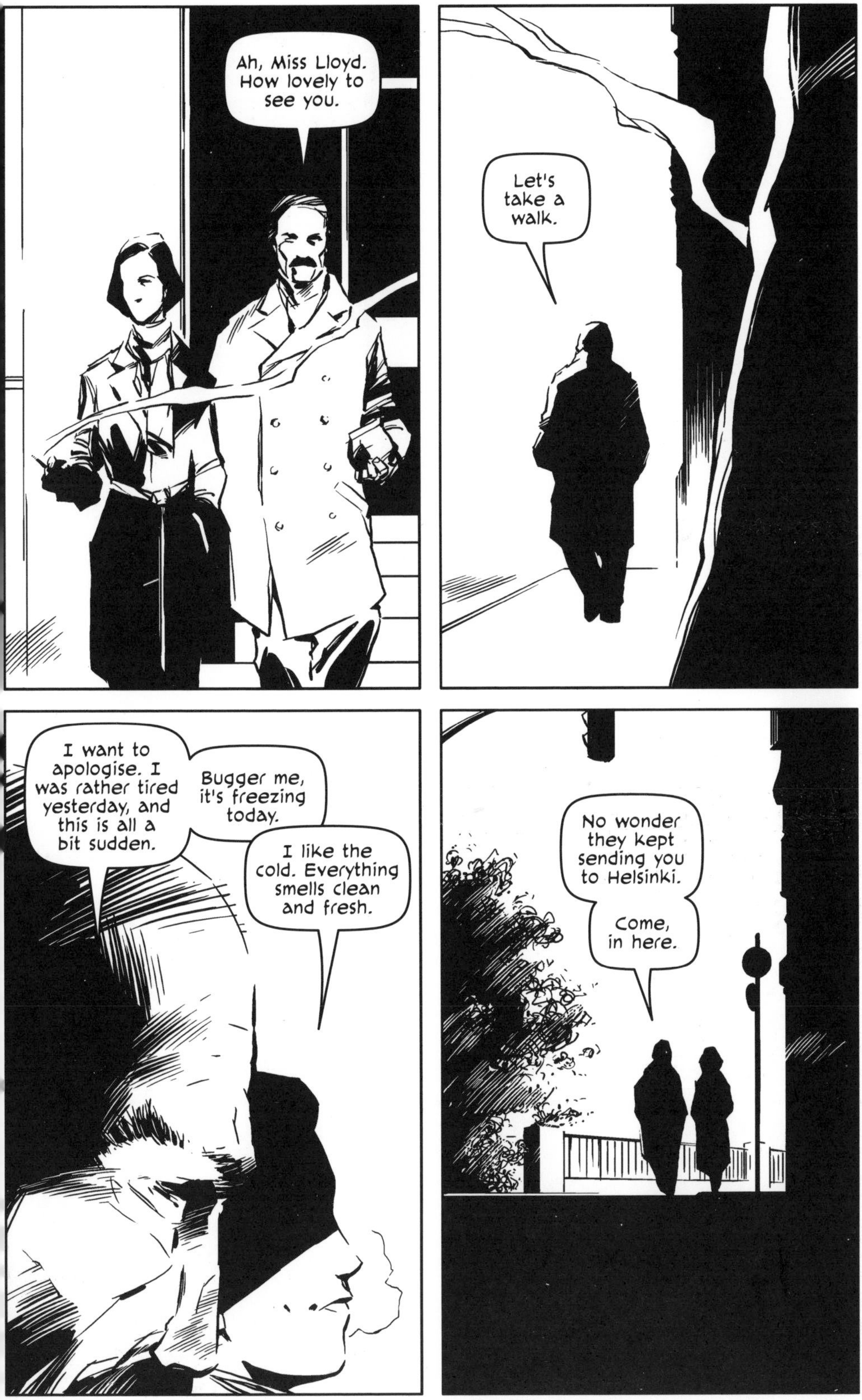

Ah, Miss Lloyd. How lovely to see you.
Let's take a walk.
I want to apologise. I was rather tired yesterday, and this is all a bit sudden.
Bugger me, it's freezing today.
I like the cold. Everything smells clean and fresh.
No wonder they kept sending you to Helsinki.
Come, in here.

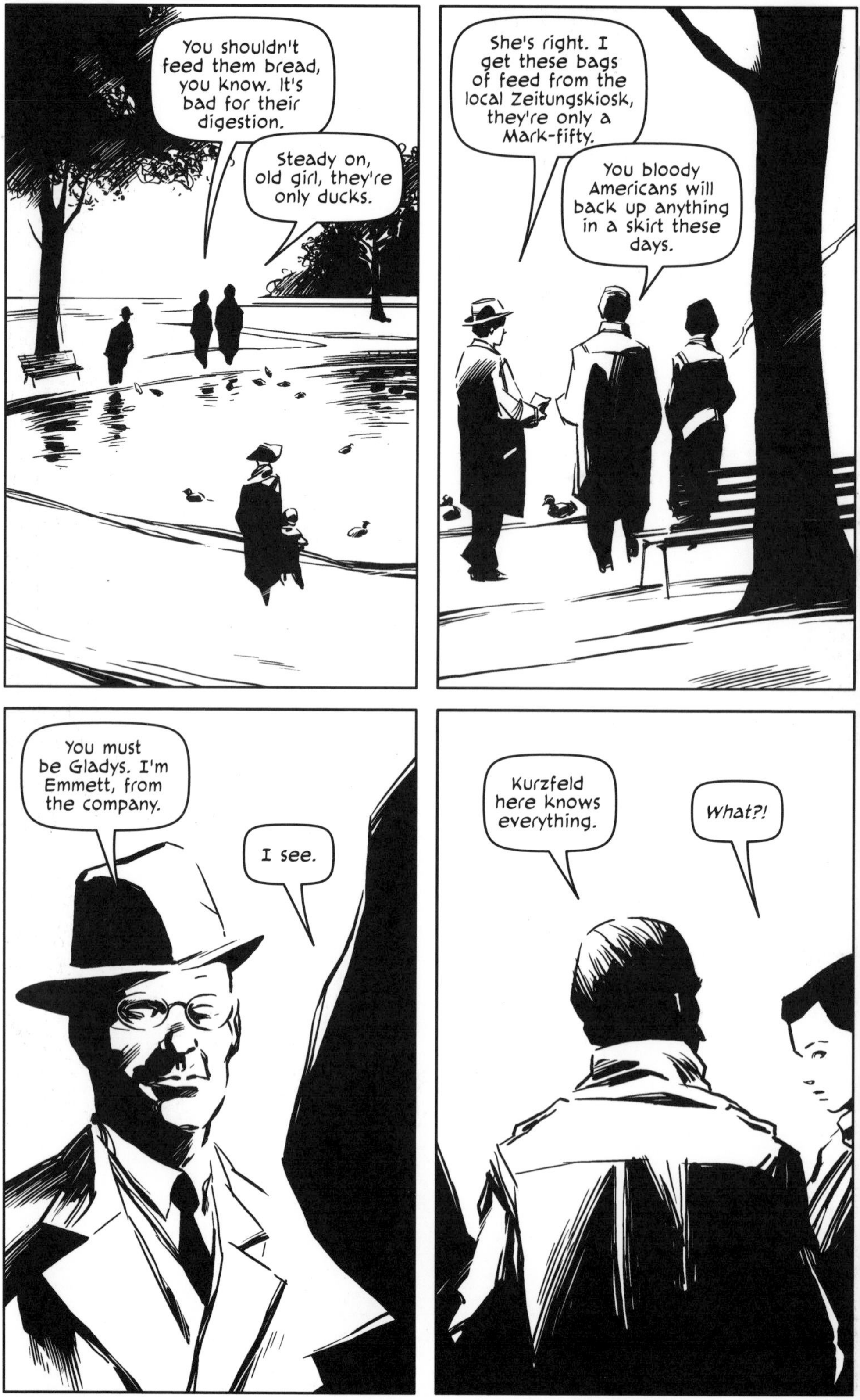
You shouldn't feed them bread, you know. It's bad for their digestion.
Steady on, old girl, they're only ducks.
She's right. I get these bags of feed from the local Zeitungskiosk, they're only a Mark-fifty.
You bloody Americans will back up anything in a skirt these days.
You must be Gladys. I'm Emmett, from the company.
I see.
Kurzfeld here knows everything.
What?!

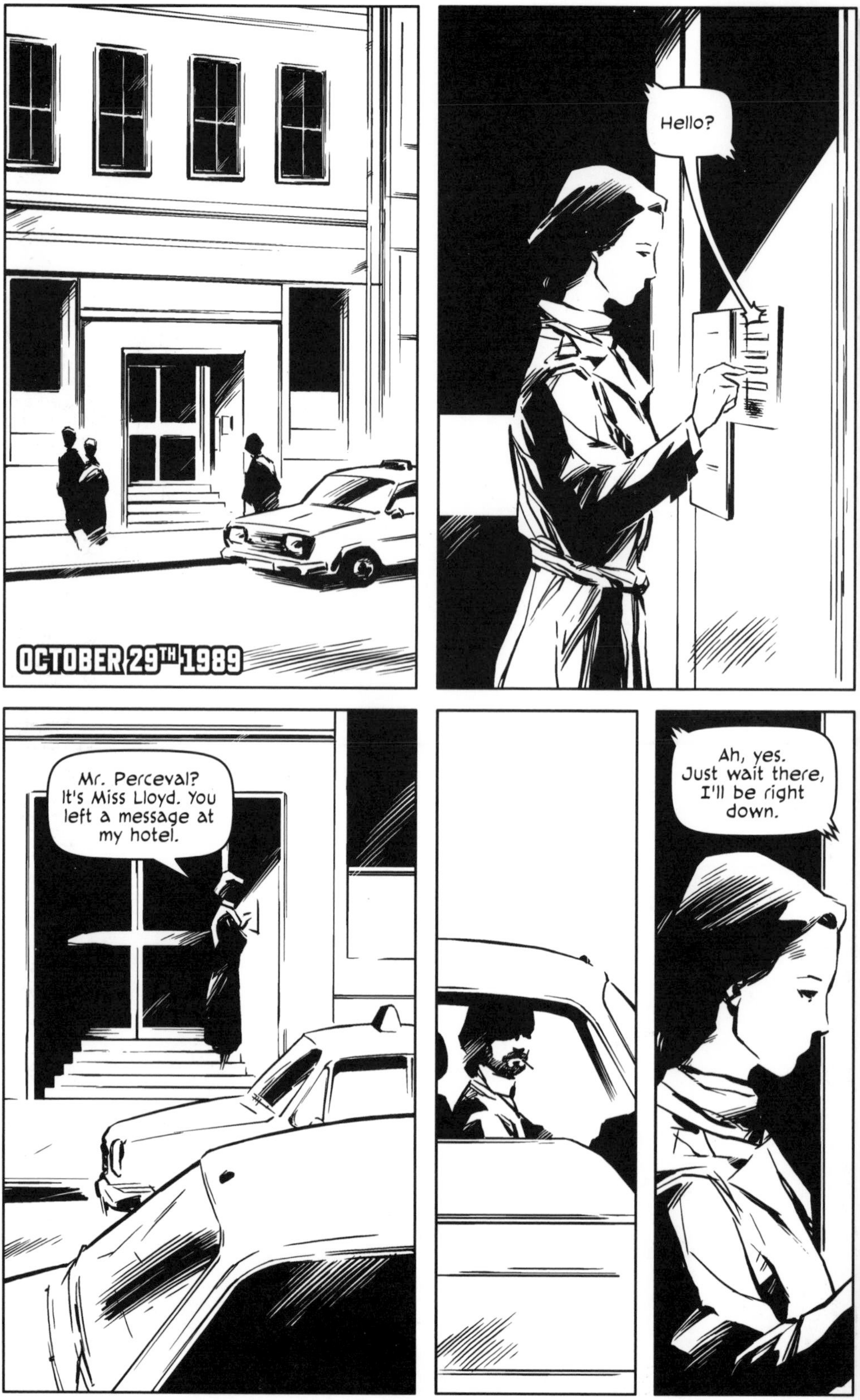
OCTOBER 29TH 1989
Hello?
Mr. Perceval? It's Miss Lloyd. You left a message at my hotel.
Ah, yes. Just wait there, I'll be right down.

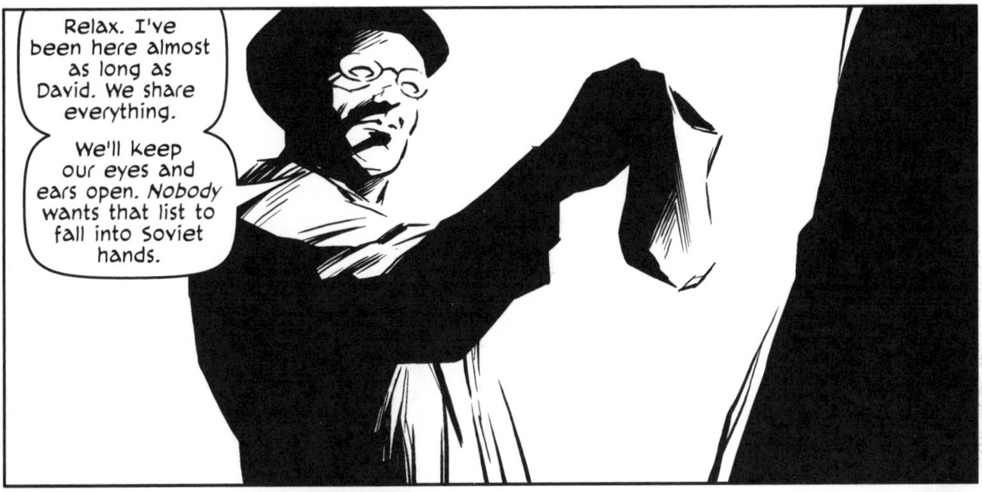
Relax. I've been here almost as long as David. We share everything.
We'll keep our eyes and ears open. *Nobody* wants that list to fall into Soviet hands.

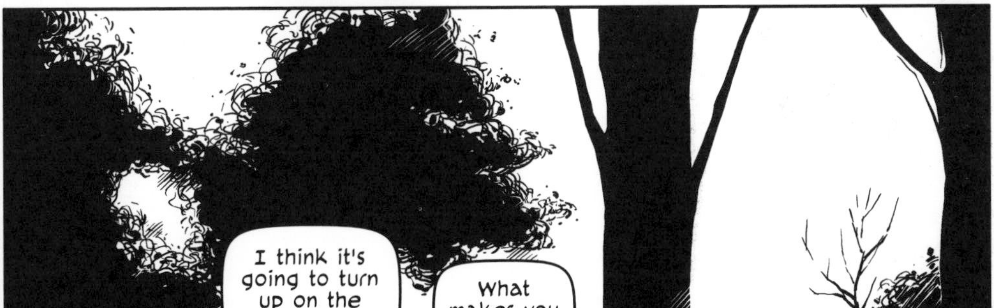
I think it's going to turn up on the black market.
What makes you so sure?

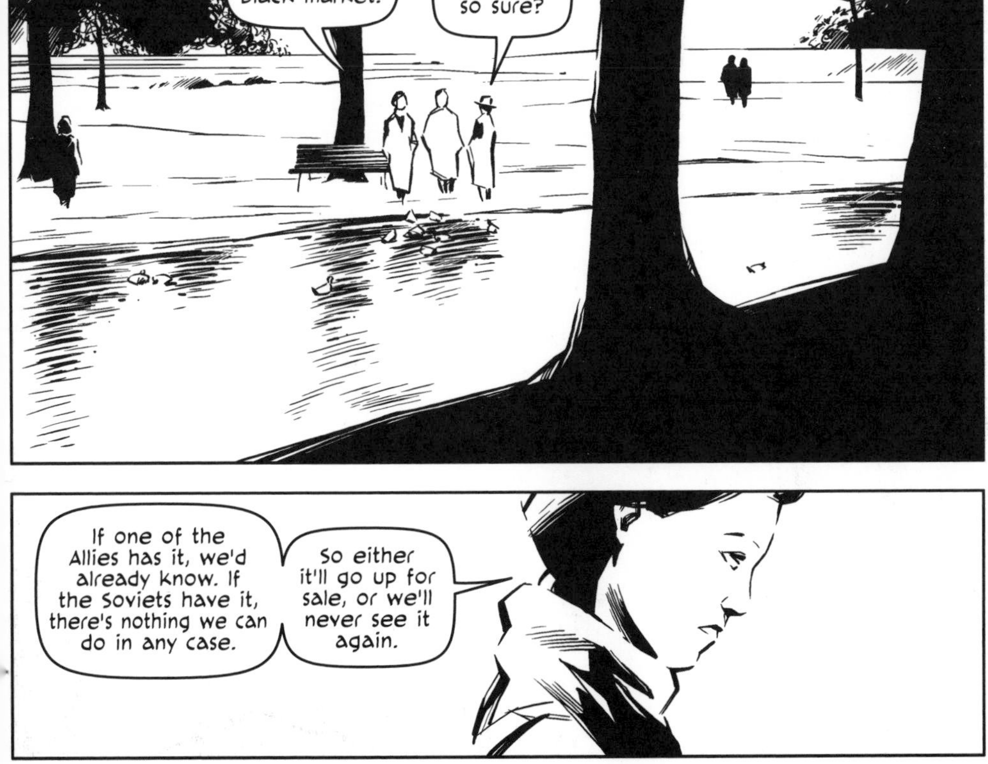
If one of the Allies has it, we'd already know. If the Soviets have it, there's nothing we can do in any case.
So either it'll go up for sale, or we'll never see it again.

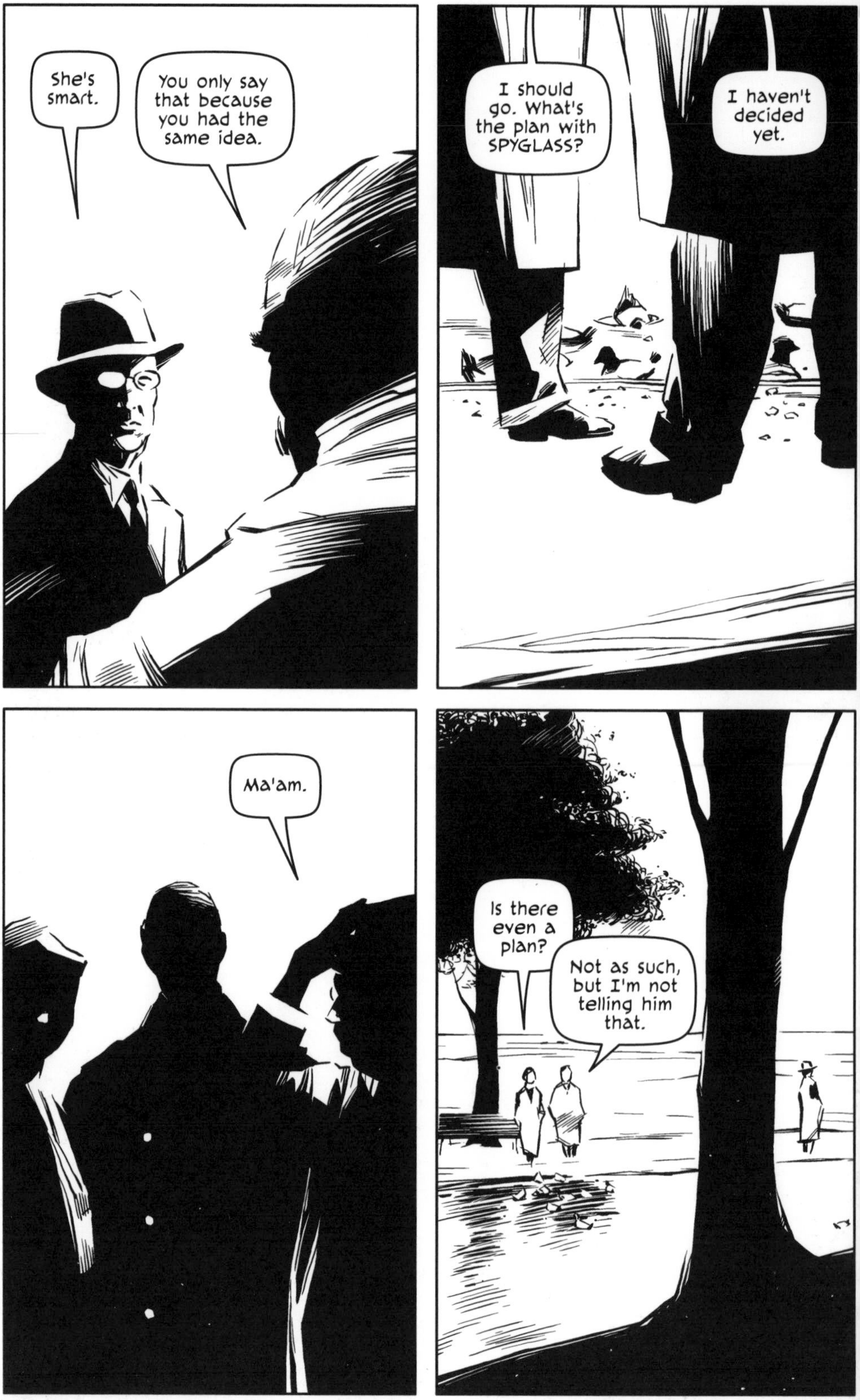
She's smart.
You only say that because you had the same idea.
I should go. What's the plan with SPYGLASS?
I haven't decided yet.
Ma'am.
Is there even a plan?
Not as such, but I'm not telling him that.

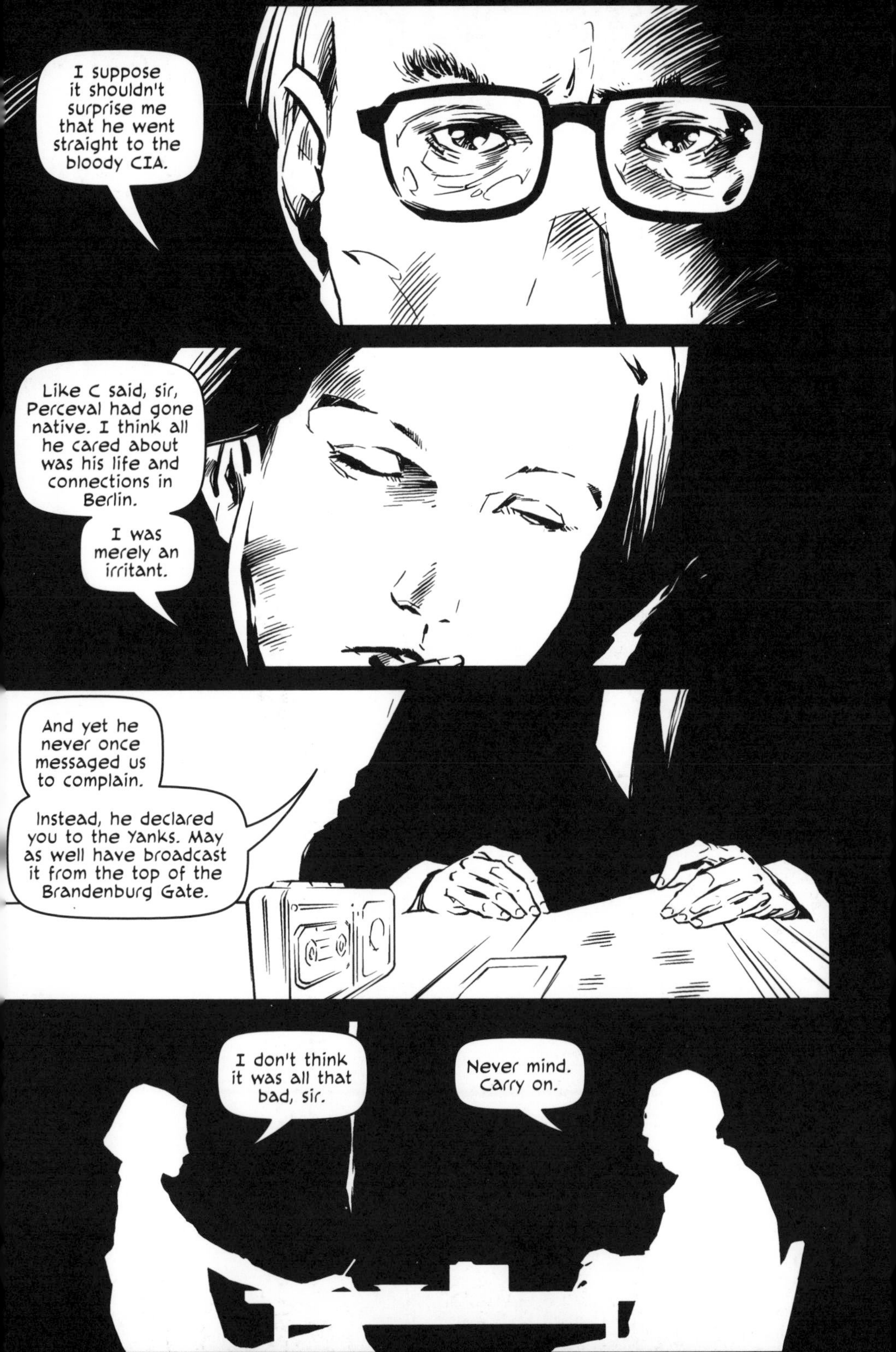
I suppose it shouldn't surprise me that he went straight to the bloody CIA.
Like C said, sir, Perceval had gone native. I think all he cared about was his life and connections in Berlin.
I was merely an irritant.
And yet he never once messaged us to complain.
Instead, he declared you to the Yanks. May as well have broadcast it from the top of the Brandenburg Gate.
I don't think it was all that bad, sir.
Never mind. Carry on.

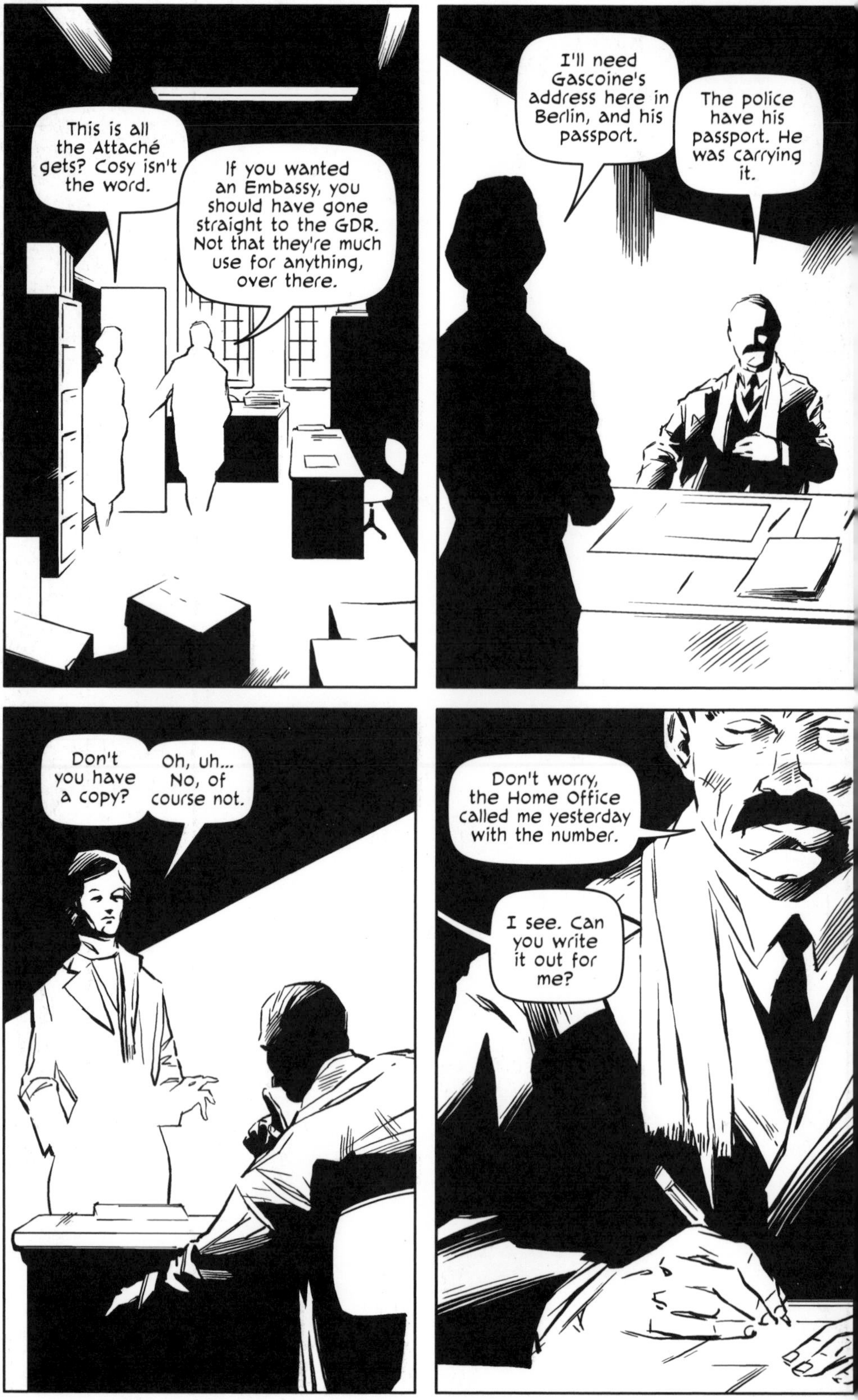
This is all the Attaché gets? Cosy isn't the word.
If you wanted an Embassy, you should have gone straight to the GDR. Not that they're much use for anything, over there.
I'll need Gascoine's address here in Berlin, and his passport.
The police have his passport. He was carrying it.
Don't you have a copy?
Oh, uh... No, of course not.
Don't worry, the Home Office called me yesterday with the number.
I see. Can you write it out for me?

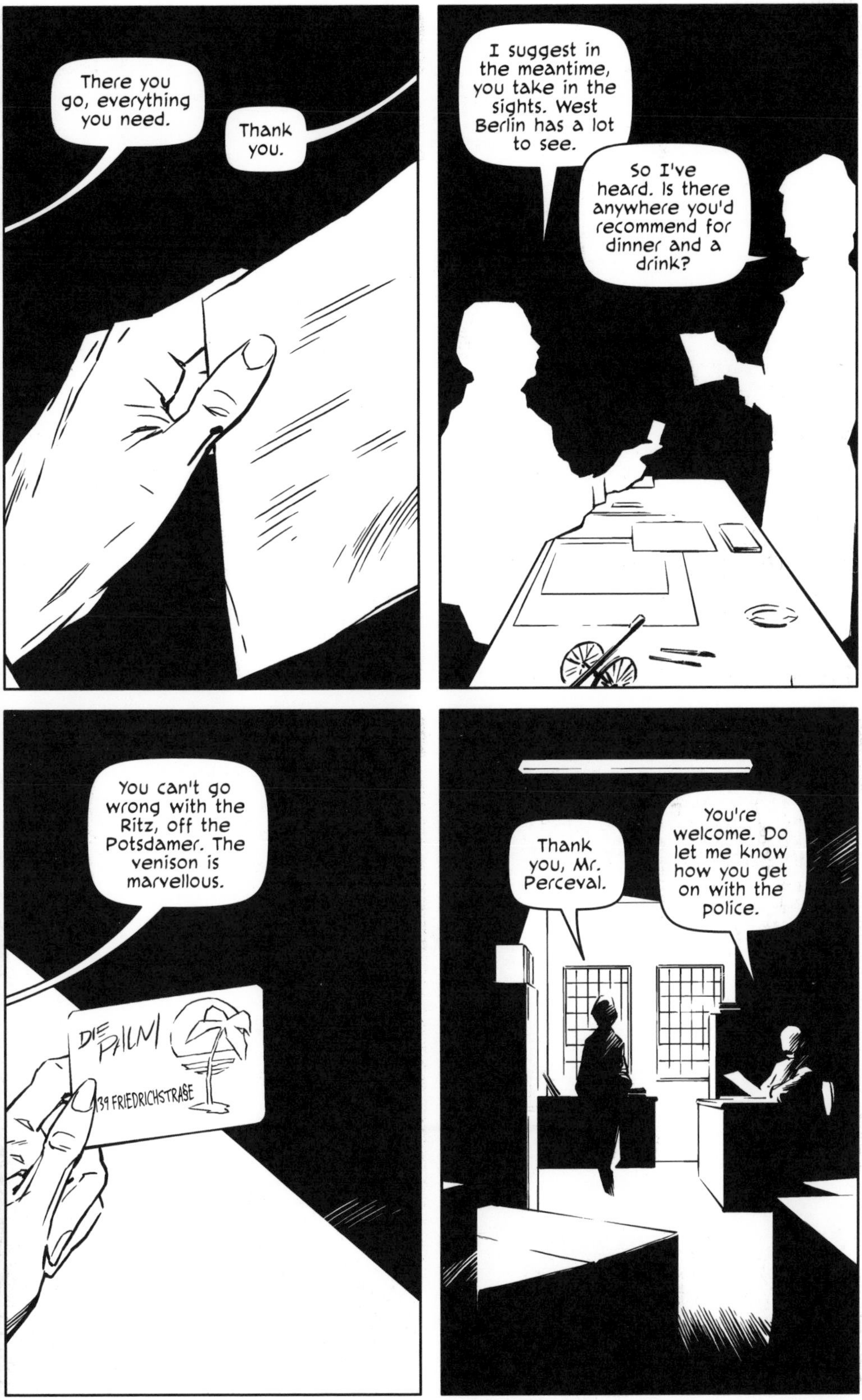
There you go, everything you need.
Thank you.
I suggest in the meantime, you take in the sights. West Berlin has a lot to see.
So I've heard. Is there anywhere you'd recommend for dinner and a drink?
You can't go wrong with the Ritz, off the Potsdamer. The venison is marvellous.
DIE PALM
39 FRIEDRICHSTRAßE
Thank you, Mr. Perceval.
You're welcome. Do let me know how you get on with the police.

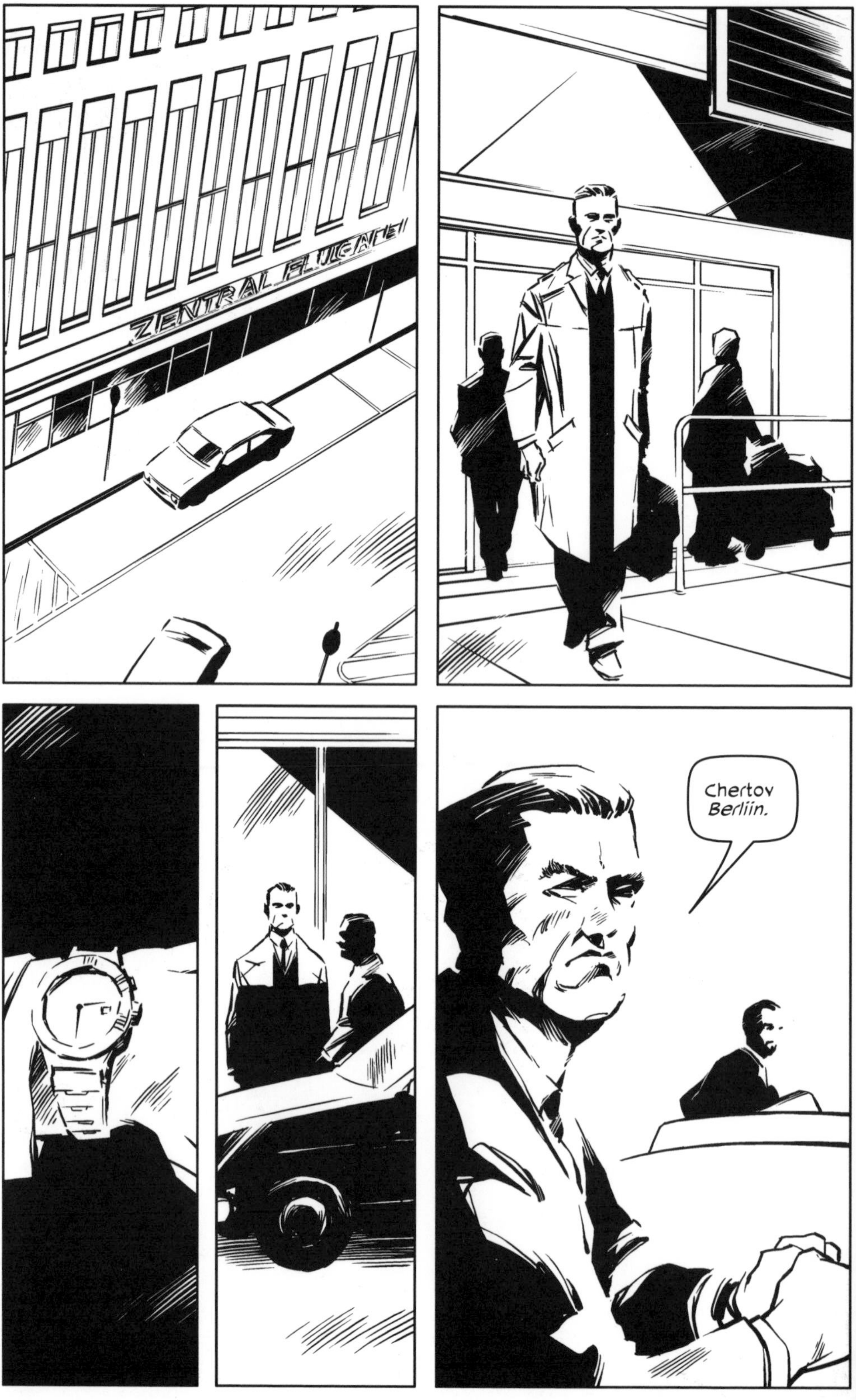
ZENTRAL FLUGHAFEN
Chertov Berliin.

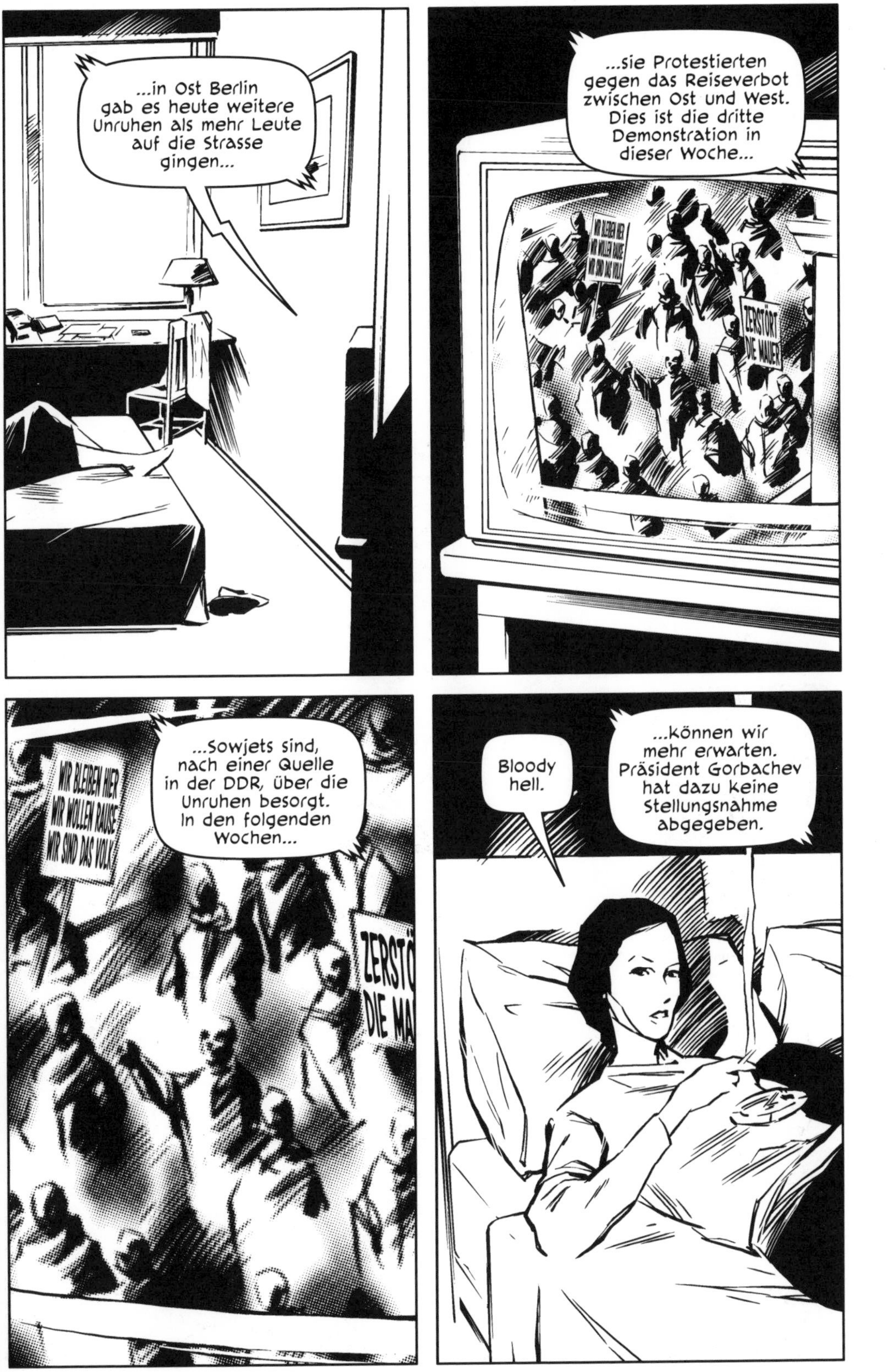
...in Ost Berlin gab es heute weitere Unruhen als mehr Leute auf die Strasse gingen...
...sie Protestierten gegen das Reiseverbot zwischen Ost und West. Dies ist die dritte Demonstration in dieser Woche...
WIR BLEIBEN HIER WIR WOLLEN RAUSE WIR SIND DAS VOLK
ZERSTÖRT DIE MAUER
...Sowjets sind, nach einer Quelle in der DDR, über die Unruhen besorgt. In den folgenden Wochen...
WIR BLEIBEN HIER WIR WOLLEN RAUSE WIR SIND DAS VOLK
Bloody hell.
...können wir mehr erwarten. Präsident Gorbachev hat dazu keine Stellungsnahme abgegeben.

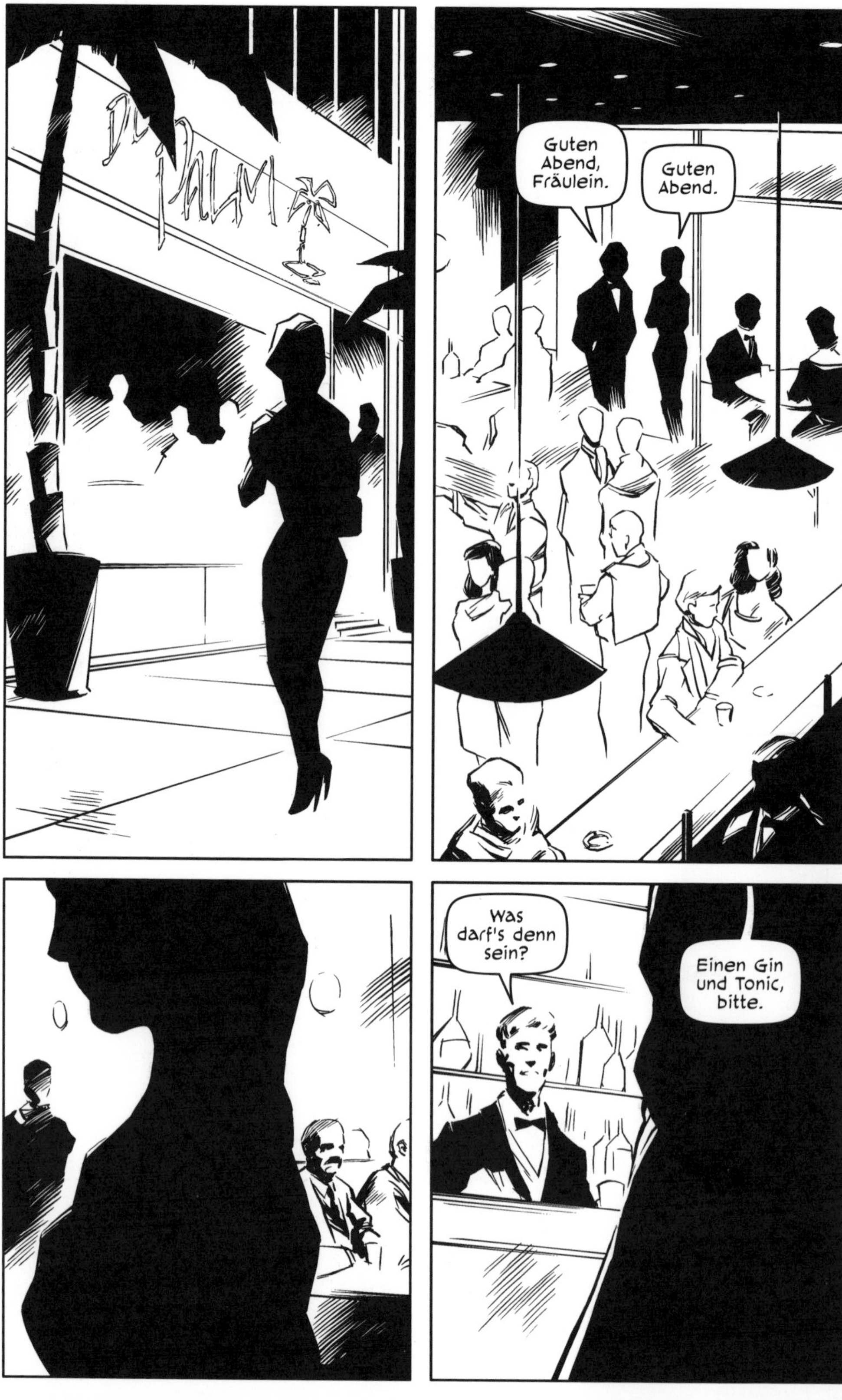
Guten Abend, Fräulein.
Guten Abend.
Was darf's denn sein?
Einen Gin und Tonic, bitte.

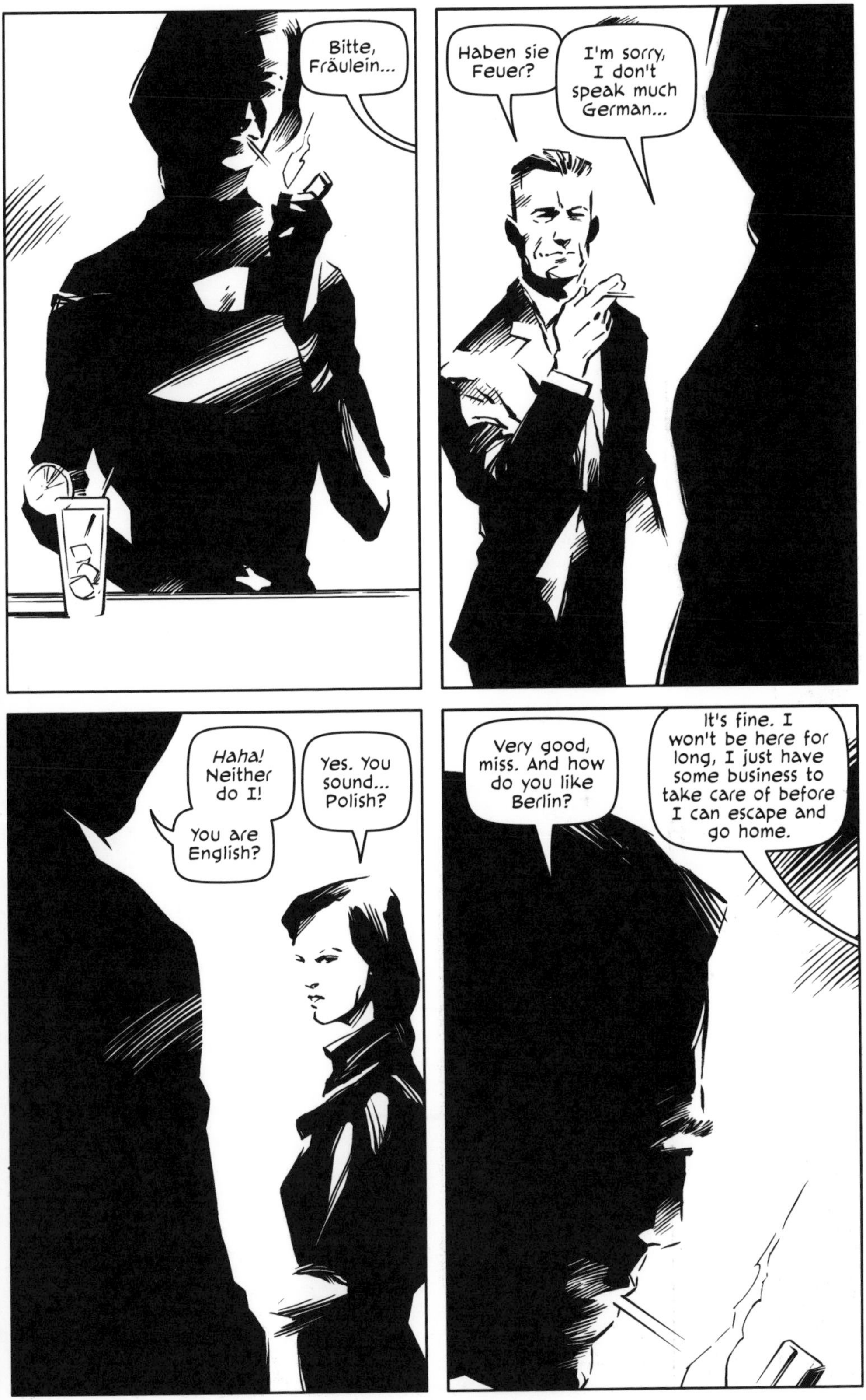
Bitte, Fräulein...
Haben sie Feuer?
I'm sorry, I don't speak much German...
Haha! Neither do I!
You are English?
Yes. You sound... Polish?
Very good, miss. And how do you like Berlin?
It's fine. I won't be here for long, I just have some business to take care of before I can escape and go home.

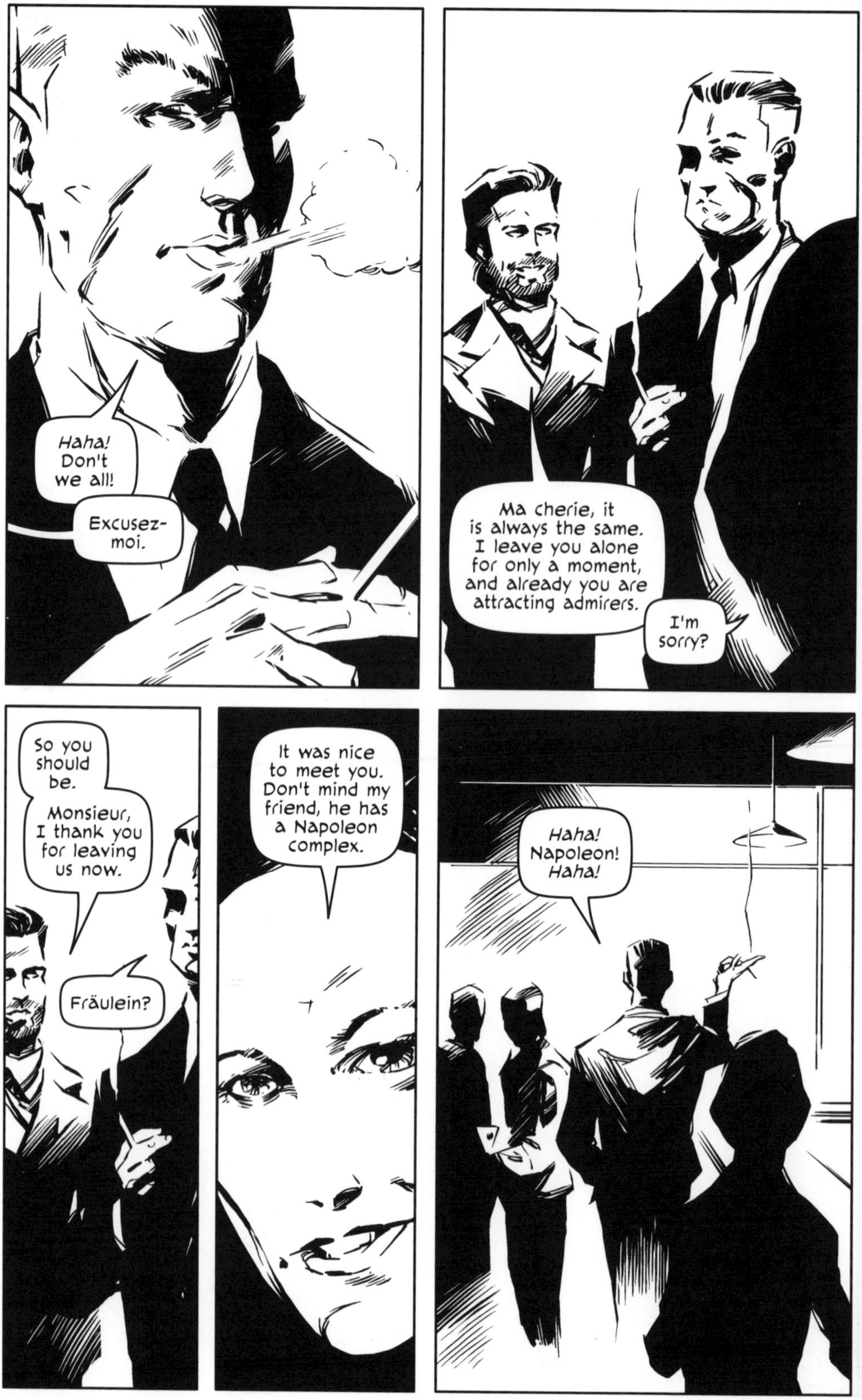
Haha! Don't we all!
Excusez-moi.
Ma cherie, it is always the same. I leave you alone for only a moment, and already you are attracting admirers.
I'm sorry?
So you should be.
Monsieur, I thank you for leaving us now.
Fräulein?
It was nice to meet you. Don't mind my friend, he has a Napoleon complex.
Haha! Napoleon! Haha!

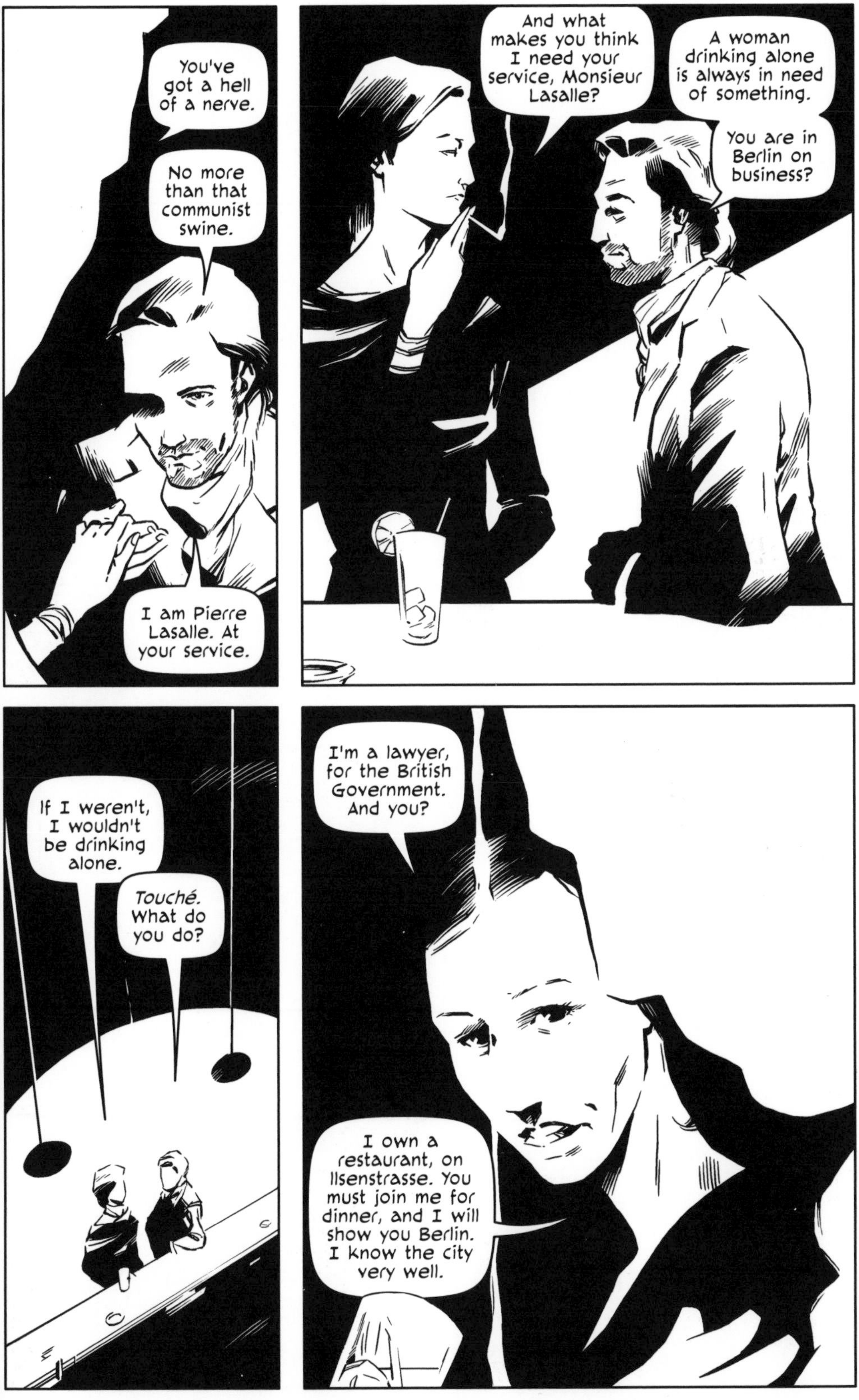

You've got a hell of a nerve.
No more than that communist swine.
I am Pierre Lasalle. At your service.
And what makes you think I need your service, Monsieur Lasalle?
A woman drinking alone is always in need of something.
You are in Berlin on business?
If I weren't, I wouldn't be drinking alone.
Touché. What do you do?
I'm a lawyer, for the British Government. And you?
I own a restaurant, on Ilsenstrasse. You must join me for dinner, and I will show you Berlin. I know the city very well.

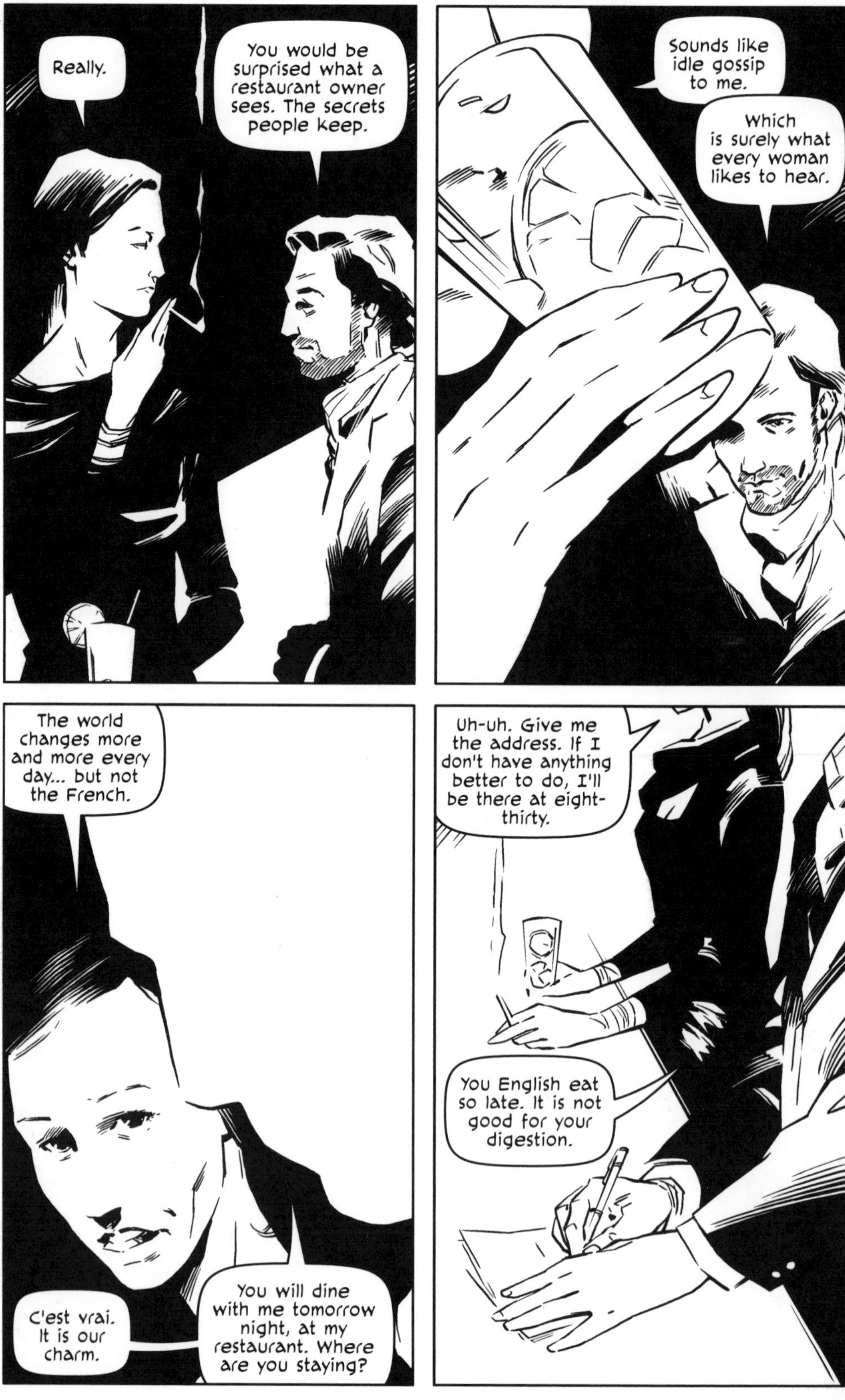
Really.
You would be surprised what a restaurant owner sees. The secrets people keep.
Sounds like idle gossip to me.
Which is surely what every woman likes to hear.
The world changes more and more every day... but not the French.
C'est vrai. It is our charm.
You will dine with me tomorrow night, at my restaurant. Where are you staying?
Uh-uh. Give me the address. If I don't have anything better to do, I'll be there at eight-thirty.
You English eat so late. It is not good for your digestion.

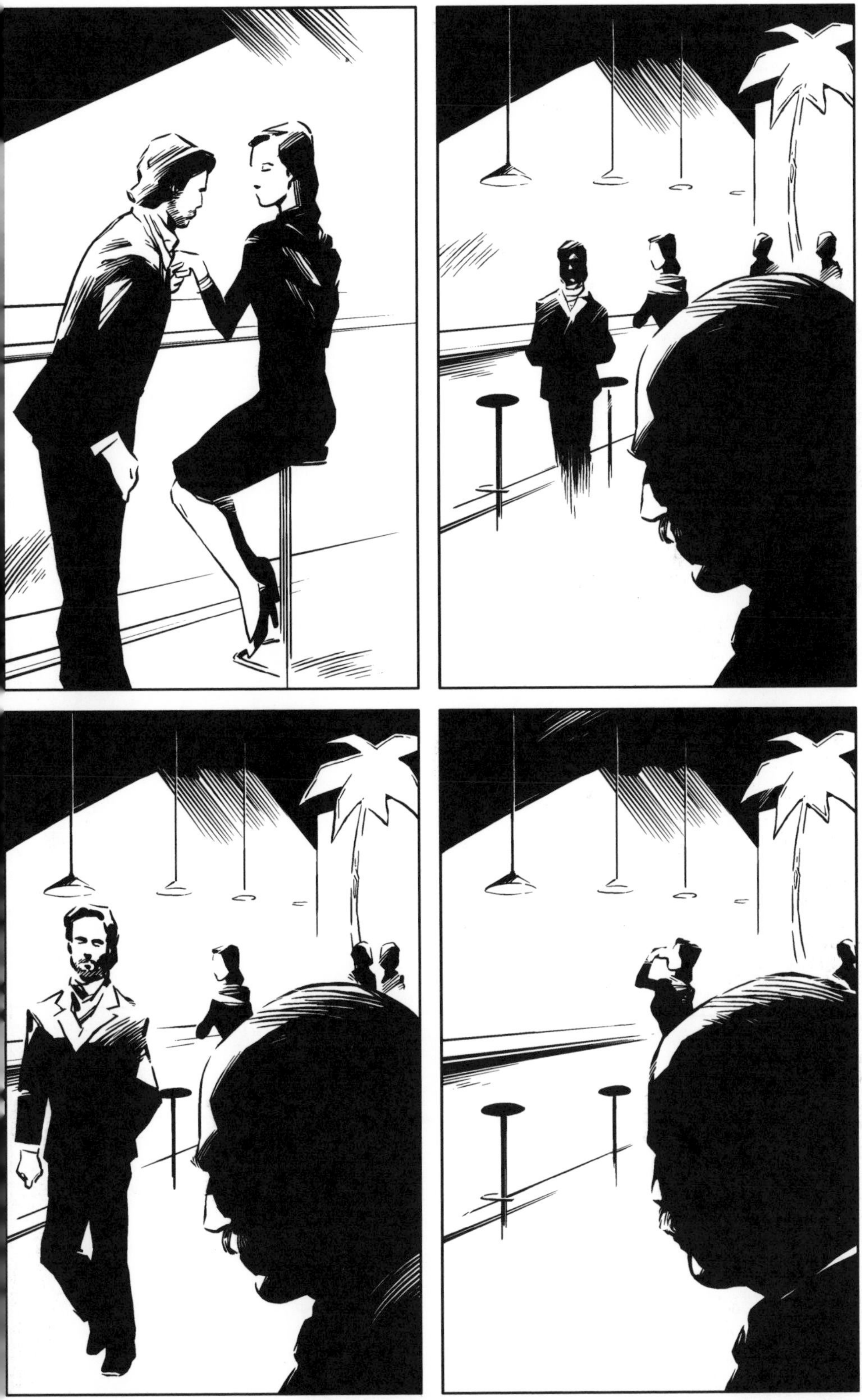

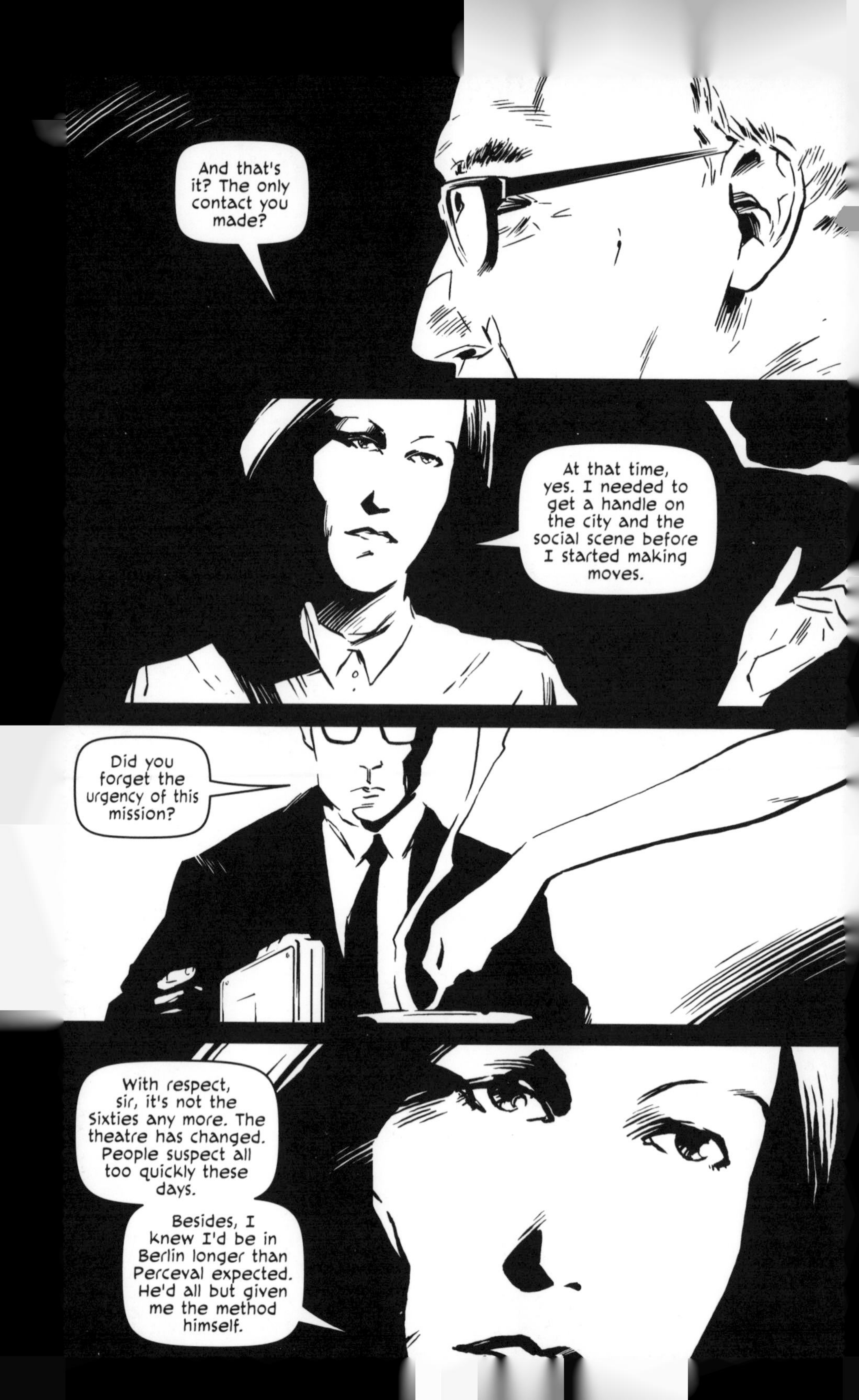

And that's it? The only contact you made?
At that time, yes. I needed to get a handle on the city and the social scene before I started making moves.
Did you forget the urgency of this mission?
With respect, sir, it's not the Sixties any more. The theatre has changed. People suspect all too quickly these days.
Besides, I knew I'd be in Berlin longer than Perceval expected. He'd all but given me the method himself.

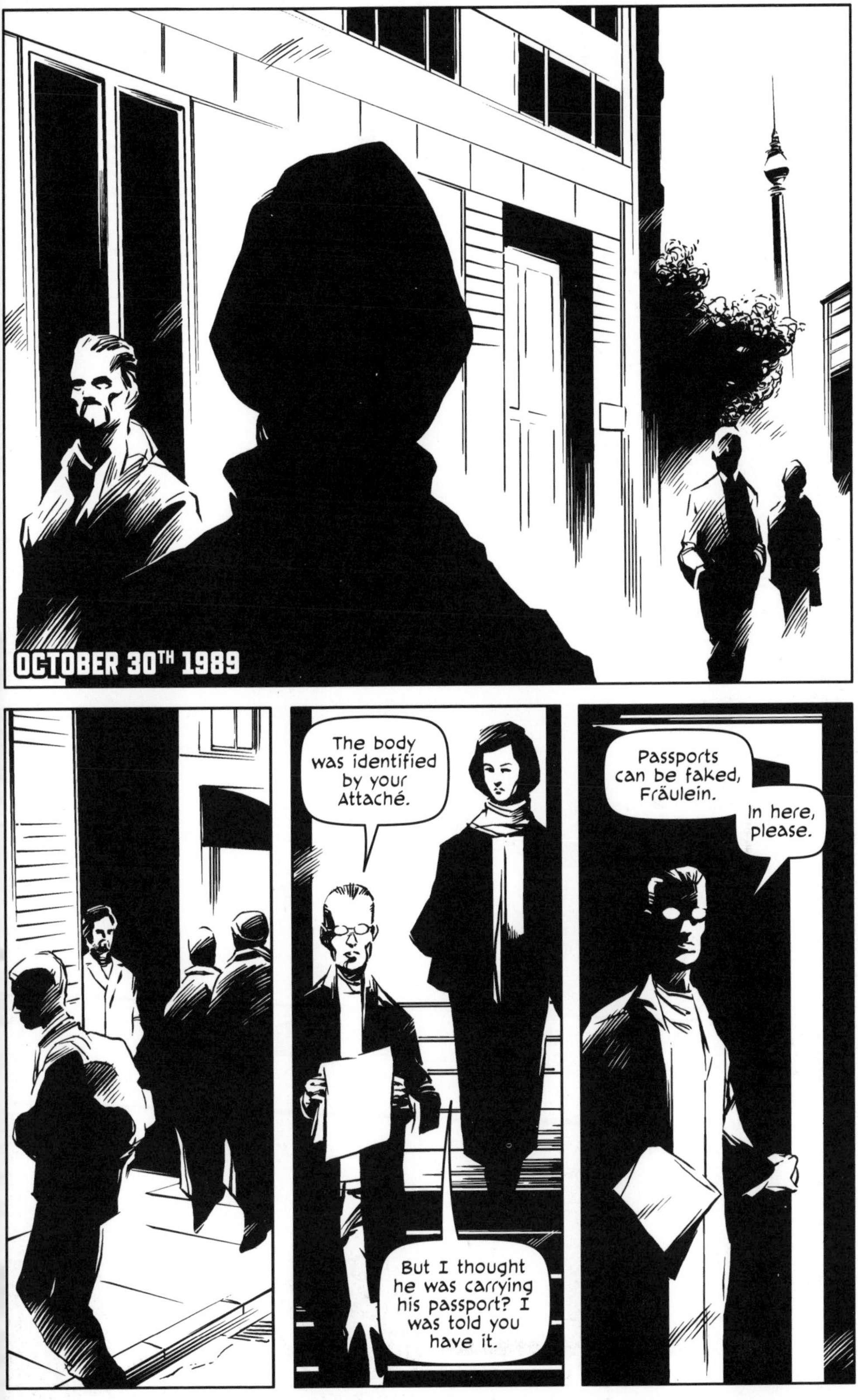
OCTOBER 30TH 1989
The body was identified by your Attaché.
But I thought he was carrying his passport? I was told you have it.
Passports can be faked, Fräulein.
In here, please.

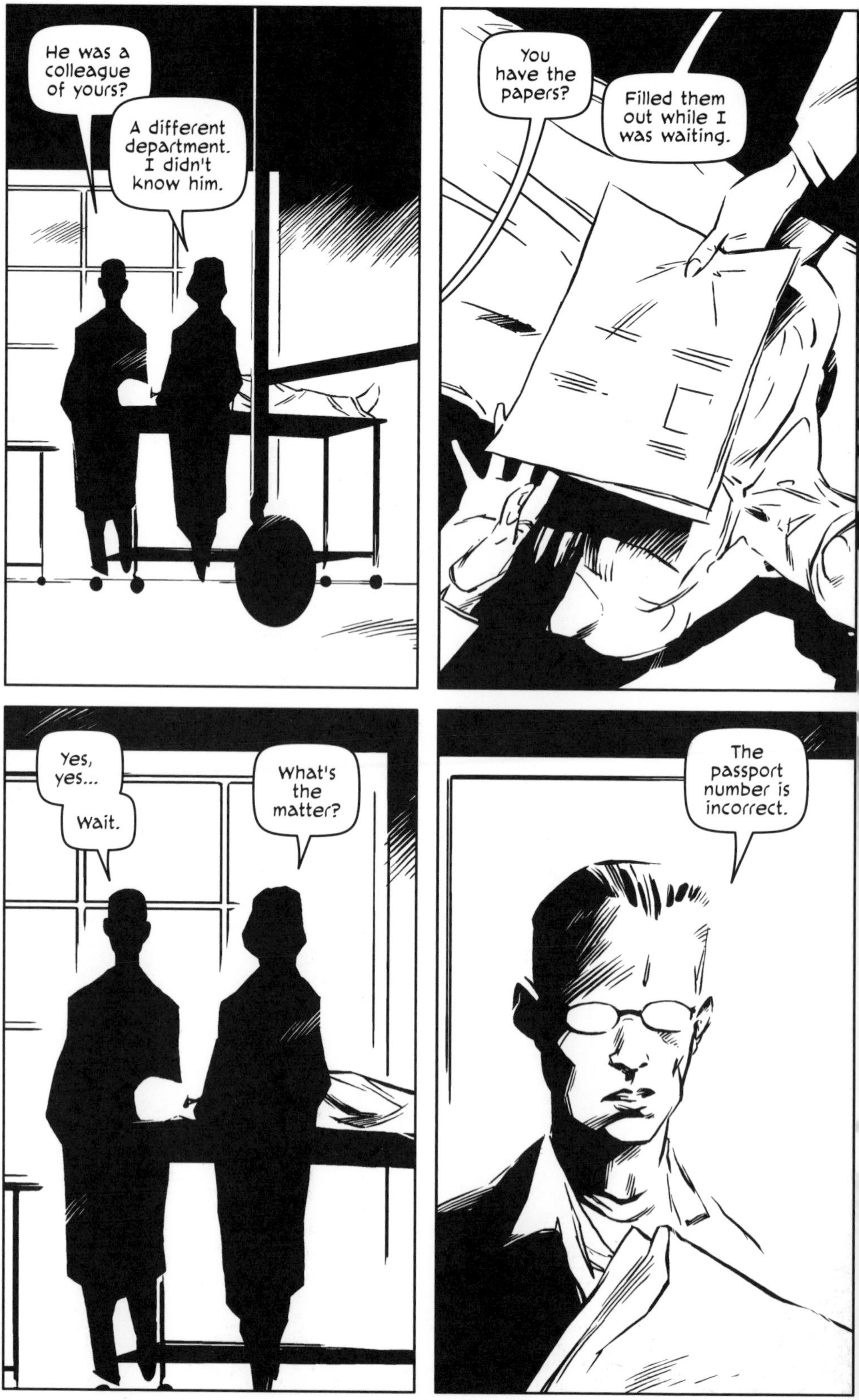
He was a colleague of yours?
A different department. I didn't know him.
You have the papers?
Filled them out while I was waiting.
Yes, yes...
Wait.
What's the matter?
The passport number is incorrect.

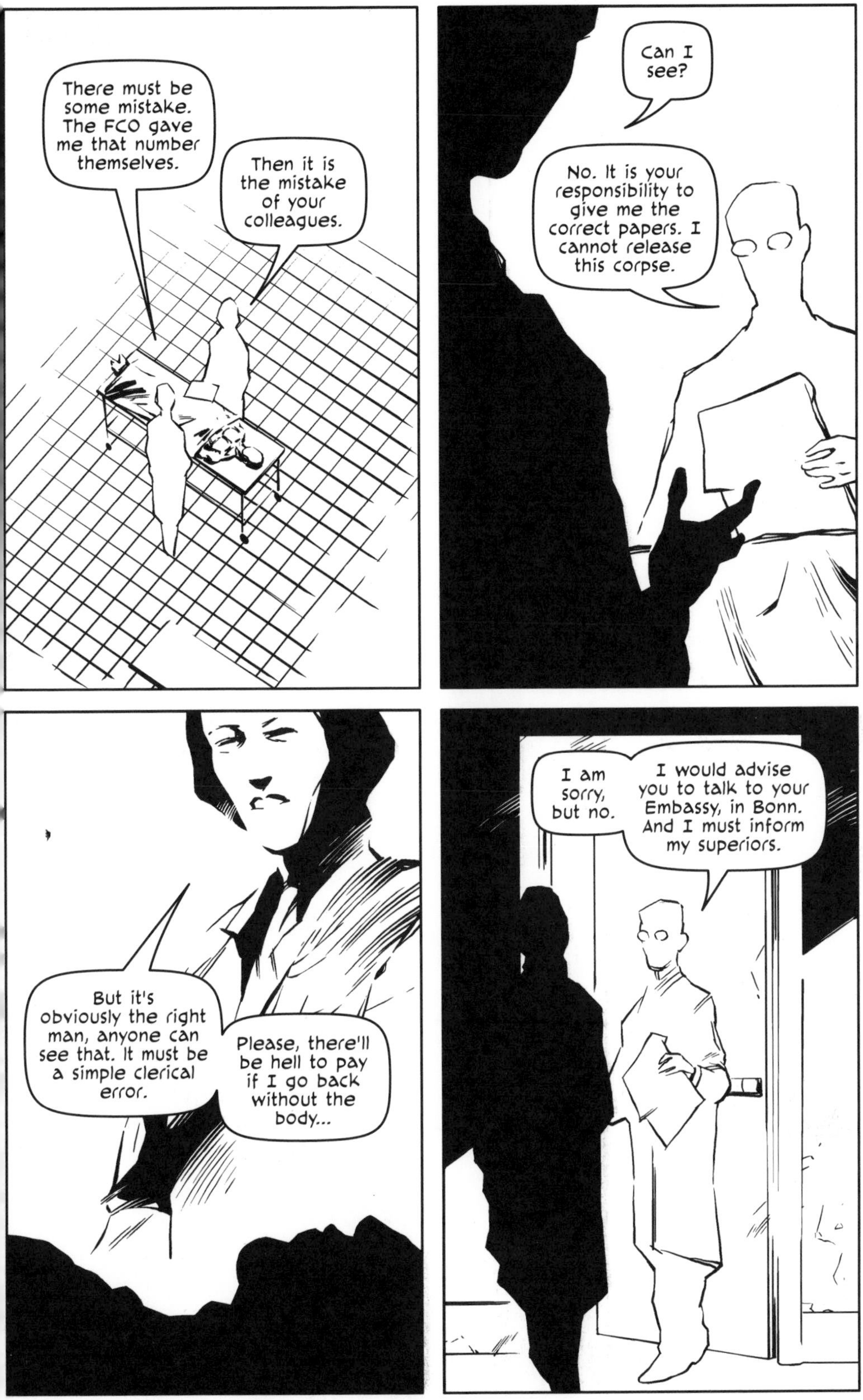
There must be some mistake. The FCO gave me that number themselves.
Then it is the mistake of your colleagues.
Can I see?
No. It is your responsibility to give me the correct papers. I cannot release this corpse.
But it's obviously the right man, anyone can see that. It must be a simple clerical error.
Please, there'll be hell to pay if I go back without the body...
I am sorry, but no.
I would advise you to talk to your Embassy, in Bonn. And I must inform my superiors.

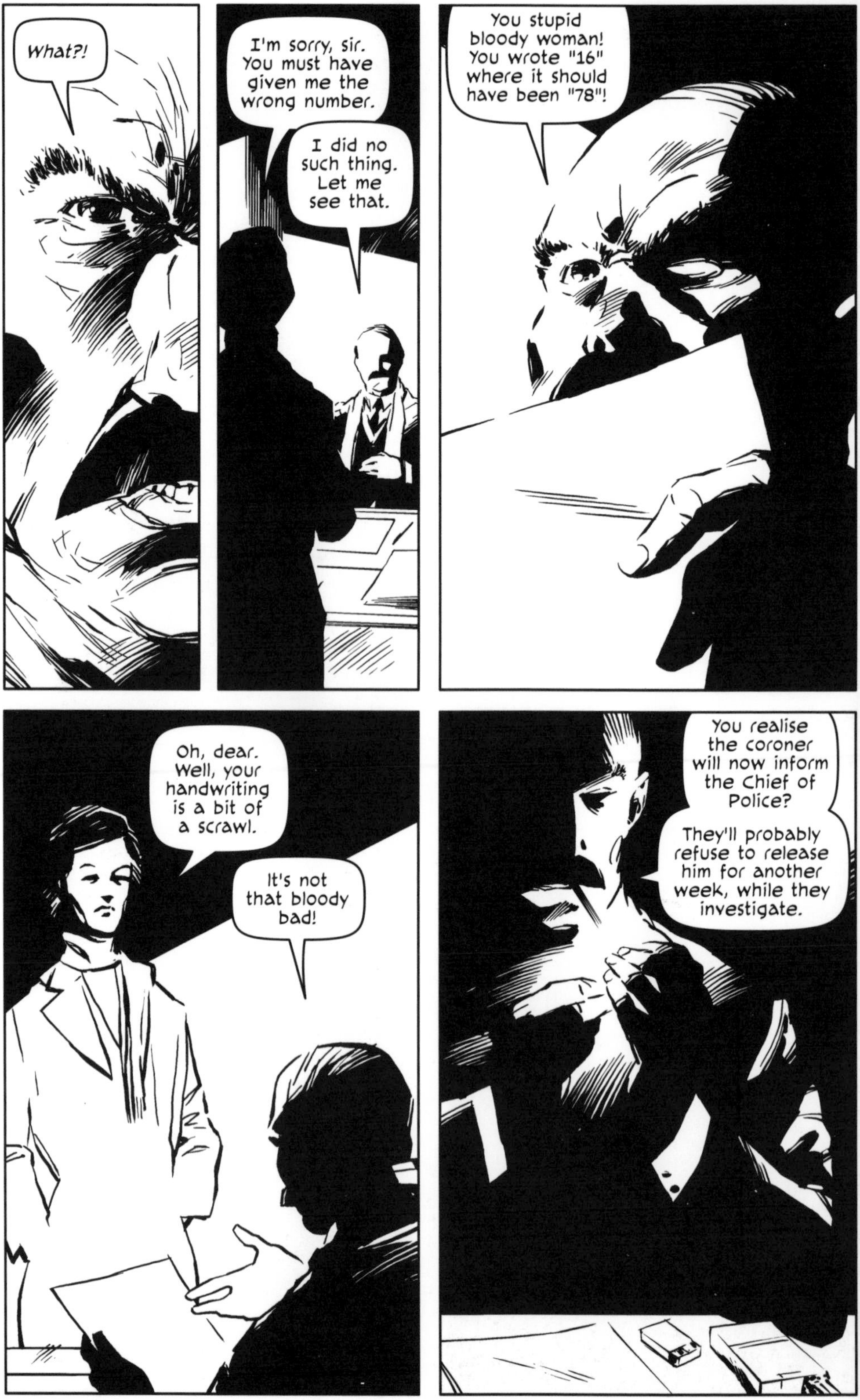
What?!
I'm sorry, sir. You must have given me the wrong number.
I did no such thing. Let me see that.
You stupid bloody woman! You wrote "16" where it should have been "78"!
Oh, dear. Well, your handwriting is a bit of a scrawl.
It's not that bloody bad!
You realise the coroner will now inform the Chief of Police?
They'll probably refuse to release him for another week, while they investigate.

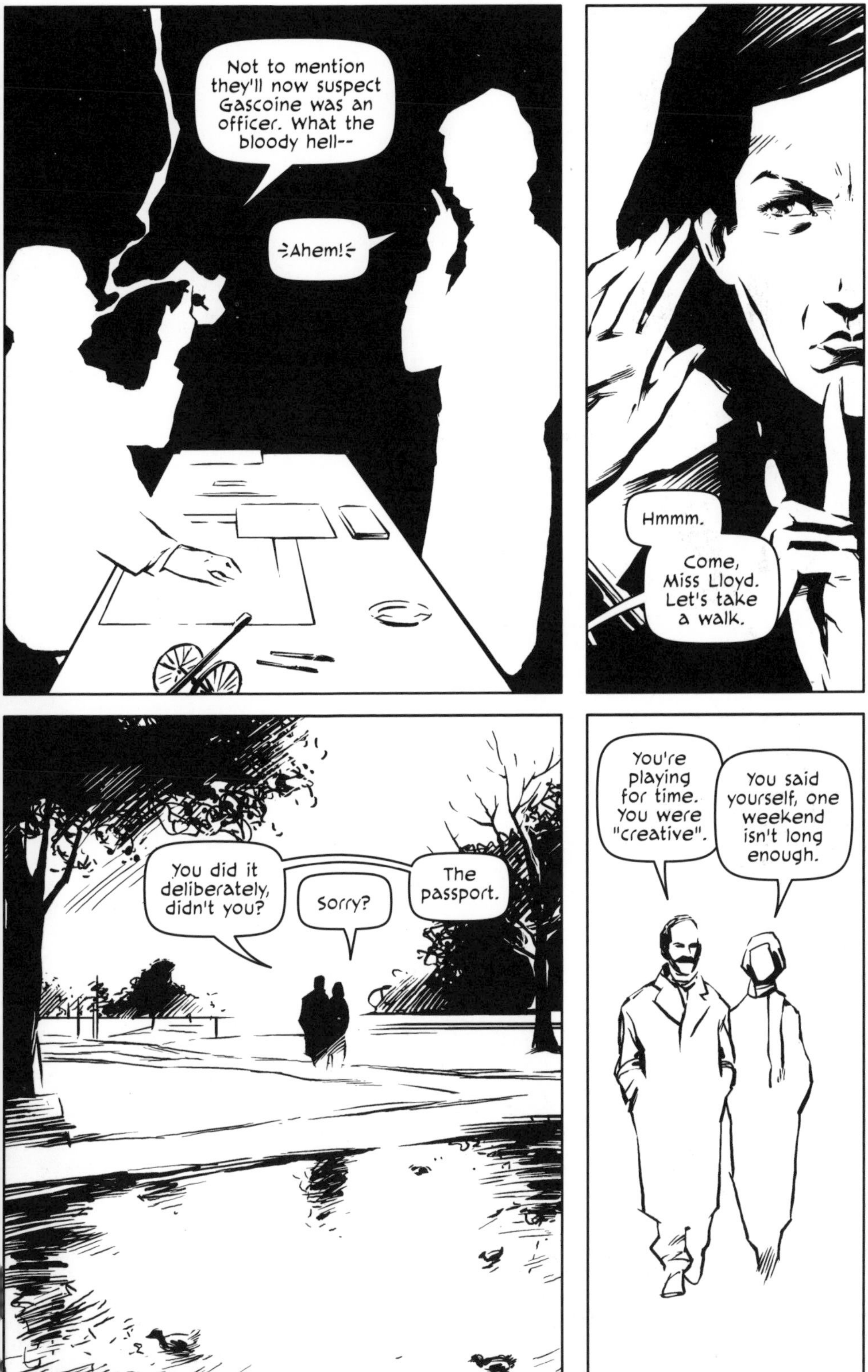
Not to mention they'll now suspect Gascoine was an officer. What the bloody hell--
Ahem!
Hmmm.
Come, Miss Lloyd. Let's take a walk.
You did it deliberately, didn't you?
Sorry?
The passport.
You're playing for time. You were "creative".
You said yourself, one weekend isn't long enough.

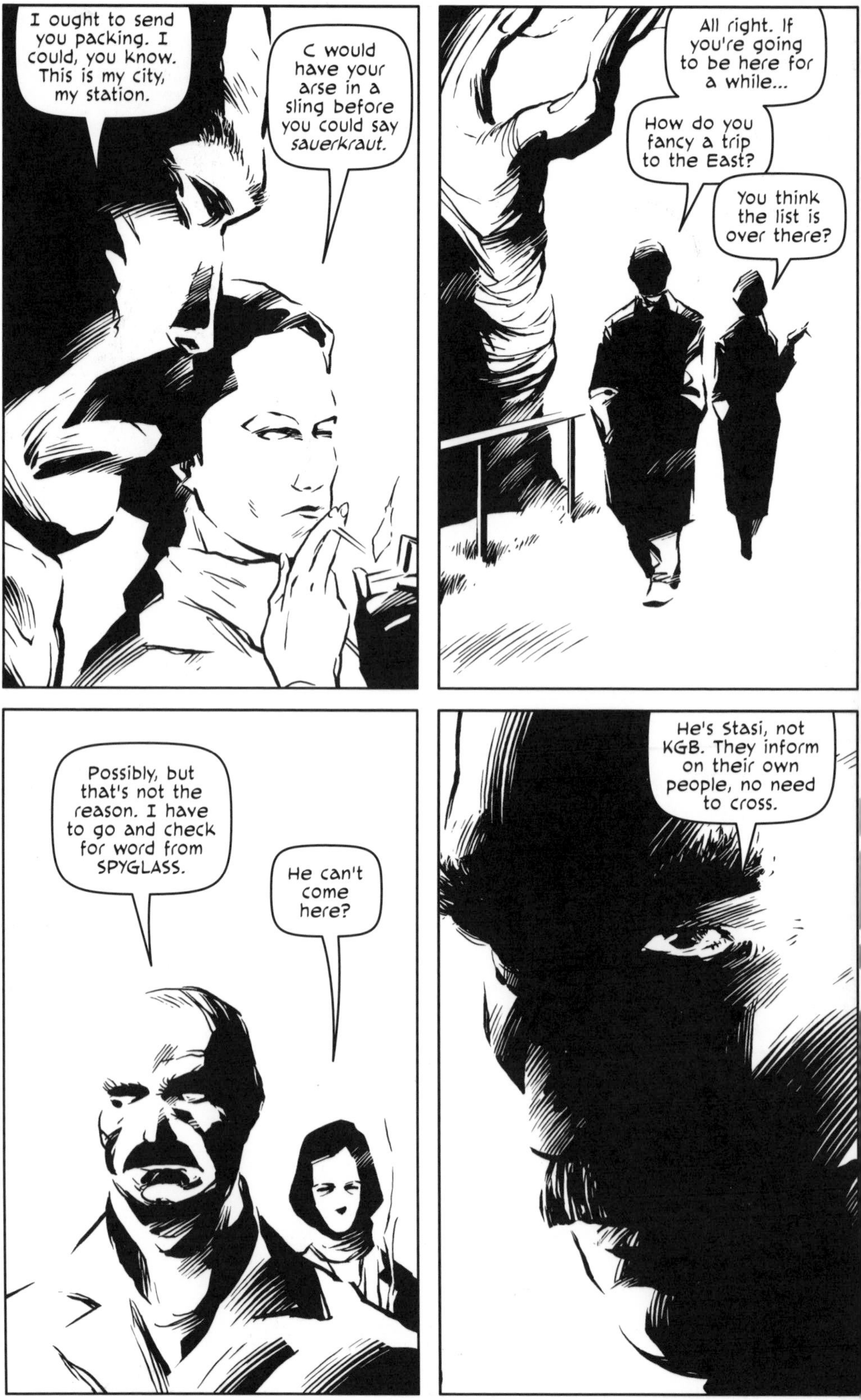
I ought to send you packing. I could, you know. This is my city, my station.
C would have your arse in a sling before you could say *sauerkraut*.
All right. If you're going to be here for a while...
How do you fancy a trip to the East?
You think the list is over there?
Possibly, but that's not the reason. I have to go and check for word from SPYGLASS.
He can't come here?
He's Stasi, not KGB. They inform on their own people, no need to cross.

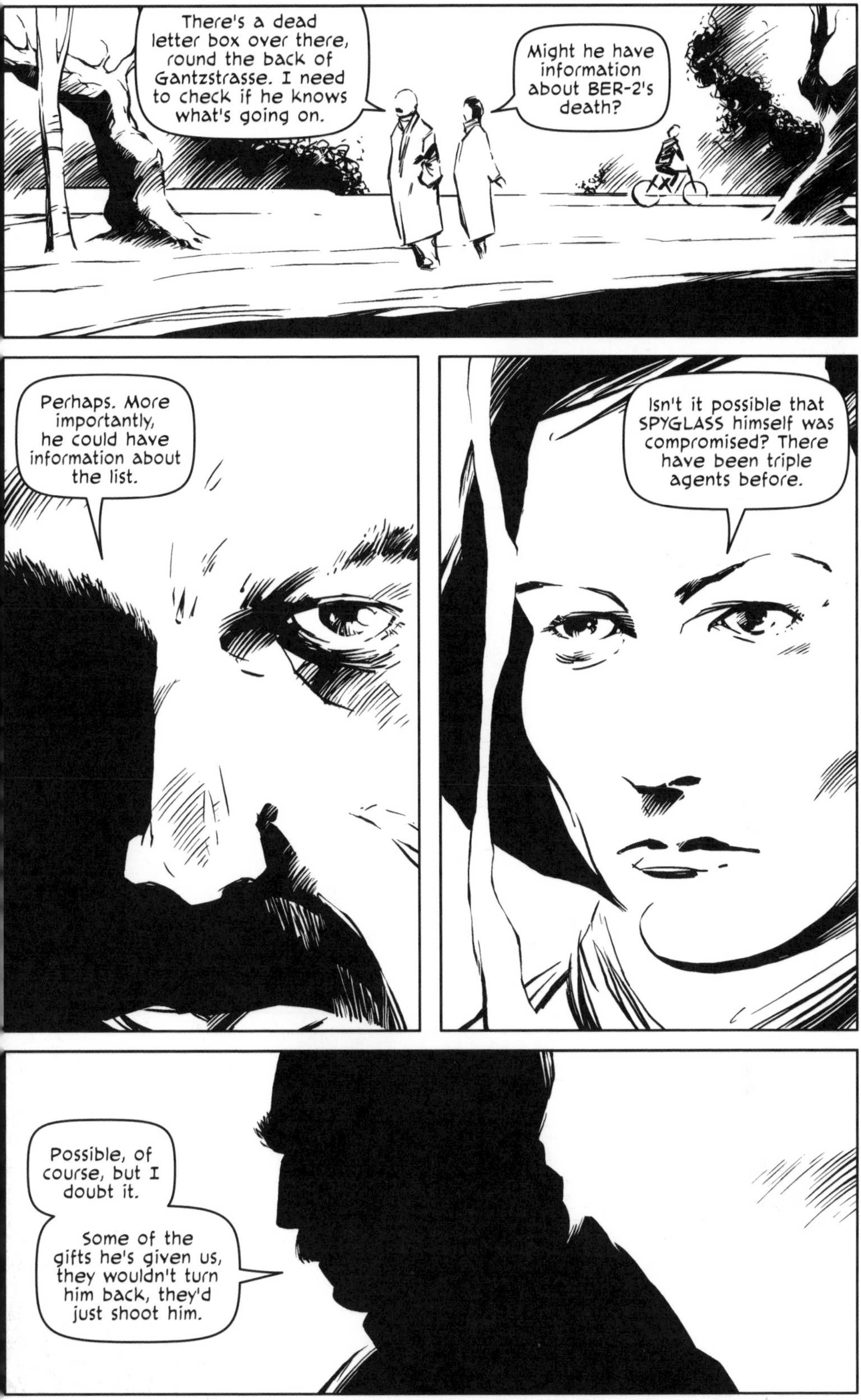
There's a dead letter box over there, round the back of Gantzstrasse. I need to check if he knows what's going on.
Might he have information about BER-2's death?
Perhaps. More importantly, he could have information about the list.
Isn't it possible that SPYGLASS himself was compromised? There have been triple agents before.
Possible, of course, but I doubt it.
Some of the gifts he's given us, they wouldn't turn him back, they'd just shoot him.

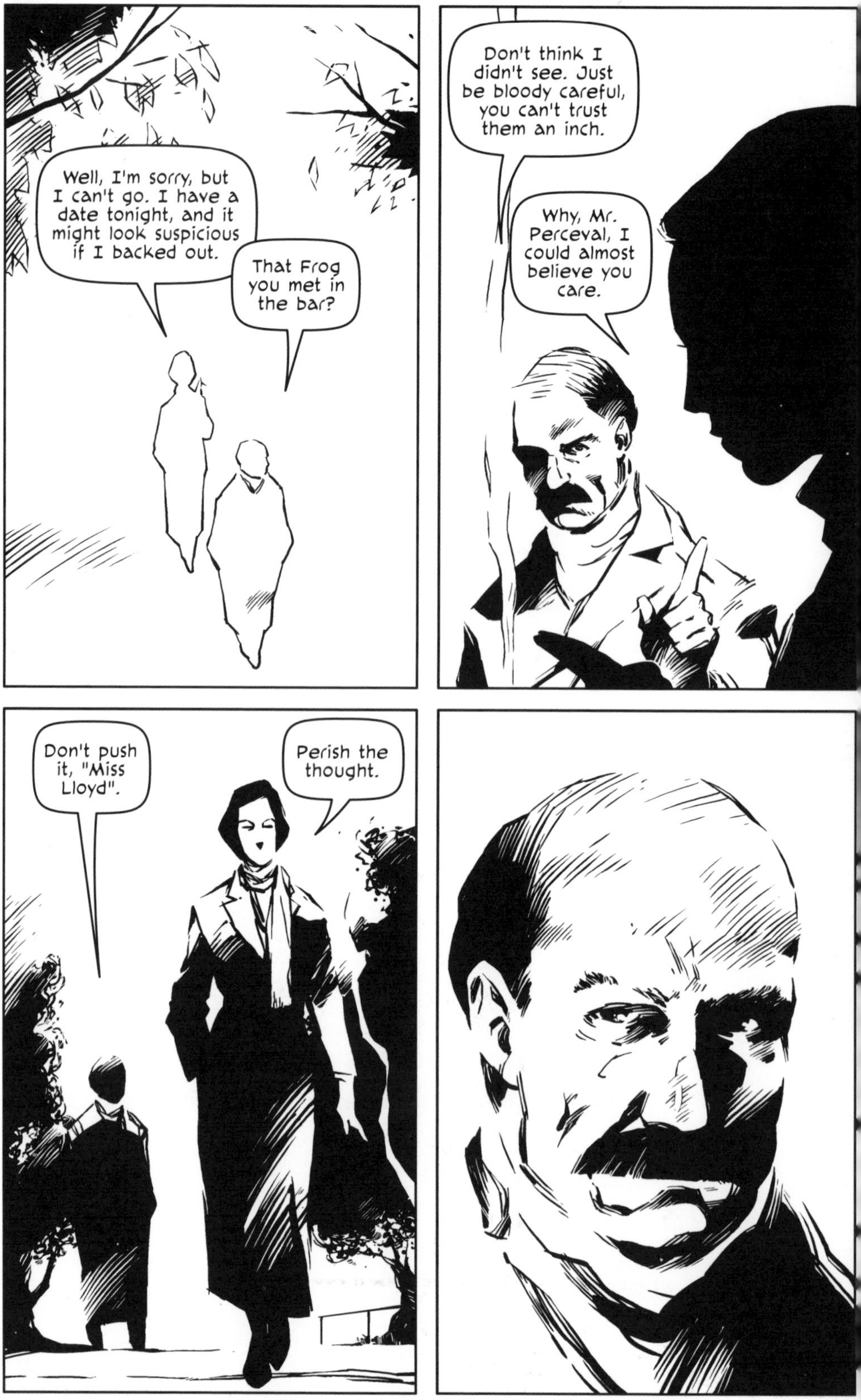
Well, I'm sorry, but I can't go. I have a date tonight, and it might look suspicious if I backed out.
That Frog you met in the bar?
Don't think I didn't see. Just be bloody careful, you can't trust them an inch.
Why, Mr. Perceval, I could almost believe you care.
Don't push it, "Miss Lloyd".
Perish the thought.

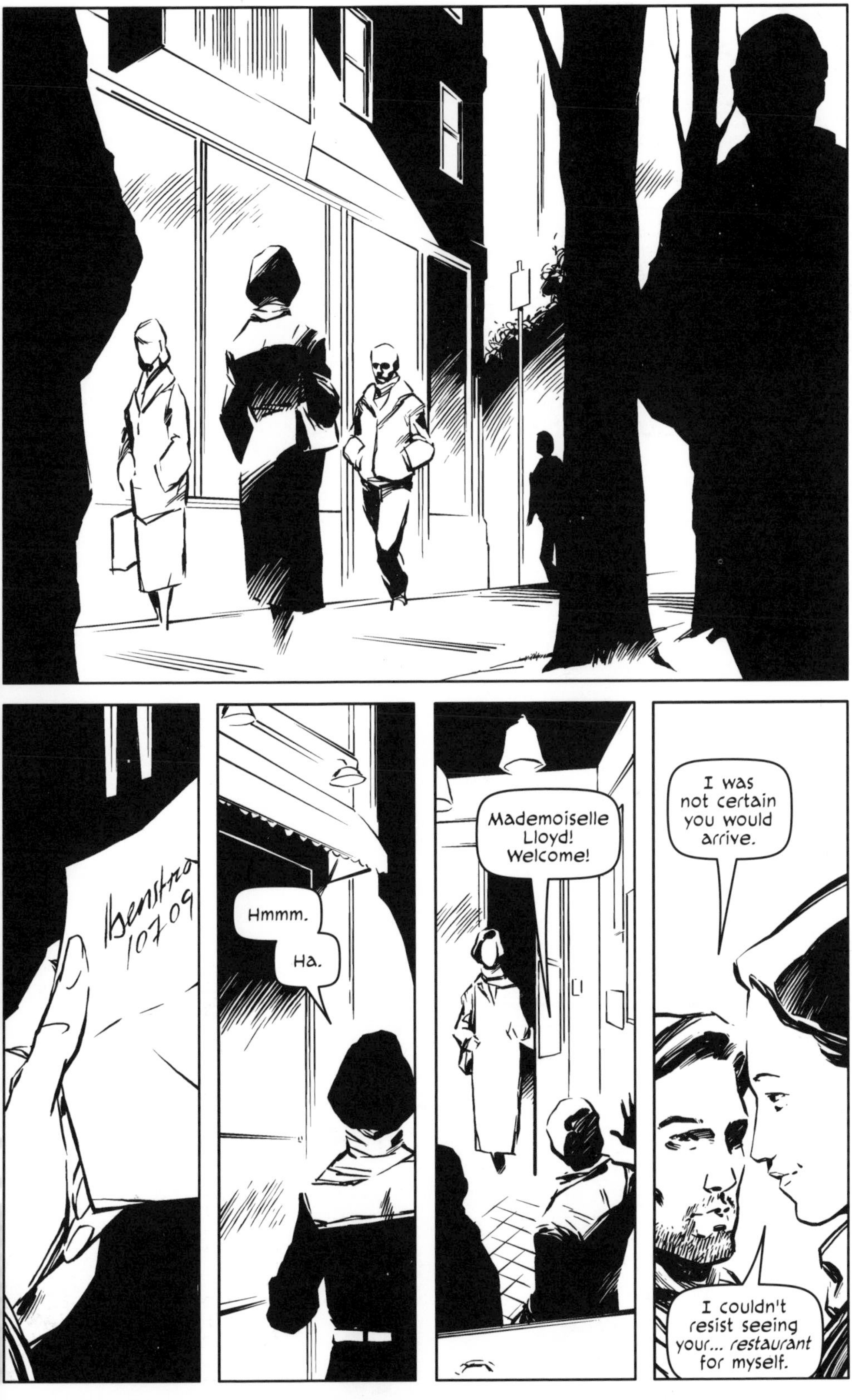
Hmmm.
Ha.
Mademoiselle Lloyd! Welcome!
I was not certain you would arrive.
I couldn't resist seeing your... *restaurant* for myself.

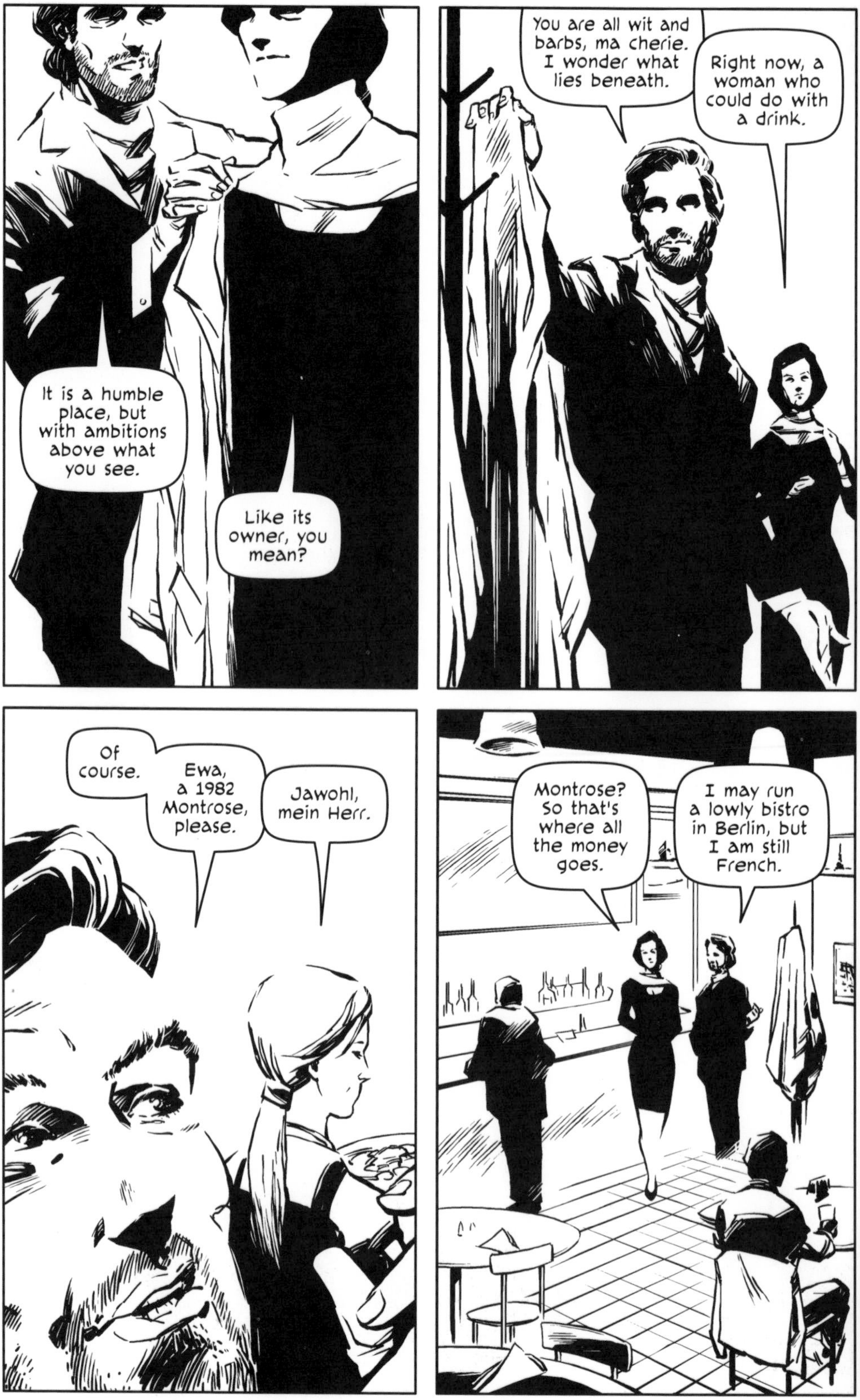
It is a humble place, but with ambitions above what you see.
Like its owner, you mean?
You are all wit and barbs, ma cherie. I wonder what lies beneath.
Right now, a woman who could do with a drink.
Of course.
Ewa, a 1982 Montrose, please.
Jawohl, mein Herr.
Montrose? So that's where all the money goes.
I may run a lowly bistro in Berlin, but I am still French.

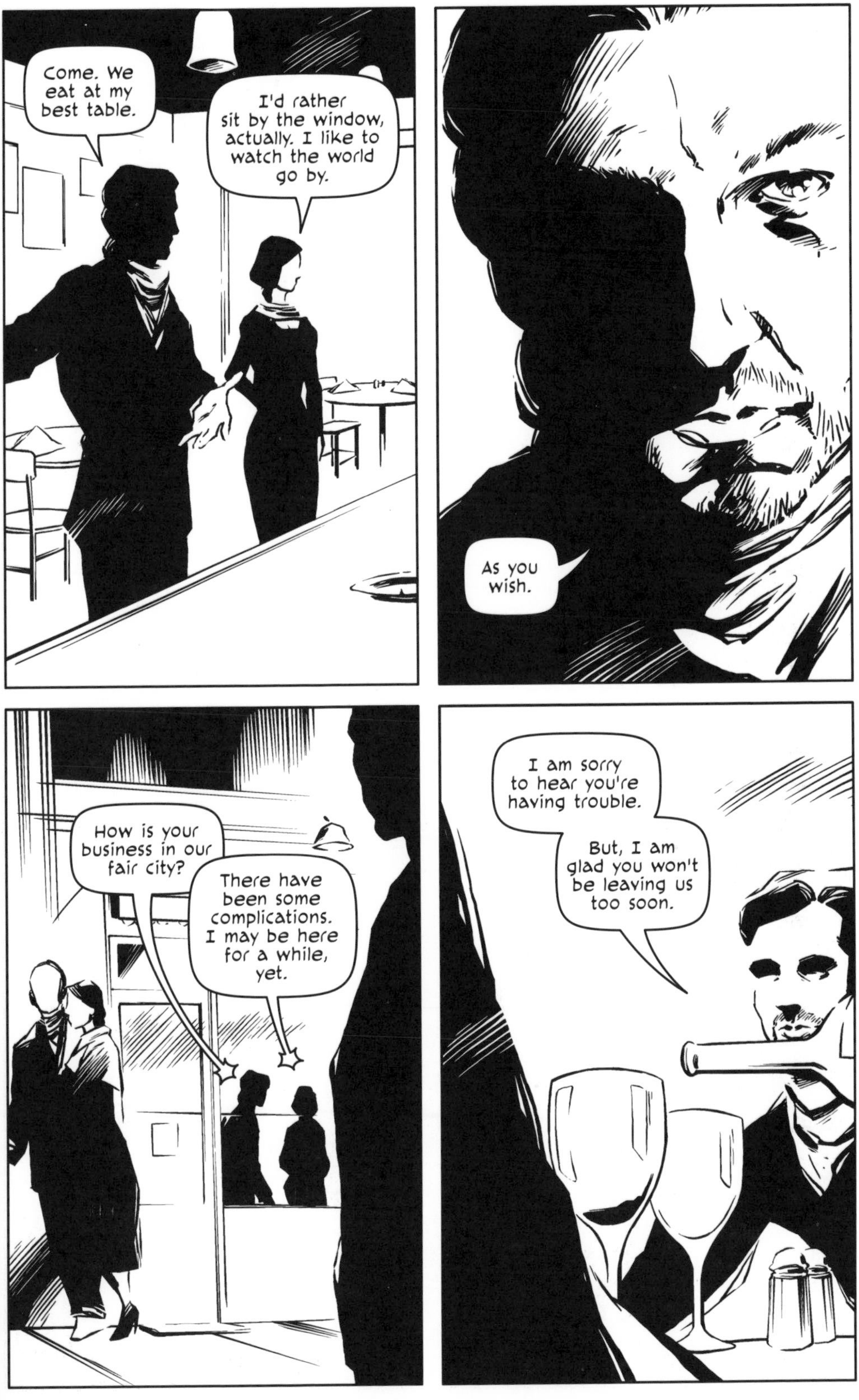
Come. We eat at my best table.
I'd rather sit by the window, actually. I like to watch the world go by.
As you wish.
How is your business in our fair city?
There have been some complications. I may be here for a while, yet.
I am sorry to hear you're having trouble.
But, I am glad you won't be leaving us too soon.

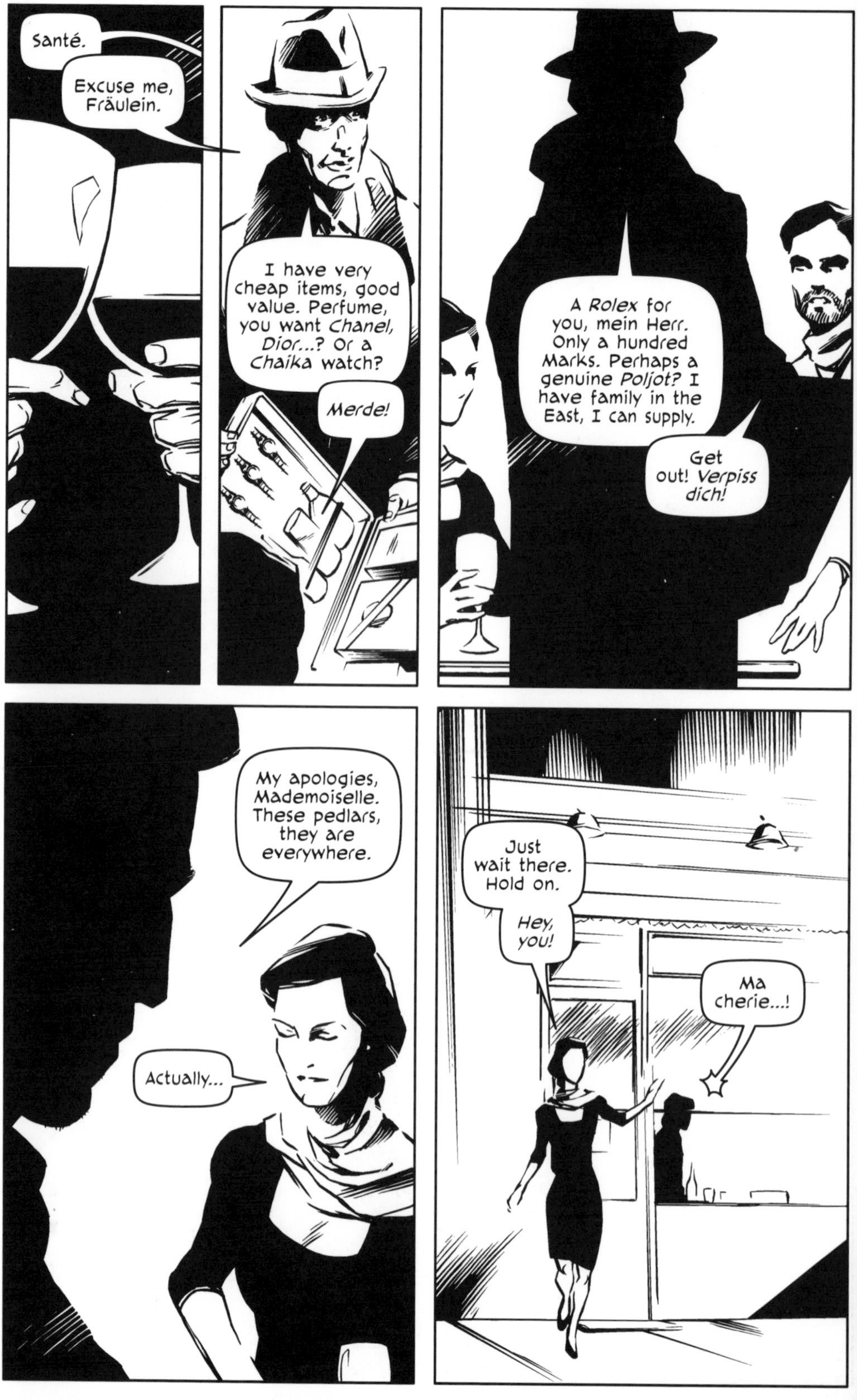
Santé.
Excuse me, Fräulein.
I have very cheap items, good value. Perfume, you want *Chanel, Dior...*? Or a *Chaika* watch?
Merde!
A *Rolex* for you, mein Herr. Only a hundred Marks. Perhaps a genuine *Poljot?* I have family in the East, I can supply.
Get out! *Verpiss dich!*
My apologies, Mademoiselle. These pedlars, they are everywhere.
Actually...
Just wait there. Hold on.
Hey, you!
Ma cherie...!

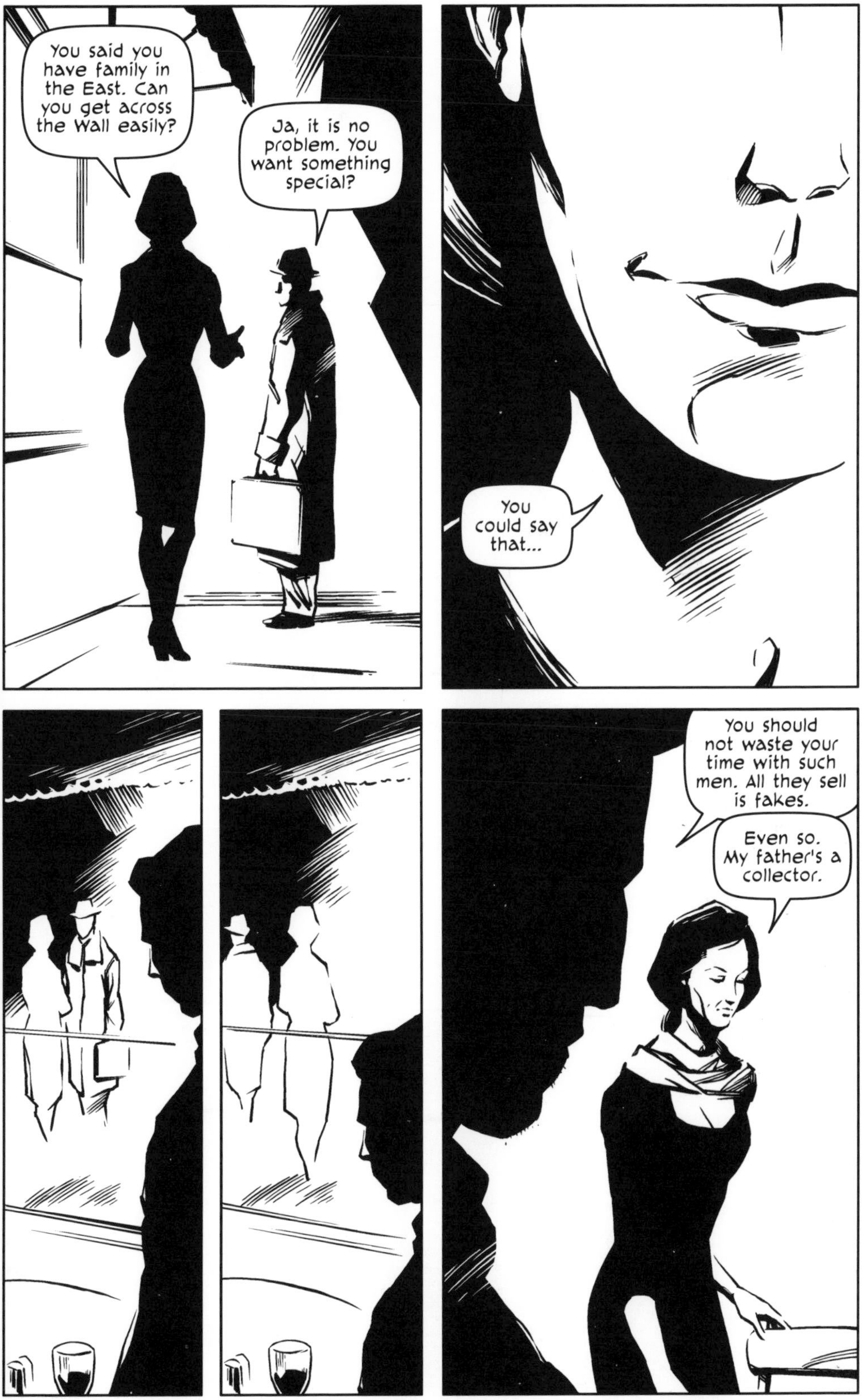
You said you have family in the East. Can you get across the Wall easily?
Ja, it is no problem. You want something special?
You could say that...
You should not waste your time with such men. All they sell is fakes.
Even so. My father's a collector.

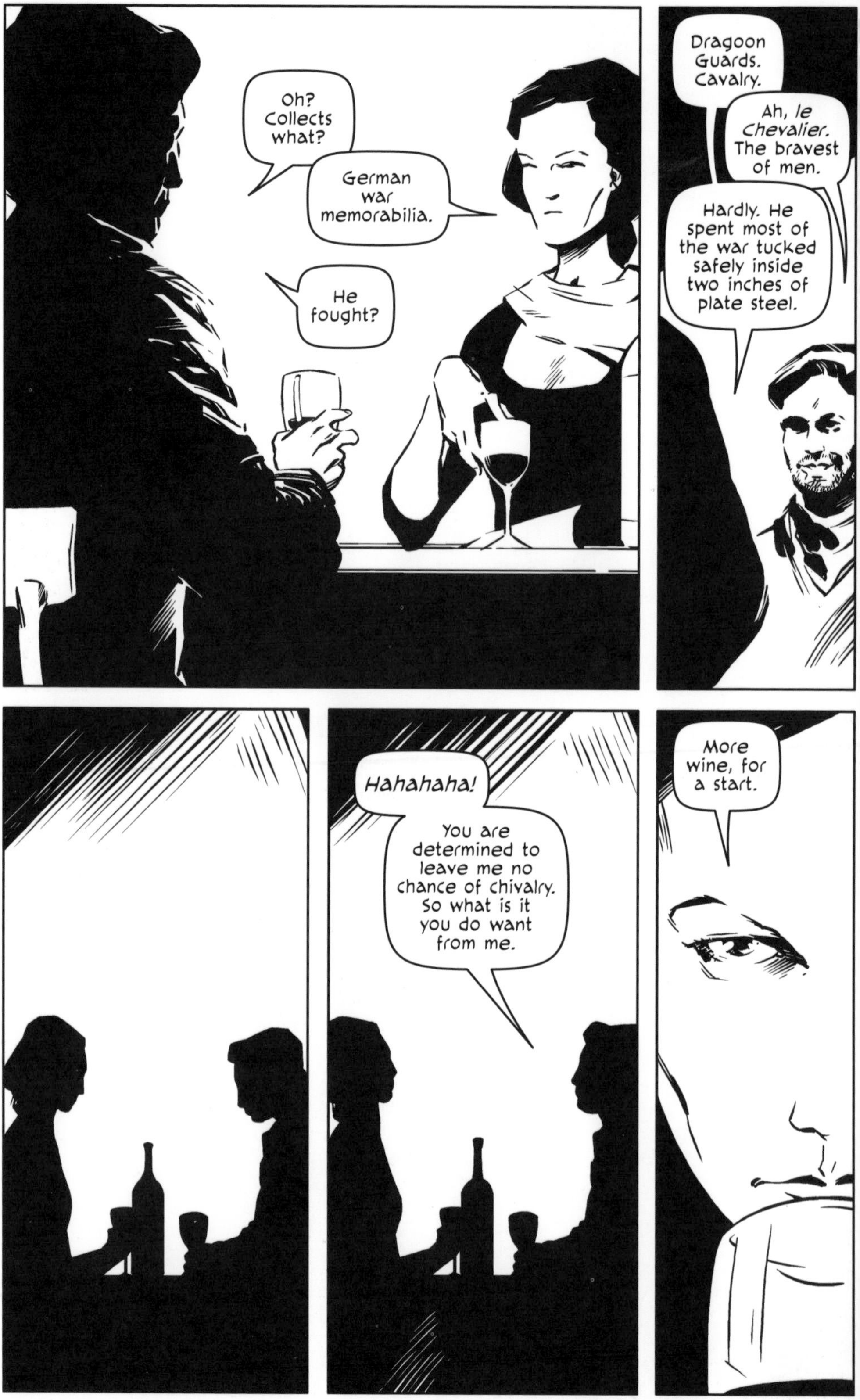
Oh? Collects what?
German war memorabilia.
He fought?
Dragoon Guards. Cavalry.
Ah, *le Chevalier.* The bravest of men.
Hardly. He spent most of the war tucked safely inside two inches of plate steel.
Hahahaha!
You are determined to leave me no chance of chivalry. So what is it you do want from me.
More wine, for a start.

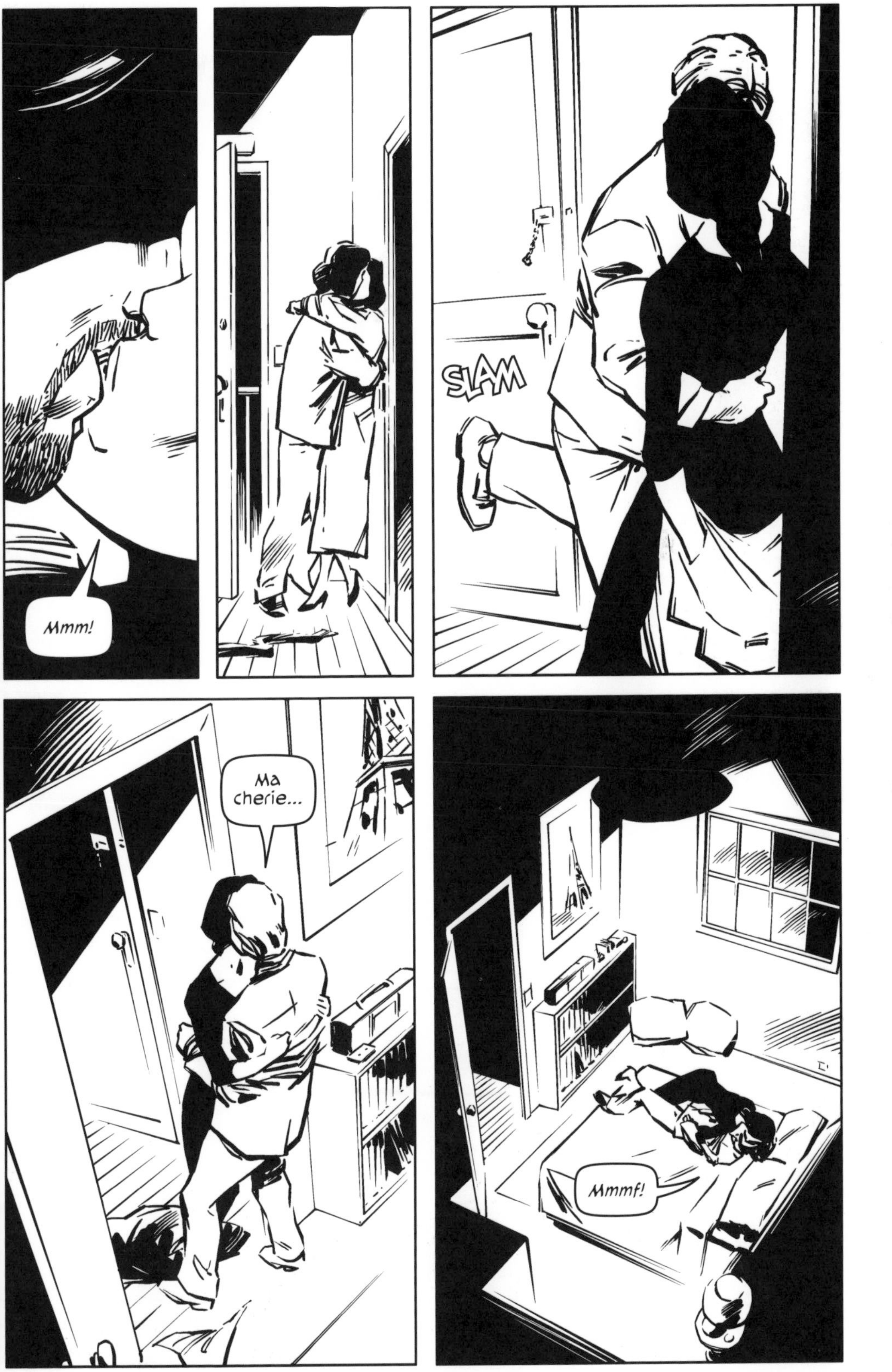
Mmm!
SLAM
Ma cherie...
Mmmf!

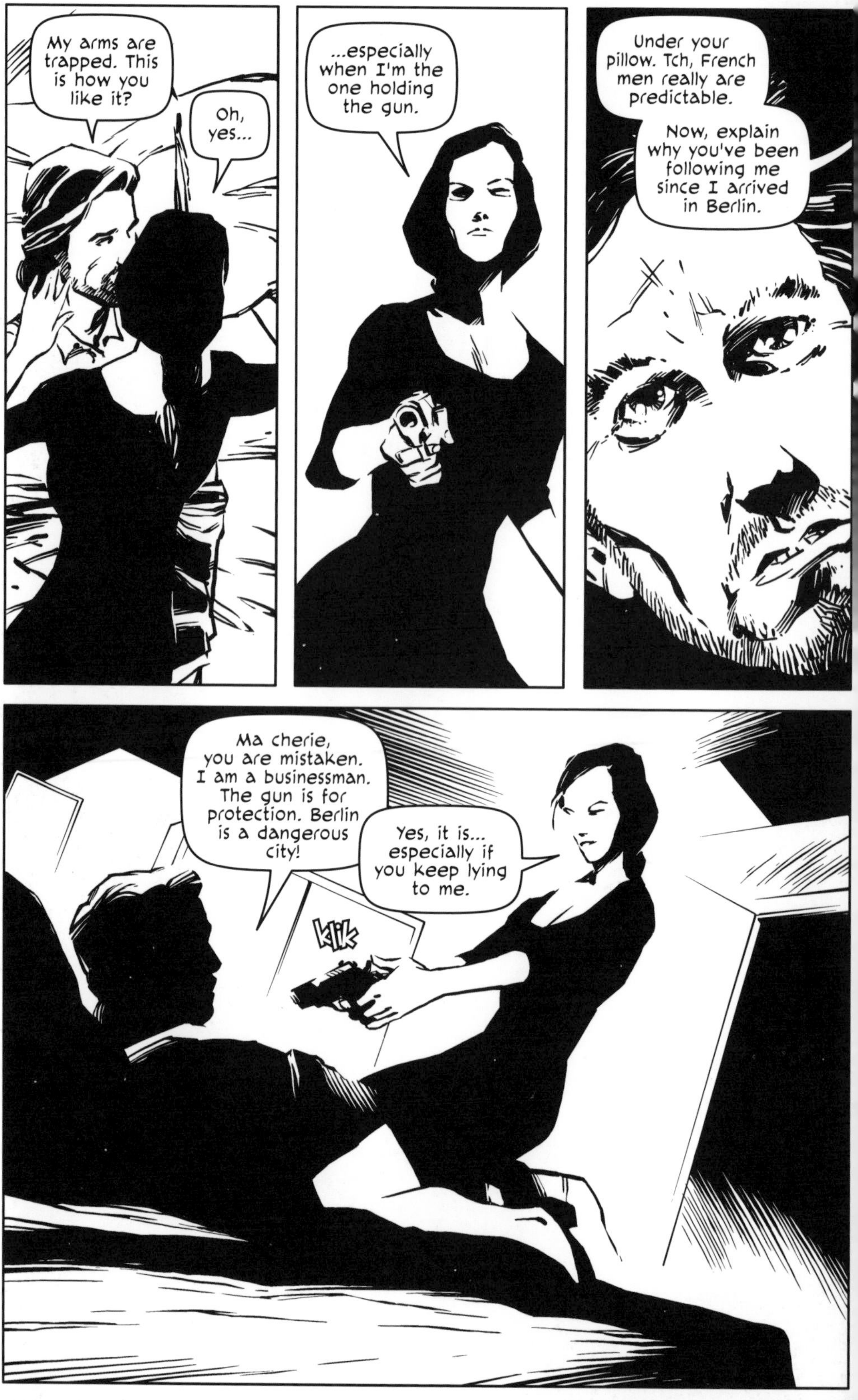
My arms are trapped. This is how you like it?
Oh, yes...
...especially when I'm the one holding the gun.
Under your pillow. Tch, French men really are predictable.
Now, explain why you've been following me since I arrived in Berlin.
Ma cherie, you are mistaken. I am a businessman. The gun is for protection. Berlin is a dangerous city!
Yes, it is... especially if you keep lying to me.
klik

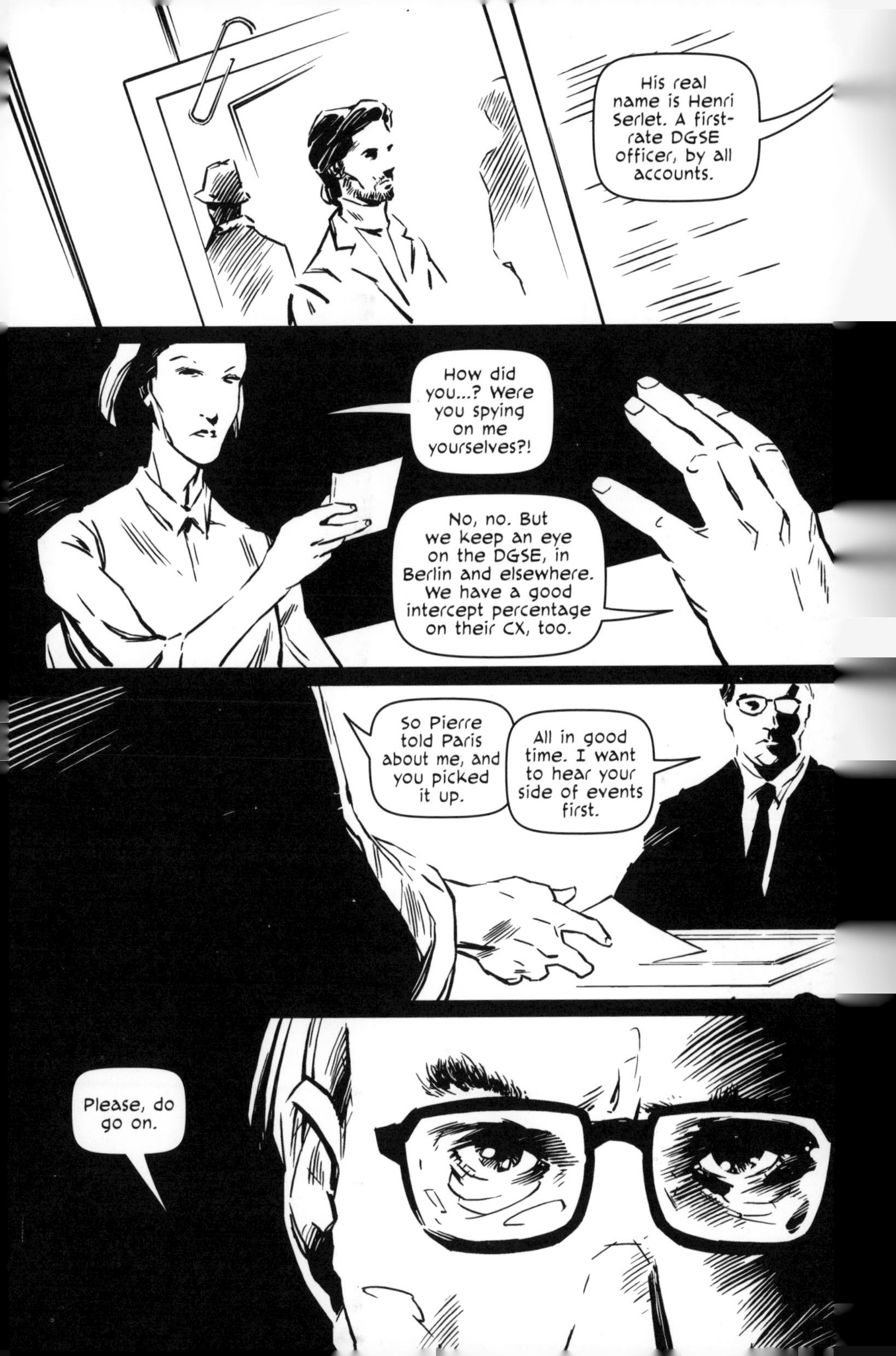
His real name is Henri Serlet. A first-rate DGSE officer, by all accounts.
How did you...? Were you spying on me yourselves?!
No, no. But we keep an eye on the DGSE, in Berlin and elsewhere. We have a good intercept percentage on their CX, too.
So Pierre told Paris about me, and you picked it up.
All in good time. I want to hear your side of events first.
Please, do go on.

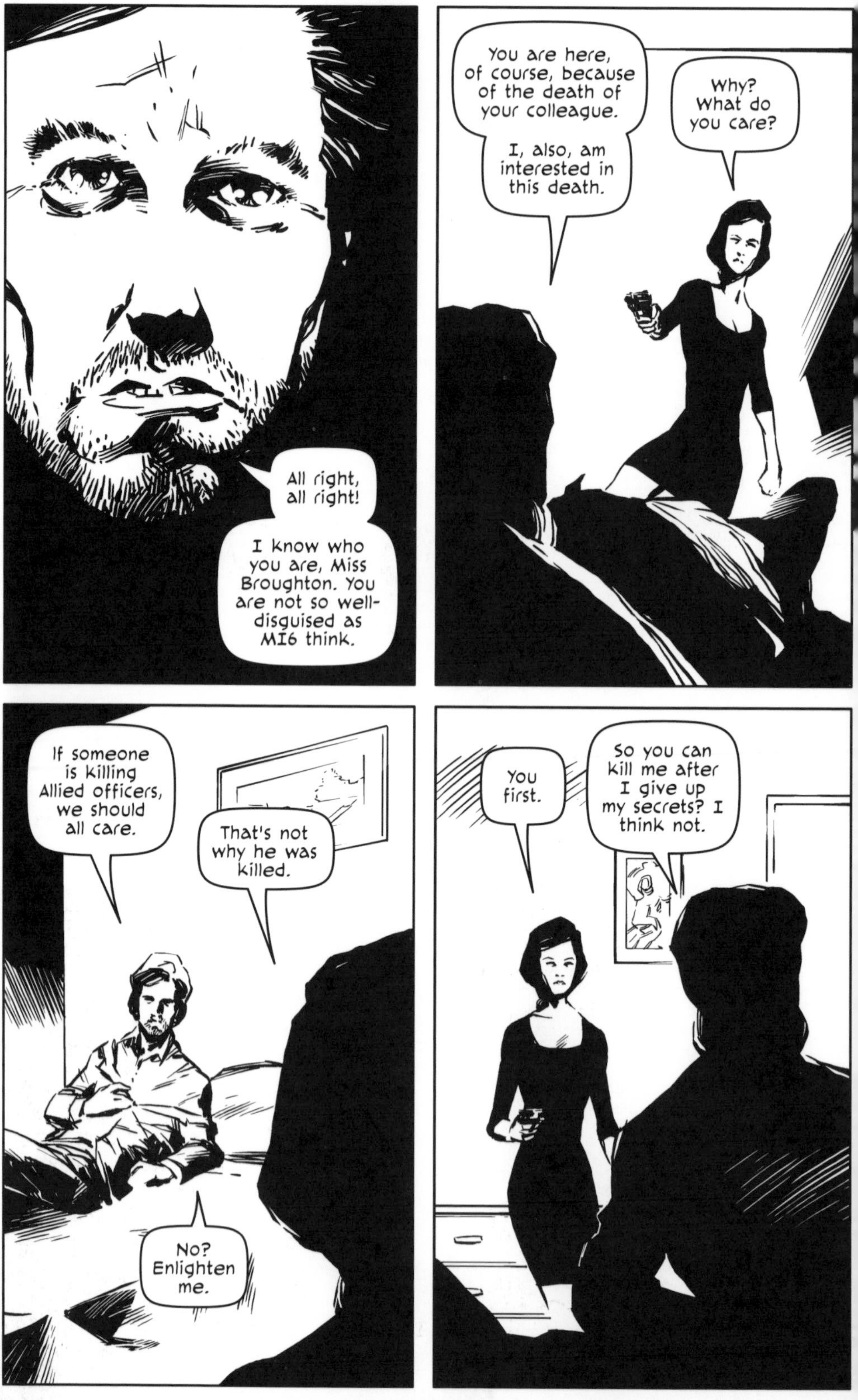
All right, all right!
I know who you are, Miss Broughton. You are not so well-disguised as MI6 think.
You are here, of course, because of the death of your colleague.
I, also, am interested in this death.
Why? What do you care?
If someone is killing Allied officers, we should all care.
That's not why he was killed.
No? Enlighten me.
You first.
So you can kill me after I give up my secrets? I think not.

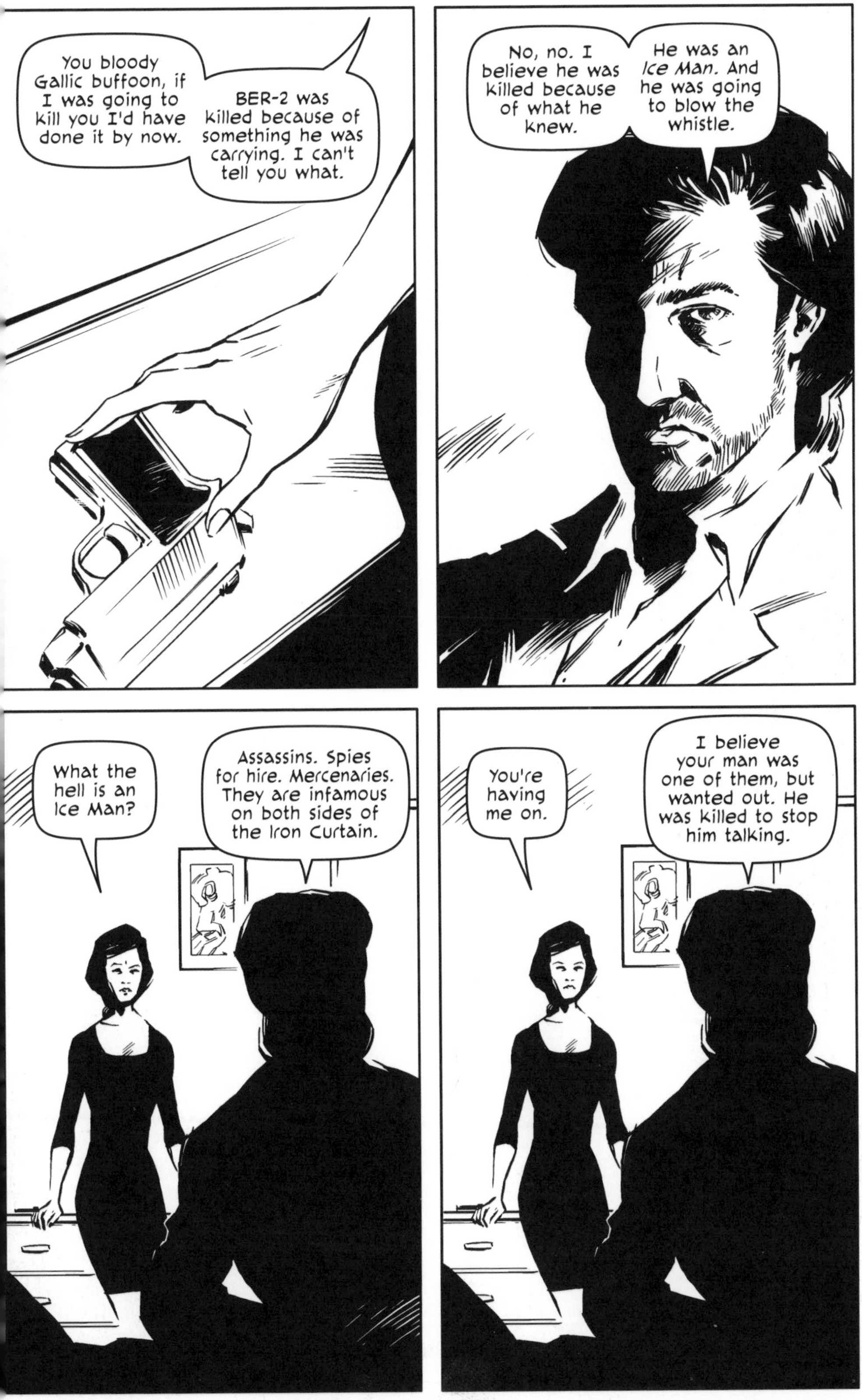

You bloody Gallic buffoon, if I was going to kill you I'd have done it by now.
BER-2 was killed because of something he was carrying. I can't tell you what.
No, no. I believe he was killed because of what he knew.
He was an *Ice Man*. And he was going to blow the whistle.
What the hell is an Ice Man?
Assassins. Spies for hire. Mercenaries. They are infamous on both sides of the Iron Curtain.
You're having me on.
I believe your man was one of them, but wanted out. He was killed to stop him talking.

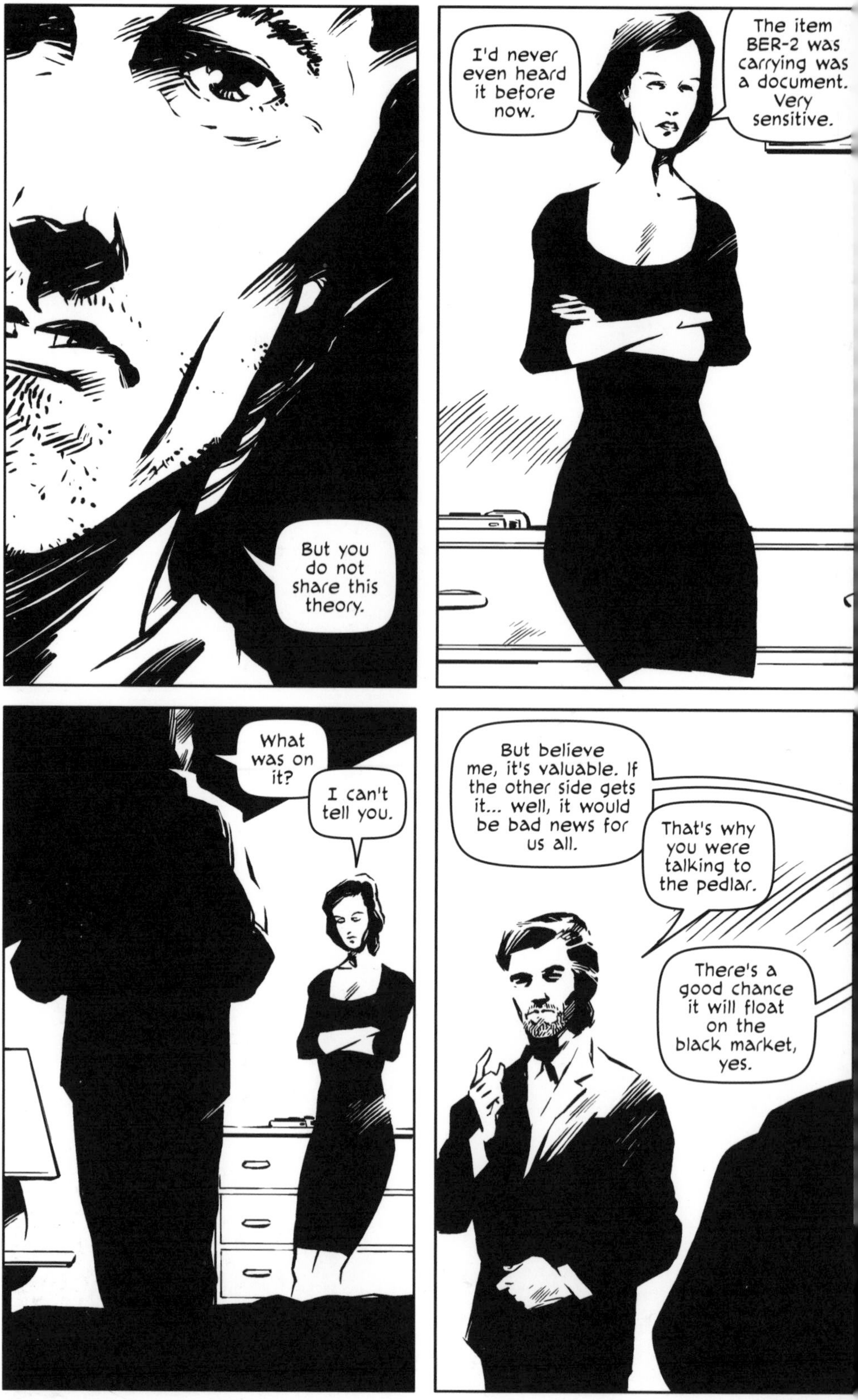
But you do not share this theory.
I'd never even heard it before now.
The item BER-2 was carrying was a document. Very sensitive.
What was on it?
I can't tell you.
But believe me, it's valuable. If the other side gets it... well, it would be bad news for us all.
That's why you were talking to the pedlar.
There's a good chance it will float on the black market, yes.

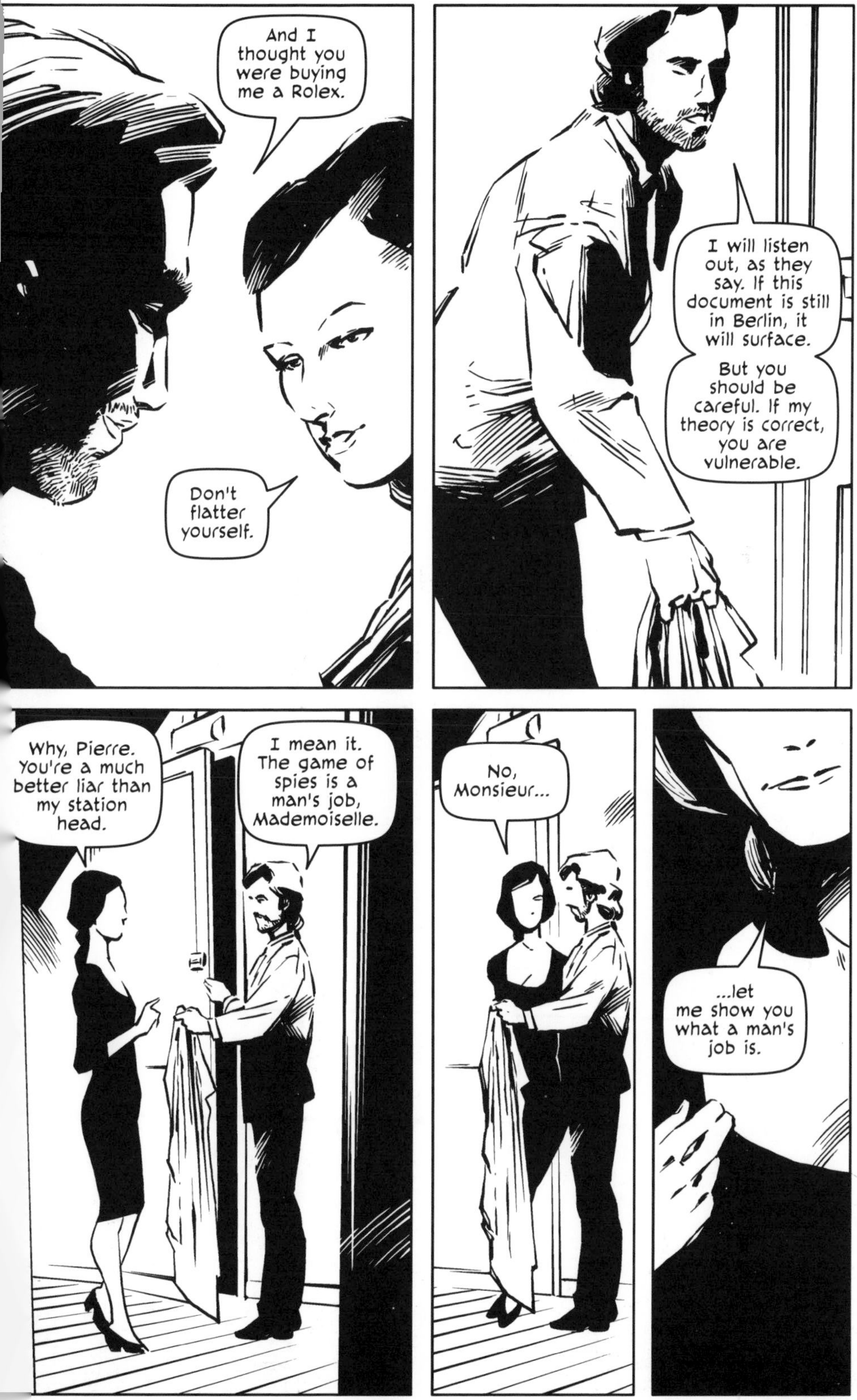
And I thought you were buying me a Rolex.
Don't flatter yourself.
I will listen out, as they say. If this document is still in Berlin, it will surface.
But you should be careful. If my theory is correct, you are vulnerable.
Why, Pierre. You're a much better liar than my station head.
I mean it. The game of spies is a man's job, Mademoiselle.
No, Monsieur...
...let me show you what a man's job is.

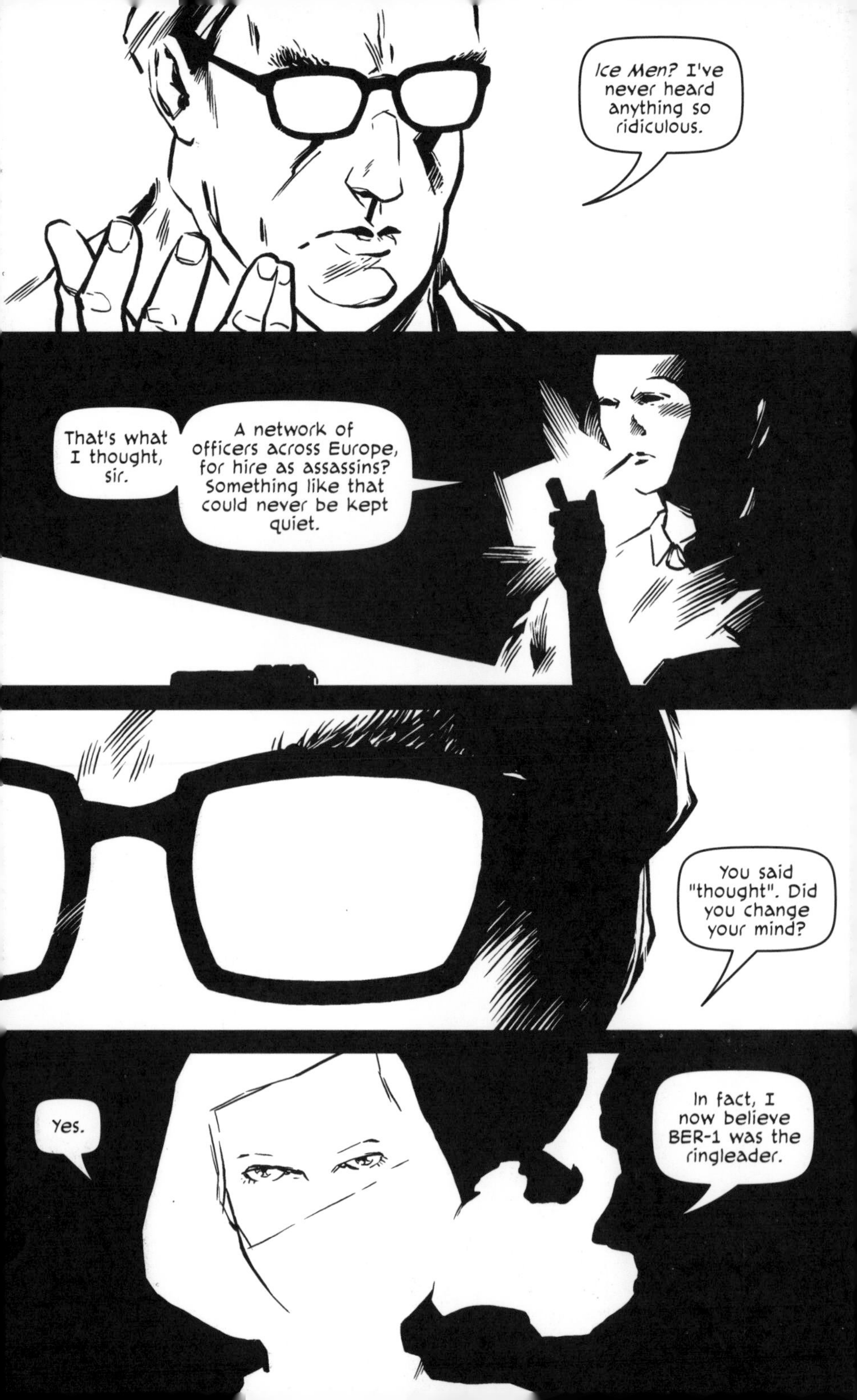
Ice Men? I've never heard anything so ridiculous.
That's what I thought, sir.
A network of officers across Europe, for hire as assassins? Something like that could never be kept quiet.
You said "thought". Did you change your mind?
Yes.
In fact, I now believe BER-1 was the ringleader.

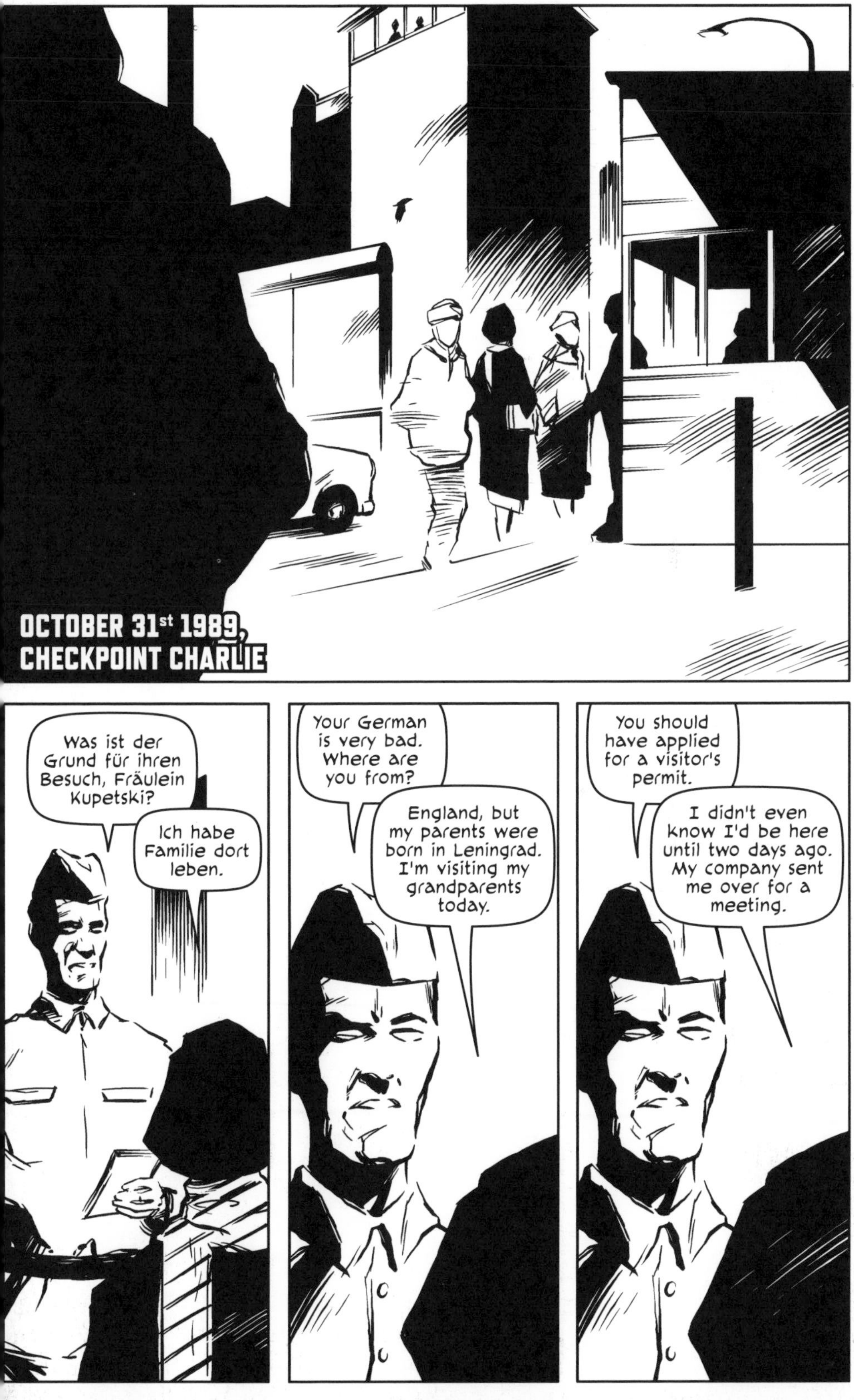
OCTOBER 31st 1989,
CHECKPOINT CHARLIE
Was ist der Grund für ihren Besuch, Fräulein Kupetski?
Ich habe Familie dort leben.
Your German is very bad. Where are you from?
England, but my parents were born in Leningrad. I'm visiting my grandparents today.
You should have applied for a visitor's permit.
I didn't even know I'd be here until two days ago. My company sent me over for a meeting.

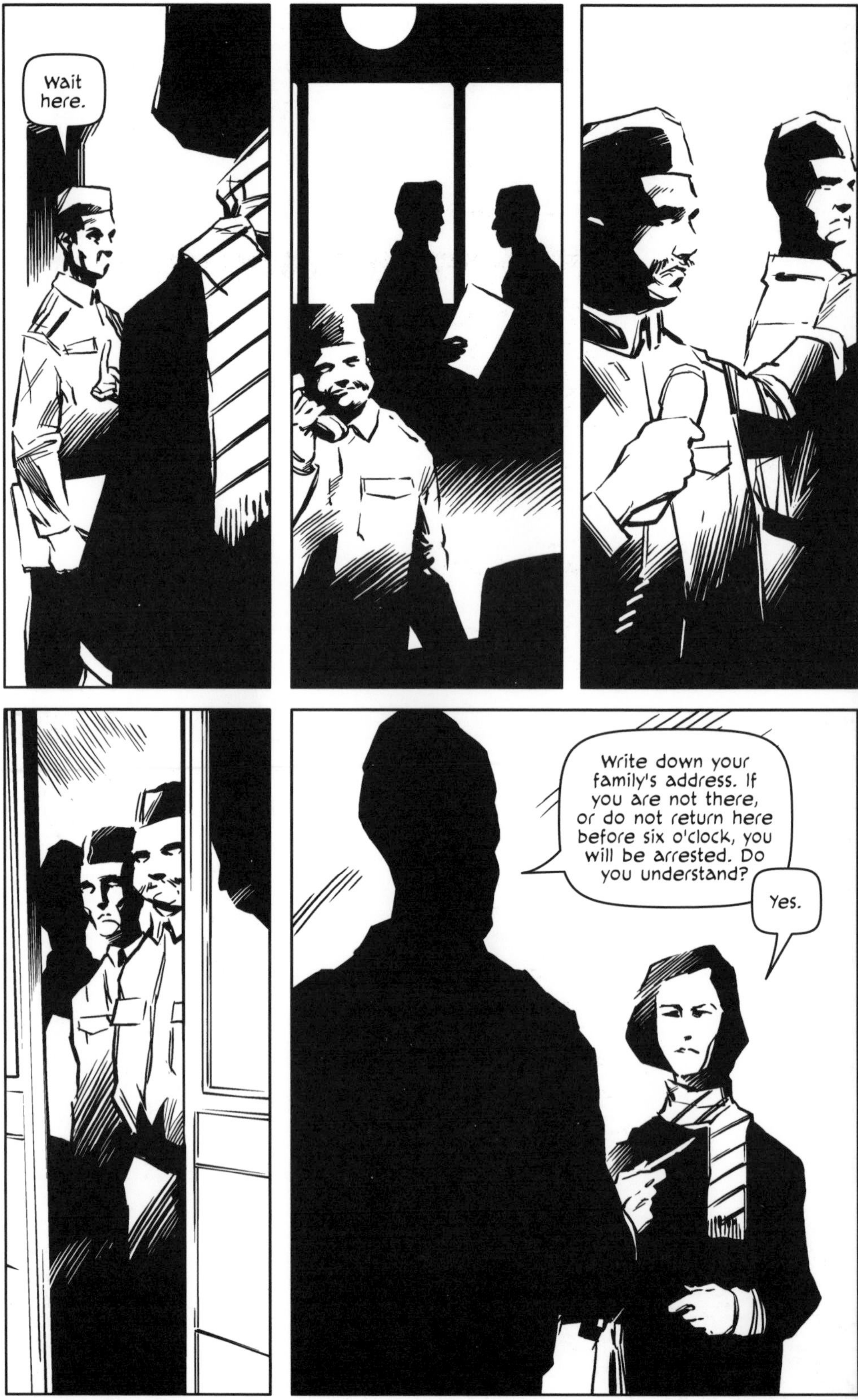
Wait here.
Write down your family's address. If you are not there, or do not return here before six o'clock, you will be arrested. Do you understand?
Yes.

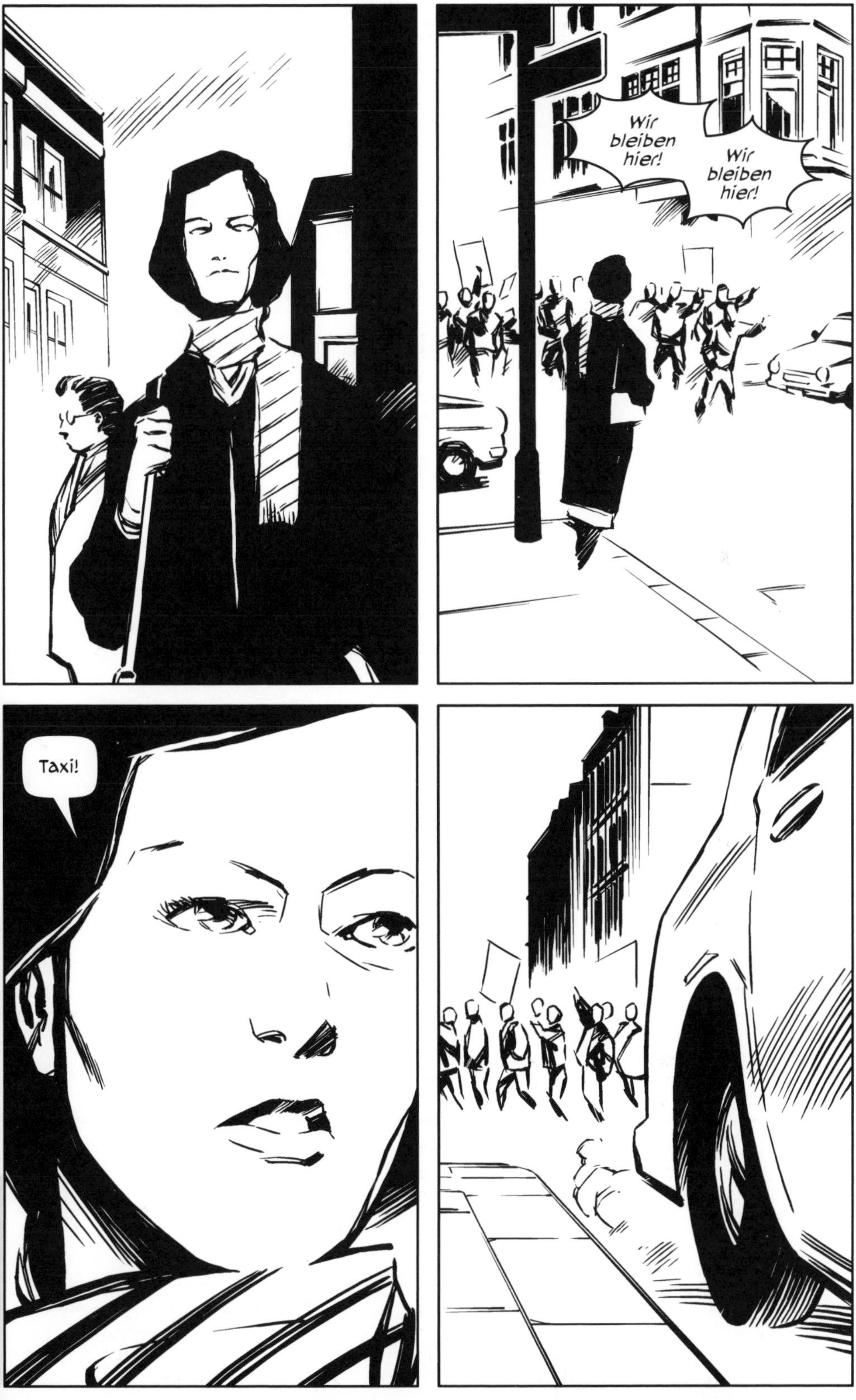
Wir bleiben hier!
Wir bleiben hier!
Taxi!

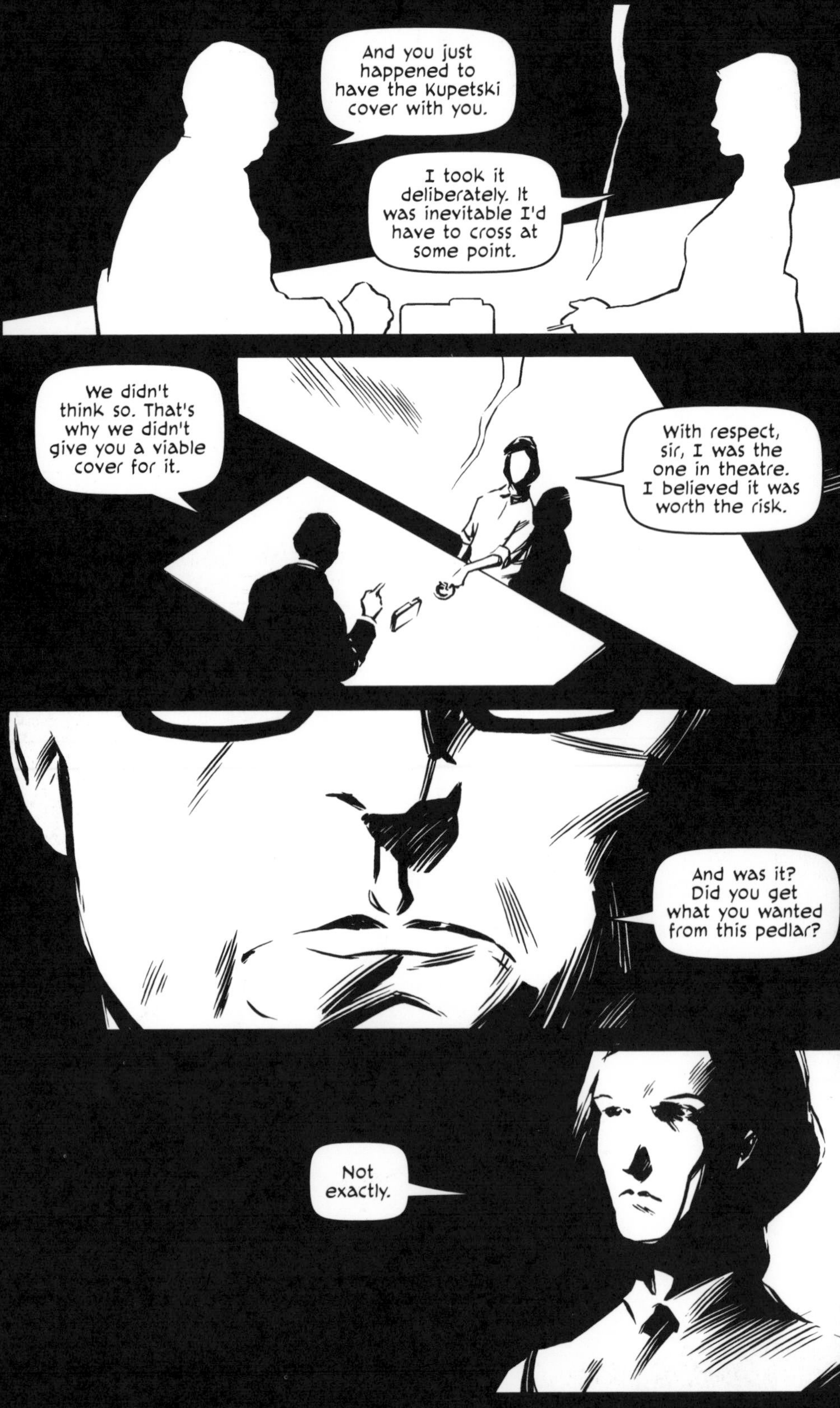
And you just happened to have the Kupetski cover with you.
I took it deliberately. It was inevitable I'd have to cross at some point.
We didn't think so. That's why we didn't give you a viable cover for it.
With respect, sir, I was the one in theatre. I believed it was worth the risk.
And was it? Did you get what you wanted from this pedlar?
Not exactly.

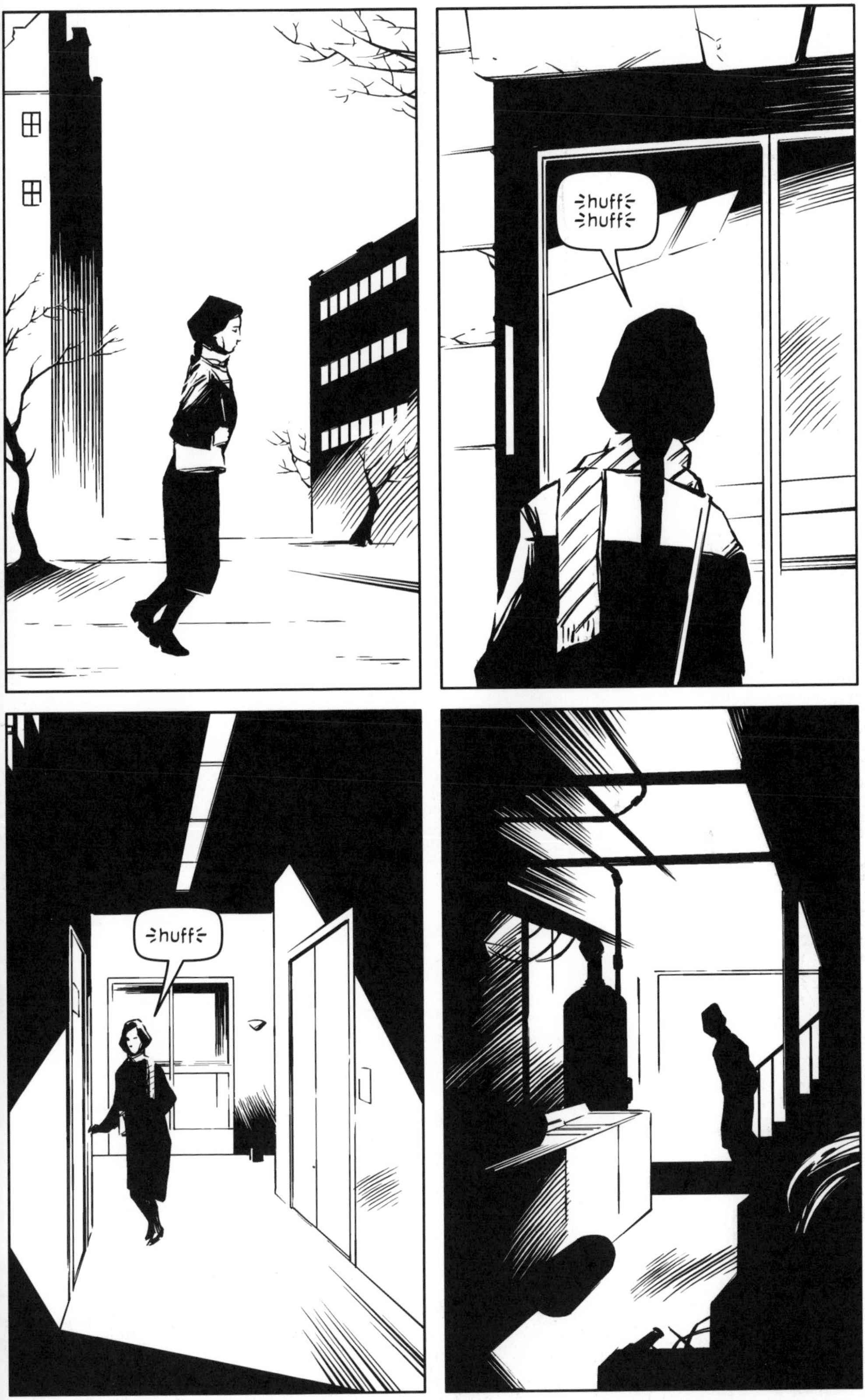
huff
huff
huff

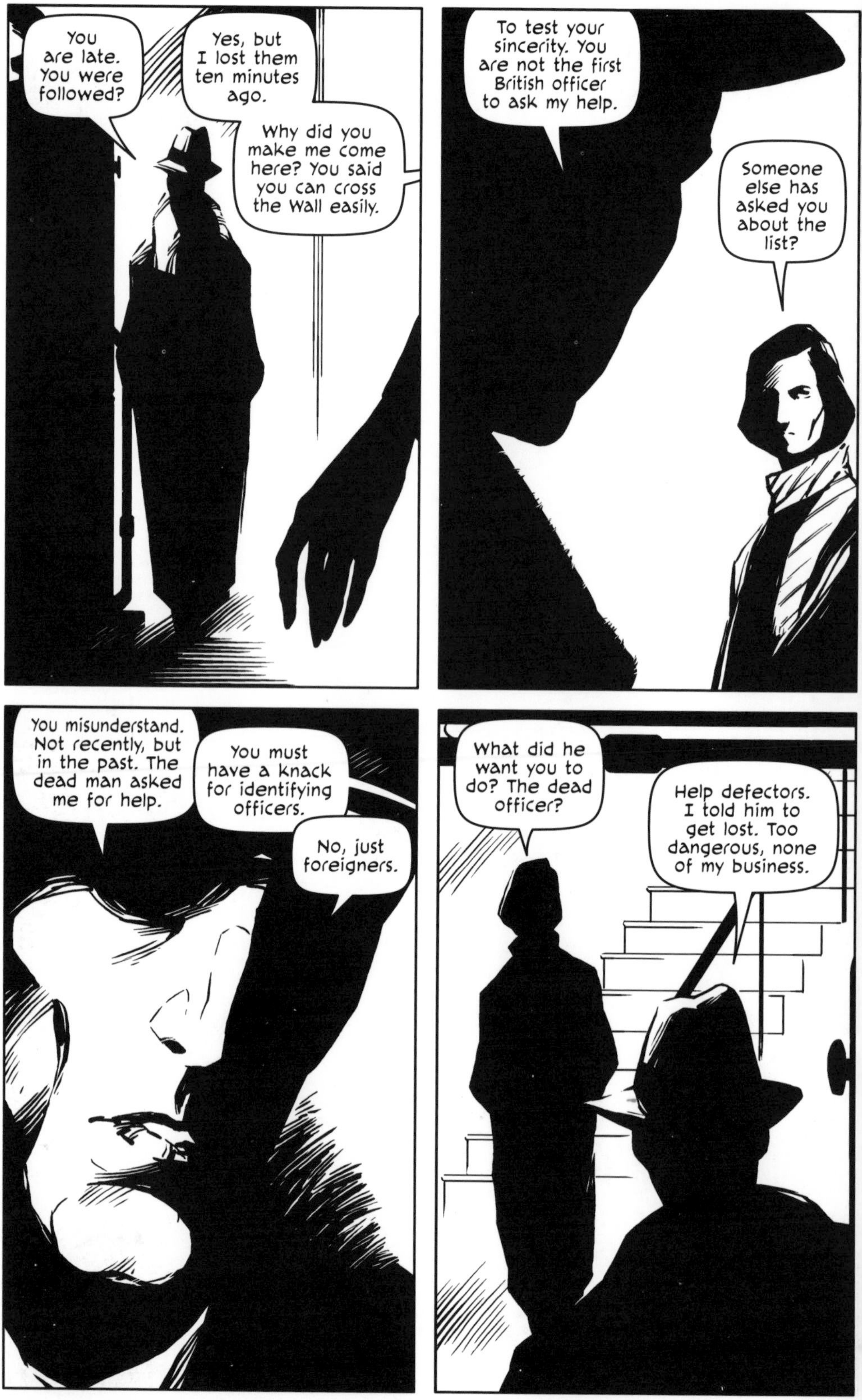
You are late. You were followed?
Yes, but I lost them ten minutes ago.
Why did you make me come here? You said you can cross the Wall easily.
To test your sincerity. You are not the first British officer to ask my help.
Someone else has asked you about the list?
You misunderstand. Not recently, but in the past. The dead man asked me for help.
You must have a knack for identifying officers.
No, just foreigners.
What did he want you to do? The dead officer?
Help defectors. I told him to get lost. Too dangerous, none of my business.

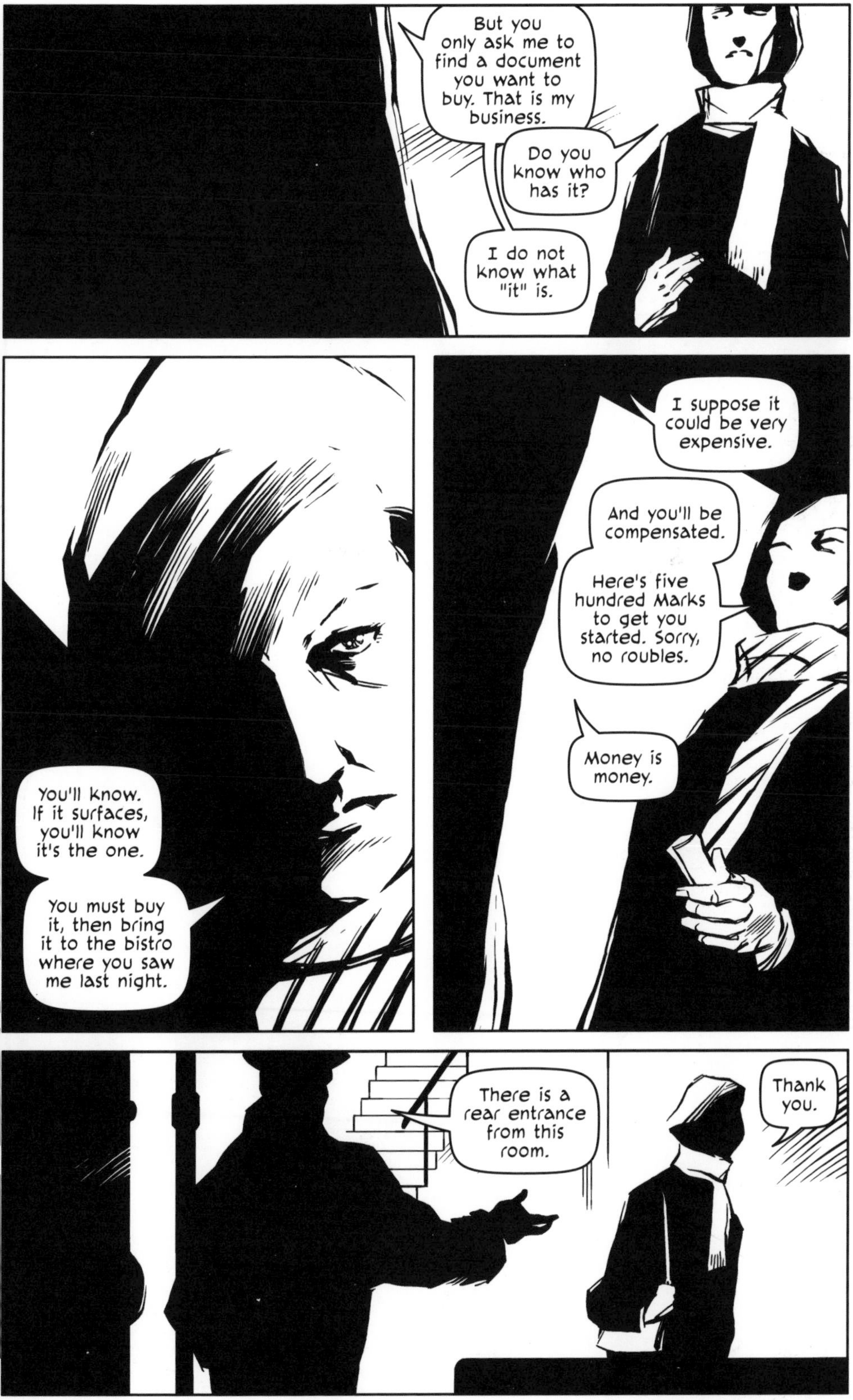
But you only ask me to find a document you want to buy. That is my business.
Do you know who has it?
I do not know what "it" is.
You'll know. If it surfaces, you'll know it's the one.
You must buy it, then bring it to the bistro where you saw me last night.
I suppose it could be very expensive.
And you'll be compensated.
Here's five hundred Marks to get you started. Sorry, no roubles.
Money is money.
There is a rear entrance from this room.
Thank you.

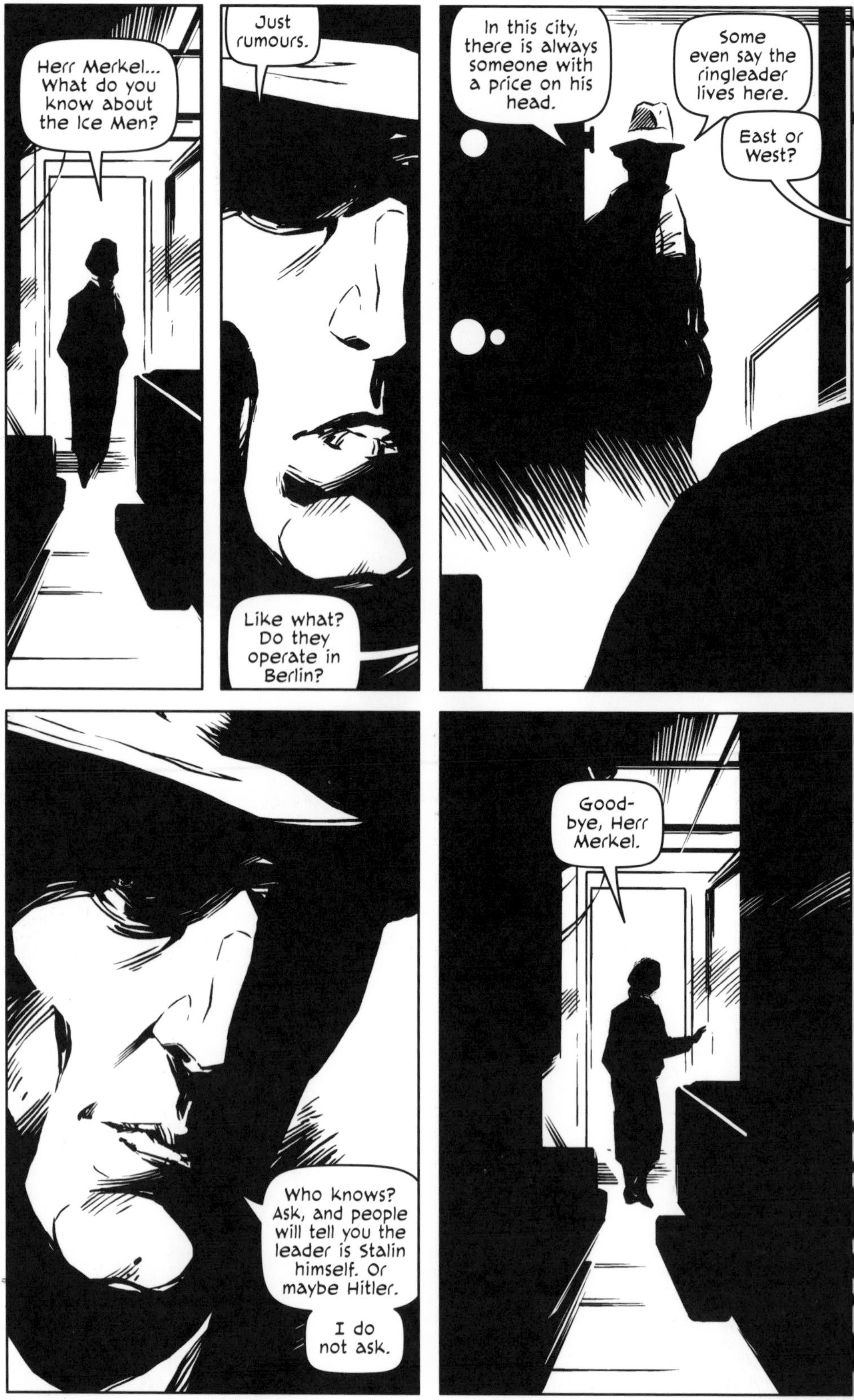
Herr Merkel... What do you know about the Ice Men?
Just rumours.
Like what? Do they operate in Berlin?
In this city, there is always someone with a price on his head.
Some even say the ringleader lives here.
East or West?
Who knows? Ask, and people will tell you the leader is Stalin himself. Or maybe Hitler.
I do not ask.
Good-bye, Herr Merkel.

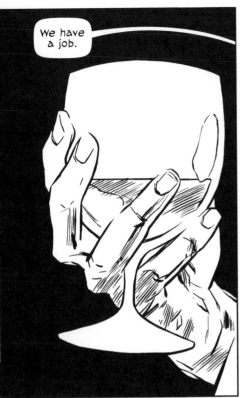

We have a job.

I'm sorry?

Our friend left me a message. He wants to come and stay with us.

Surely that's your area.

Actually, it was James' expertise.

So I was right. He's been compromised.

No, but he's petrified he will be. I told you, the Wall won't last much longer. Haven't you seen the protests on the news?

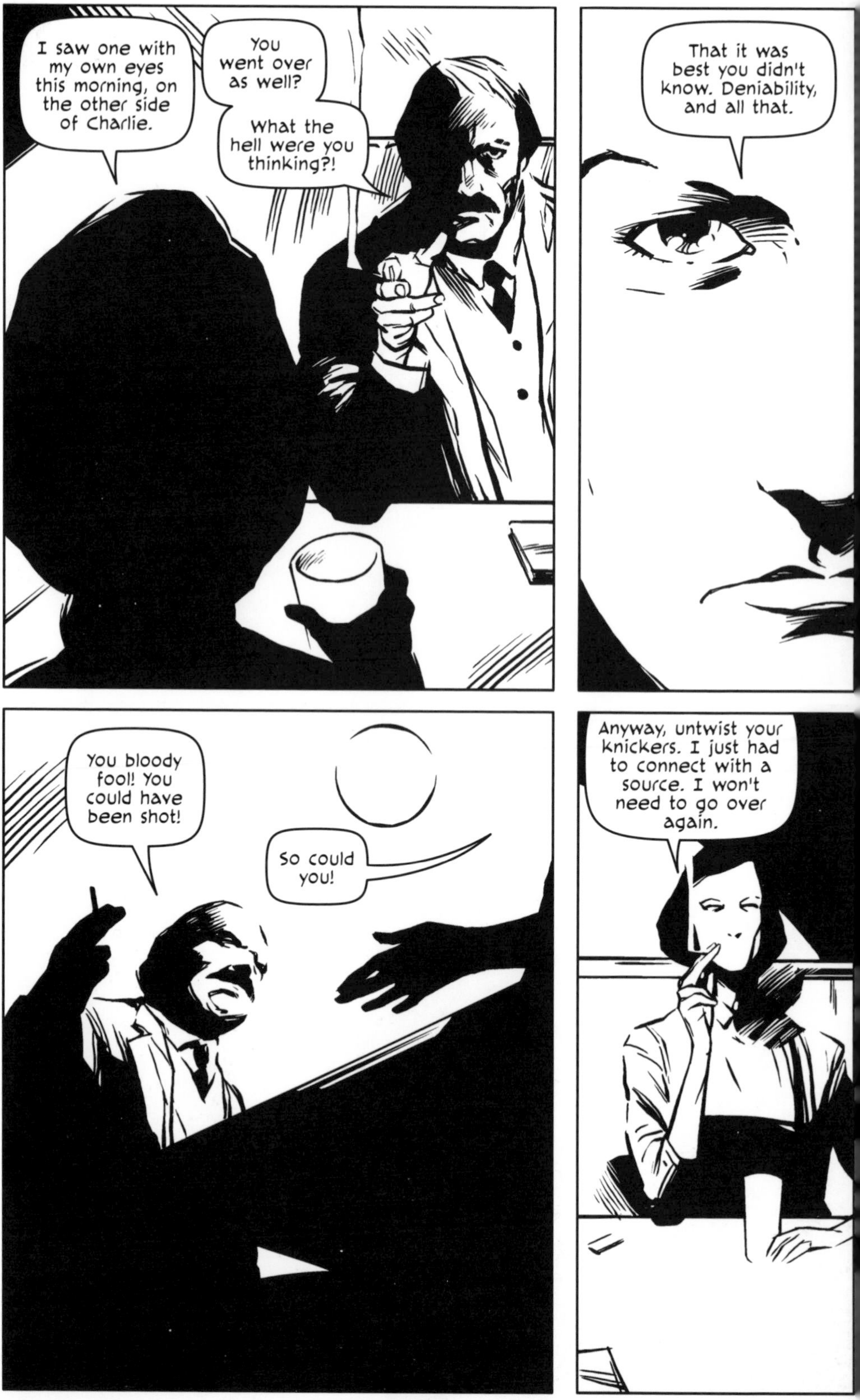
I saw one with my own eyes this morning, on the other side of Charlie.
You went over as well?
What the hell were you thinking?!
That it was best you didn't know. Deniability, and all that.
You bloody fool! You could have been shot!
So could you!
Anyway, untwist your knickers. I just had to connect with a source. I won't need to go over again.

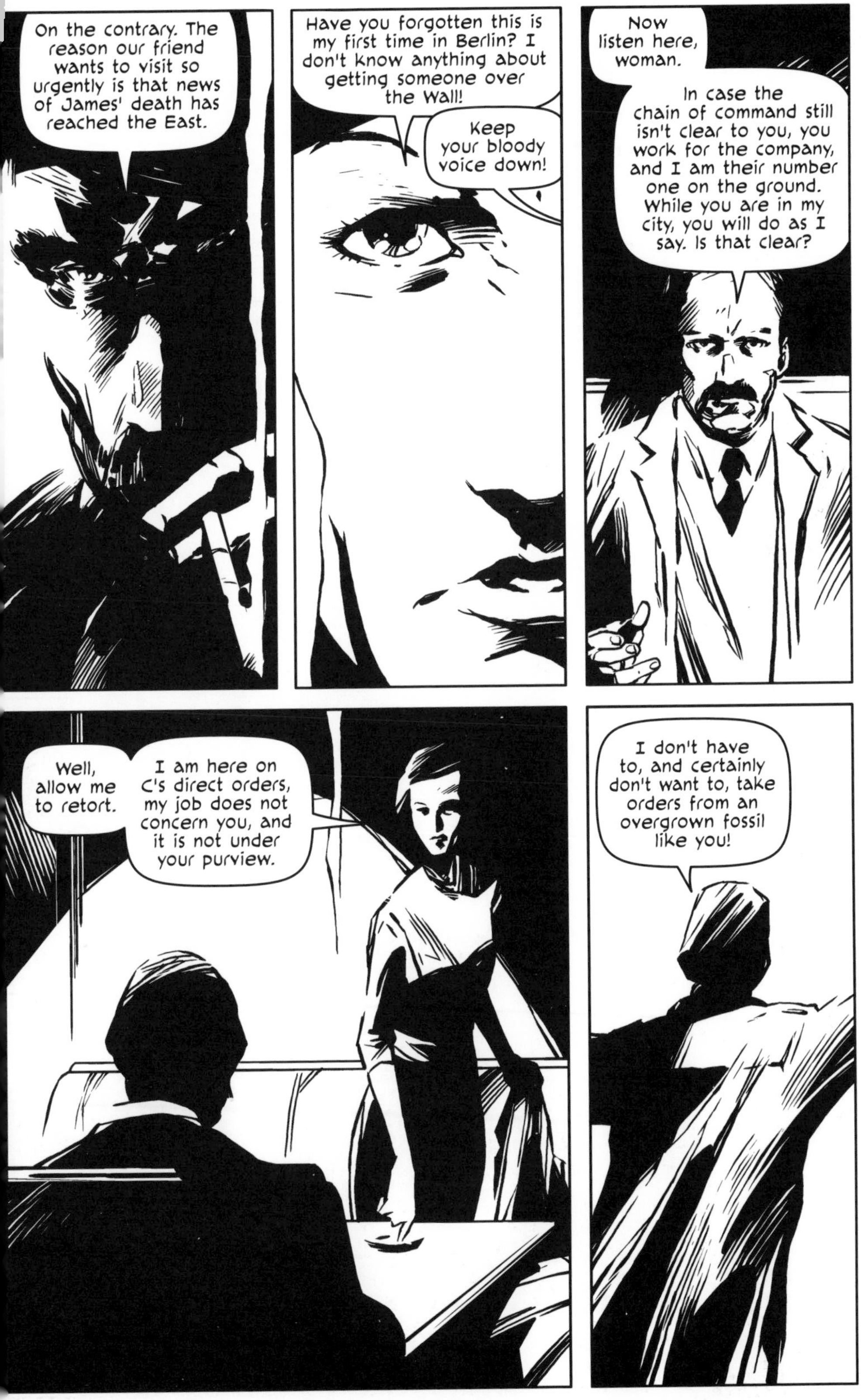
On the contrary. The reason our friend wants to visit so urgently is that news of James' death has reached the East.
Have you forgotten this is my first time in Berlin? I don't know anything about getting someone over the Wall!
Keep your bloody voice down!
Now listen here, woman.
In case the chain of command still isn't clear to you, you work for the company, and I am their number one on the ground. While you are in my city, you will do as I say. Is that clear?
Well, allow me to retort.
I am here on C's direct orders, my job does not concern you, and it is not under your purview.
I don't have to, and certainly don't want to, take orders from an overgrown fossil like you!

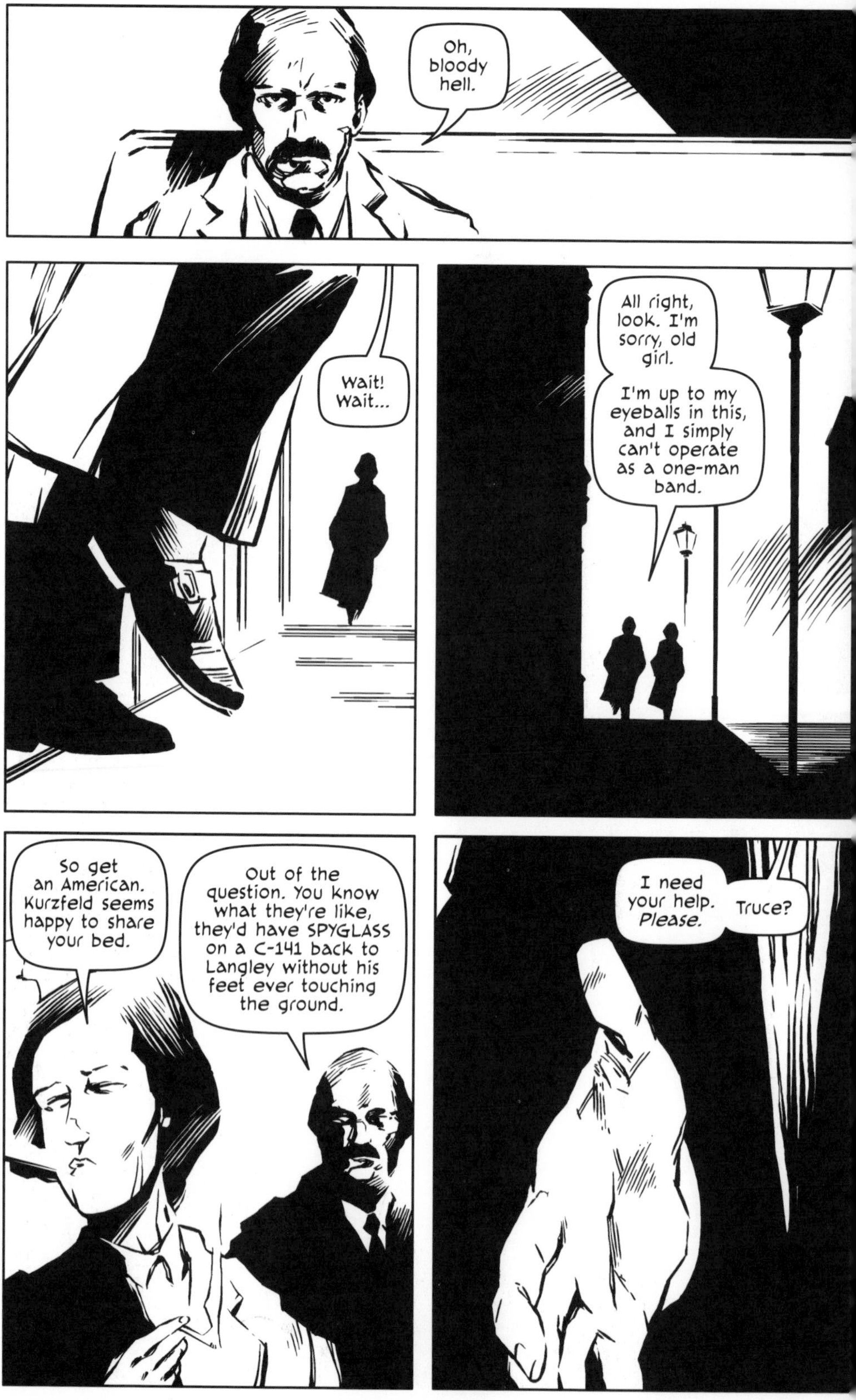
Oh, bloody hell.
Wait! Wait...
All right, look. I'm sorry, old girl.
I'm up to my eyeballs in this, and I simply can't operate as a one-man band.
So get an American. Kurzfeld seems happy to share your bed.
Out of the question. You know what they're like, they'd have SPYGLASS on a C-141 back to Langley without his feet ever touching the ground.
I need your help. *Please.*
Truce?

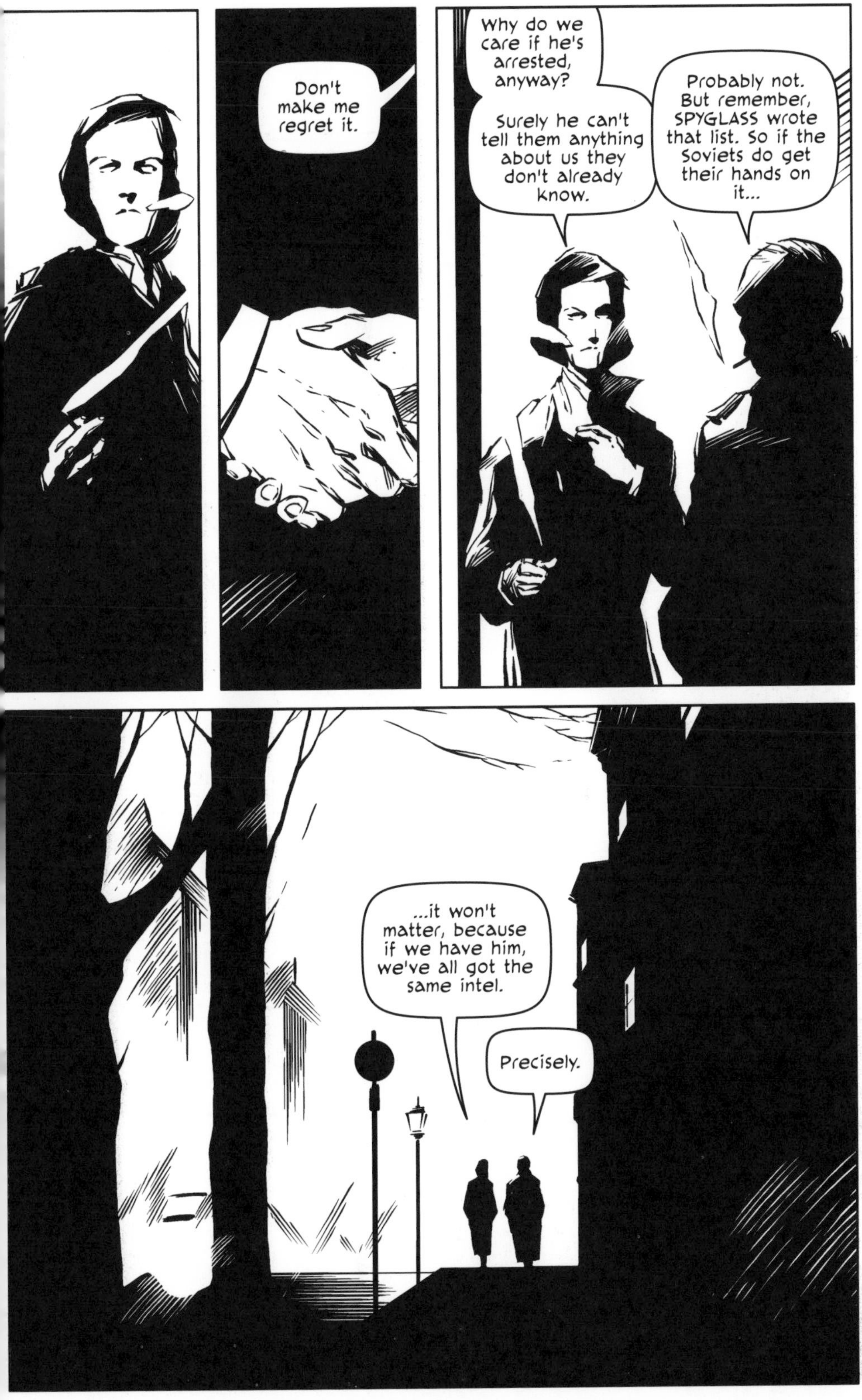
Don't make me regret it.
Why do we care if he's arrested, anyway?
Surely he can't tell them anything about us they don't already know.
Probably not. But remember, SPYGLASS wrote that list. So if the Soviets do get their hands on it...
...it won't matter, because if we have him, we've all got the same intel.
Precisely.

One advantage is that Ivan won't be expecting a breakout.

Not now, with the holes in Hungary and Czechoslovakia.

And I know you're green, but I can make allowances for that.

I'm not "green", you bloody dinosaur. I've crossed the Iron Curtain more times than you've wished Maggie Thatcher dead.

Just not here. Not in Berlin.

Well, anyway, we have routes in place. But I'm concerned they haven't been used for a while.

You think they might have been blown.

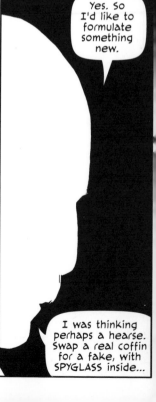

Yes. So I'd like to formulate something new.

I was thinking perhaps a hearse. Swap a real coffin for a fake, with SPYGLASS inside...

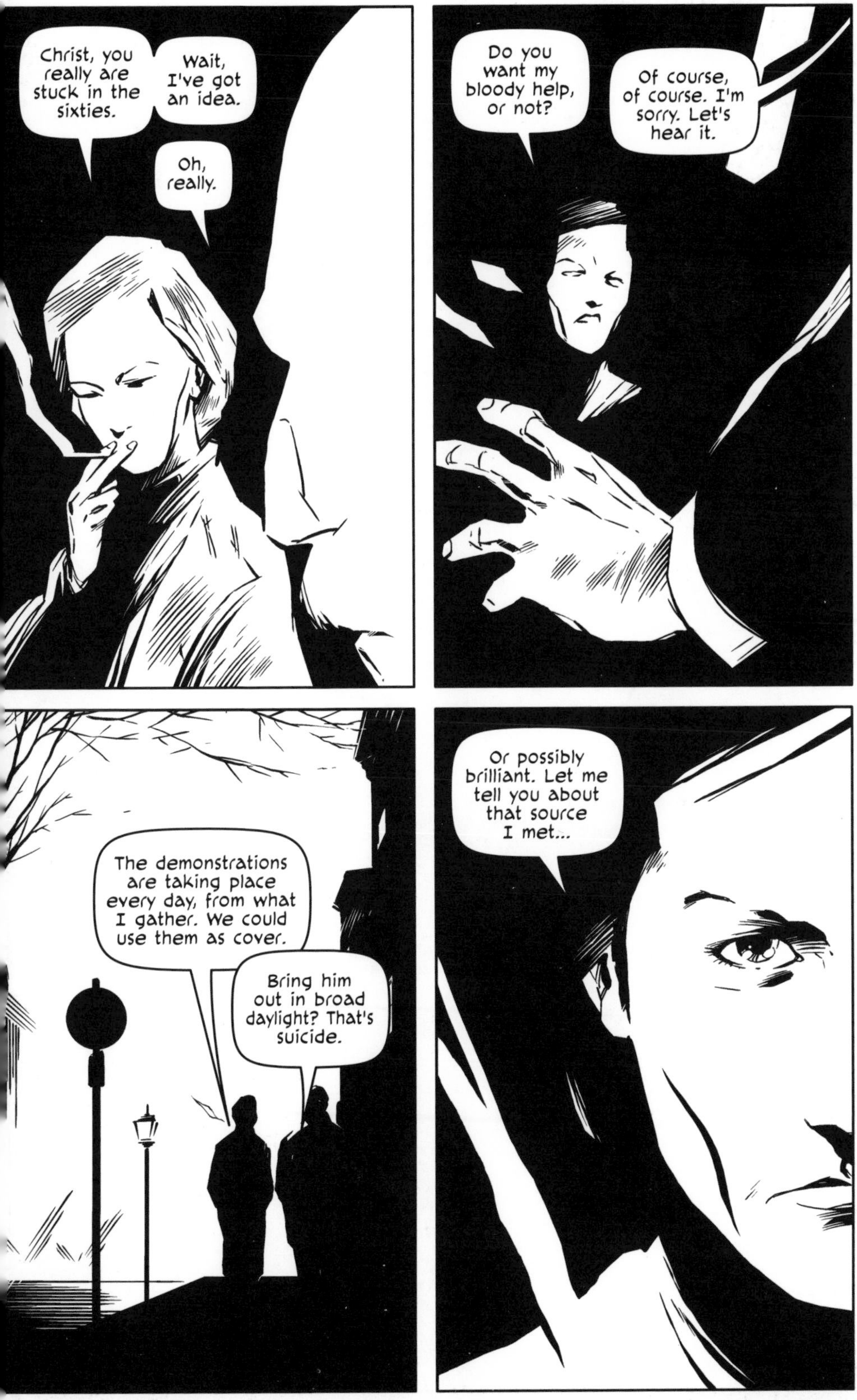
Christ, you really are stuck in the sixties.
Wait, I've got an idea.
Oh, really.
Do you want my bloody help, or not?
Of course, of course. I'm sorry. Let's hear it.
The demonstrations are taking place every day, from what I gather. We could use them as cover.
Bring him out in broad daylight? That's suicide.
Or possibly brilliant. Let me tell you about that source I met...

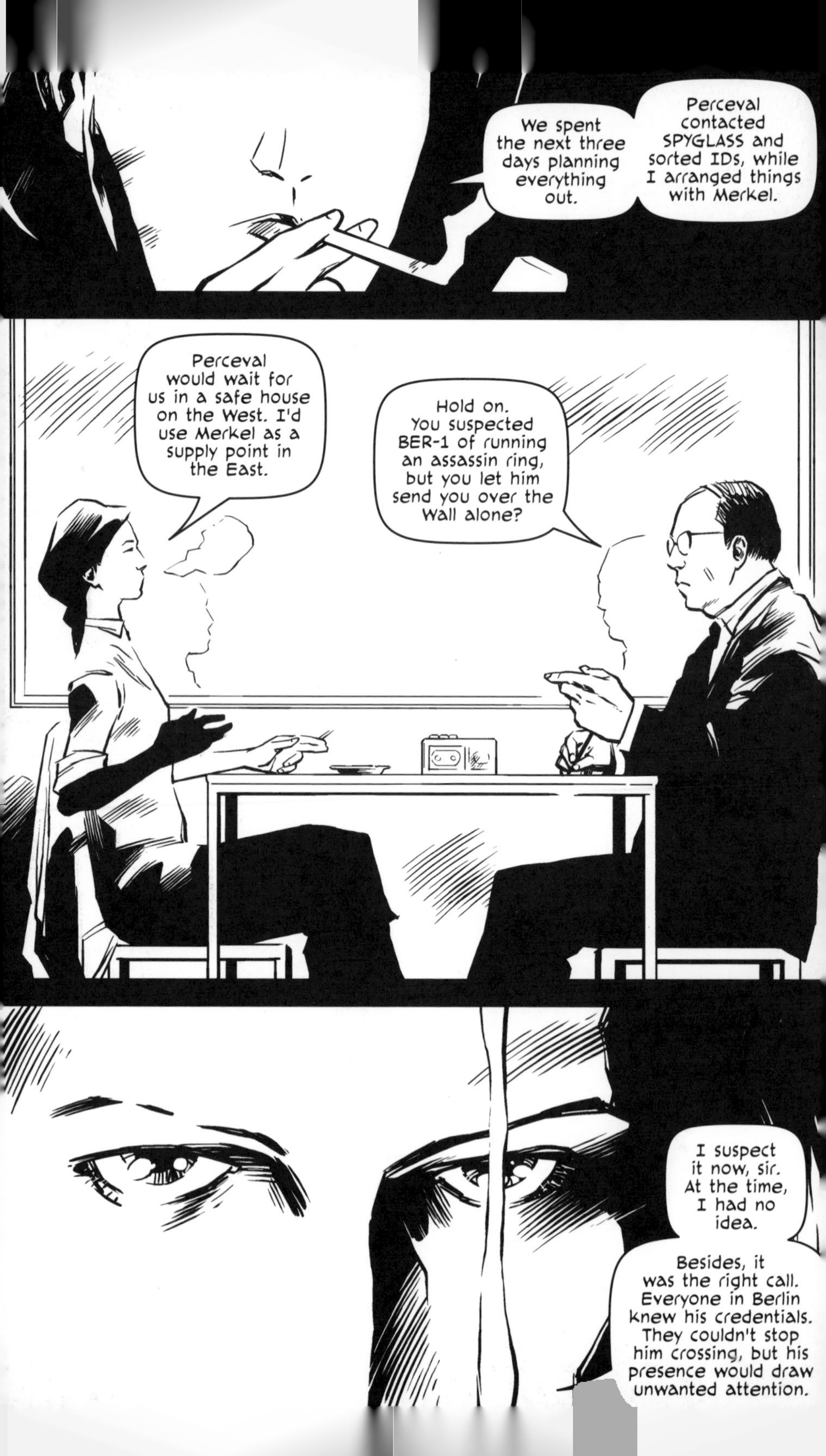
We spent the next three days planning everything out.
Perceval contacted SPYGLASS and sorted IDs, while I arranged things with Merkel.
Perceval would wait for us in a safe house on the West. I'd use Merkel as a supply point in the East.
Hold on. You suspected BER-1 of running an assassin ring, but you let him send you over the Wall alone?
I suspect it now, sir. At the time, I had no idea.
Besides, it was the right call. Everyone in Berlin knew his credentials. They couldn't stop him crossing, but his presence would draw unwanted attention.

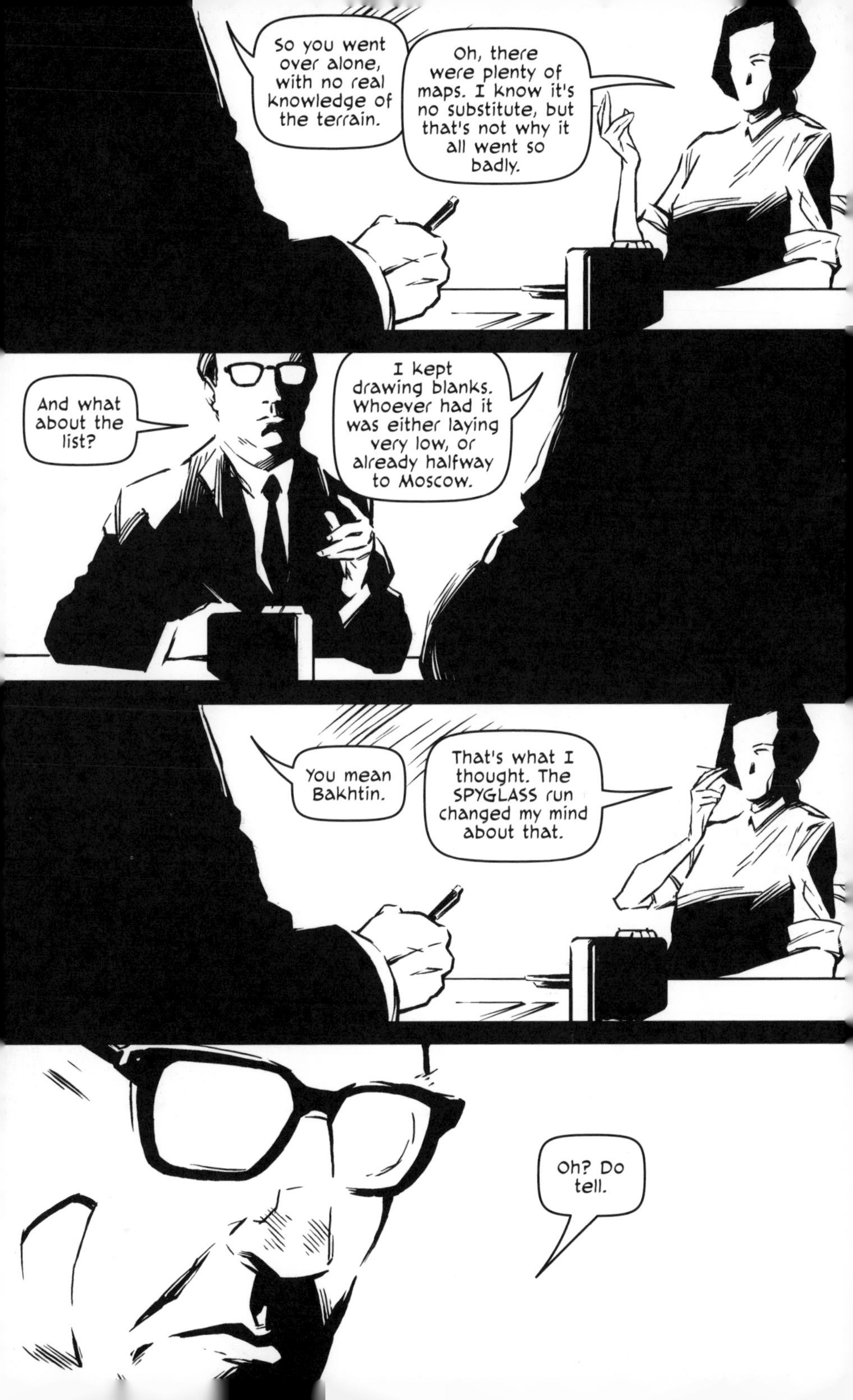
So you went over alone, with no real knowledge of the terrain.
Oh, there were plenty of maps. I know it's no substitute, but that's not why it all went so badly.
And what about the list?
I kept drawing blanks. Whoever had it was either laying very low, or already halfway to Moscow.
You mean Bakhtin.
That's what I thought. The SPYGLASS run changed my mind about that.
Oh? Do tell.

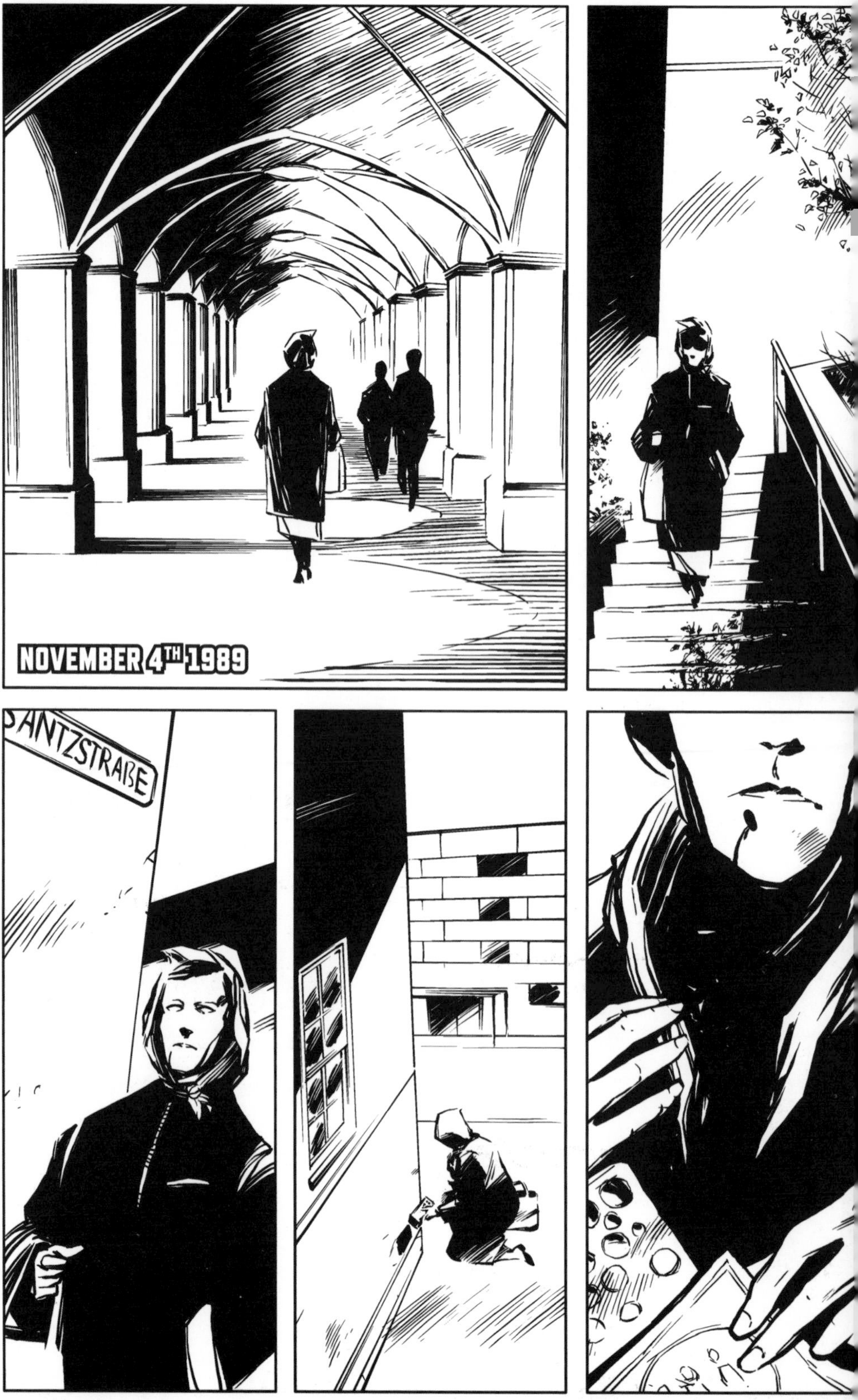
NOVEMBER 4TH 1989
ANTZSTRAßE

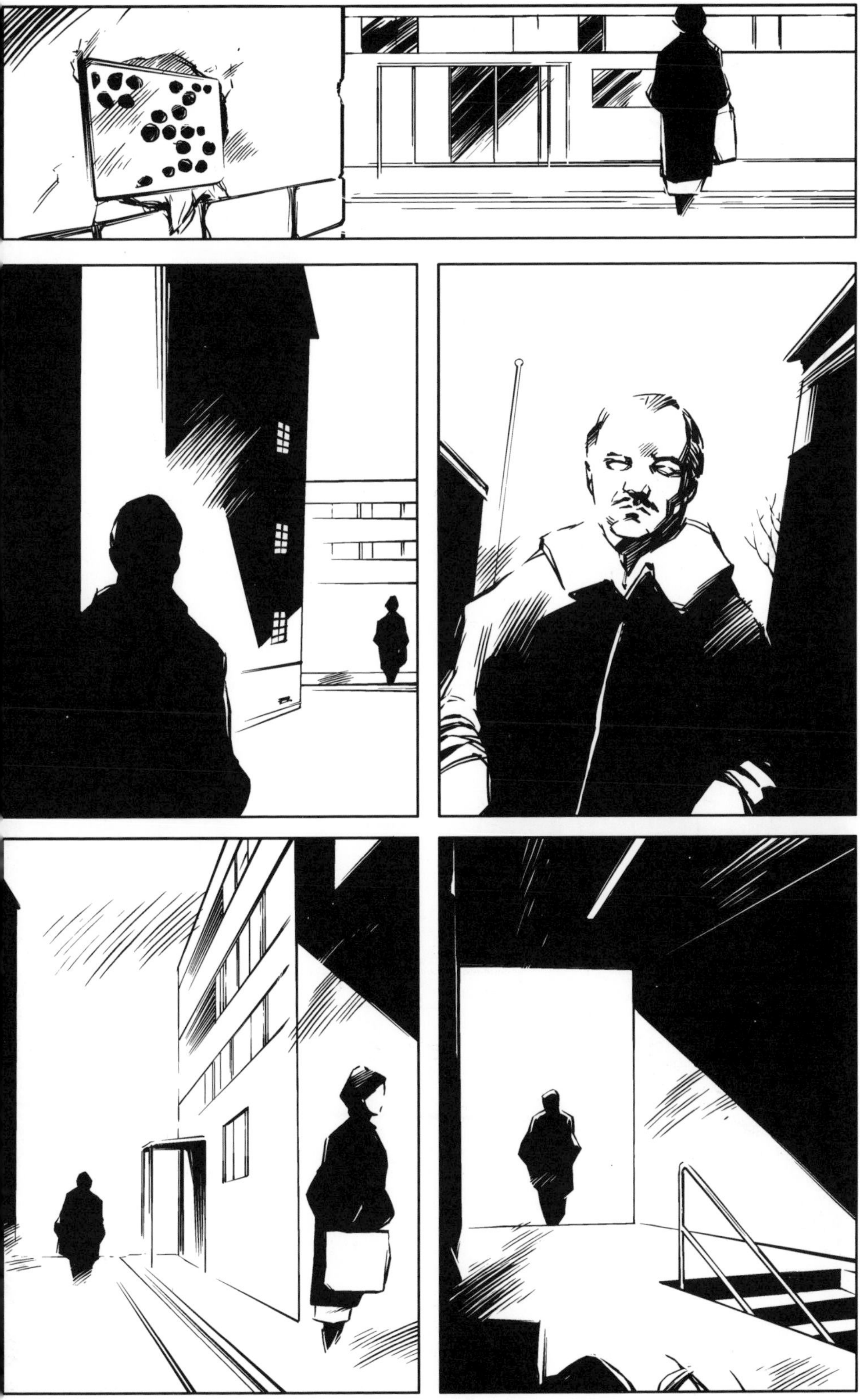

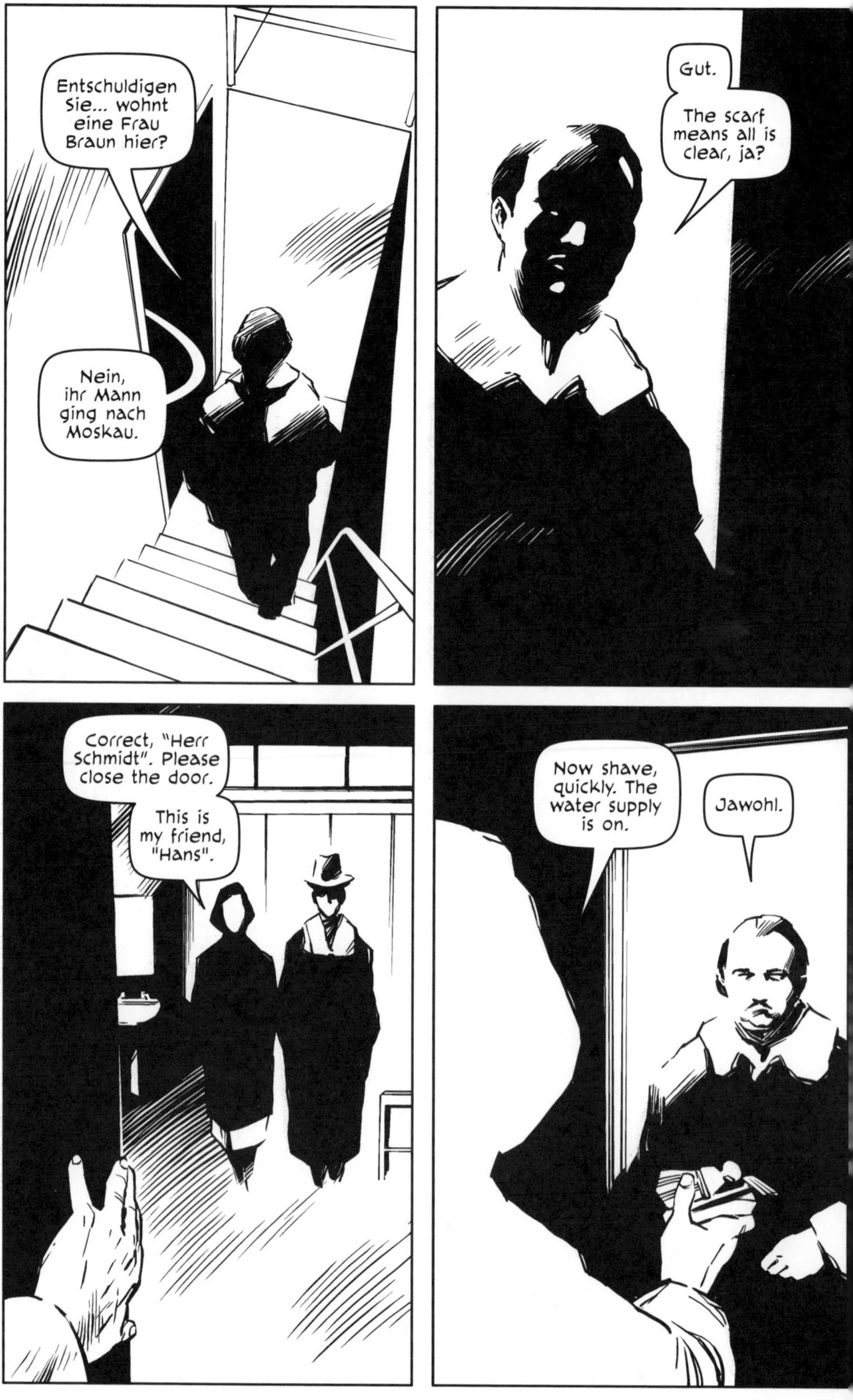
Entschuldigen Sie... wohnt eine Frau Braun hier?
Nein, ihr Mann ging nach Moskau.
Gut.
The scarf means all is clear, ja?
Correct, "Herr Schmidt". Please close the door.
This is my friend, "Hans".
Now shave, quickly. The water supply is on.
Jawohl.

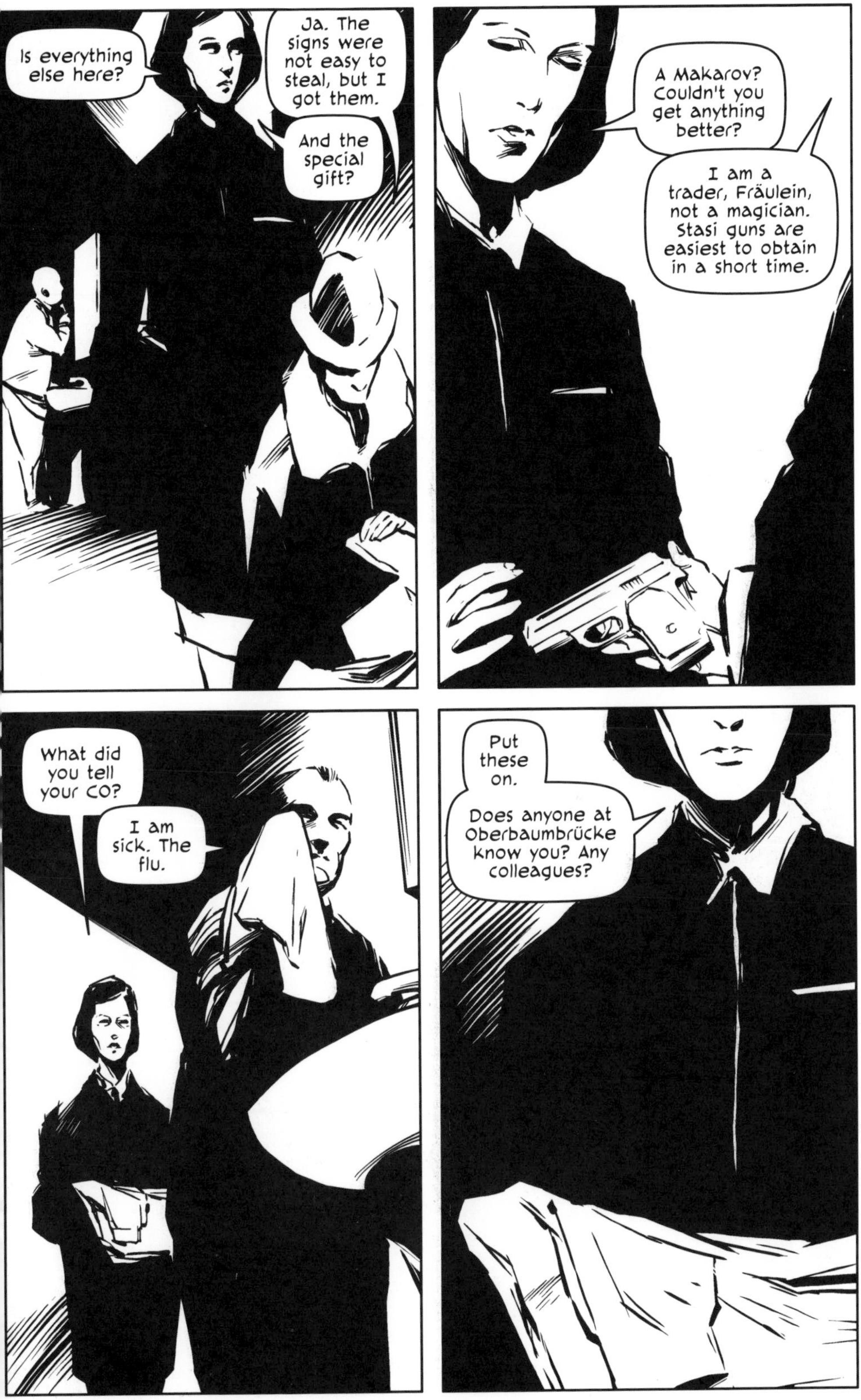
Is everything else here?
Ja. The signs were not easy to steal, but I got them.
And the special gift?
A Makarov? Couldn't you get anything better?
I am a trader, Fräulein, not a magician. Stasi guns are easiest to obtain in a short time.
What did you tell your CO?
I am sick. The flu.
Put these on.
Does anyone at Oberbaumbrücke know you? Any colleagues?

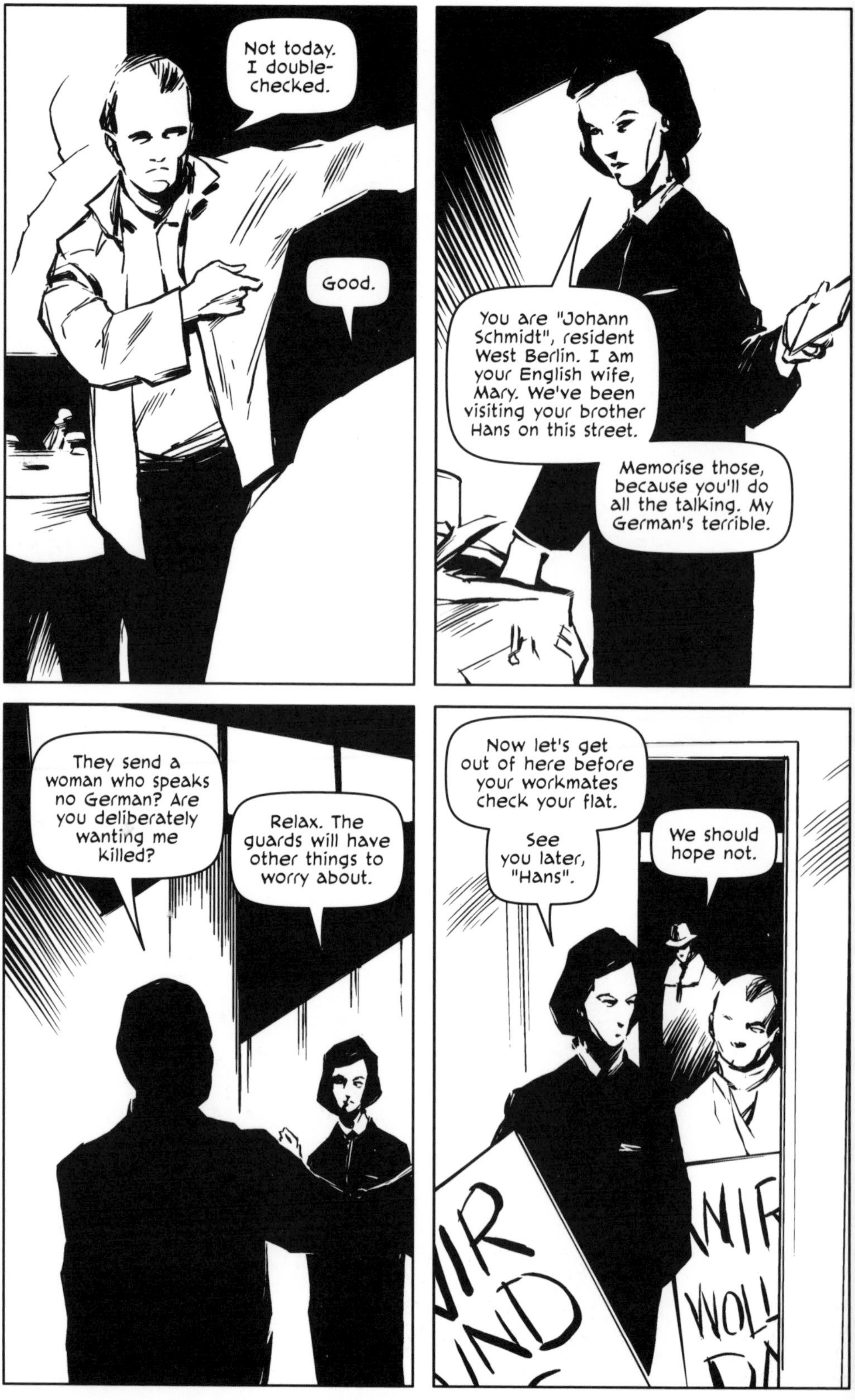
Not today. I double-checked.
Good.
You are "Johann Schmidt", resident West Berlin. I am your English wife, Mary. We've been visiting your brother Hans on this street.
Memorise those, because you'll do all the talking. My German's terrible.
They send a woman who speaks no German? Are you deliberately wanting me killed?
Relax. The guards will have other things to worry about.
Now let's get out of here before your workmates check your flat.
See you later, "Hans".
We should hope not.

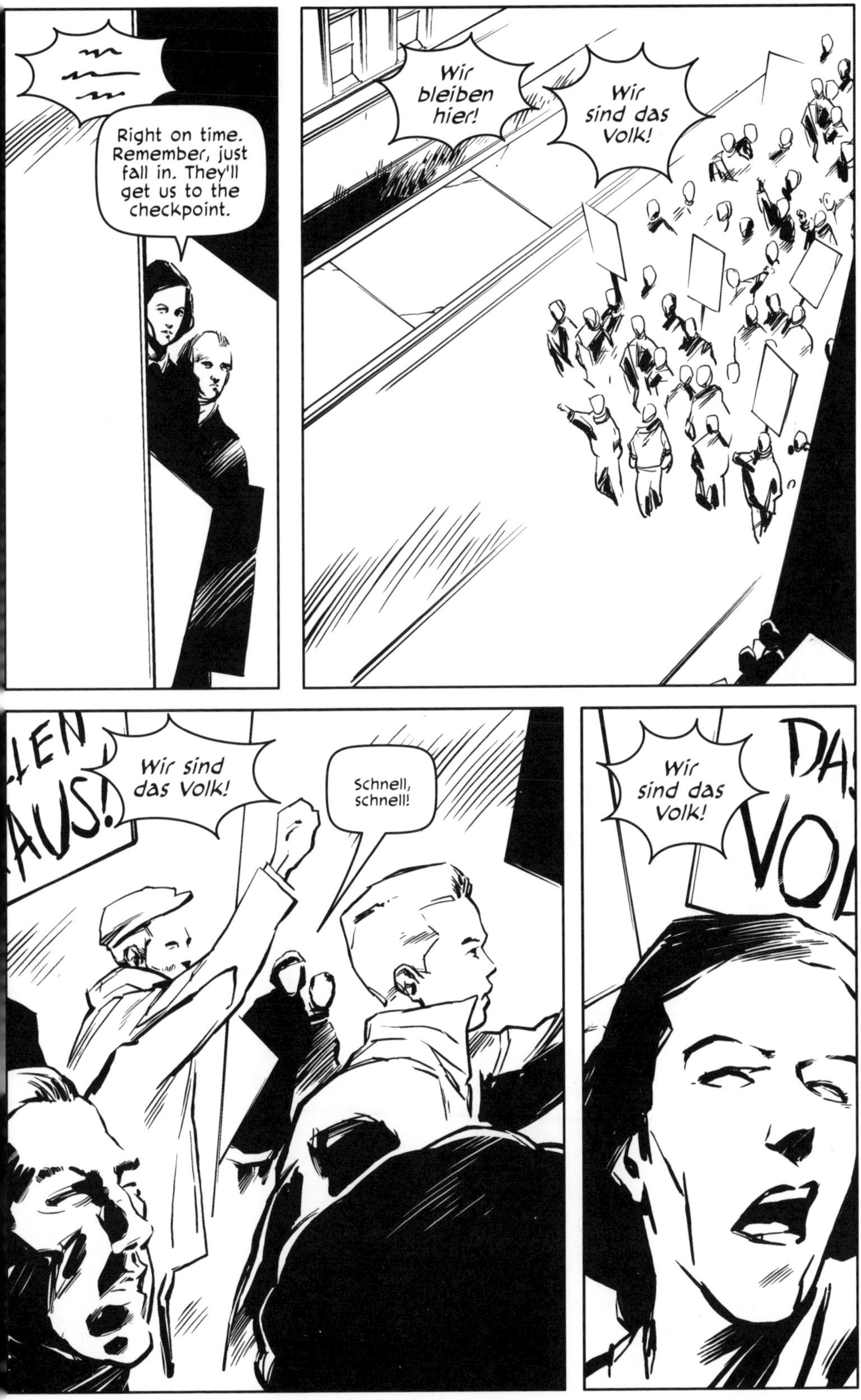
Right on time. Remember, just fall in. They'll get us to the checkpoint.
Wir bleiben hier!
Wir sind das Volk!
Wir sind das Volk!
Schnell, schnell!
Wir sind das Volk!

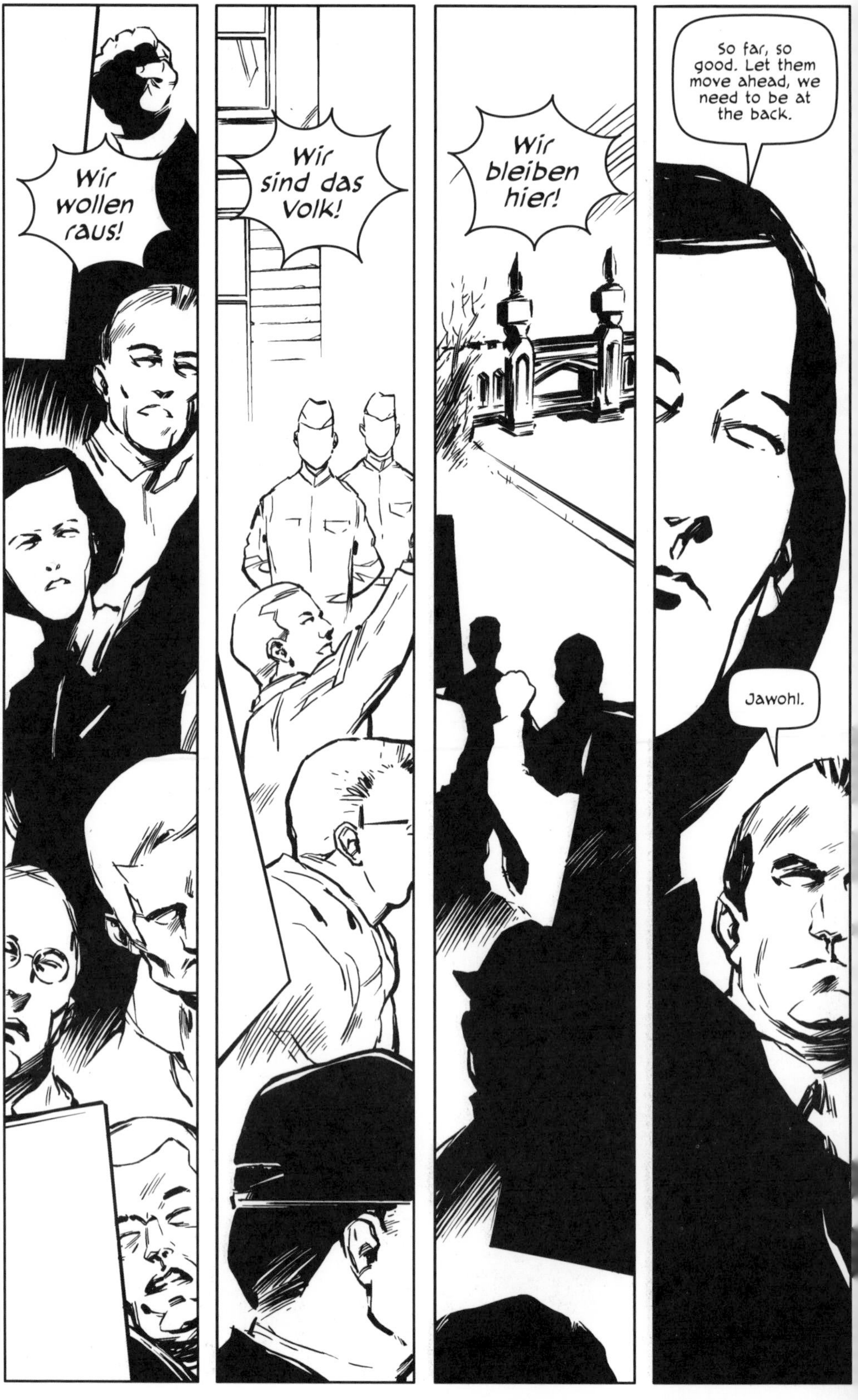
Wir wollen raus!
Wir sind das Volk!
Wir bleiben hier!
So far, so good. Let them move ahead, we need to be at the back.
Jawohl.

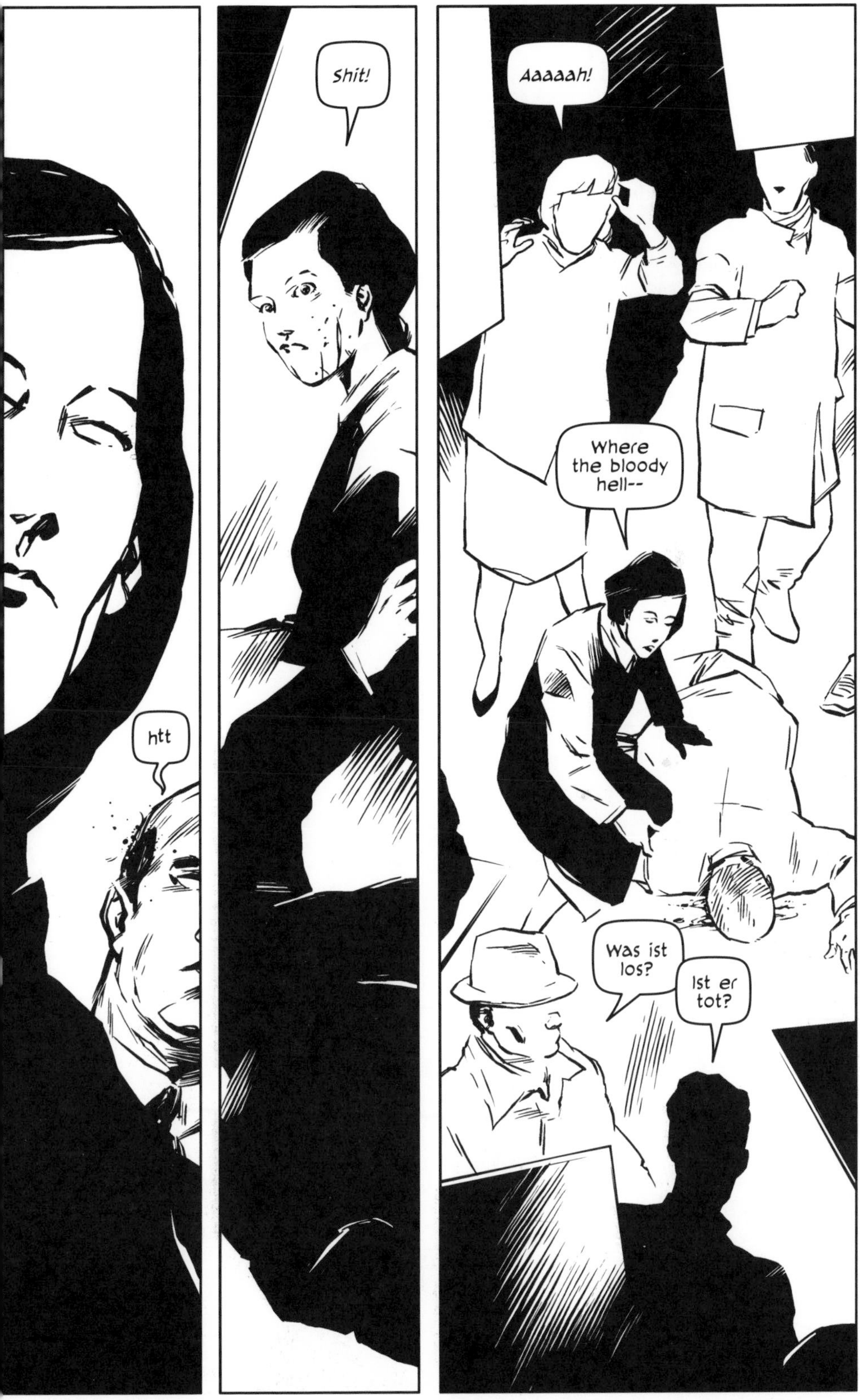
htt
Shit!
Aaaaah!
Where the bloody hell--
Was ist los?
Ist er tot?

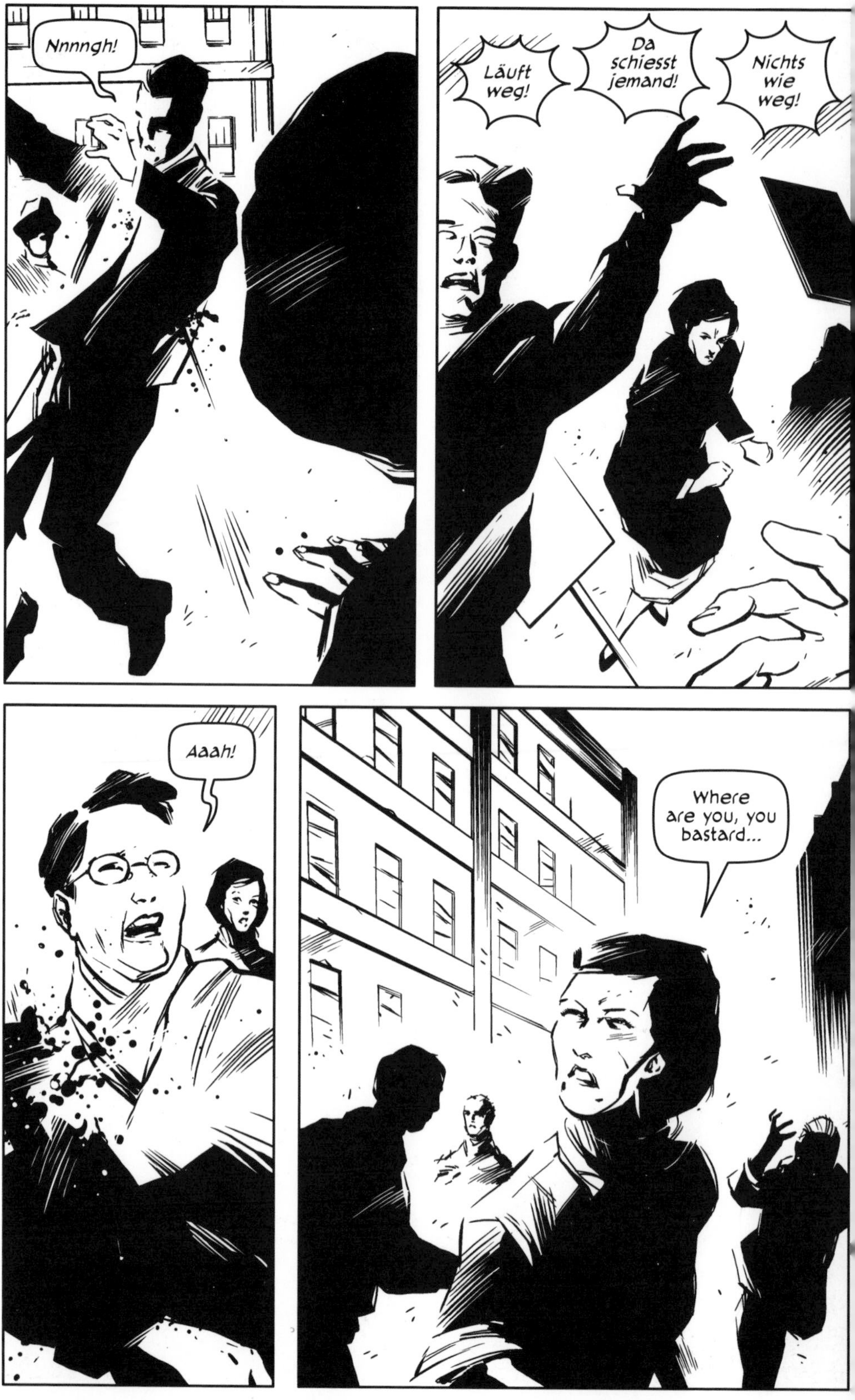

Nnnngh!
Läuft weg!
Da schiesst jemand!
Nichts wie weg!
Aaah!
Where are you, you bastard...

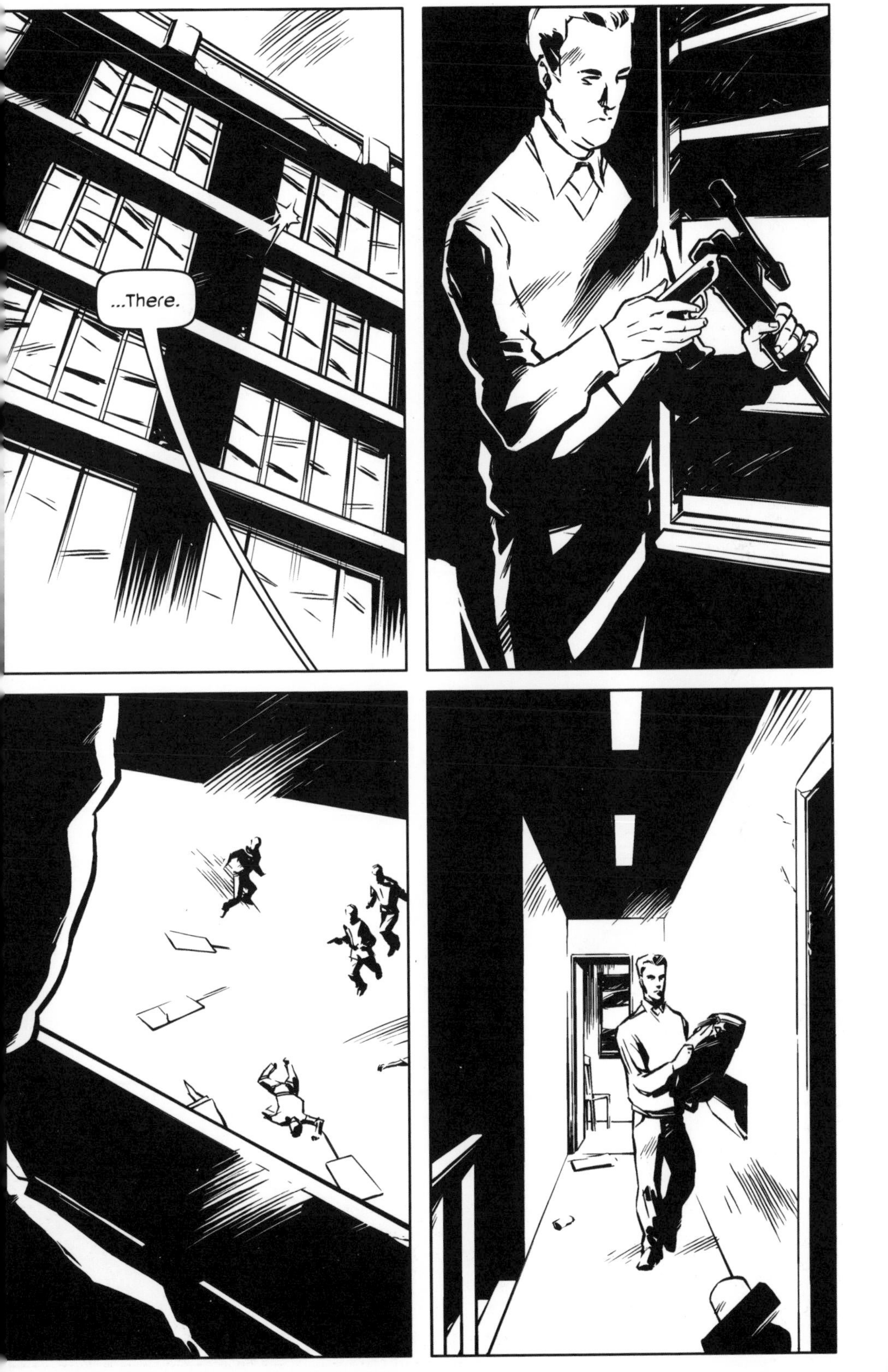
...There.

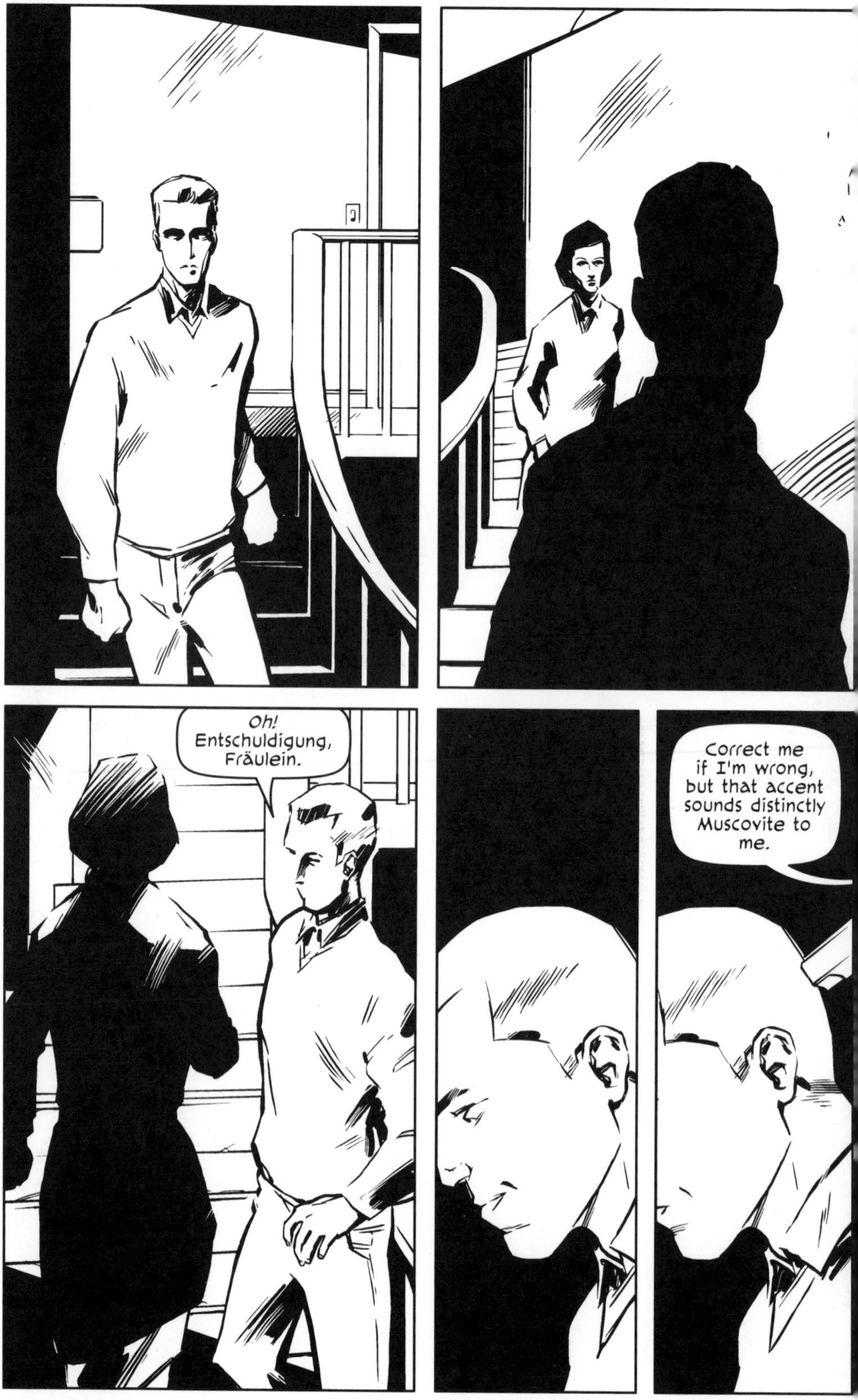
Oh! Entschuldigung, Fräulein.
Correct me if I'm wrong, but that accent sounds distinctly Muscovite to me.

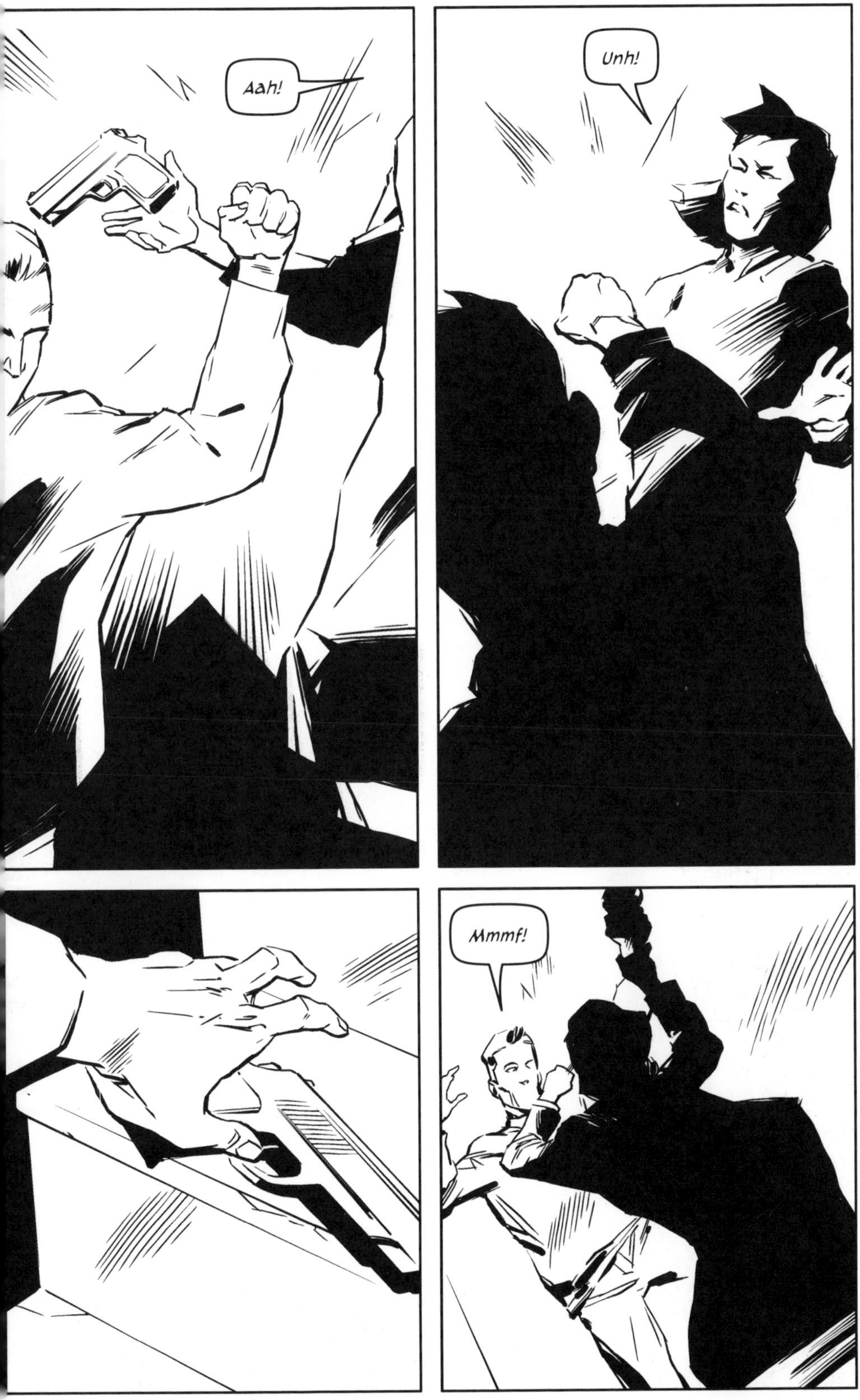
Aah!
Unh!
Mmmf!

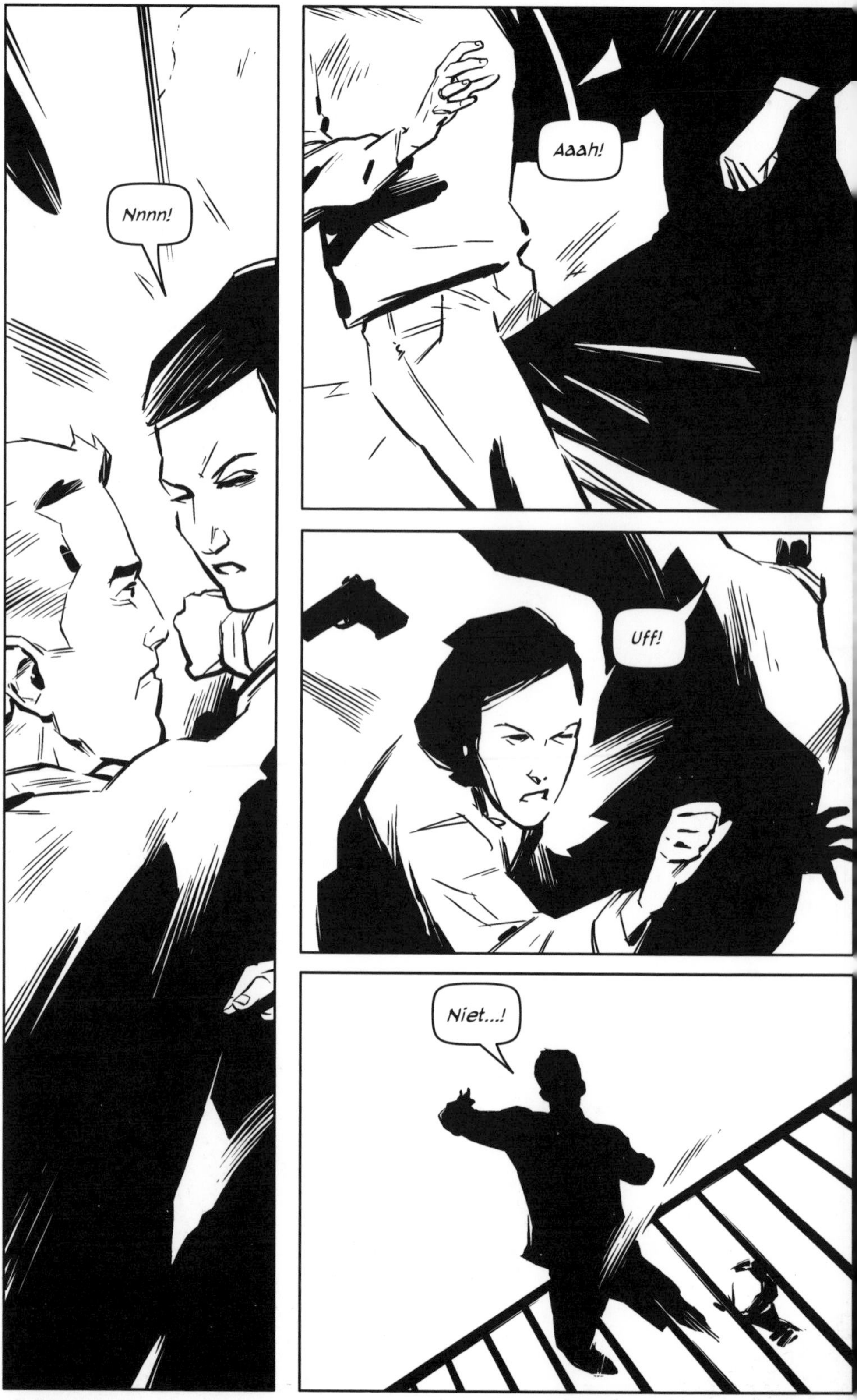
Nnnn!
Aaah!
Uff!
Niet...!

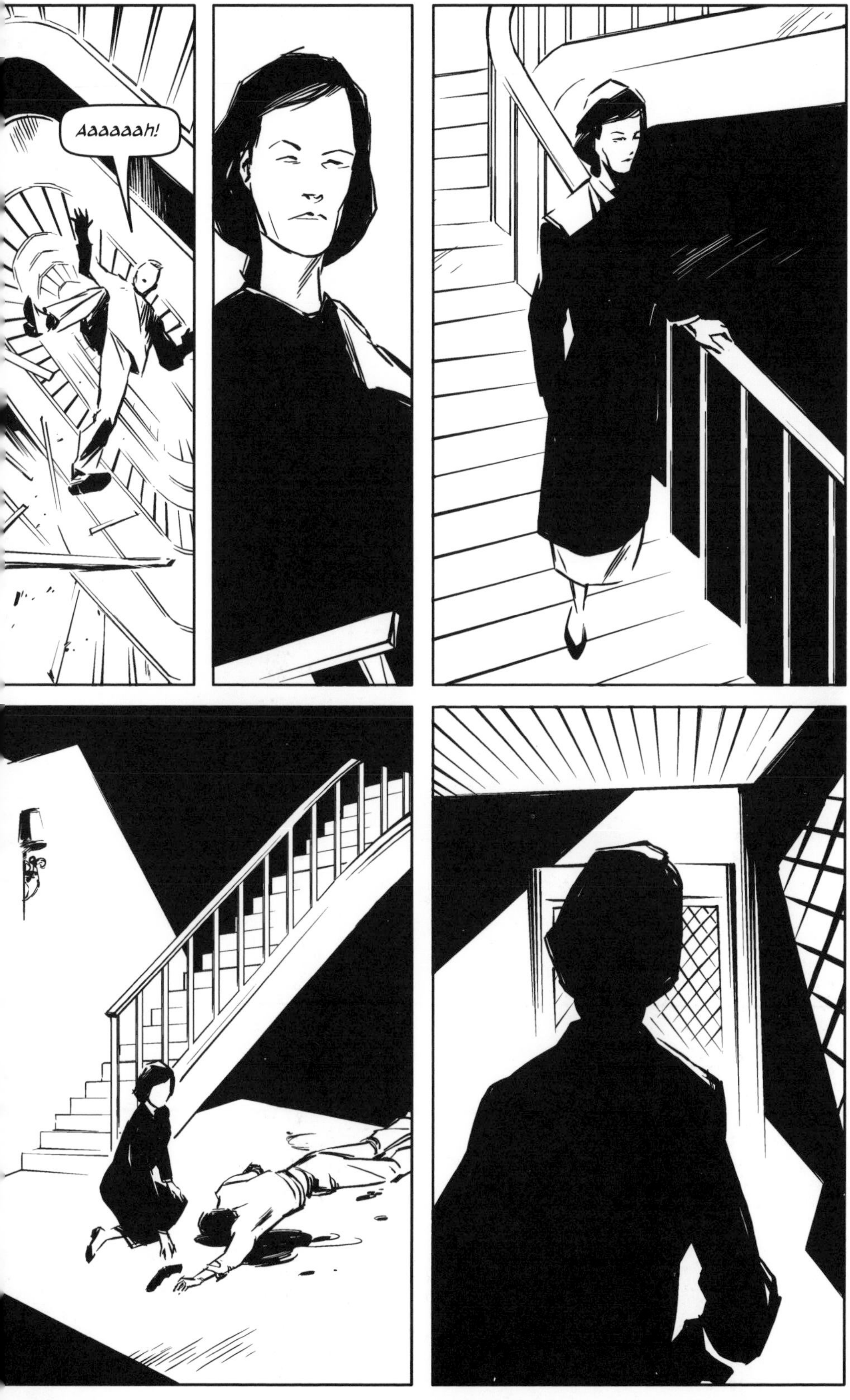
Aaaaaah!

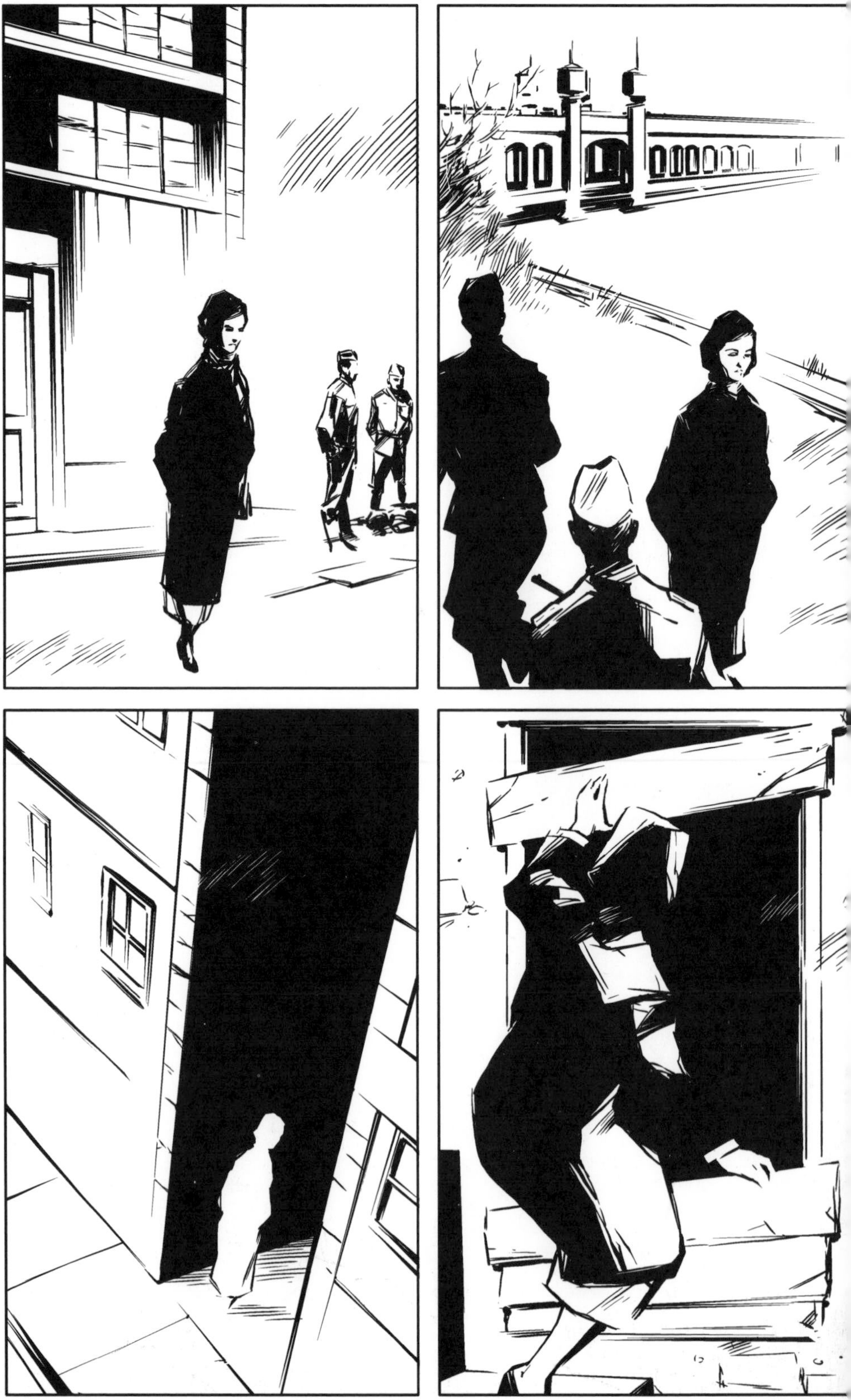

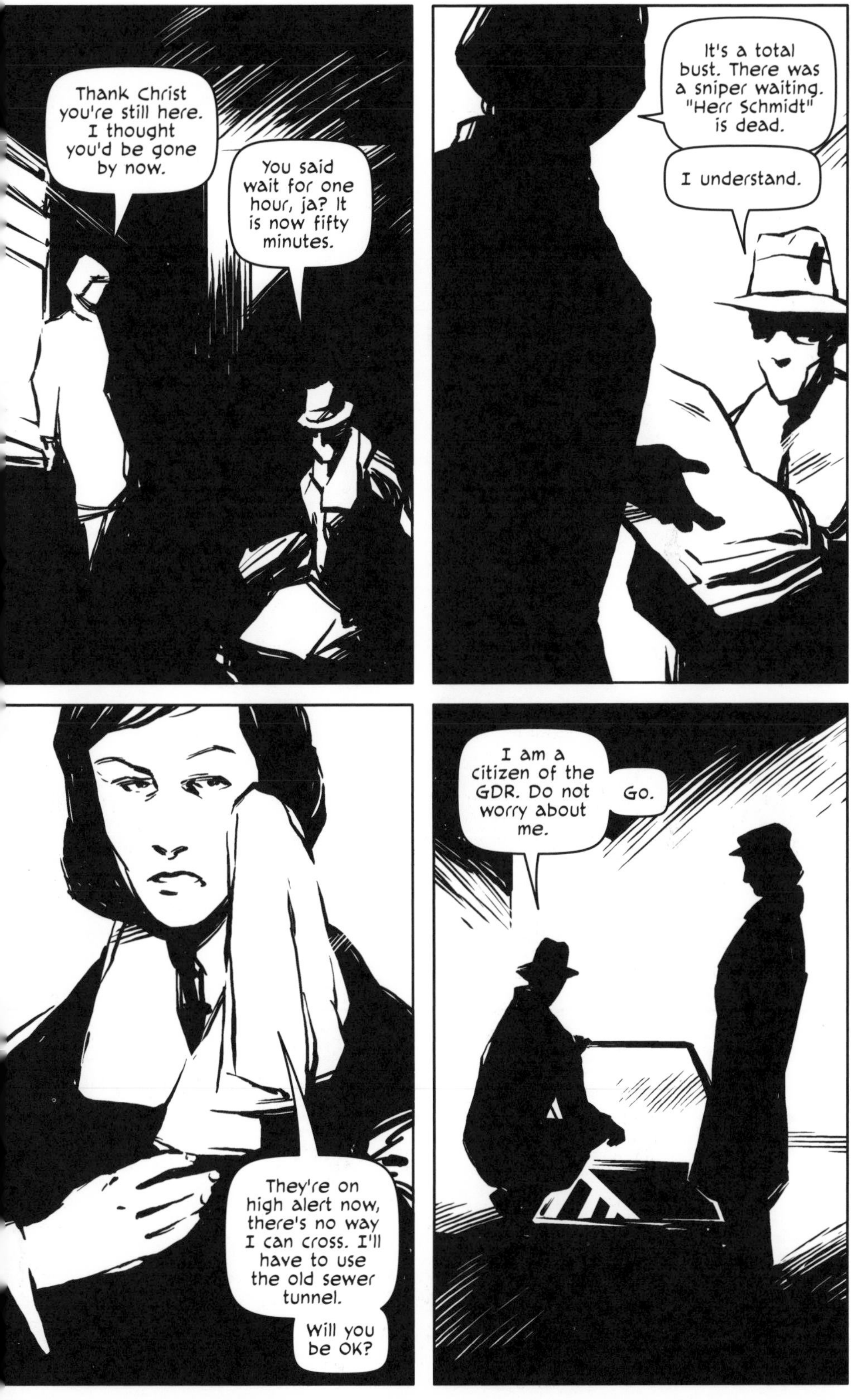
Thank Christ you're still here. I thought you'd be gone by now.
You said wait for one hour, ja? It is now fifty minutes.
It's a total bust. There was a sniper waiting. "Herr Schmidt" is dead.
I understand.
They're on high alert now, there's no way I can cross. I'll have to use the old sewer tunnel.
Will you be OK?
I am a citizen of the GDR. Do not worry about me.
Go.

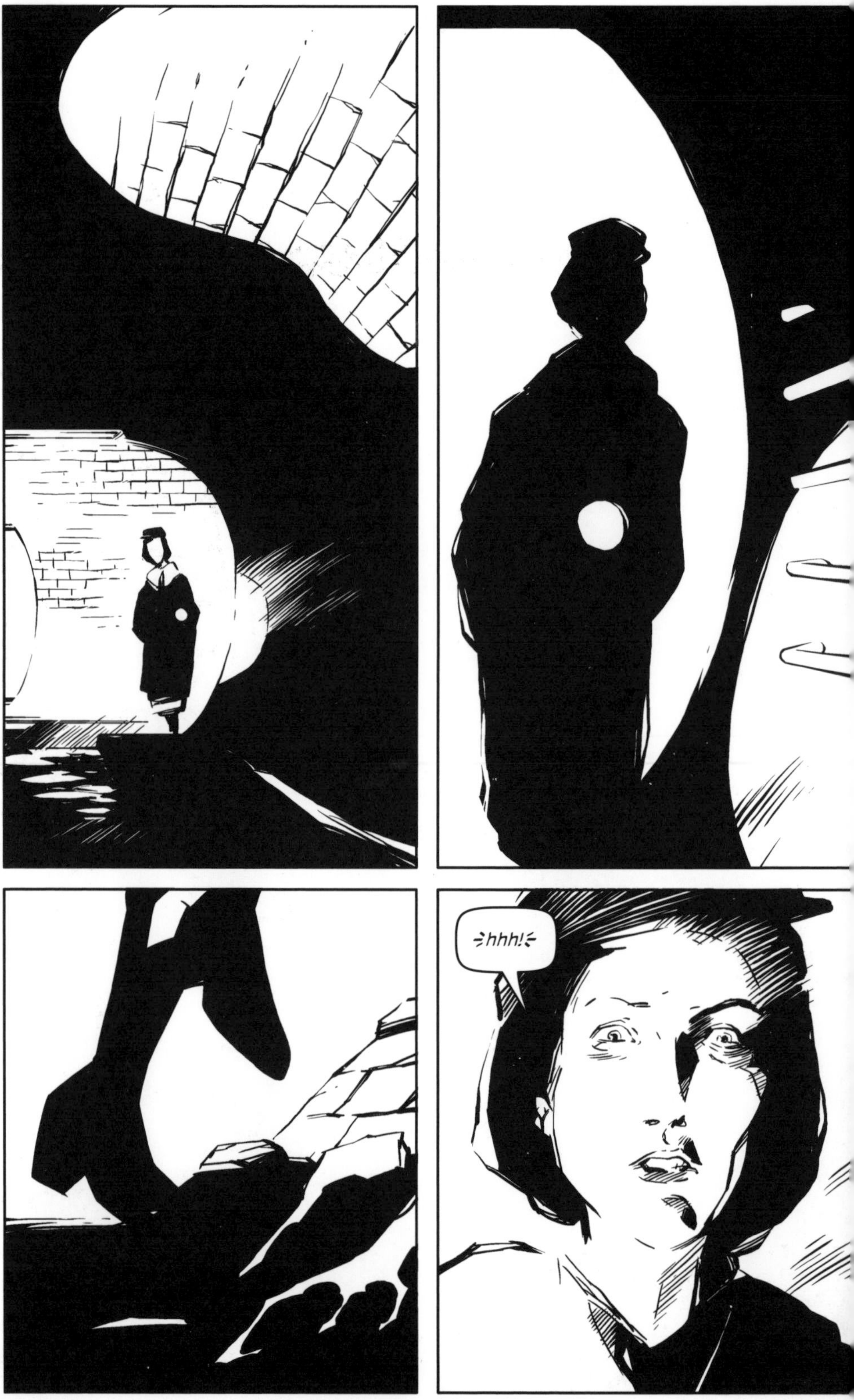

hhh!

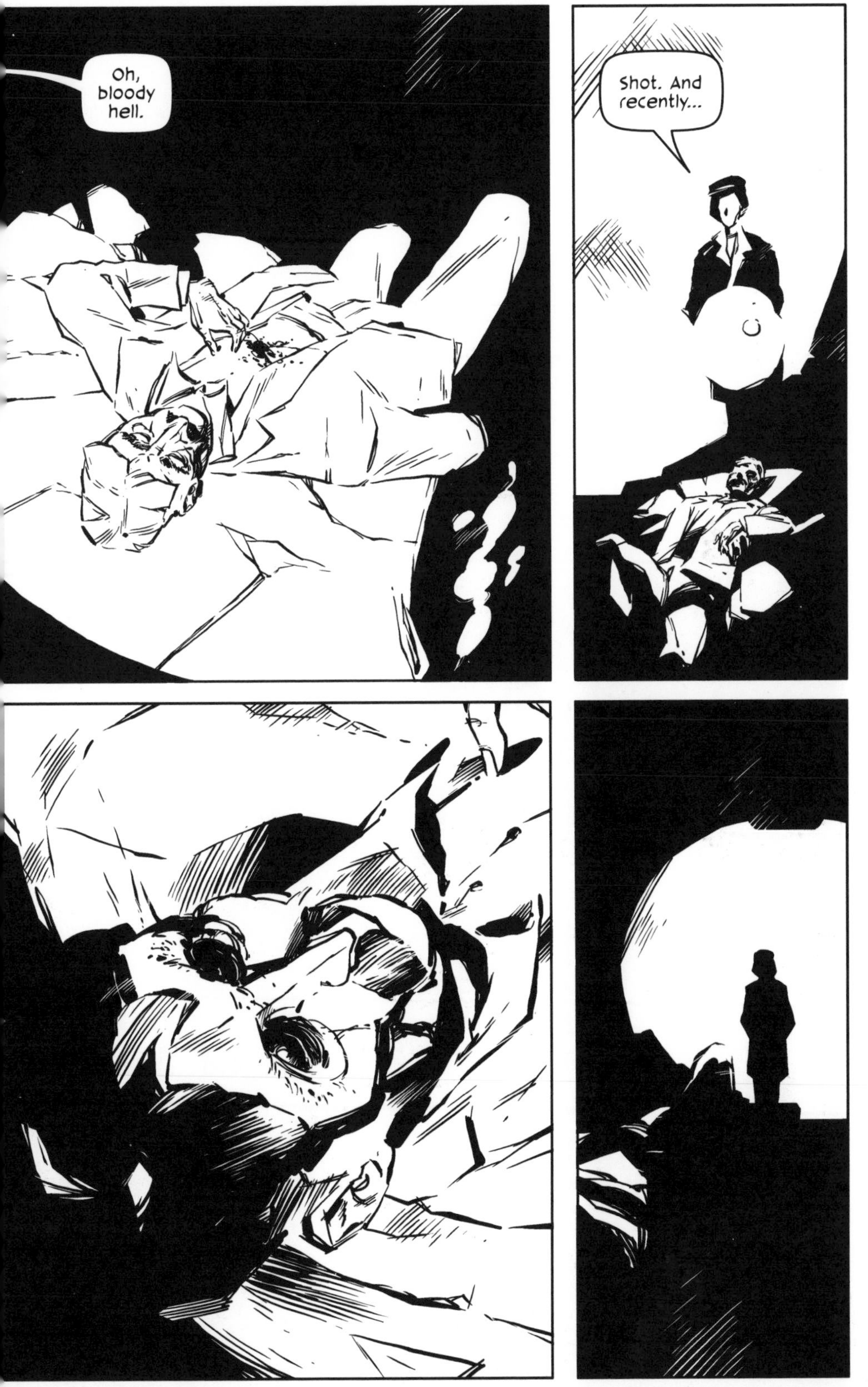
Oh, bloody hell.
Shot. And recently...

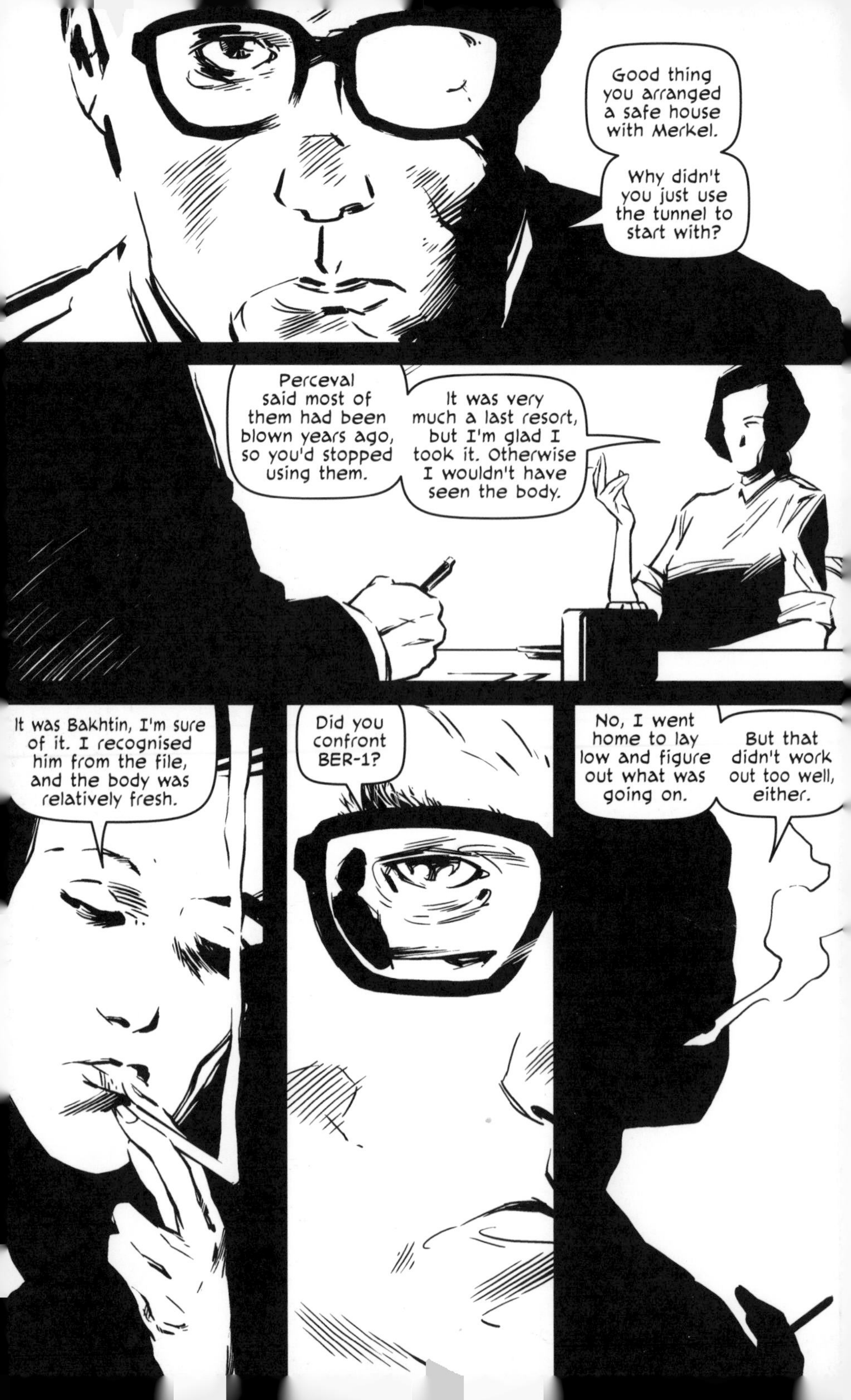
Good thing you arranged a safe house with Merkel.
Why didn't you just use the tunnel to start with?
Perceval said most of them had been blown years ago, so you'd stopped using them.
It was very much a last resort, but I'm glad I took it. Otherwise I wouldn't have seen the body.
It was Bakhtin, I'm sure of it. I recognised him from the file, and the body was relatively fresh.
Did you confront BER-1?
No, I went home to lay low and figure out what was going on.
But that didn't work out too well, either.

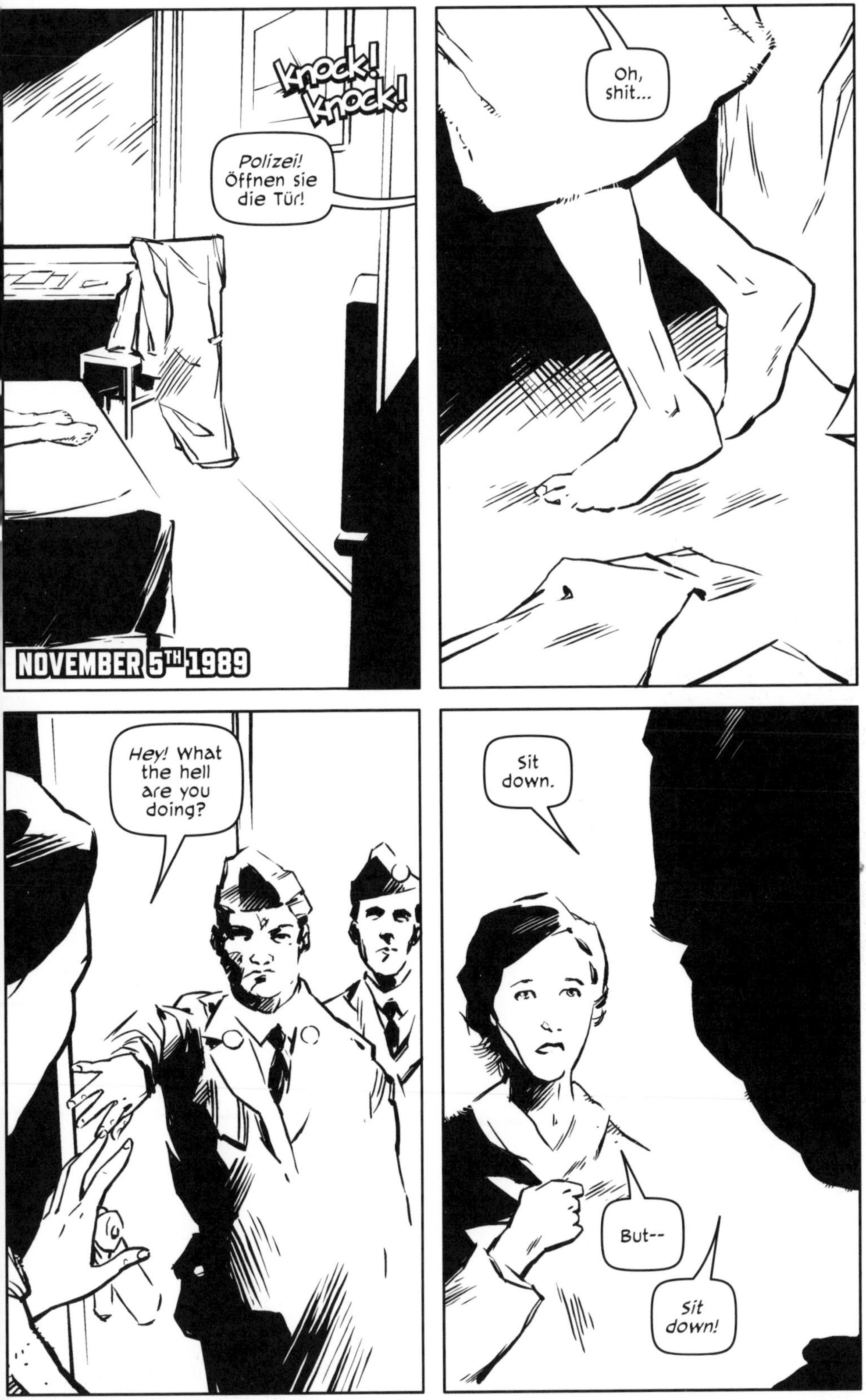
knock! knock!
Polizei! Öffnen sie die Tür!
NOVEMBER 5TH 1989
Oh, shit...
Hey! What the hell are you doing?
Sit down.
But--
Sit down!

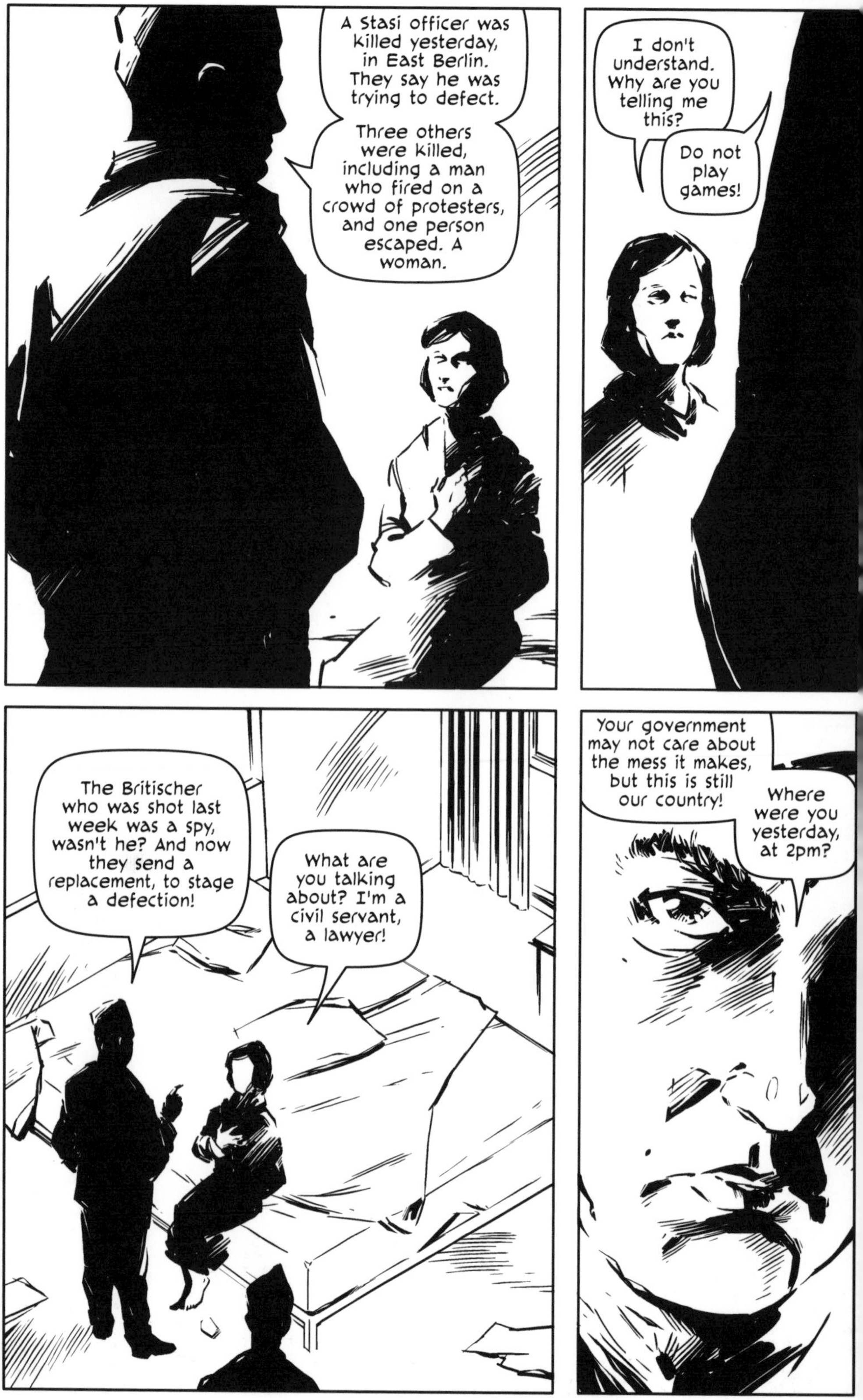
A Stasi officer was killed yesterday, in East Berlin. They say he was trying to defect.
Three others were killed, including a man who fired on a crowd of protesters, and one person escaped. A woman.
I don't understand. Why are you telling me this?
Do not play games!
The Britischer who was shot last week was a spy, wasn't he? And now they send a replacement, to stage a defection!
What are you talking about? I'm a civil servant, a lawyer!
Your government may not care about the mess it makes, but this is still our country!
Where were you yesterday, at 2pm?

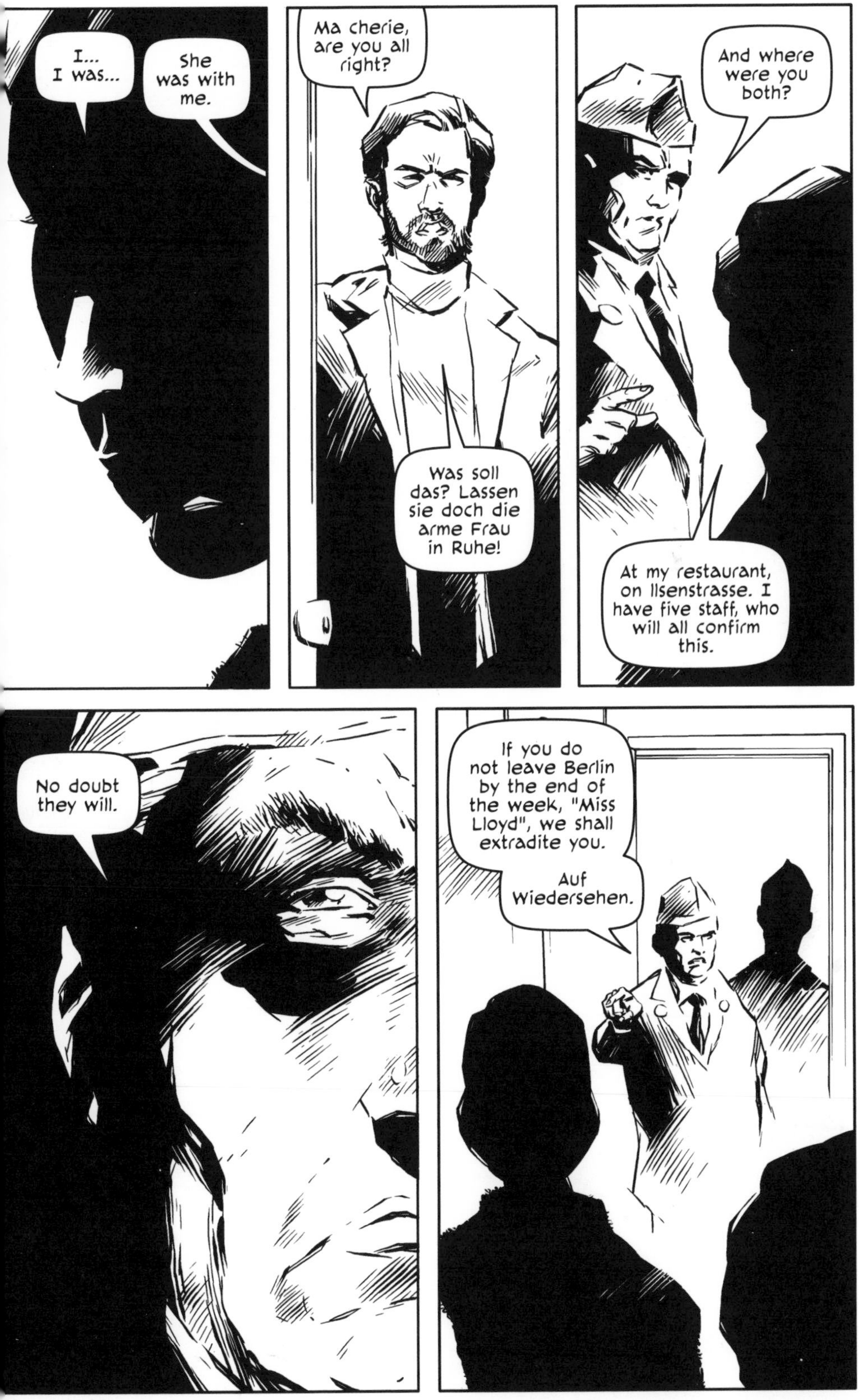
I... I was...
She was with me.
Ma cherie, are you all right?
Was soll das? Lassen sie doch die arme Frau in Ruhe!
And where were you both?
At my restaurant, on Ilsenstrasse. I have five staff, who will all confirm this.
No doubt they will.
If you do not leave Berlin by the end of the week, "Miss Lloyd", we shall extradite you.
Auf Wiedersehen.

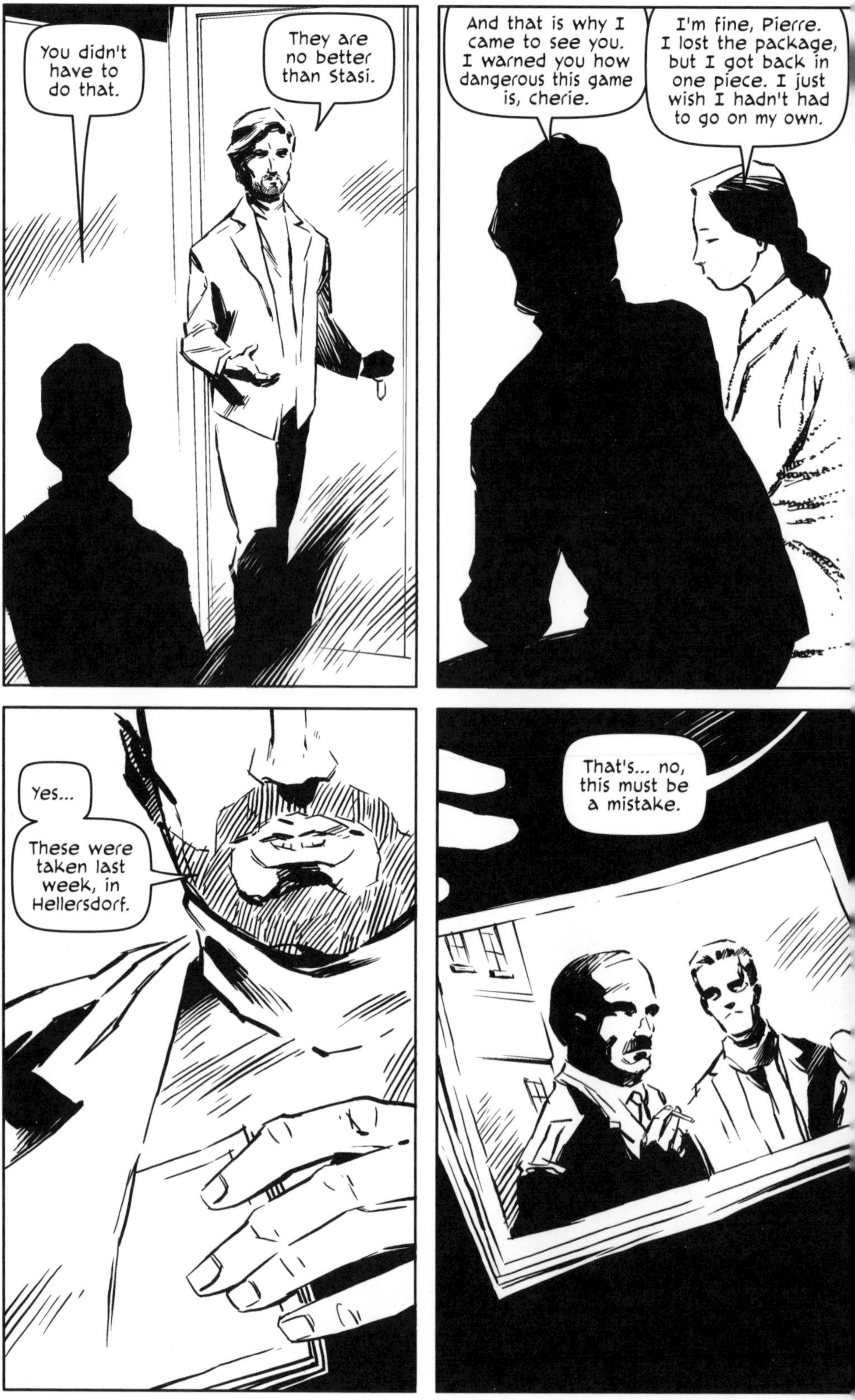
You didn't have to do that.
They are no better than Stasi.
And that is why I came to see you. I warned you how dangerous this game is, cherie.
I'm fine, Pierre. I lost the package, but I got back in one piece. I just wish I hadn't had to go on my own.
Yes...
These were taken last week, in Hellersdorf.
That's... no, this must be a mistake.

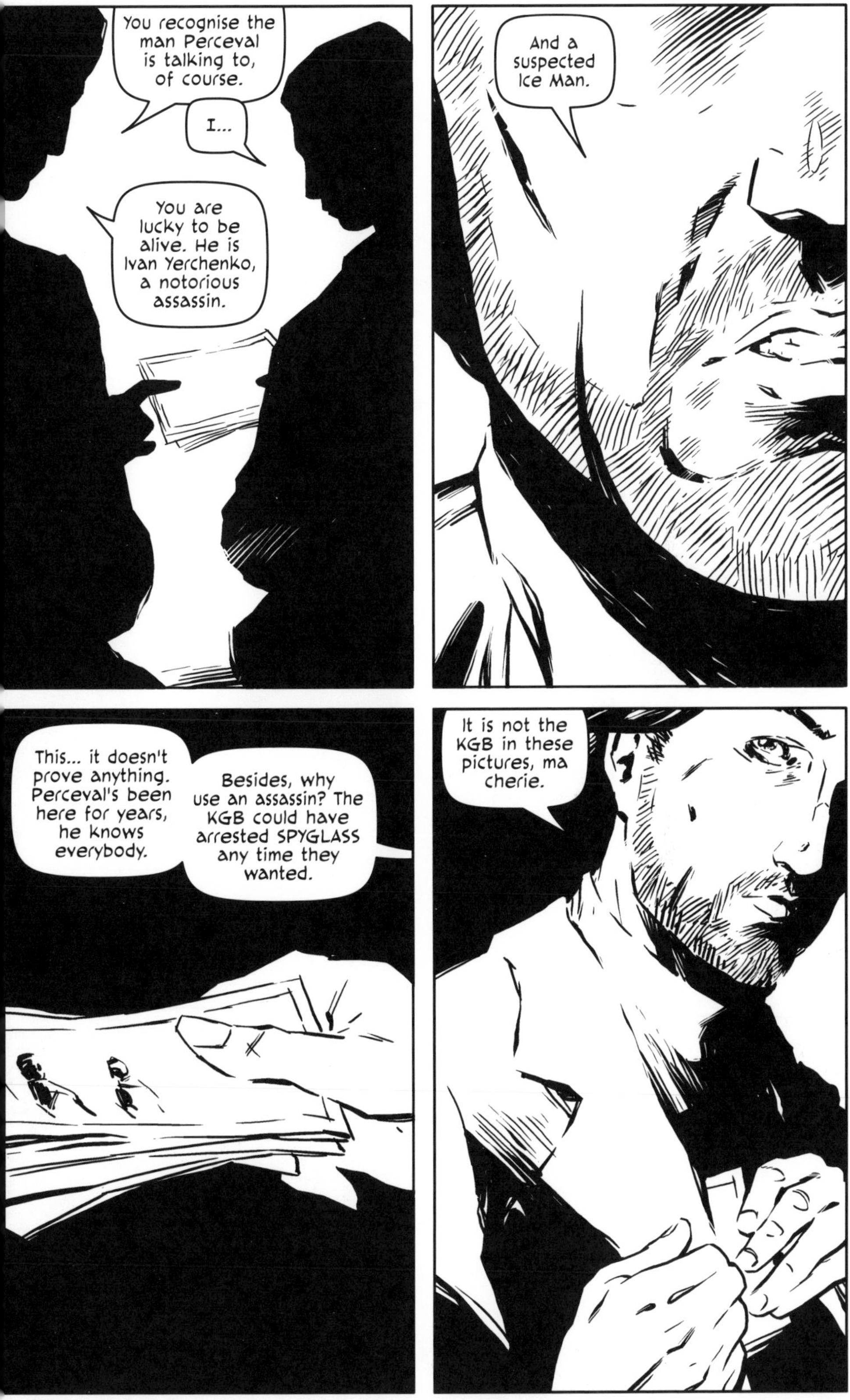

You recognise the man Perceval is talking to, of course.
I...
You are lucky to be alive. He is Ivan Yerchenko, a notorious assassin.
And a suspected Ice Man.
This... it doesn't prove anything. Perceval's been here for years, he knows everybody.
Besides, why use an assassin? The KGB could have arrested SPYGLASS any time they wanted.
It is not the KGB in these pictures, ma cherie.

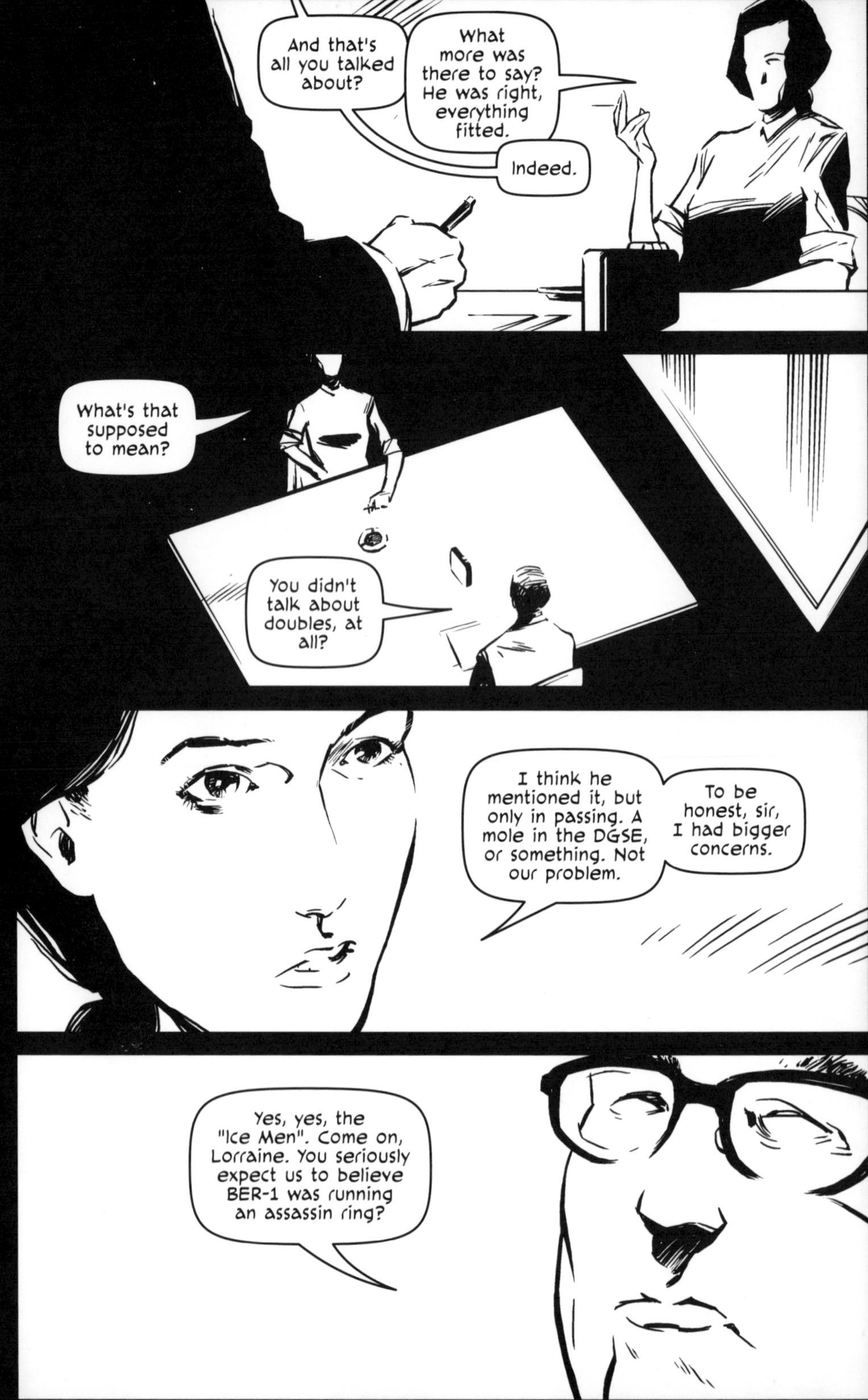

And that's all you talked about?
What more was there to say? He was right, everything fitted.
Indeed.
What's that supposed to mean?
You didn't talk about doubles, at all?
I think he mentioned it, but only in passing. A mole in the DGSE, or something. Not our problem.
To be honest, sir, I had bigger concerns.
Yes, yes, the "Ice Men". Come on, Lorraine. You seriously expect us to believe BER-1 was running an assassin ring?

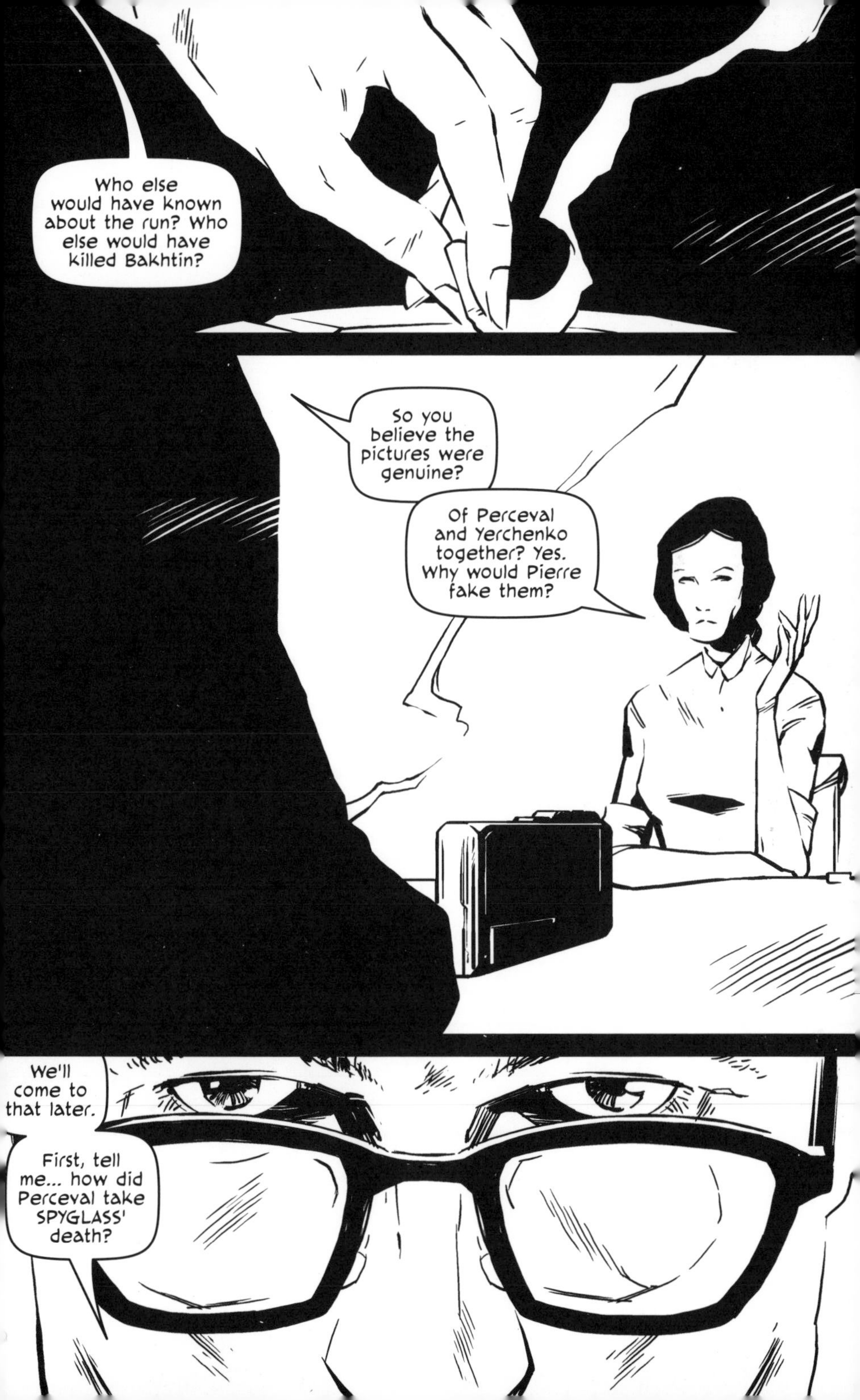
Who else would have known about the run? Who else would have killed Bakhtin?
So you believe the pictures were genuine?
Of Perceval and Yerchenko together? Yes. Why would Pierre fake them?
We'll come to that later.
First, tell me... how did Perceval take SPYGLASS' death?

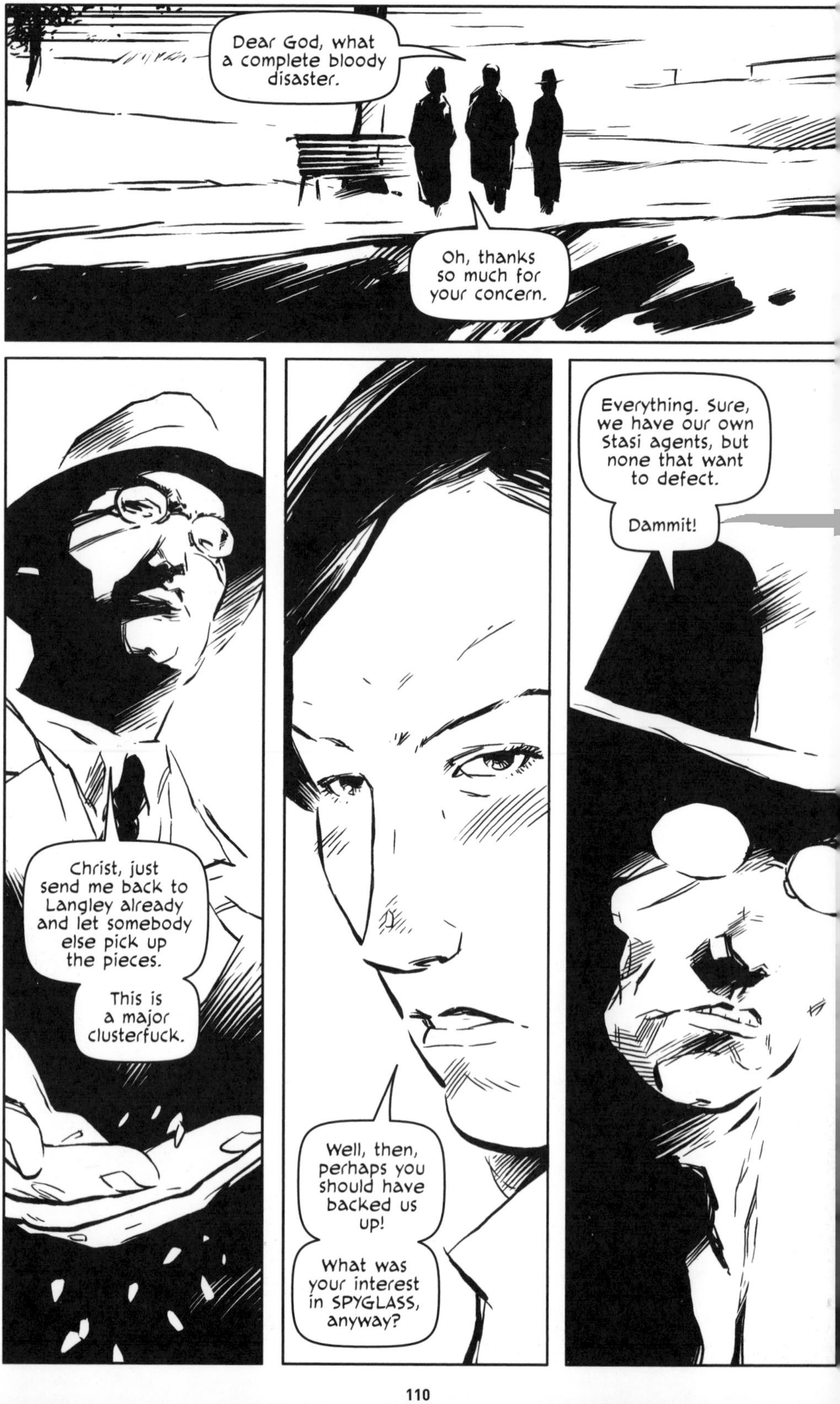
Dear God, what a complete bloody disaster.
Oh, thanks so much for your concern.
Christ, just send me back to Langley already and let somebody else pick up the pieces.
This is a major clusterfuck.
Well, then, perhaps you should have backed us up!
What was your interest in SPYGLASS, anyway?
Everything. Sure, we have our own Stasi agents, but none that want to defect.
Dammit!

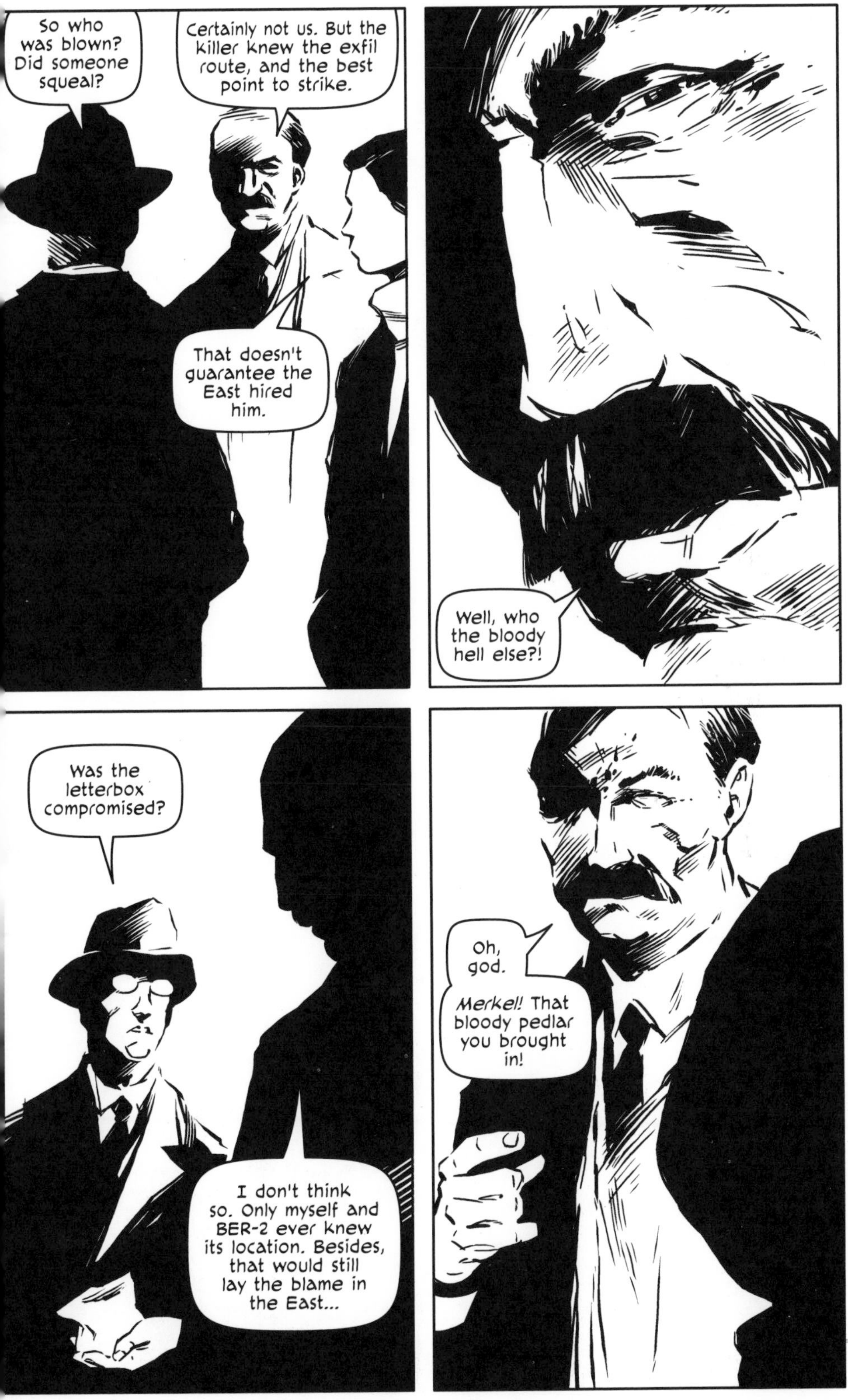
So who was blown? Did someone squeal?
Certainly not us. But the killer knew the exfil route, and the best point to strike.
That doesn't guarantee the East hired him.
Well, who the bloody hell else?!
Was the letterbox compromised?
I don't think so. Only myself and BER-2 ever knew its location. Besides, that would still lay the blame in the East...
Oh, god.
Merkel! That bloody pedlar you brought in!

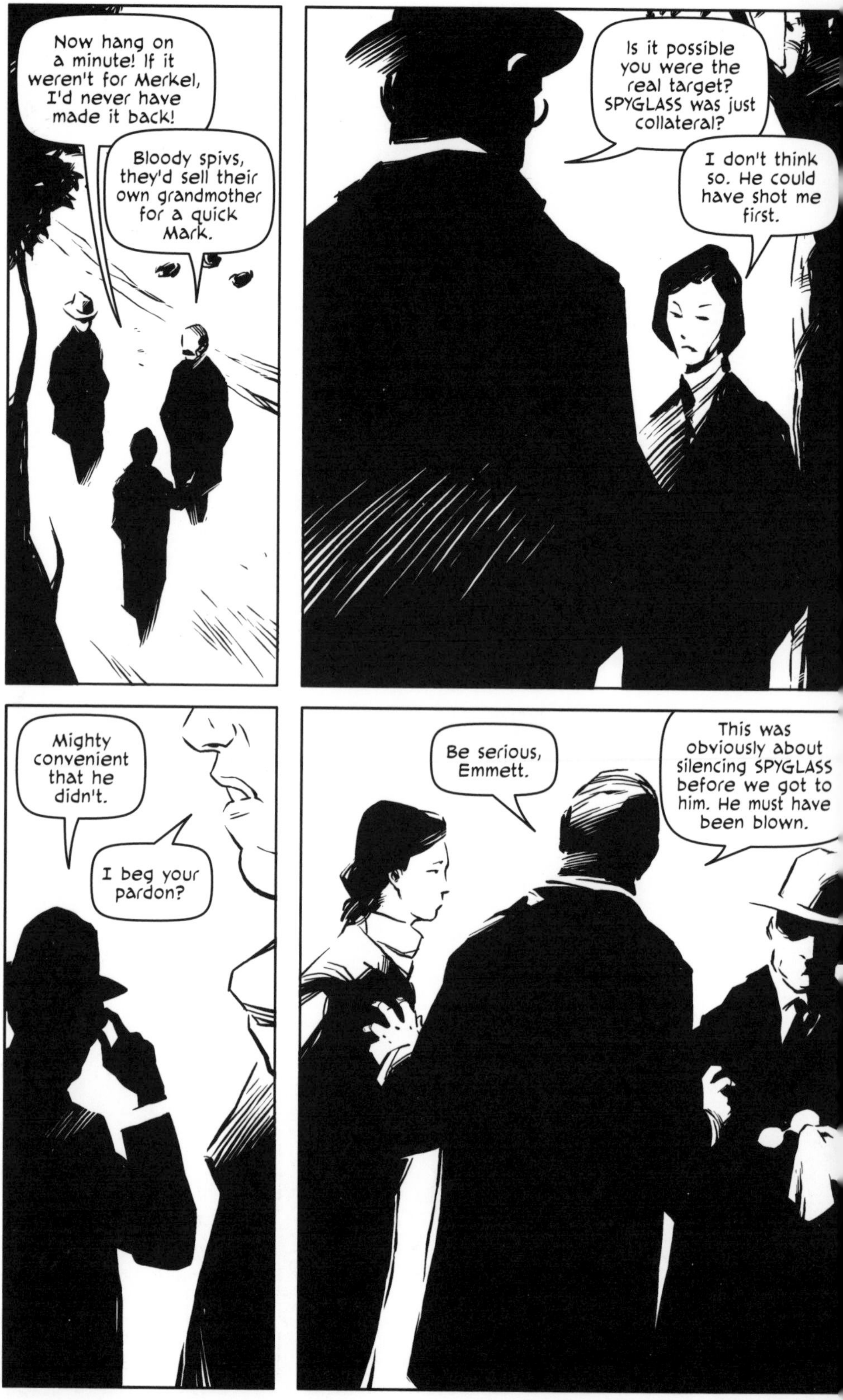
Now hang on a minute! If it weren't for Merkel, I'd never have made it back!
Bloody spivs, they'd sell their own grandmother for a quick Mark.
Is it possible you were the real target? SPYGLASS was just collateral?
I don't think so. He could have shot me first.
Mighty convenient that he didn't.
I beg your pardon?
Be serious, Emmett.
This was obviously about silencing SPYGLASS before we got to him. He must have been blown.

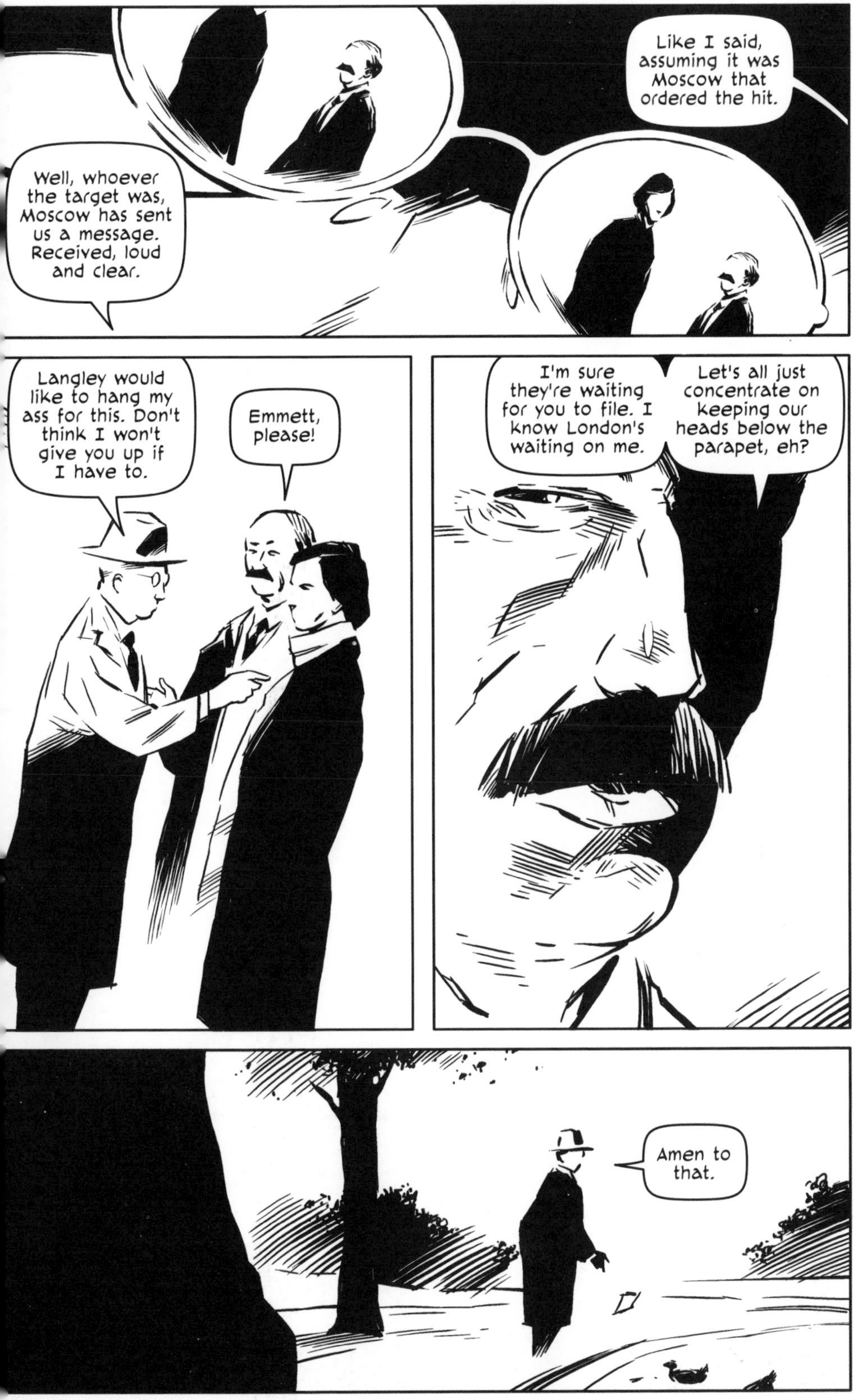
Like I said, assuming it was Moscow that ordered the hit.
Well, whoever the target was, Moscow has sent us a message. Received, loud and clear.
Langley would like to hang my ass for this. Don't think I won't give you up if I have to.
Emmett, please!
I'm sure they're waiting for you to file. I know London's waiting on me.
Let's all just concentrate on keeping our heads below the parapet, eh?
Amen to that.

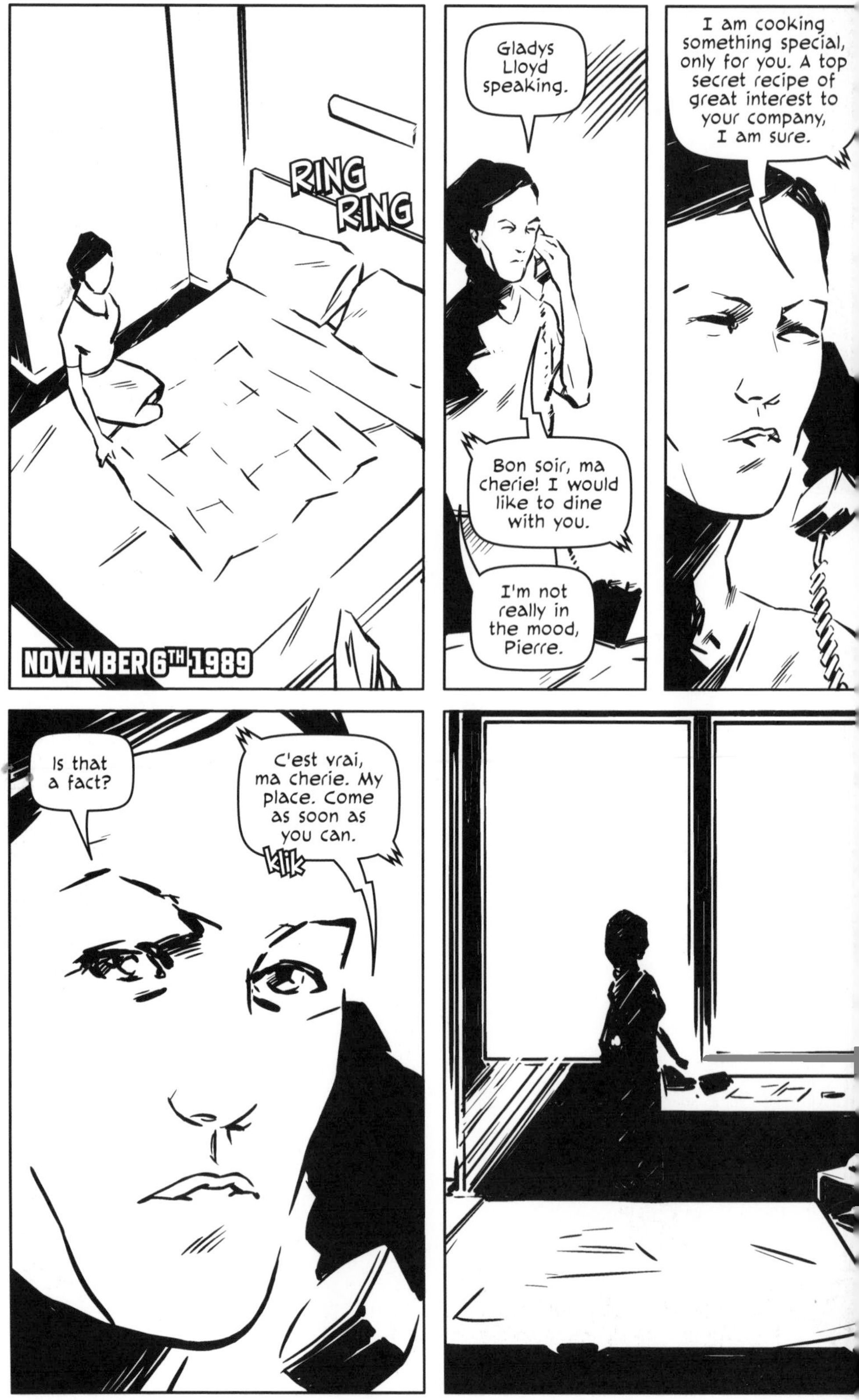
RING RING
NOVEMBER 6TH 1989
Gladys Lloyd speaking.
Bon soir, ma cherie! I would like to dine with you.
I'm not really in the mood, Pierre.
I am cooking something special, only for you. A top secret recipe of great interest to your company, I am sure.
Is that a fact?
C'est vrai, ma cherie. My place. Come as soon as you can.
klik

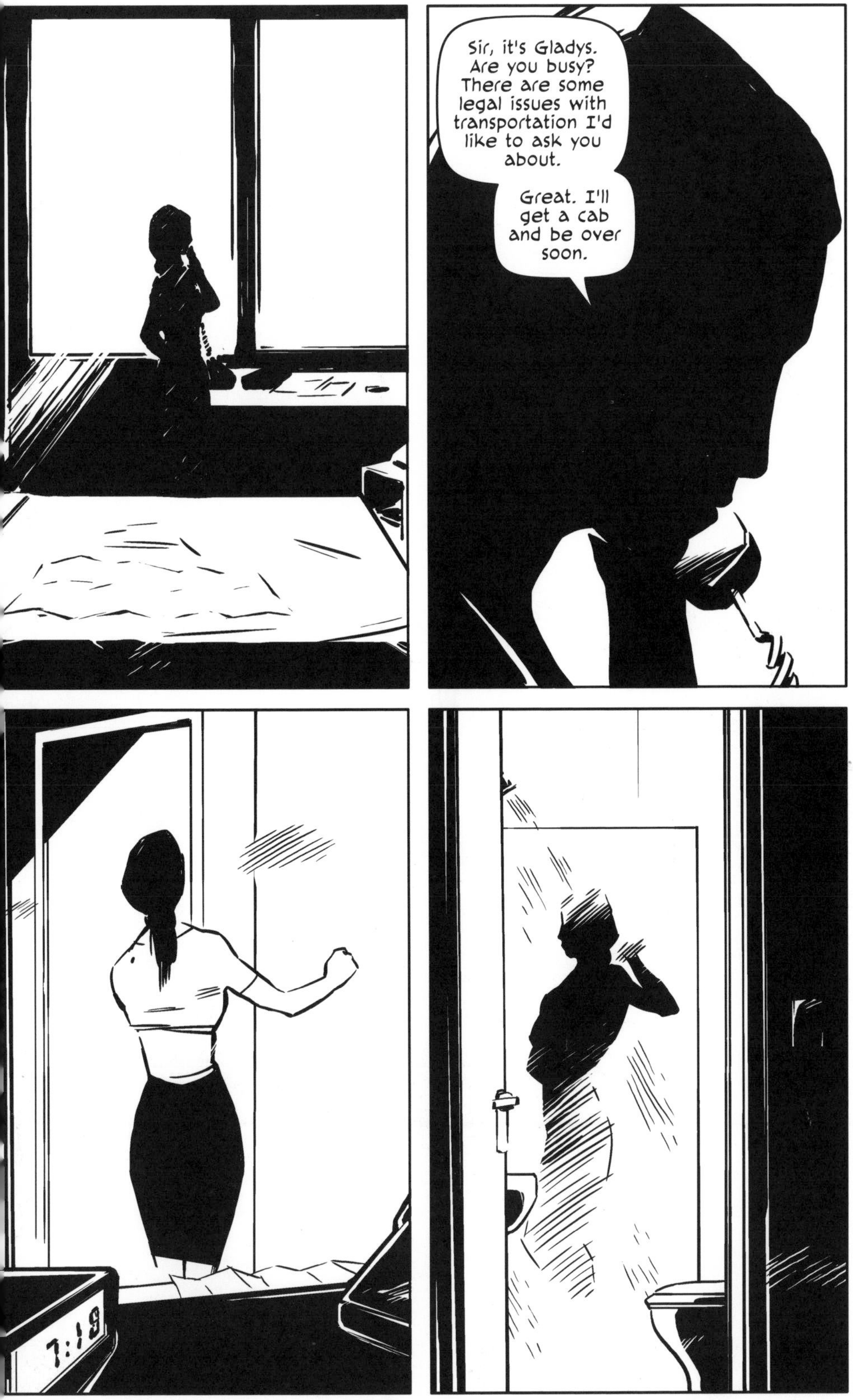
Sir, it's Gladys. Are you busy? There are some legal issues with transportation I'd like to ask you about.
Great. I'll get a cab and be over soon.
7:19

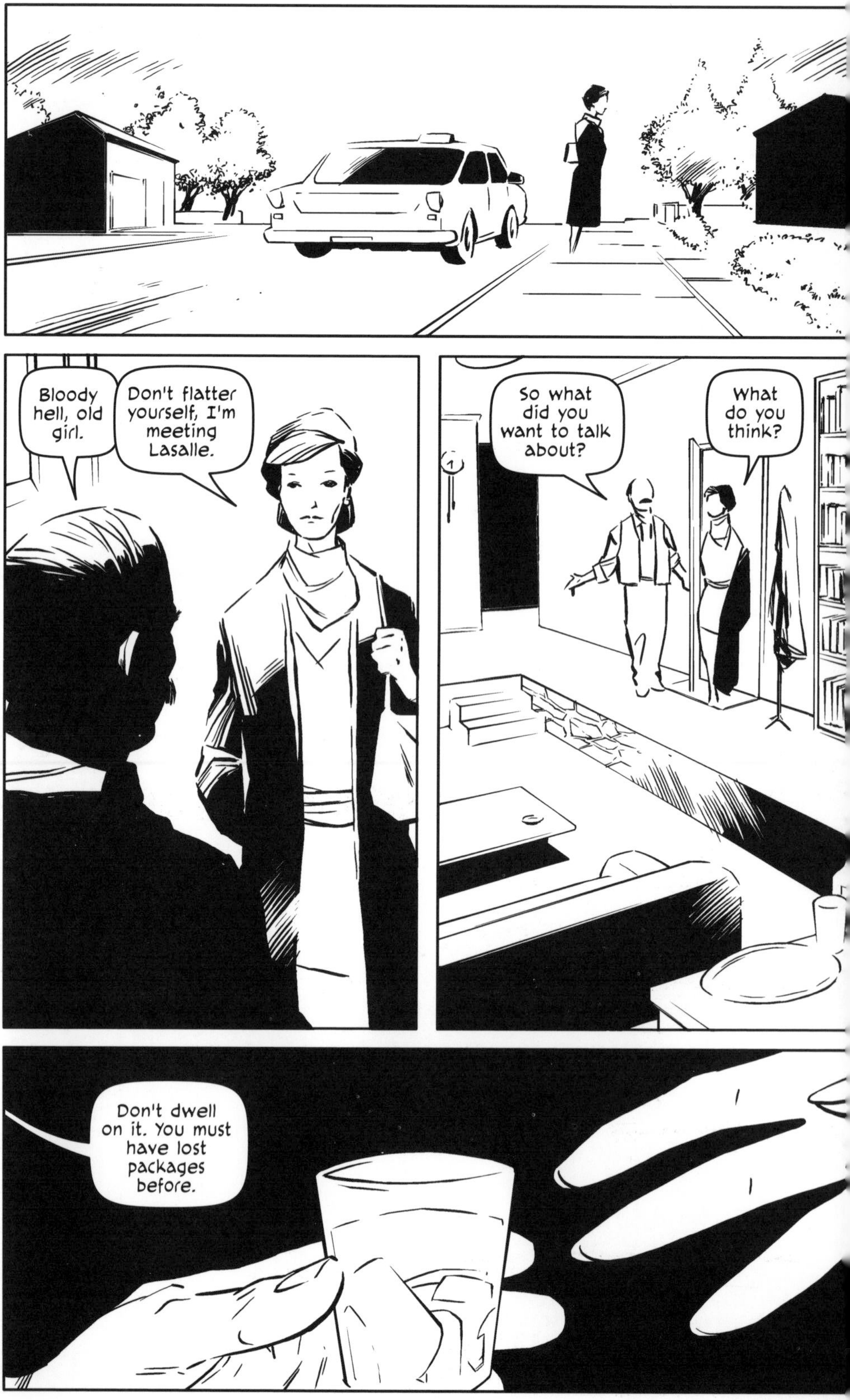
Bloody hell, old girl.
Don't flatter yourself, I'm meeting Lasalle.
So what did you want to talk about?
What do you think?
Don't dwell on it. You must have lost packages before.

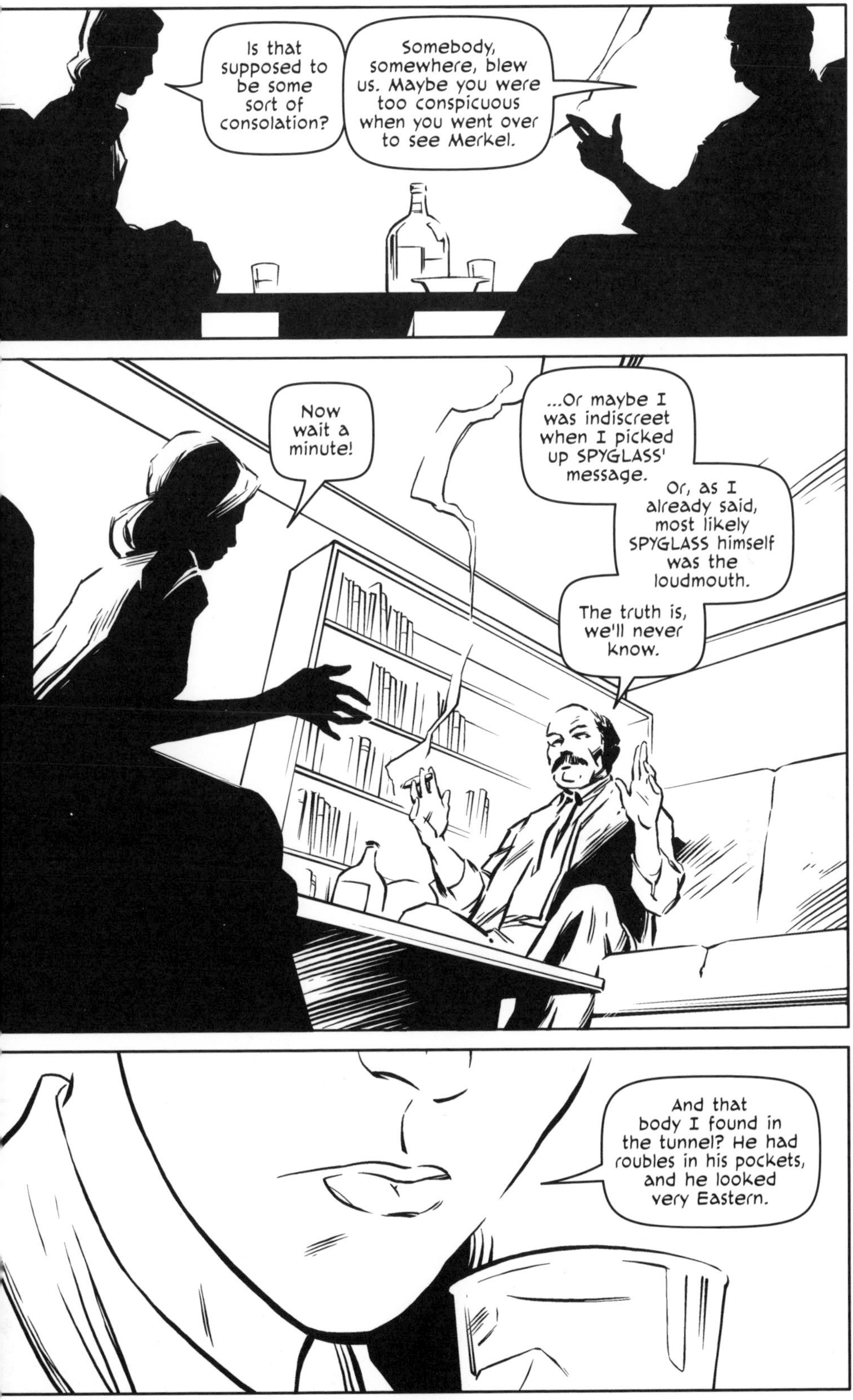
Is that supposed to be some sort of consolation?
Somebody, somewhere, blew us. Maybe you were too conspicuous when you went over to see Merkel.
Now wait a minute!
...Or maybe I was indiscreet when I picked up SPYGLASS' message.
Or, as I already said, most likely SPYGLASS himself was the loudmouth.
The truth is, we'll never know.
And that body I found in the tunnel? He had roubles in his pockets, and he looked very Eastern.

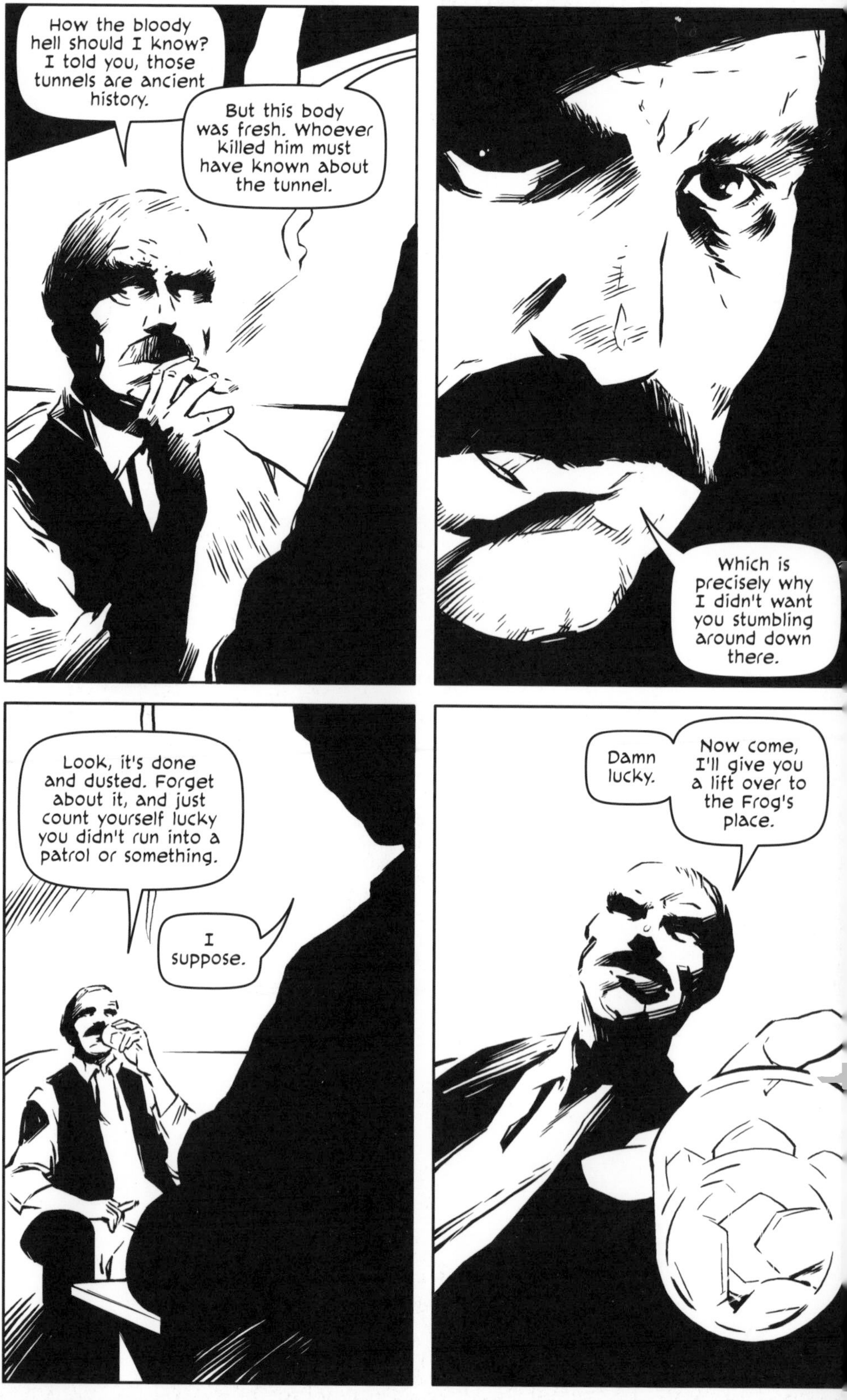
How the bloody hell should I know? I told you, those tunnels are ancient history.
But this body was fresh. Whoever killed him must have known about the tunnel.
Which is precisely why I didn't want you stumbling around down there.
Look, it's done and dusted. Forget about it, and just count yourself lucky you didn't run into a patrol or something.
I suppose.
Damn lucky.
Now come, I'll give you a lift over to the Frog's place.

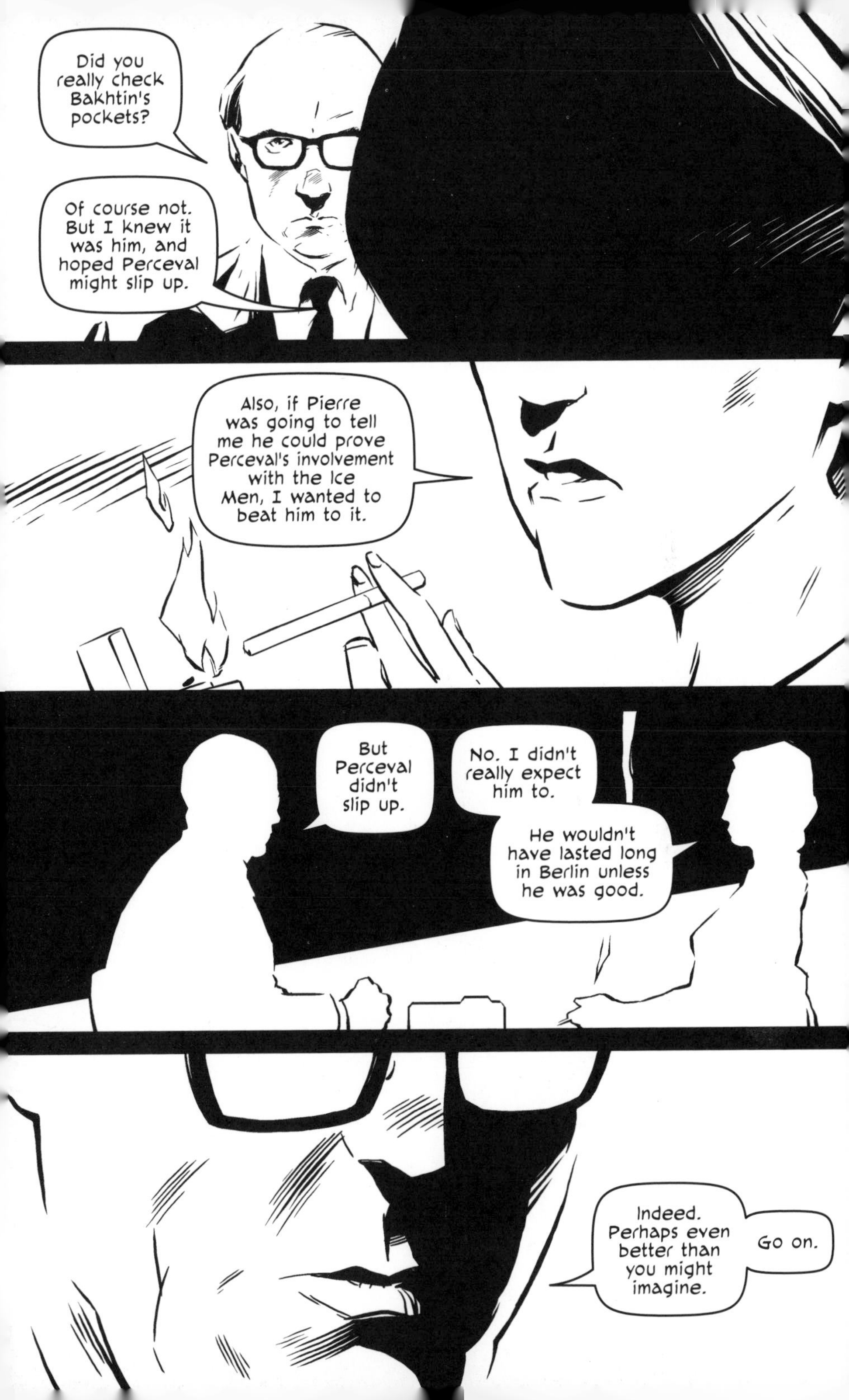
Did you really check Bakhtin's pockets?
Of course not. But I knew it was him, and hoped Perceval might slip up.
Also, if Pierre was going to tell me he could prove Perceval's involvement with the Ice Men, I wanted to beat him to it.
But Perceval didn't slip up.
No. I didn't really expect him to.
He wouldn't have lasted long in Berlin unless he was good.
Indeed. Perhaps even better than you might imagine.
Go on.

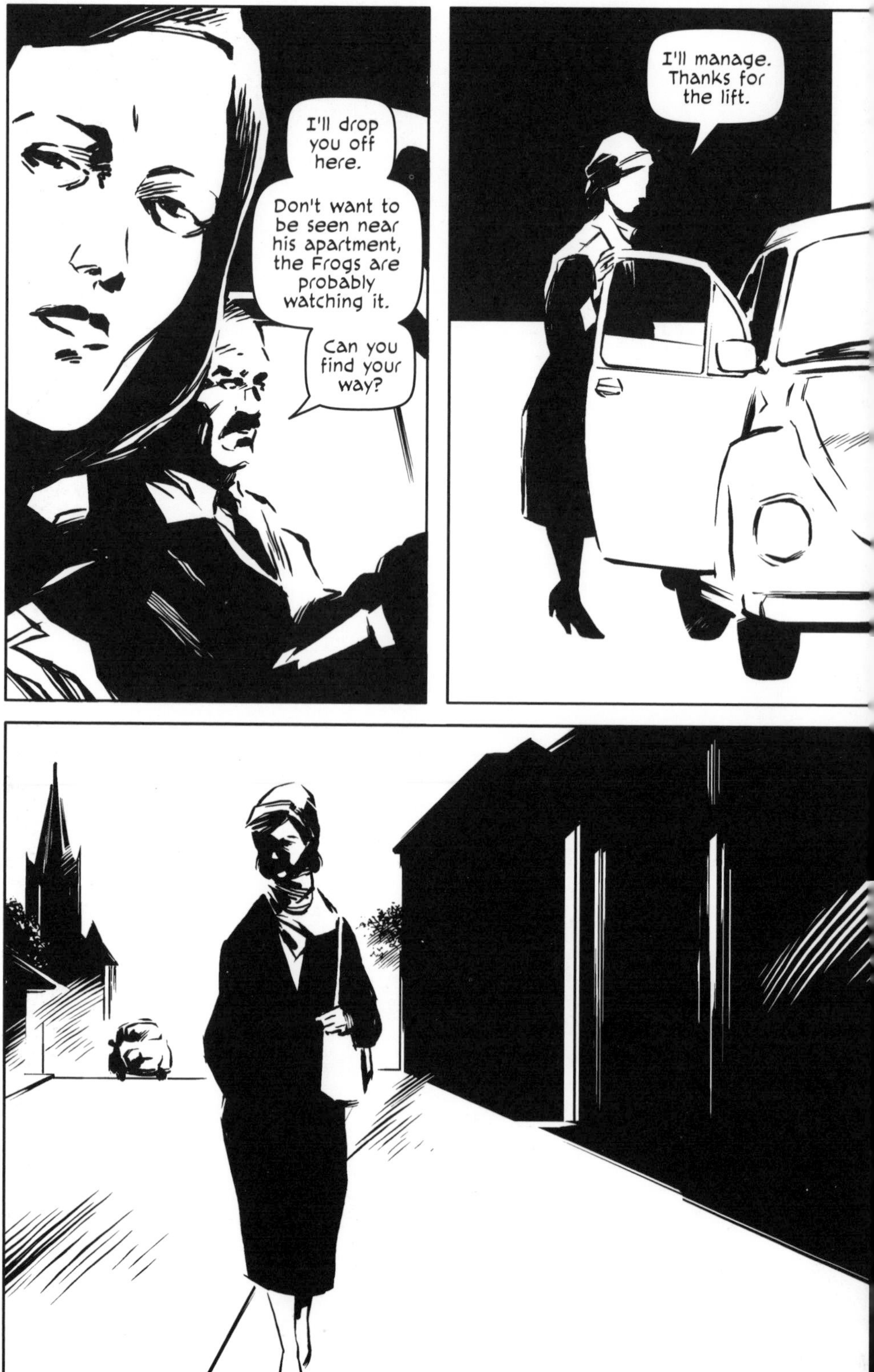
I'll drop you off here.
Don't want to be seen near his apartment, the Frogs are probably watching it.
Can you find your way?
I'll manage. Thanks for the lift.

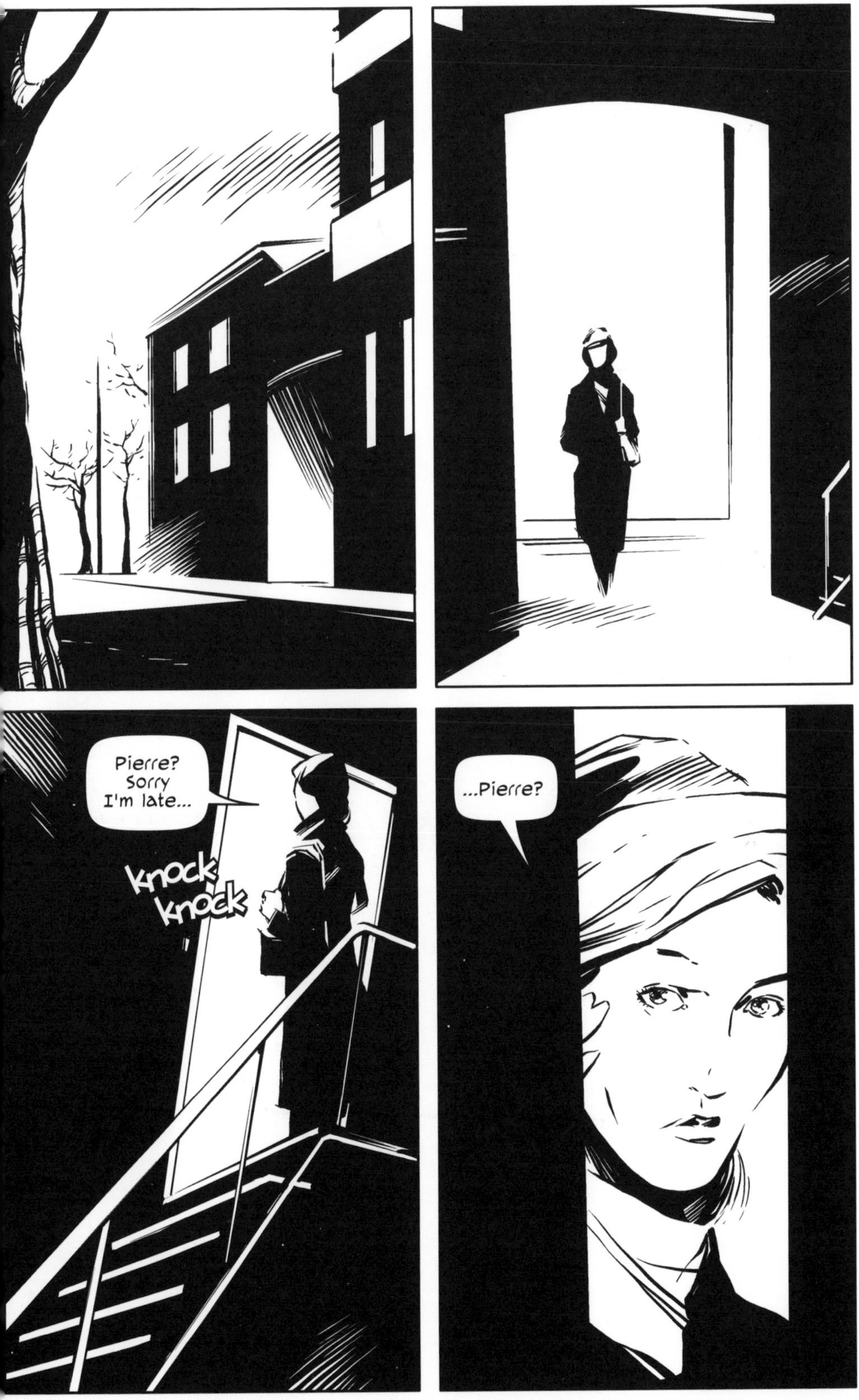
Pierre? Sorry I'm late...
knock knock
...Pierre?

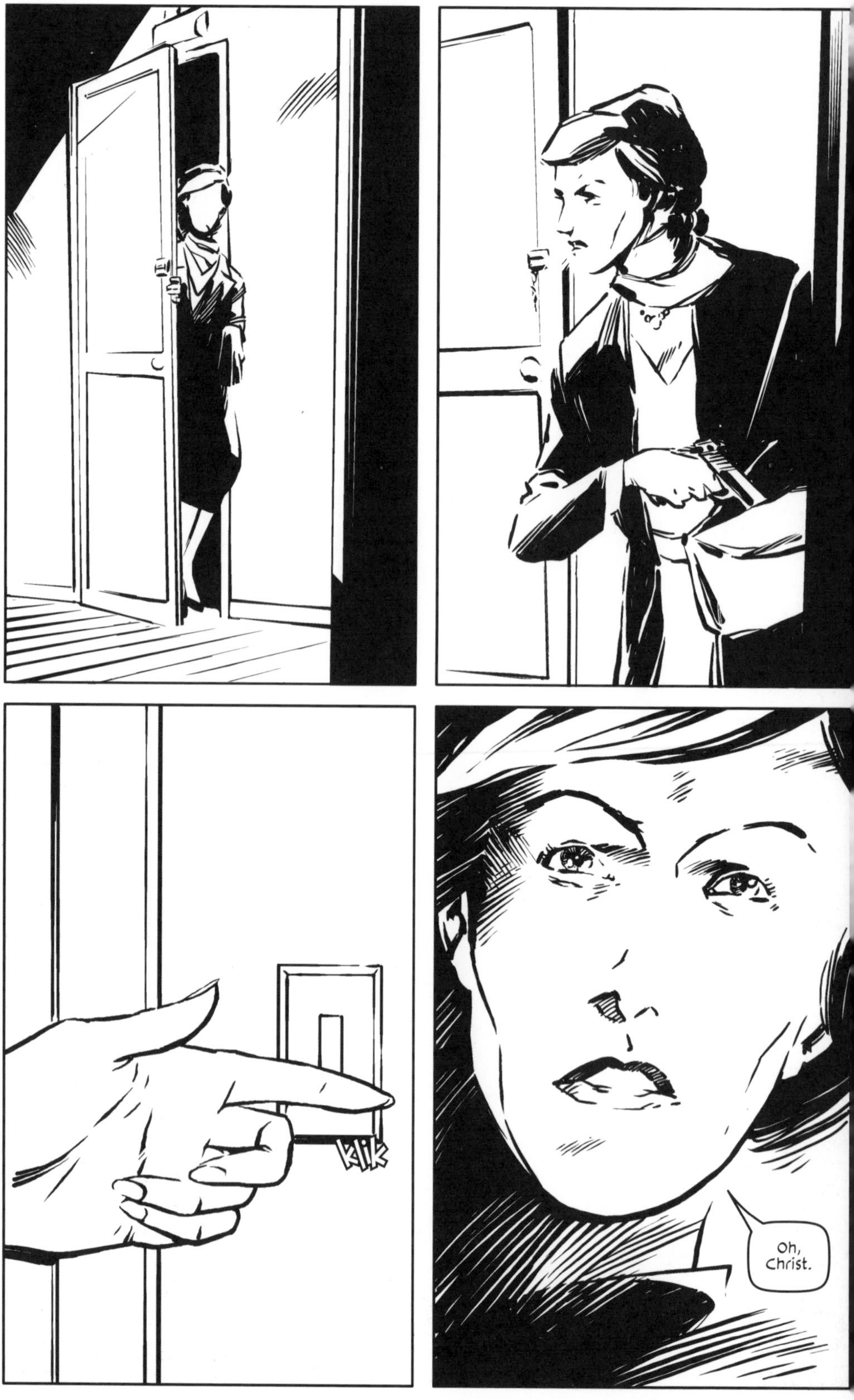

klik
Oh, Christ.

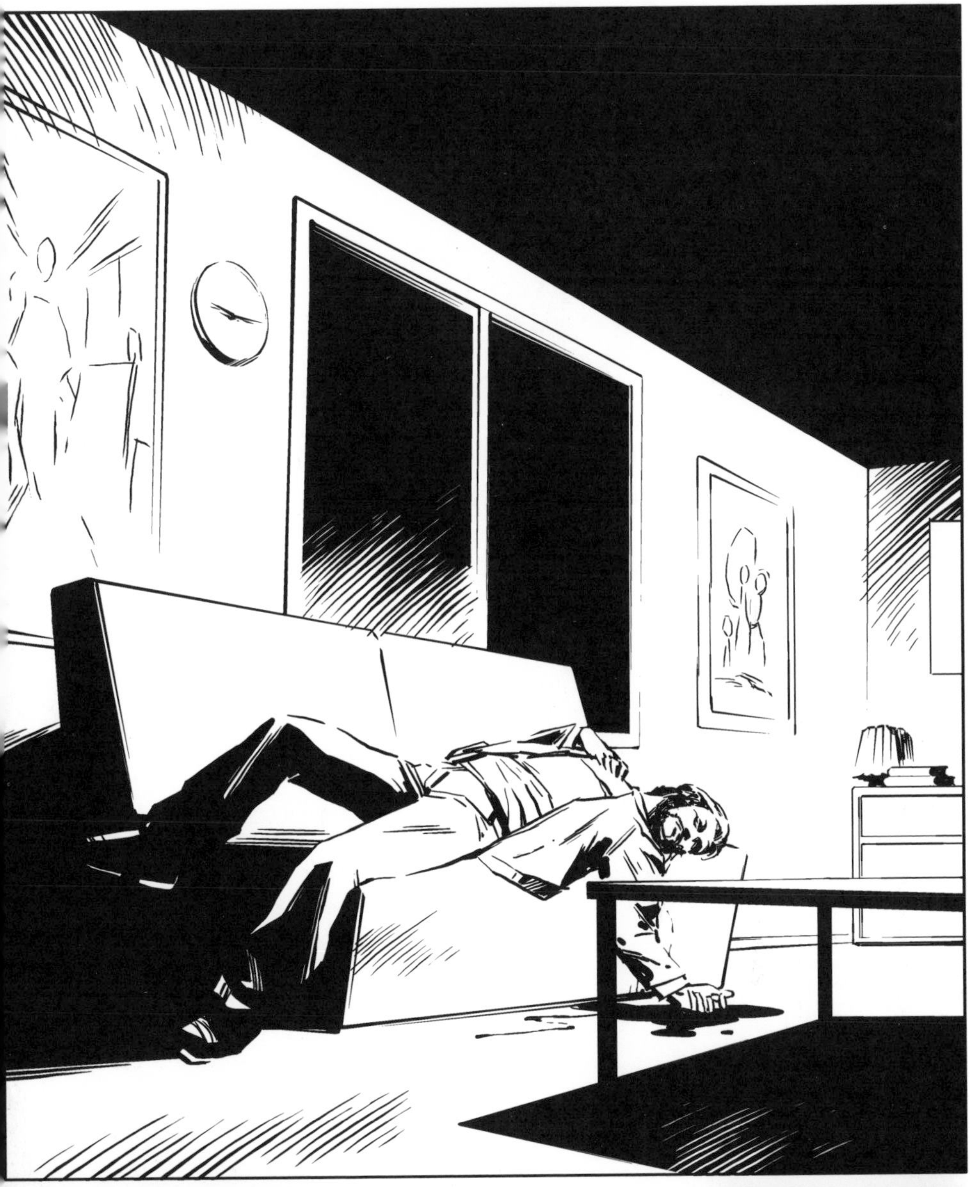

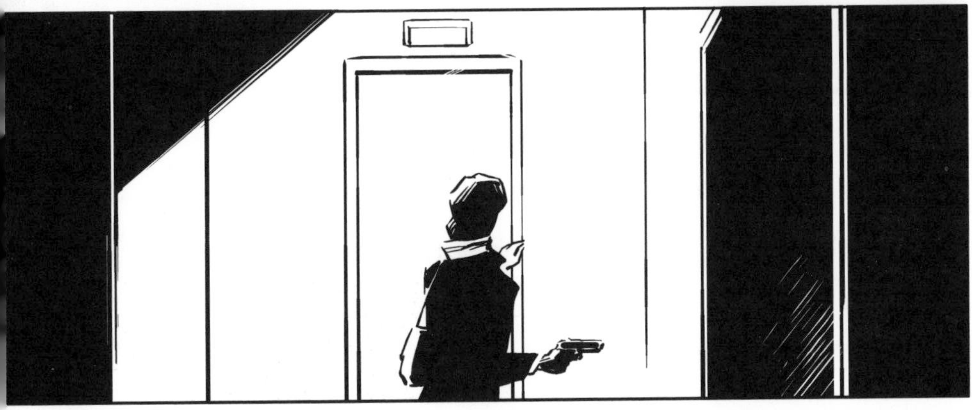

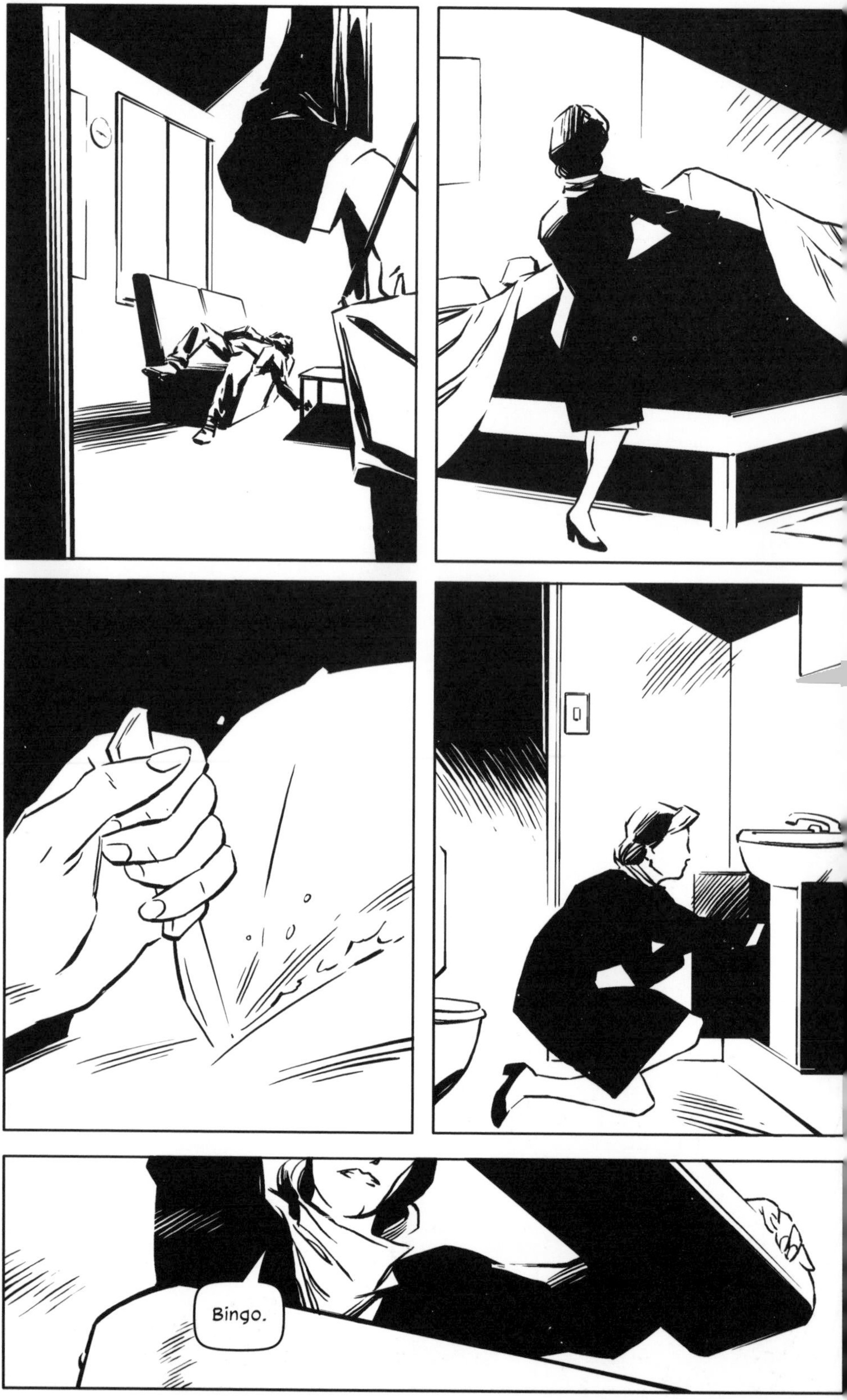
Bingo.

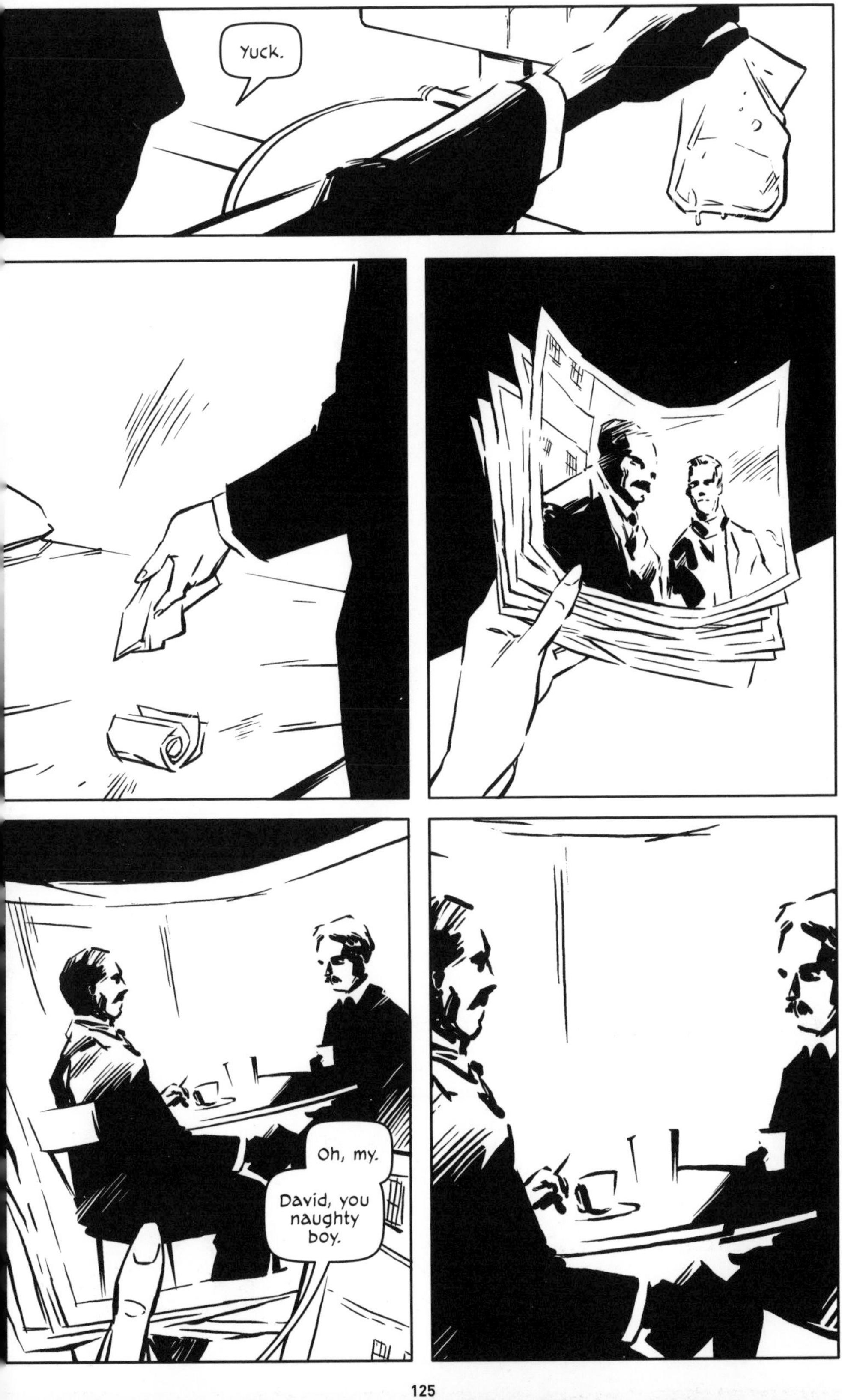
YUCK.
Oh, my.
David, you naughty boy.

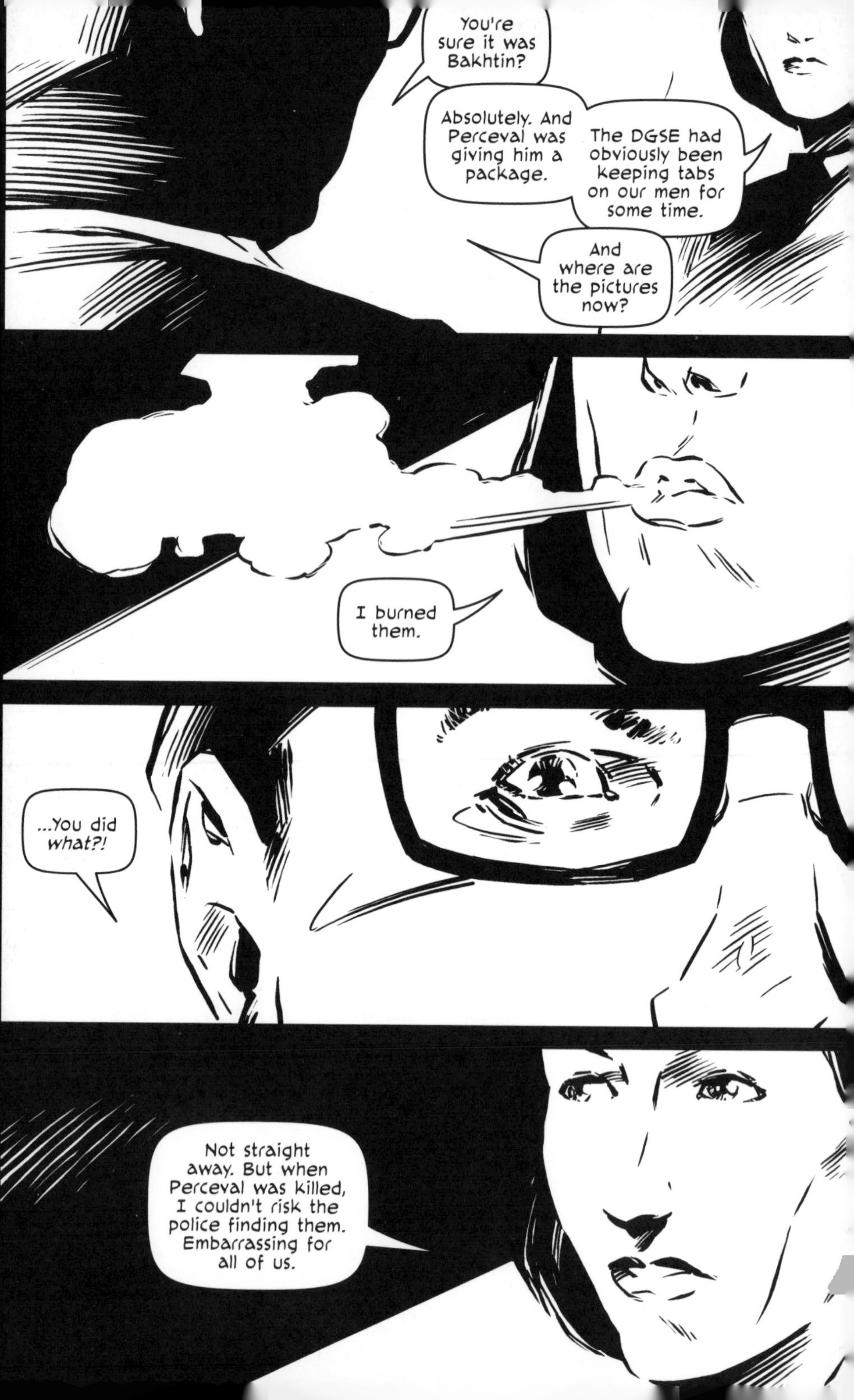

You're sure it was Bakhtin?
Absolutely. And Perceval was giving him a package.
The DGSE had obviously been keeping tabs on our men for some time.
And where are the pictures now?
I burned them.
...You did *what?!*
Not straight away. But when Perceval was killed, I couldn't risk the police finding them. Embarrassing for all of us.

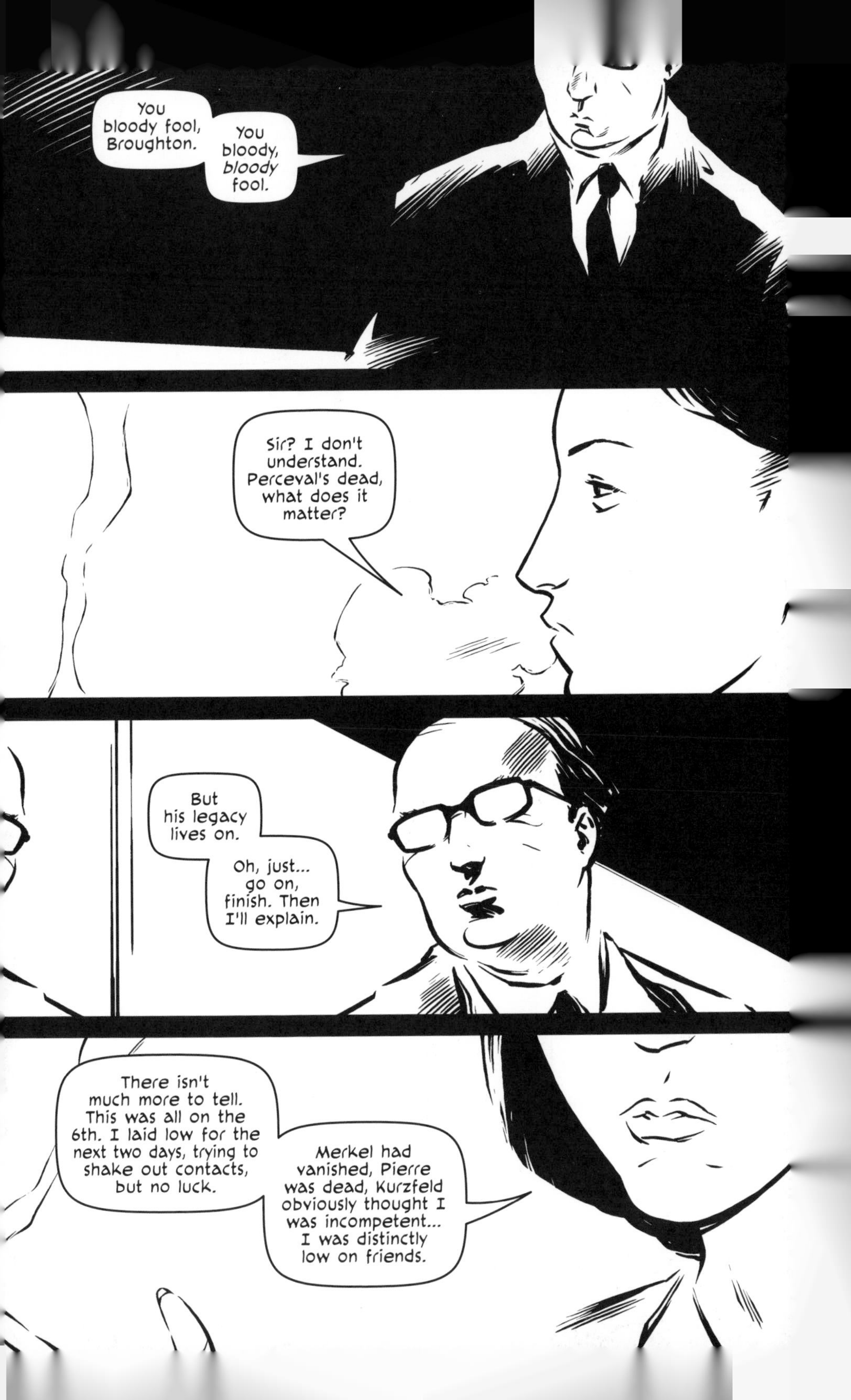
You bloody fool, Broughton.
You bloody, *bloody* fool.
Sir? I don't understand. Perceval's dead, what does it matter?
But his legacy lives on.
Oh, just... go on, finish. Then I'll explain.
There isn't much more to tell. This was all on the 6th. I laid low for the next two days, trying to shake out contacts, but no luck.
Merkel had vanished, Pierre was dead, Kurzfeld obviously thought I was incompetent... I was distinctly low on friends.

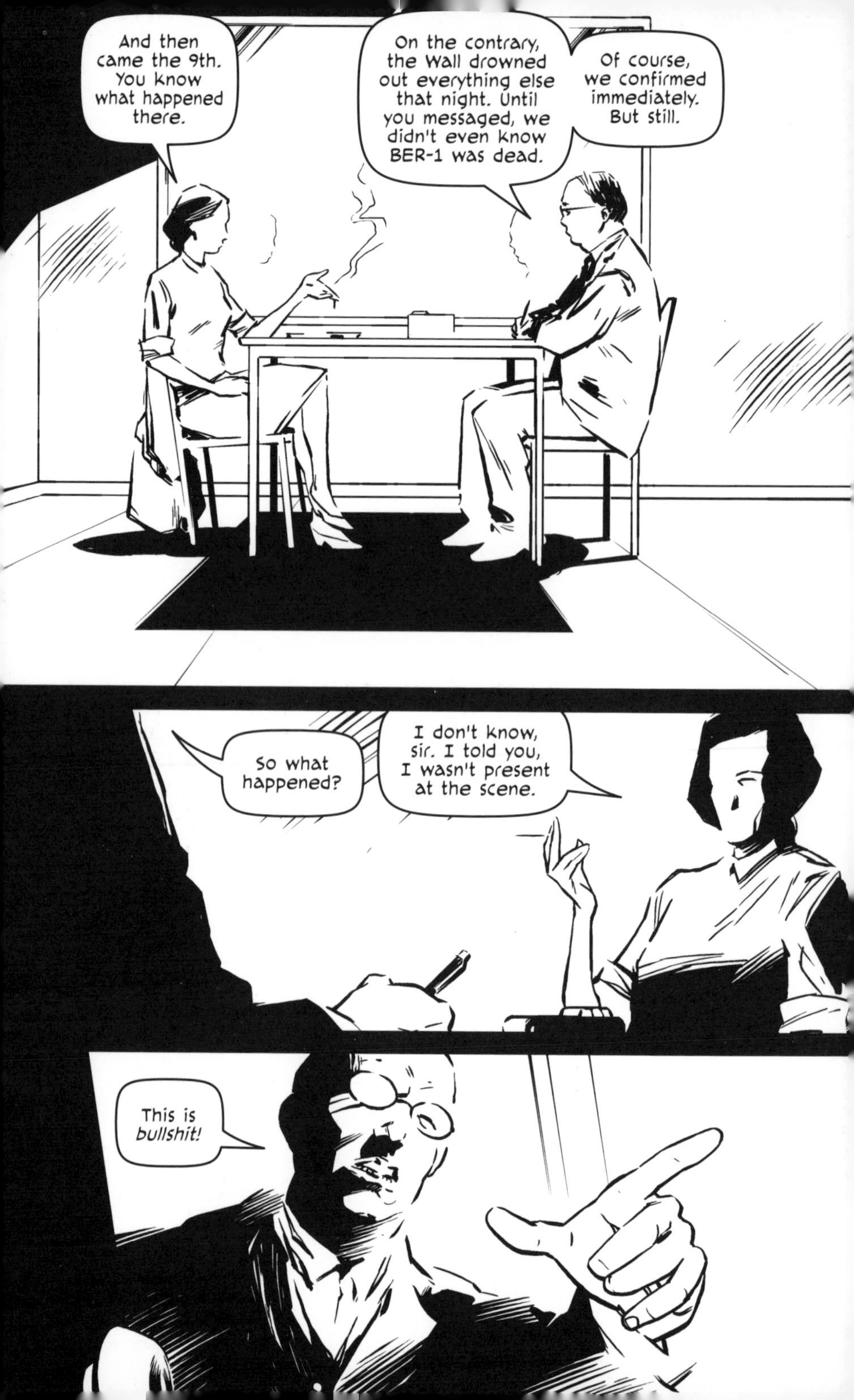
And then came the 9th. You know what happened there.
On the contrary, the Wall drowned out everything else that night. Until you messaged, we didn't even know BER-1 was dead.
Of course, we confirmed immediately. But still.
So what happened?
I don't know, sir. I told you, I wasn't present at the scene.
This is *bullshit!*

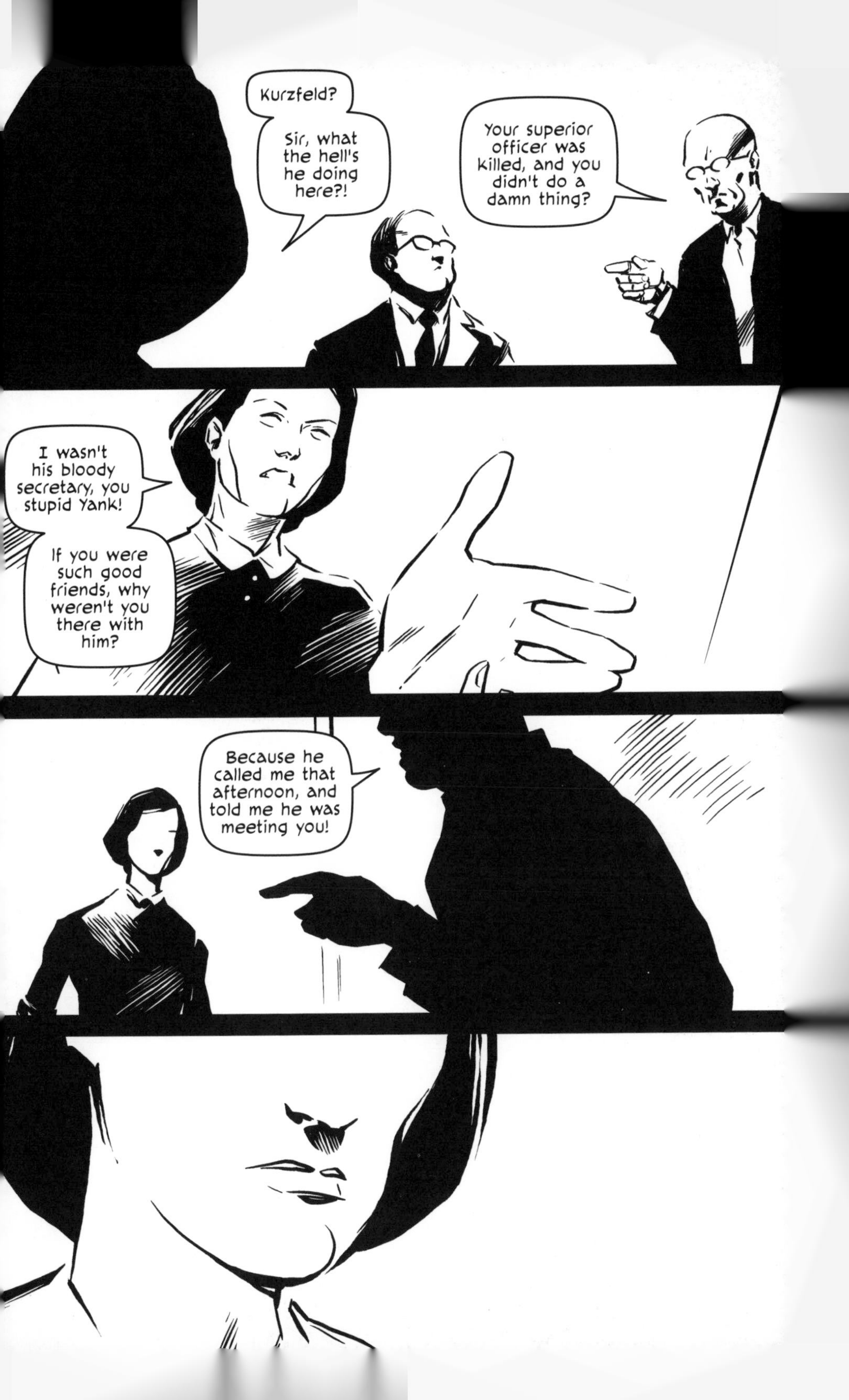
Kurzfeld?
Sir, what the hell's he doing here?!
Your superior officer was killed, and you didn't do a damn thing?
I wasn't his bloody secretary, you stupid Yank!
If you were such good friends, why weren't you there with him?
Because he called me that afternoon, and told me he was meeting you!

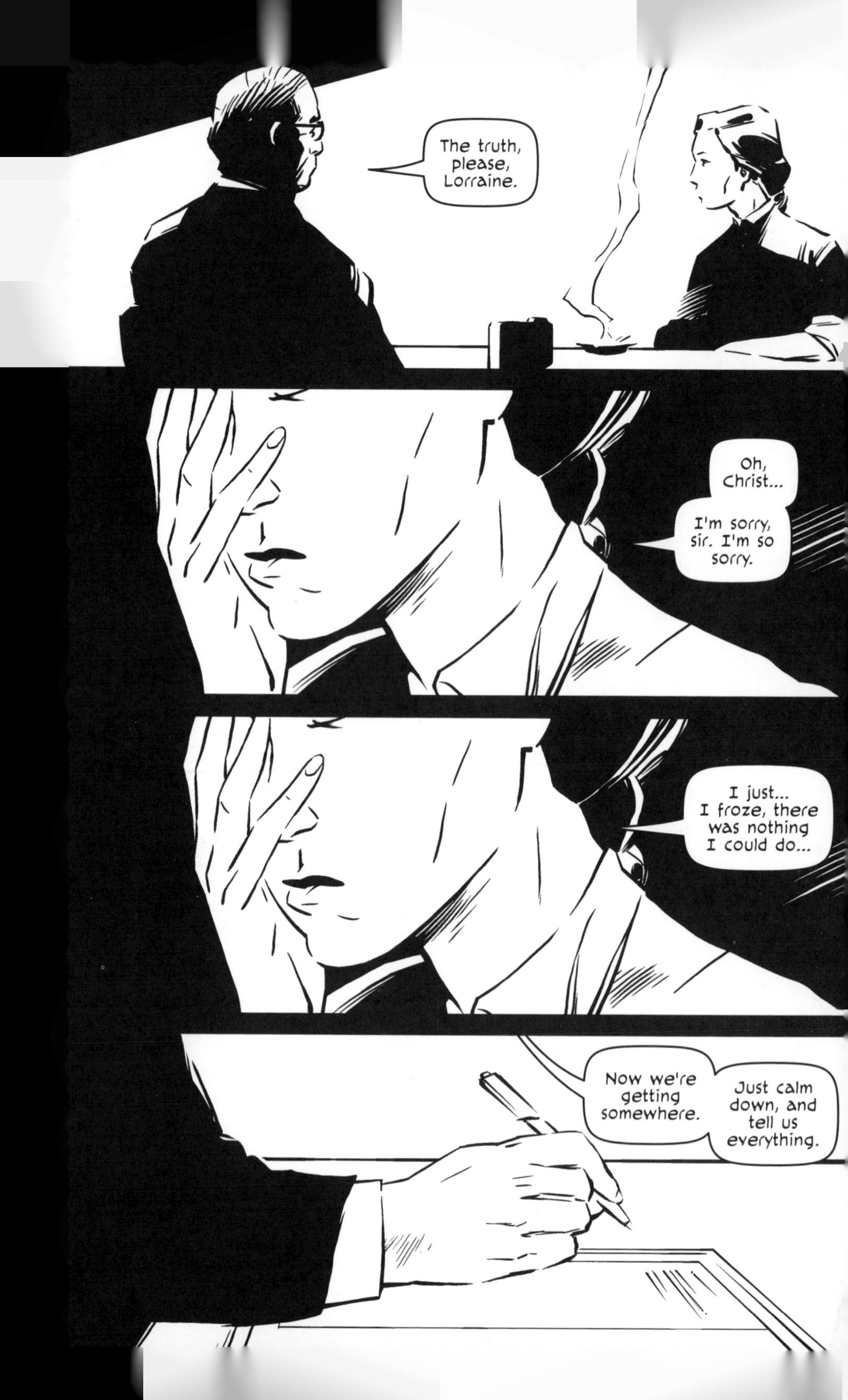
The truth, please, Lorraine.
Oh, Christ...
I'm sorry, sir. I'm so sorry.
I just... I froze, there was nothing I could do...
Now we're getting somewhere.
Just calm down, and tell us everything.

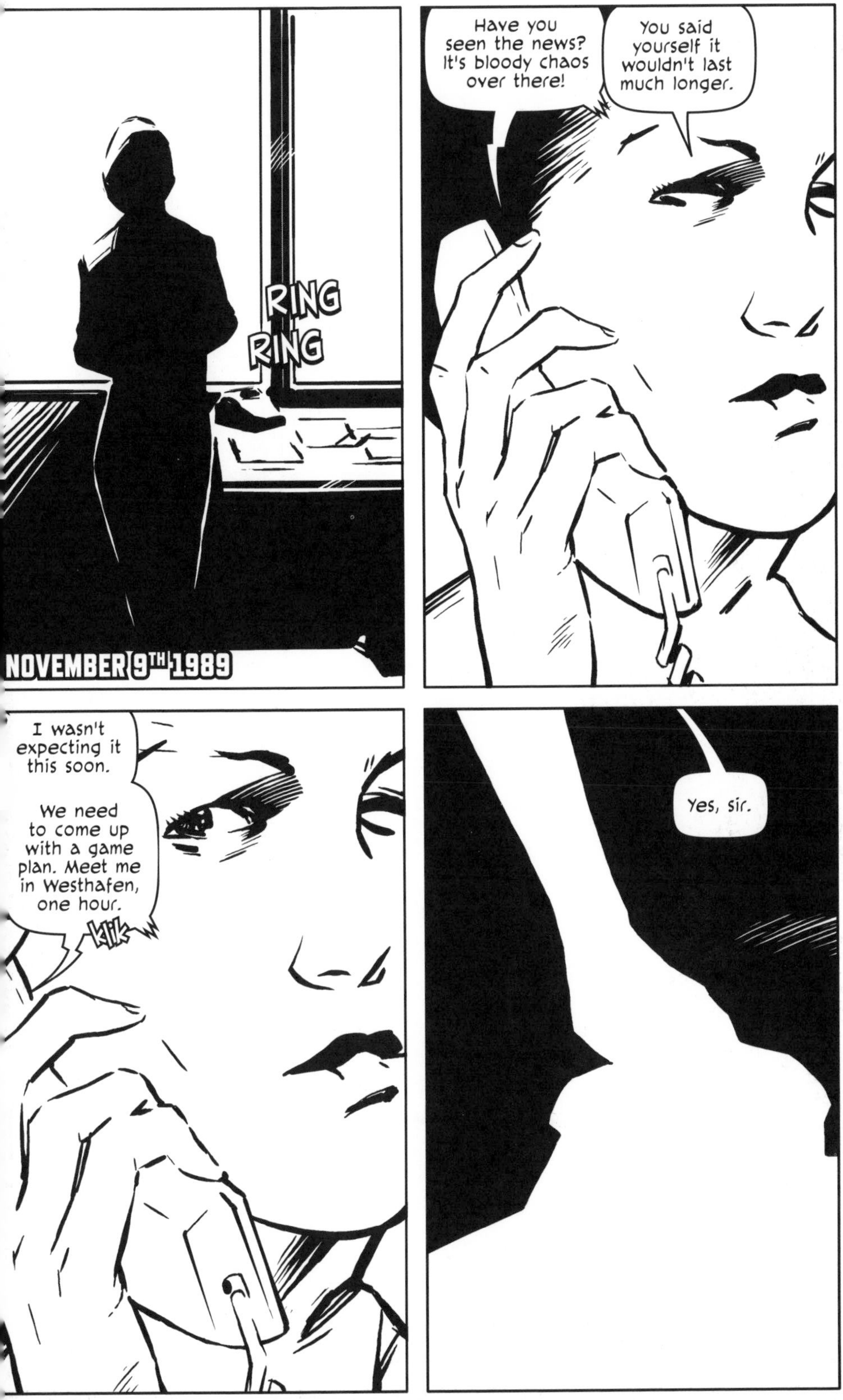
RING
RING
NOVEMBER 9TH 1989
Have you seen the news? It's bloody chaos over there!
You said yourself it wouldn't last much longer.
I wasn't expecting it this soon.
We need to come up with a game plan. Meet me in Westhafen, one hour.
klik
Yes, sir.

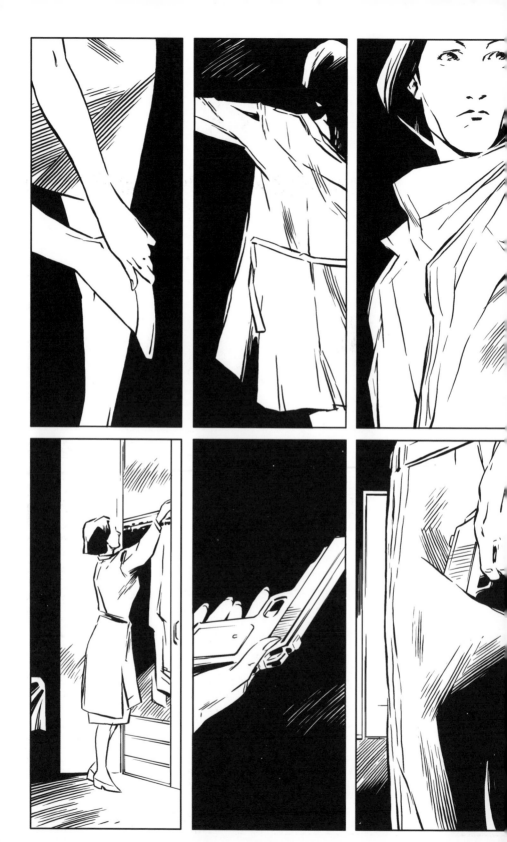

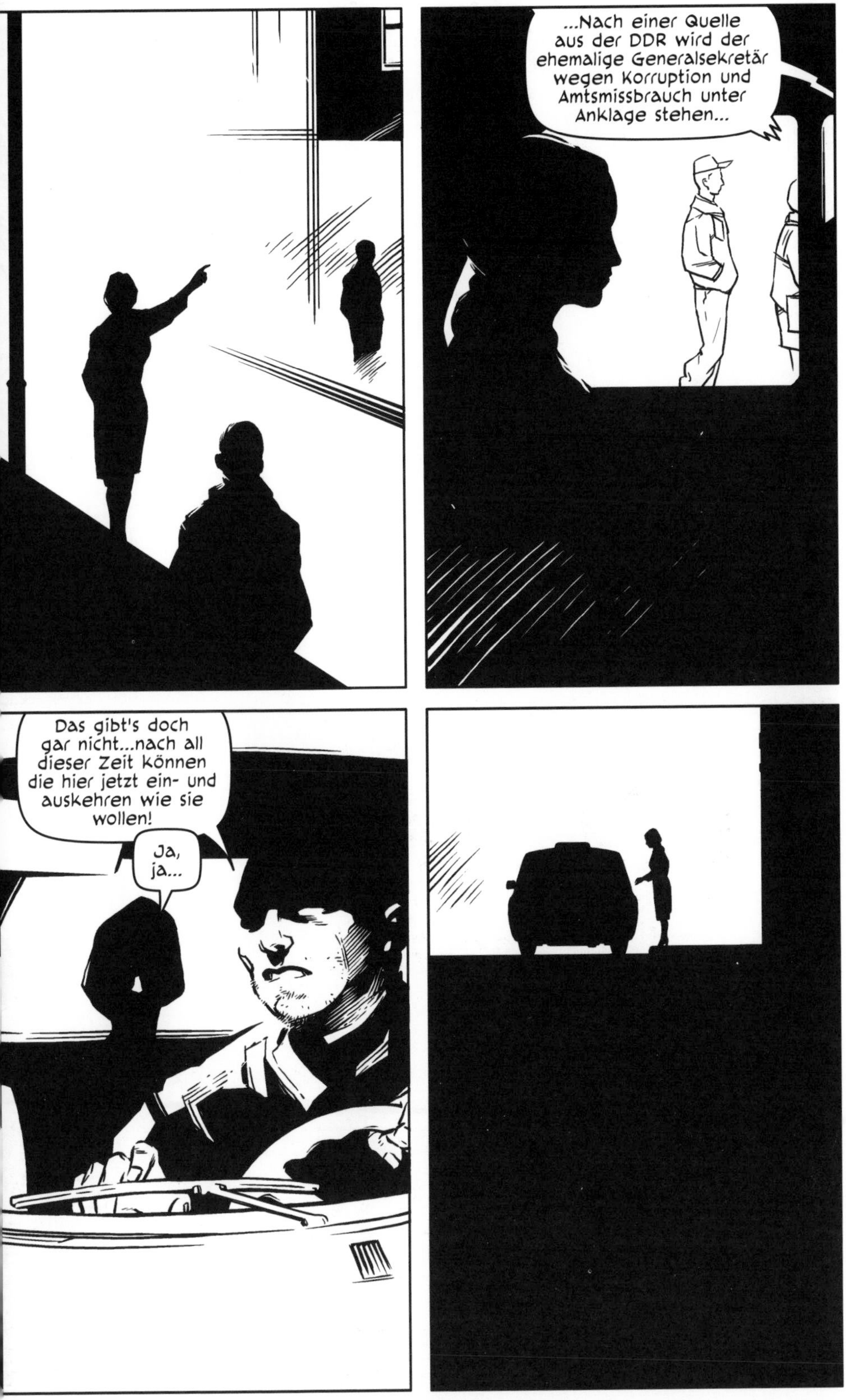
...Nach einer Quelle aus der DDR wird der ehemalige Generalsekretär wegen Korruption und Amtsmissbrauch unter Anklage stehen...
Das gibt's doch gar nicht...nach all dieser Zeit können die hier jetzt ein- und auskehren wie sie wollen!
Ja, ja...

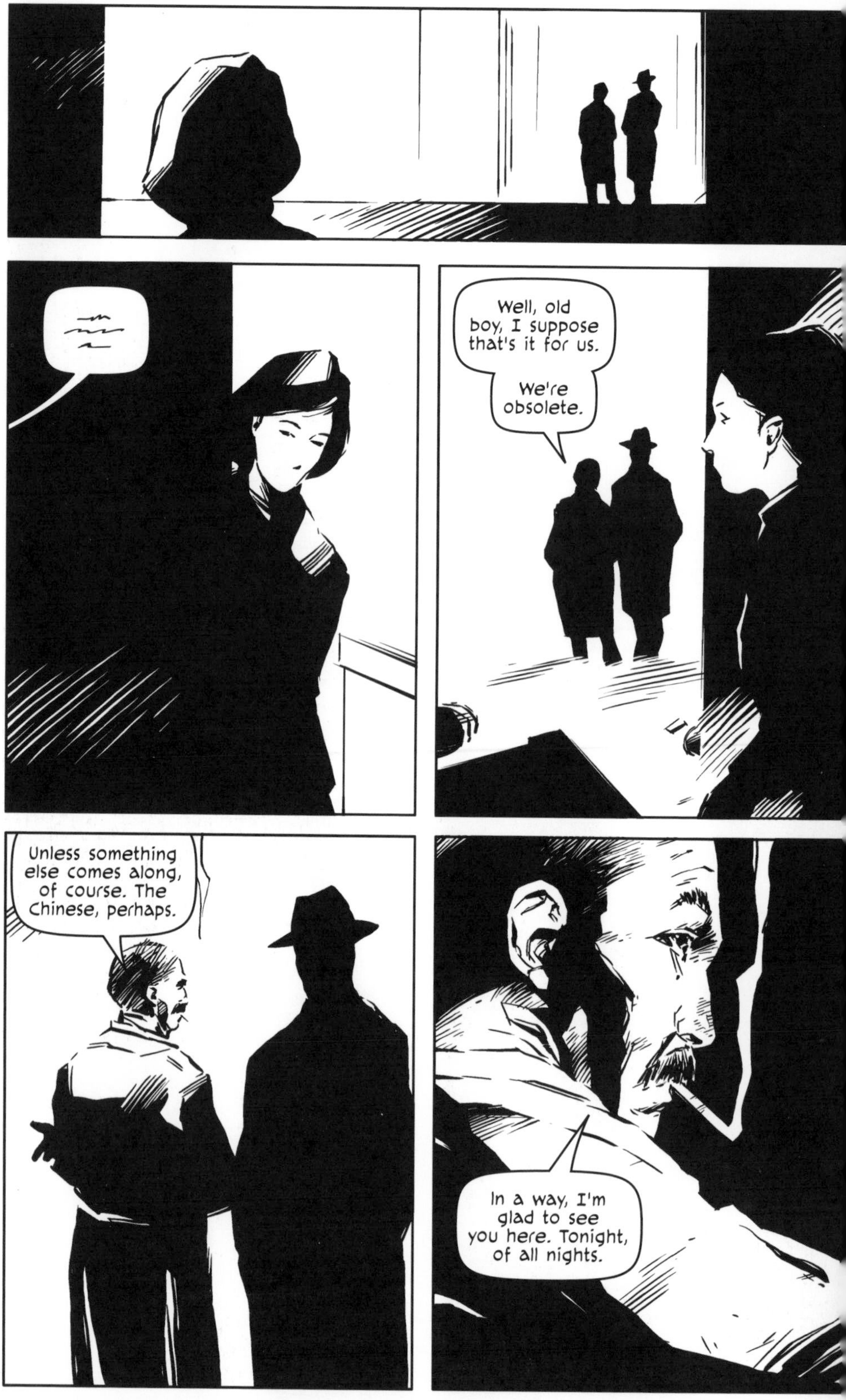
Well, old boy, I suppose that's it for us.
We're obsolete.
Unless something else comes along, of course. The Chinese, perhaps.
In a way, I'm glad to see you here. Tonight, of all nights.

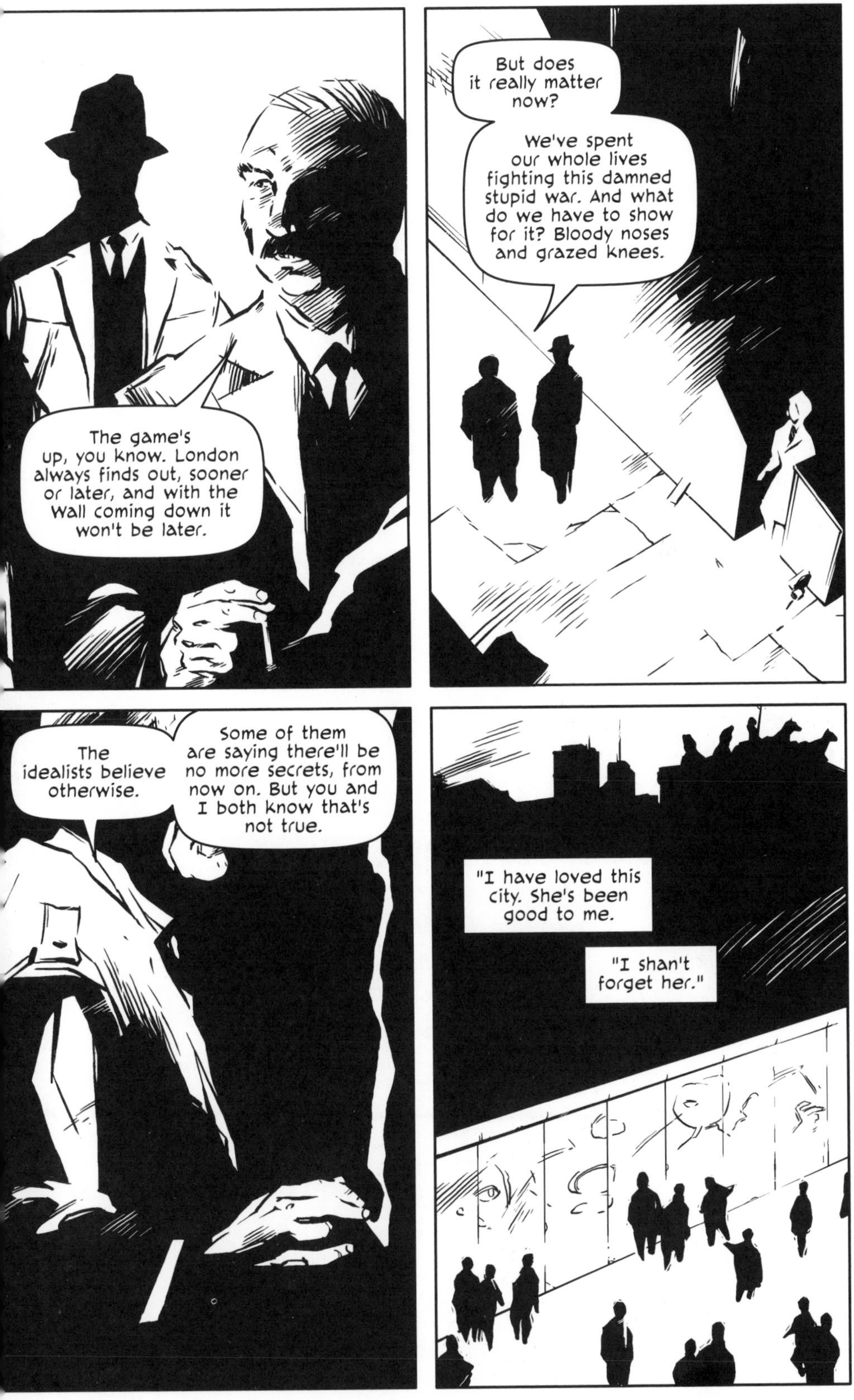
The game's up, you know. London always finds out, sooner or later, and with the Wall coming down it won't be later.
But does it really matter now?
We've spent our whole lives fighting this damned stupid war. And what do we have to show for it? Bloody noses and grazed knees.
The idealists believe otherwise.
Some of them are saying there'll be no more secrets, from now on. But you and I both know that's not true.
"I have loved this city. She's been good to me.
"I shan't forget her."

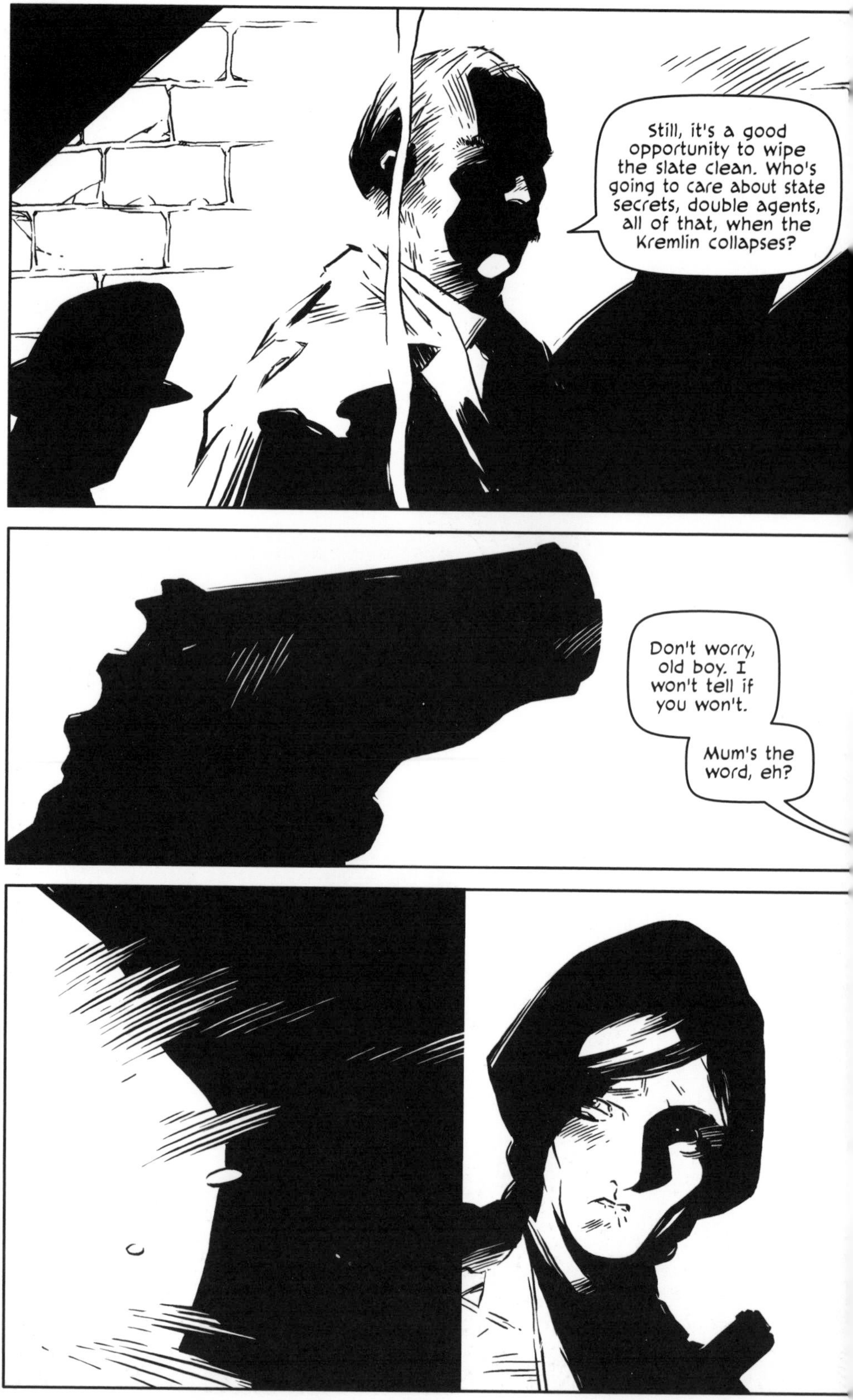
Still, it's a good opportunity to wipe the slate clean. Who's going to care about state secrets, double agents, all of that, when the Kremlin collapses?
Don't worry, old boy. I won't tell if you won't.
Mum's the word, eh?

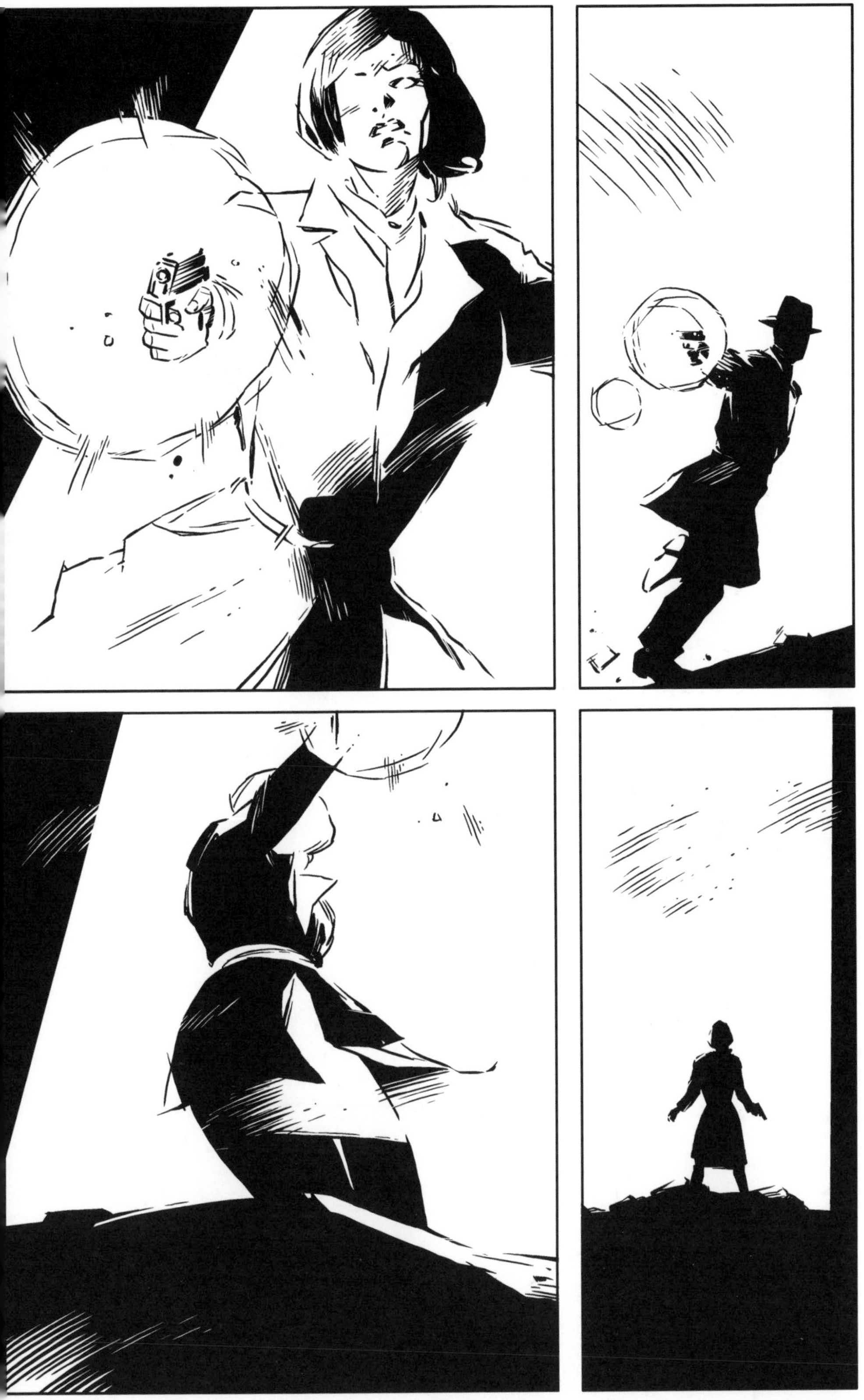

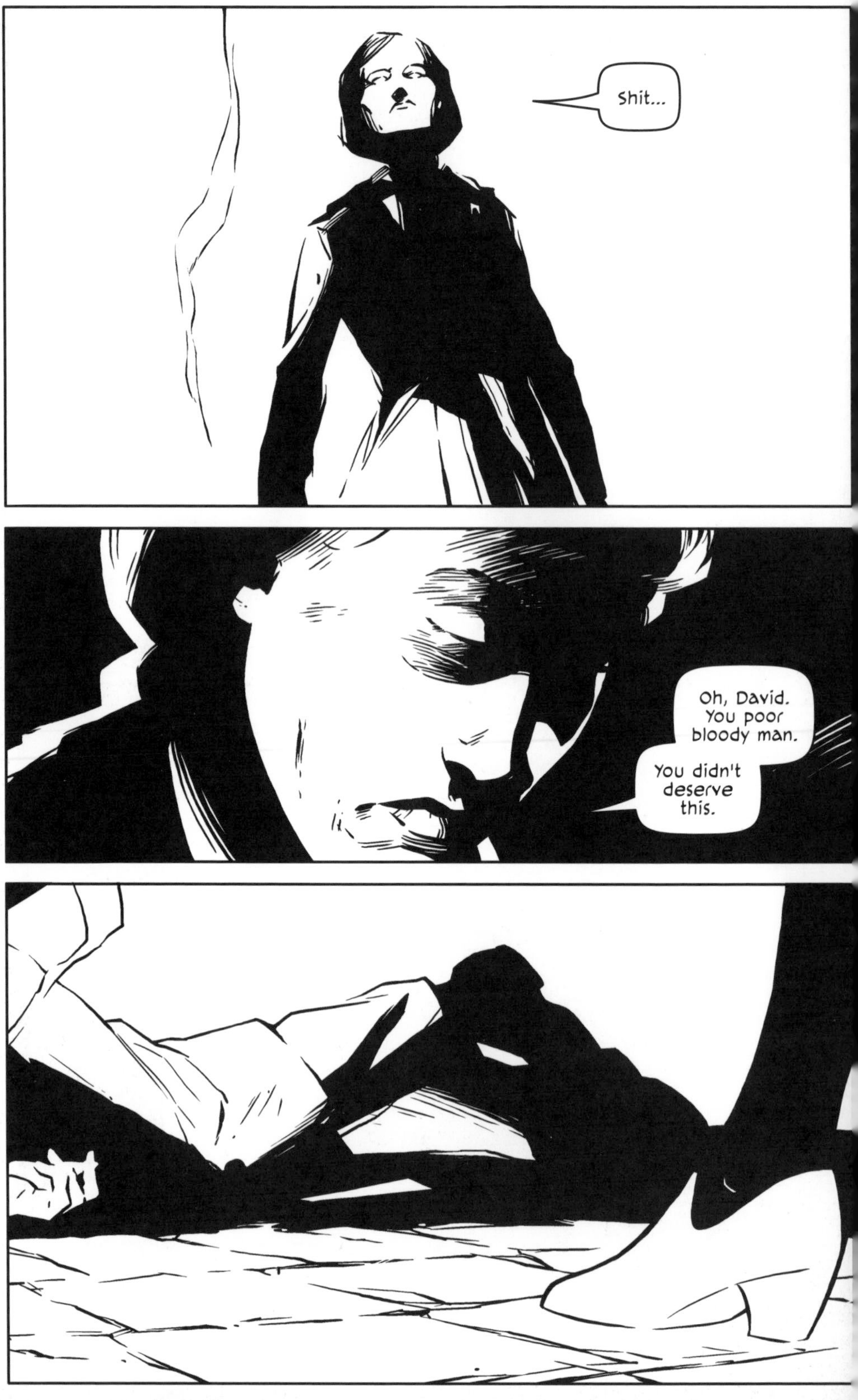
Shit...
Oh, David. You poor bloody man.
You didn't deserve this.

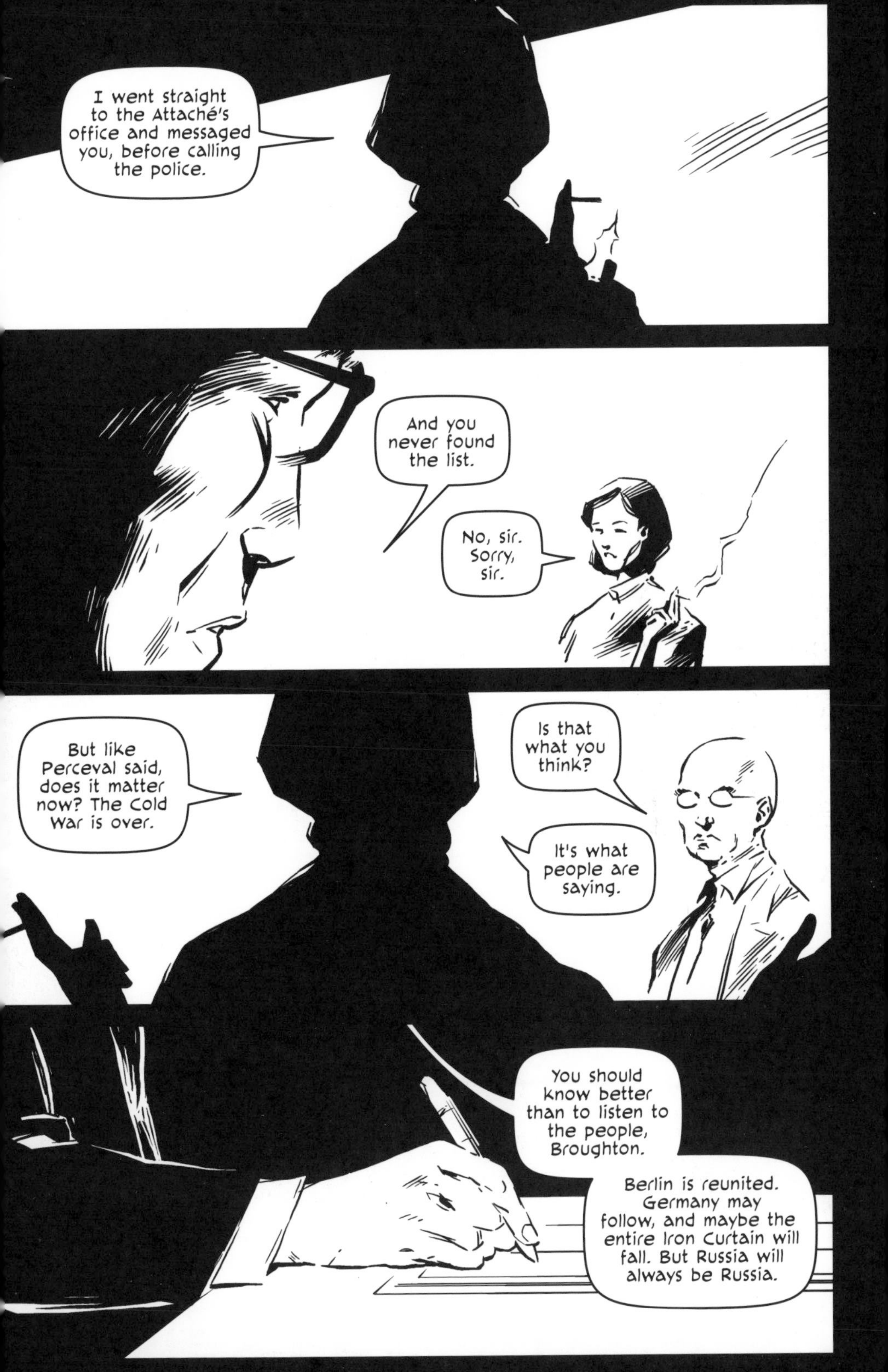
I went straight to the Attaché's office and messaged you, before calling the police.
And you never found the list.
No, sir. Sorry, sir.
But like Perceval said, does it matter now? The Cold War is over.
Is that what you think?
It's what people are saying.
You should know better than to listen to the people, Broughton.
Berlin is reunited. Germany may follow, and maybe the entire Iron Curtain will fall. But Russia will always be Russia.

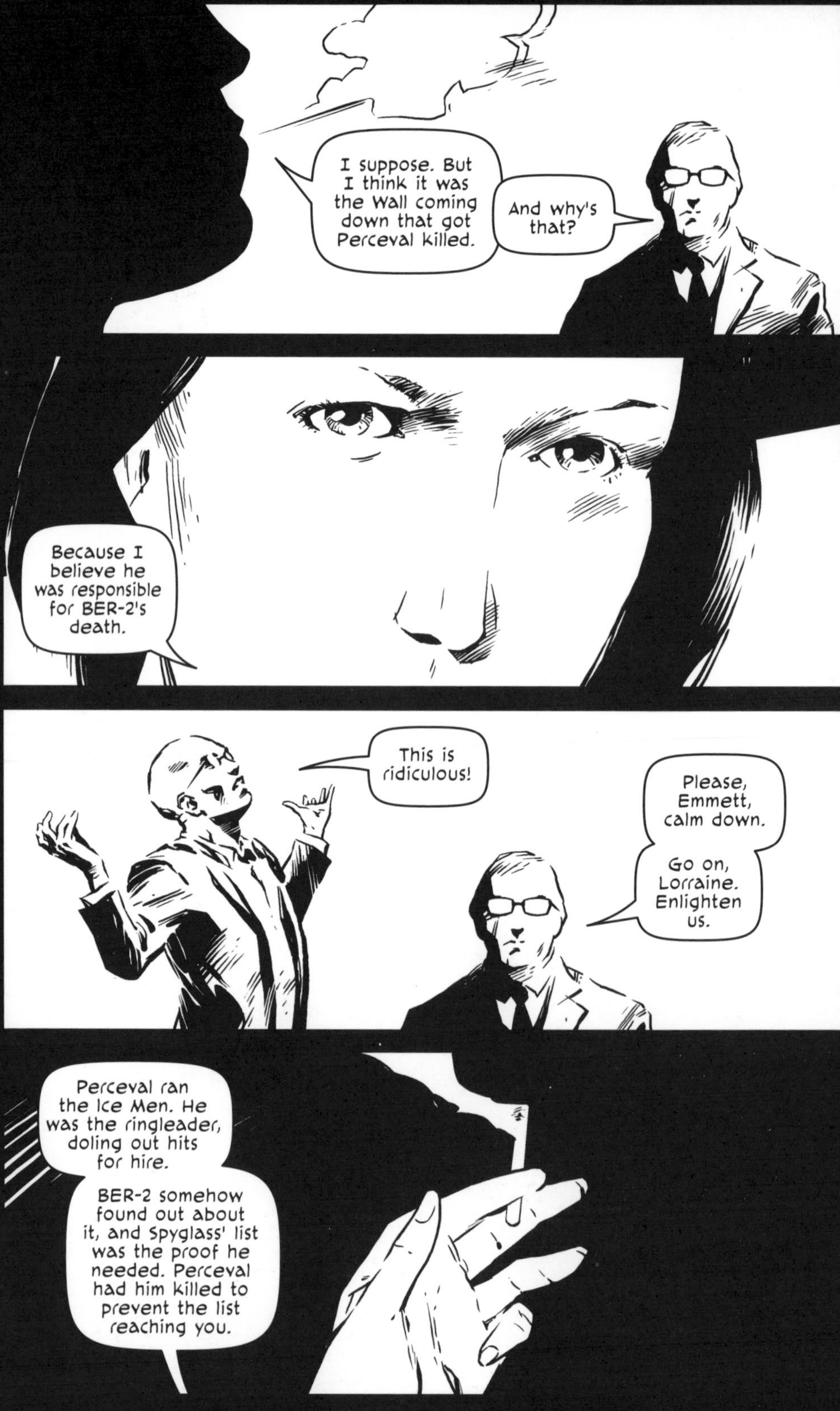
I suppose. But I think it was the Wall coming down that got Perceval killed.
And why's that?
Because I believe he was responsible for BER-2's death.
This is ridiculous!
Please, Emmett, calm down.
Go on, Lorraine. Enlighten us.
Perceval ran the Ice Men. He was the ringleader, doling out hits for hire.
BER-2 somehow found out about it, and Spyglass' list was the proof he needed. Perceval had him killed to prevent the list reaching you.

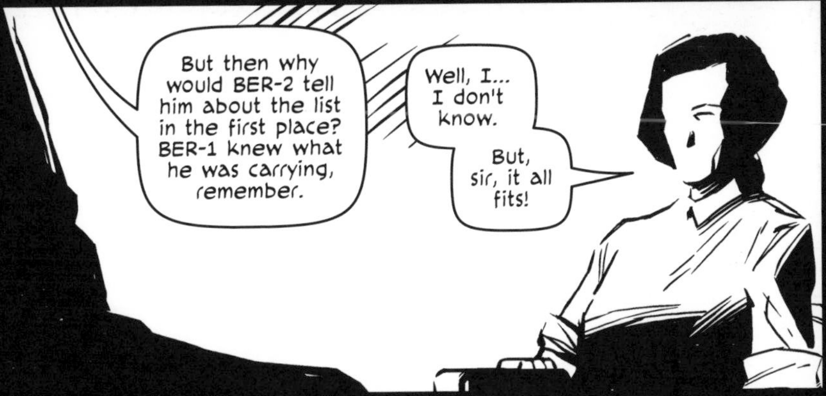
But then why would BER-2 tell him about the list in the first place? BER-1 knew what he was carrying, remember.
Well, I... I don't know.
But, sir, it all fits!

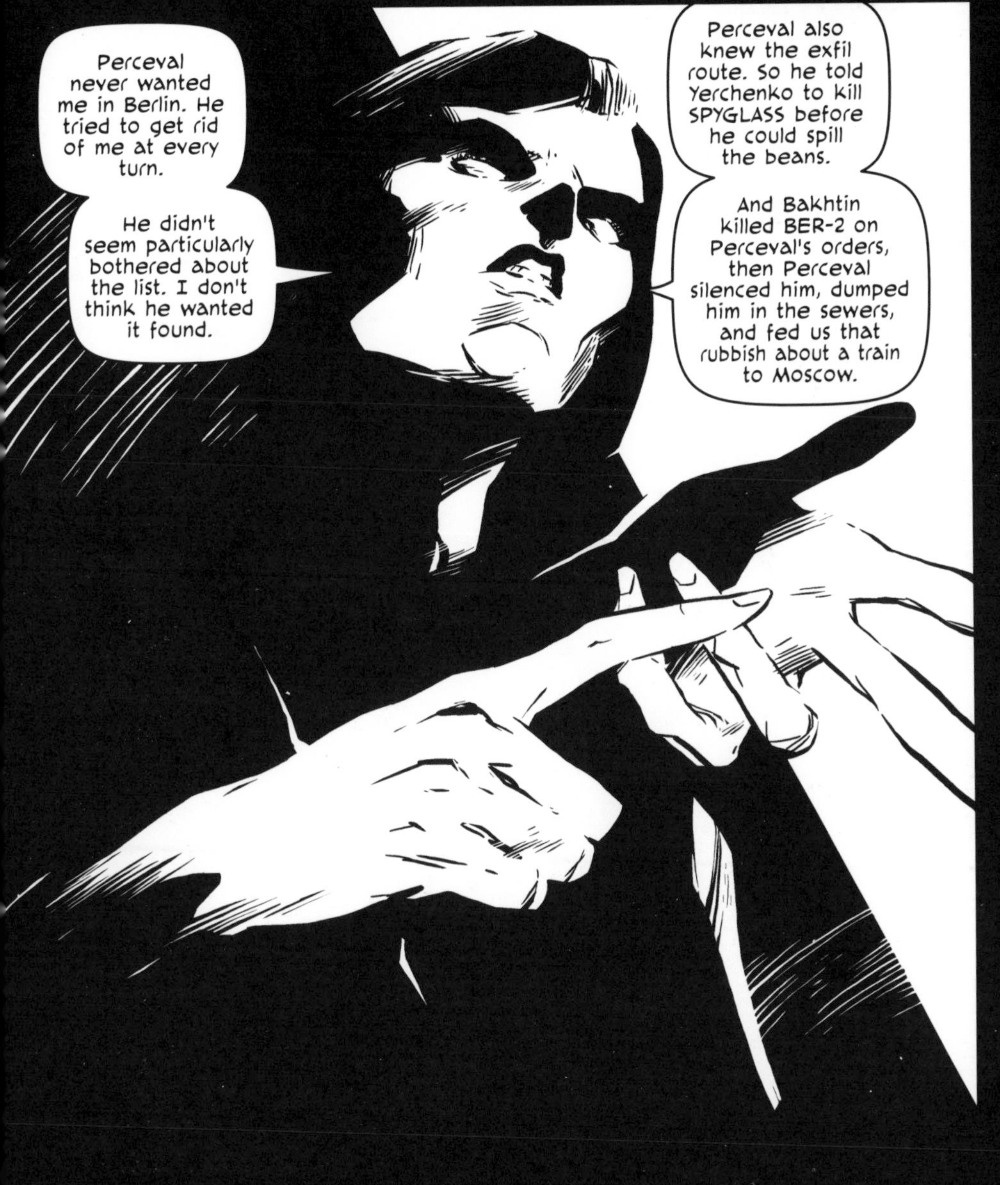
Perceval never wanted me in Berlin. He tried to get rid of me at every turn.
He didn't seem particularly bothered about the list. I don't think he wanted it found.
Perceval also knew the exfil route. So he told Yerchenko to kill SPYGLASS before he could spill the beans.
And Bakhtin killed BER-2 on Perceval's orders, then Perceval silenced him, dumped him in the sewers, and fed us that rubbish about a train to Moscow.

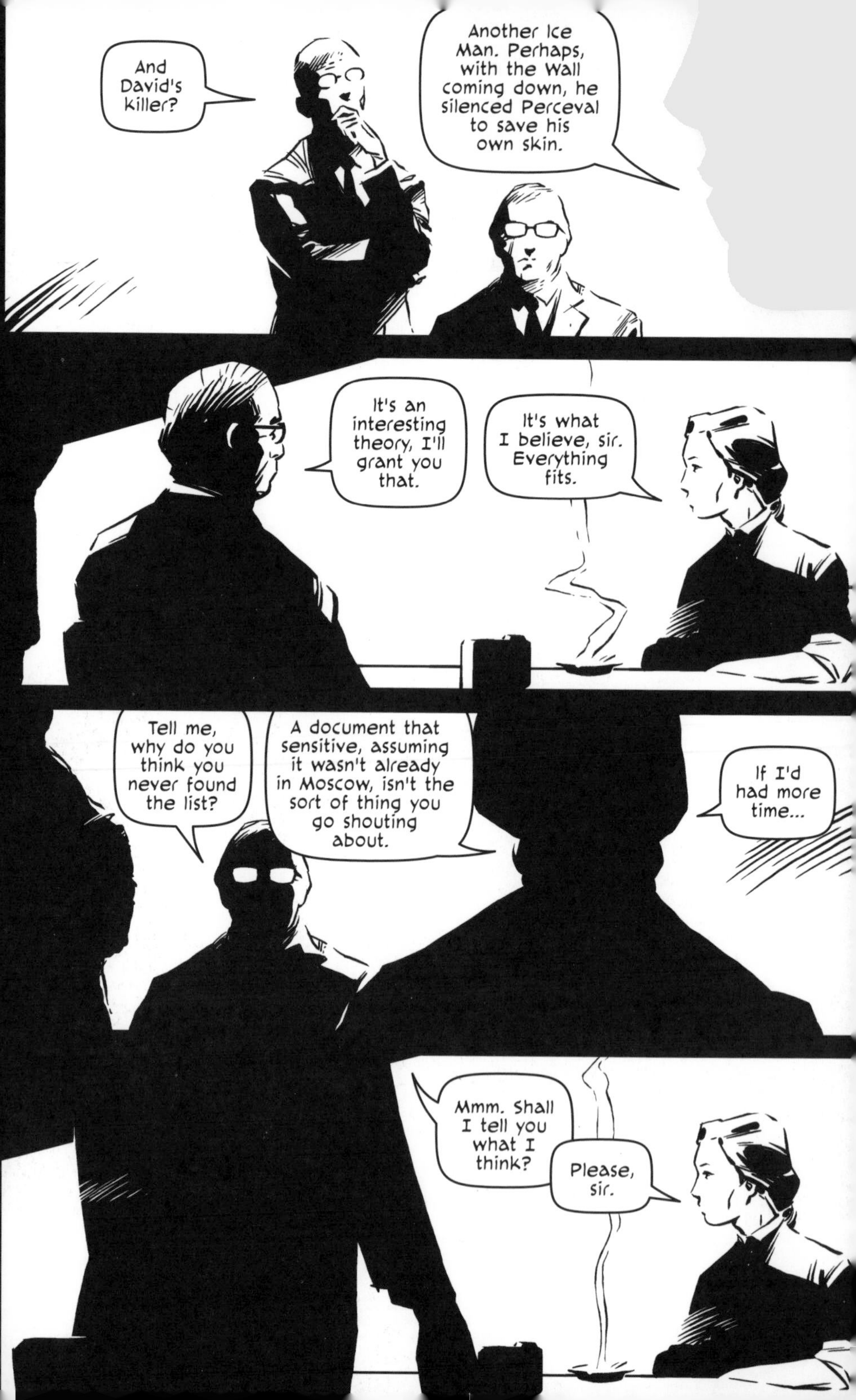
And David's killer?
Another Ice Man. Perhaps, with the Wall coming down, he silenced Perceval to save his own skin.
It's an interesting theory, I'll grant you that.
It's what I believe, sir. Everything fits.
Tell me, why do you think you never found the list?
A document that sensitive, assuming it wasn't already in Moscow, isn't the sort of thing you go shouting about.
If I'd had more time...
Mmm. Shall I tell you what I think?
Please, sir.

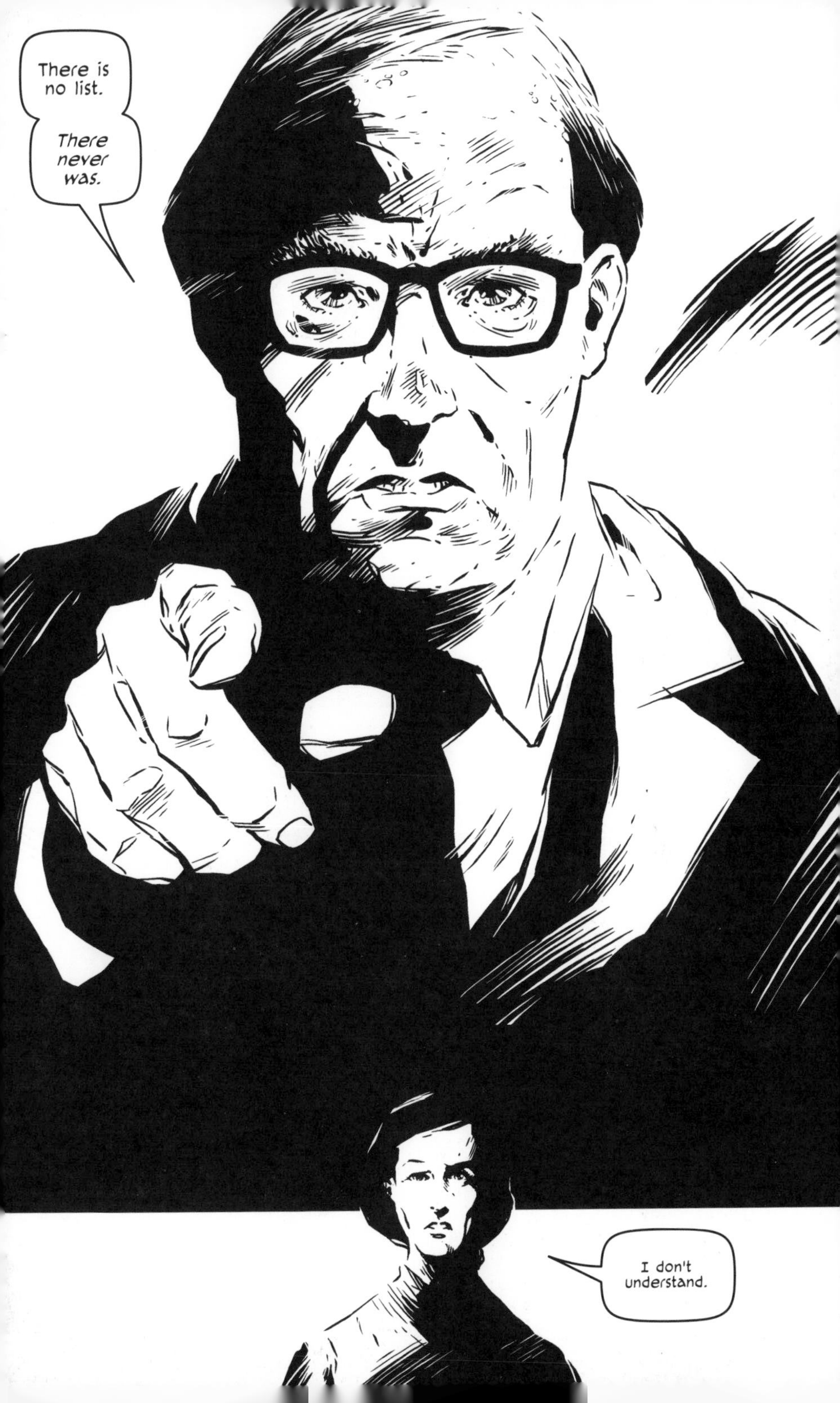
There is no list.
There never was.
I don't understand.

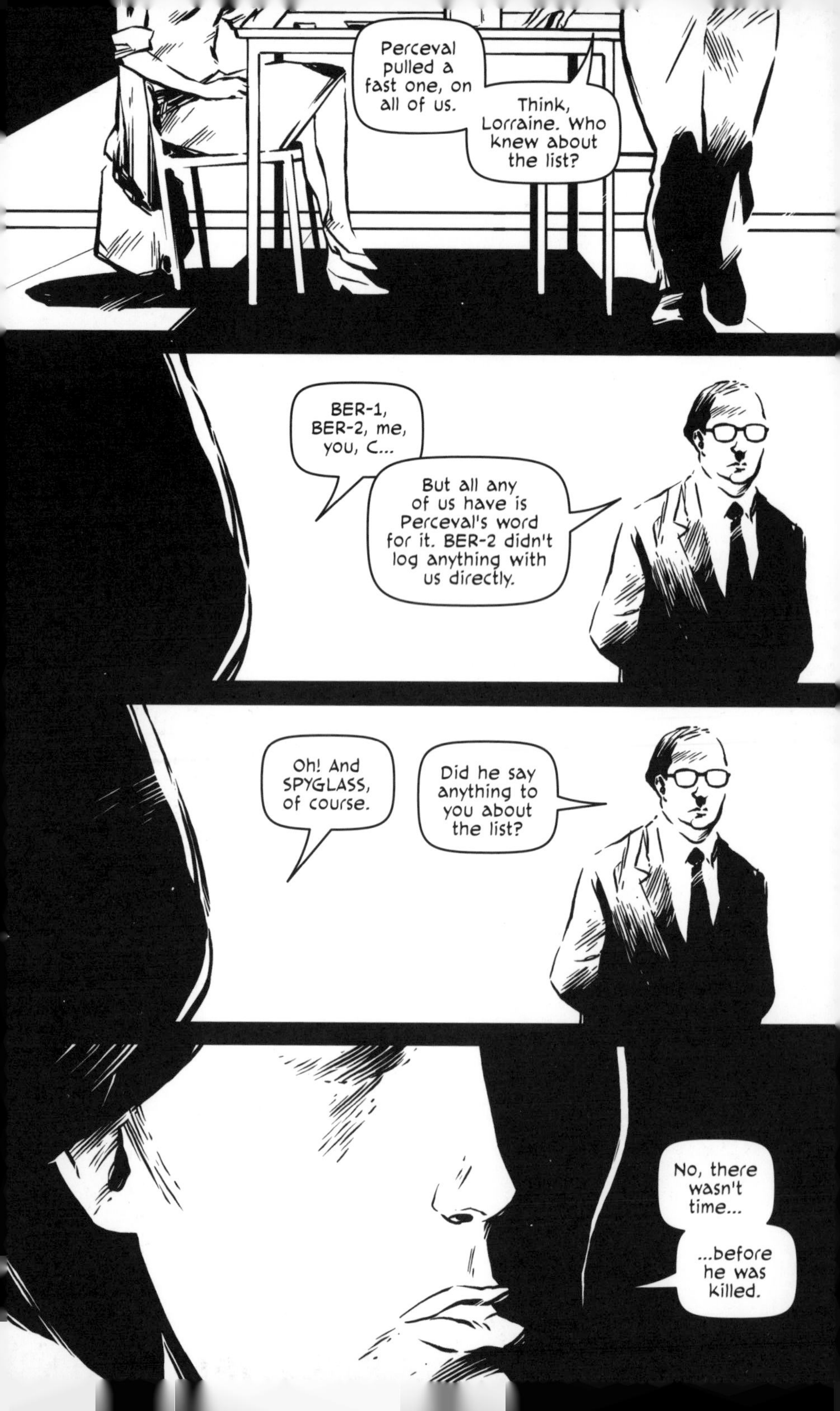

Perceval pulled a fast one, on all of us.
Think, Lorraine. Who knew about the list?
BER-1, BER-2, me, you, C...
But all any of us have is Perceval's word for it. BER-2 didn't log anything with us directly.
Oh! And SPYGLASS, of course.
Did he say anything to you about the list?
No, there wasn't time...
...before he was killed.

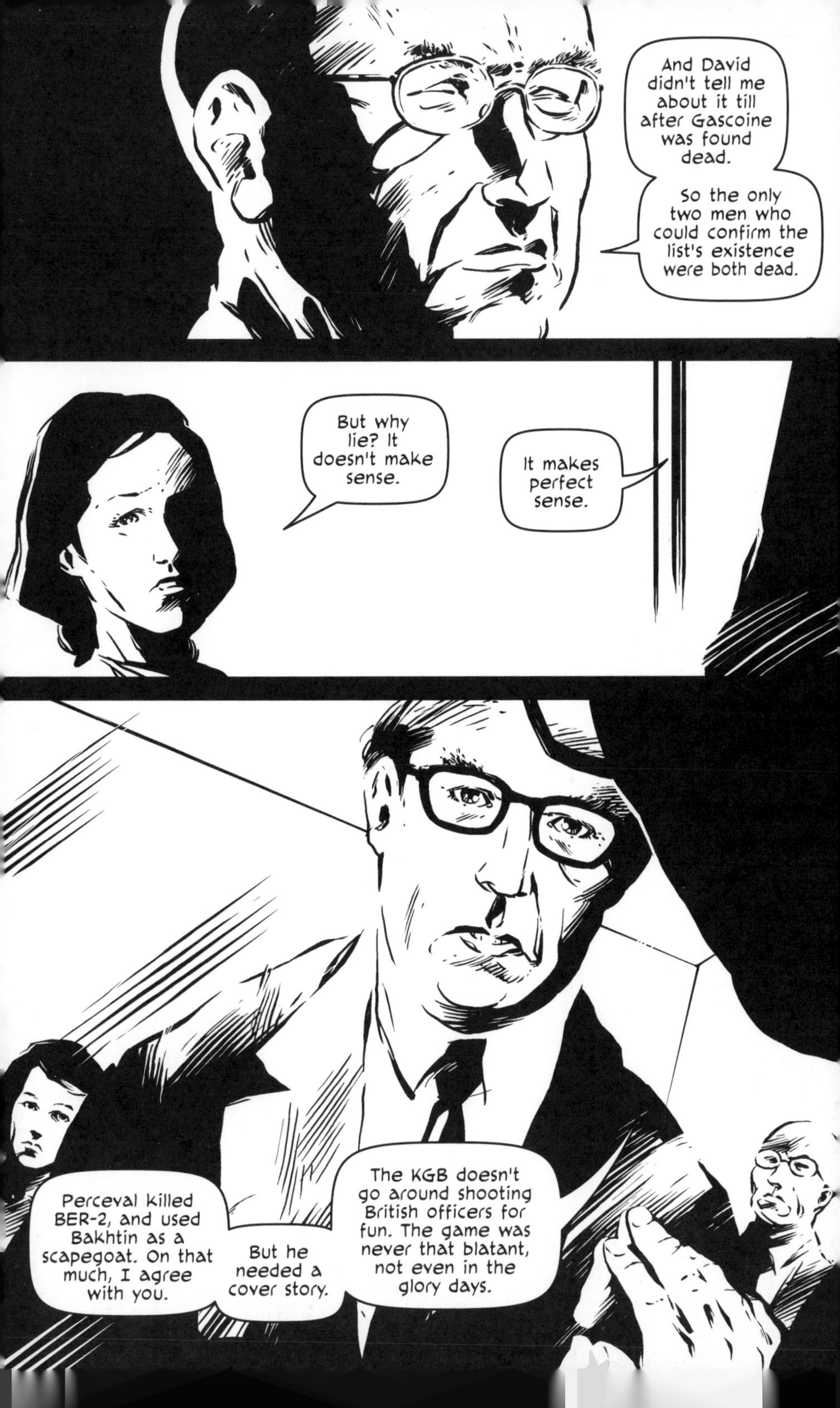
And David didn't tell me about it till after Gascoine was found dead.
So the only two men who could confirm the list's existence were both dead.
But why lie? It doesn't make sense.
It makes perfect sense.
Perceval killed BER-2, and used Bakhtin as a scapegoat. On that much, I agree with you.
But he needed a cover story.
The KGB doesn't go around shooting British officers for fun. The game was never that blatant, not even in the glory days.

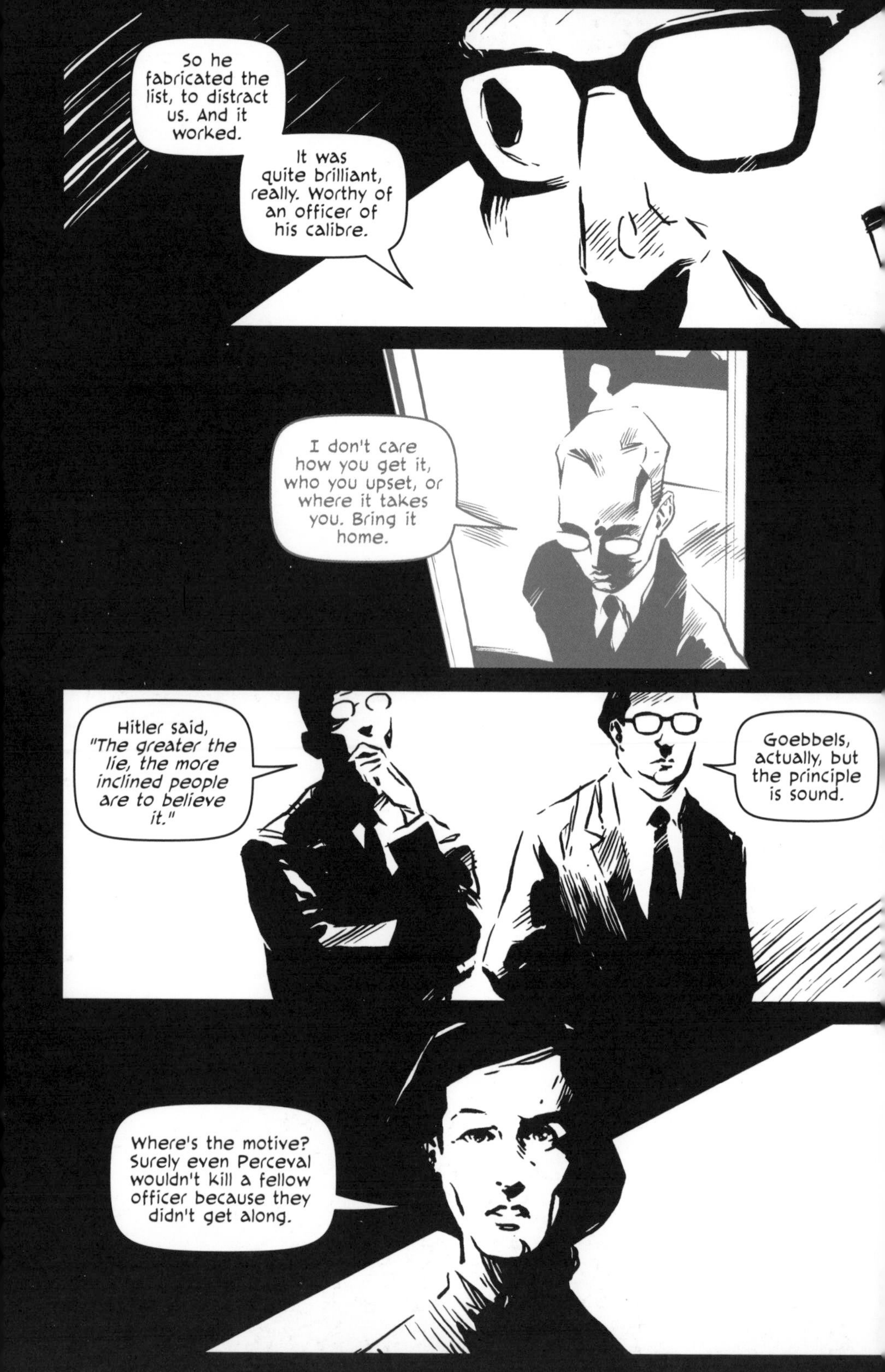
So he fabricated the list, to distract us. And it worked.
It was quite brilliant, really. Worthy of an officer of his calibre.
I don't care how you get it, who you upset, or where it takes you. Bring it home.
Hitler said, *"The greater the lie, the more inclined people are to believe it."*
Goebbels, actually, but the principle is sound.
Where's the motive? Surely even Perceval wouldn't kill a fellow officer because they didn't get along.

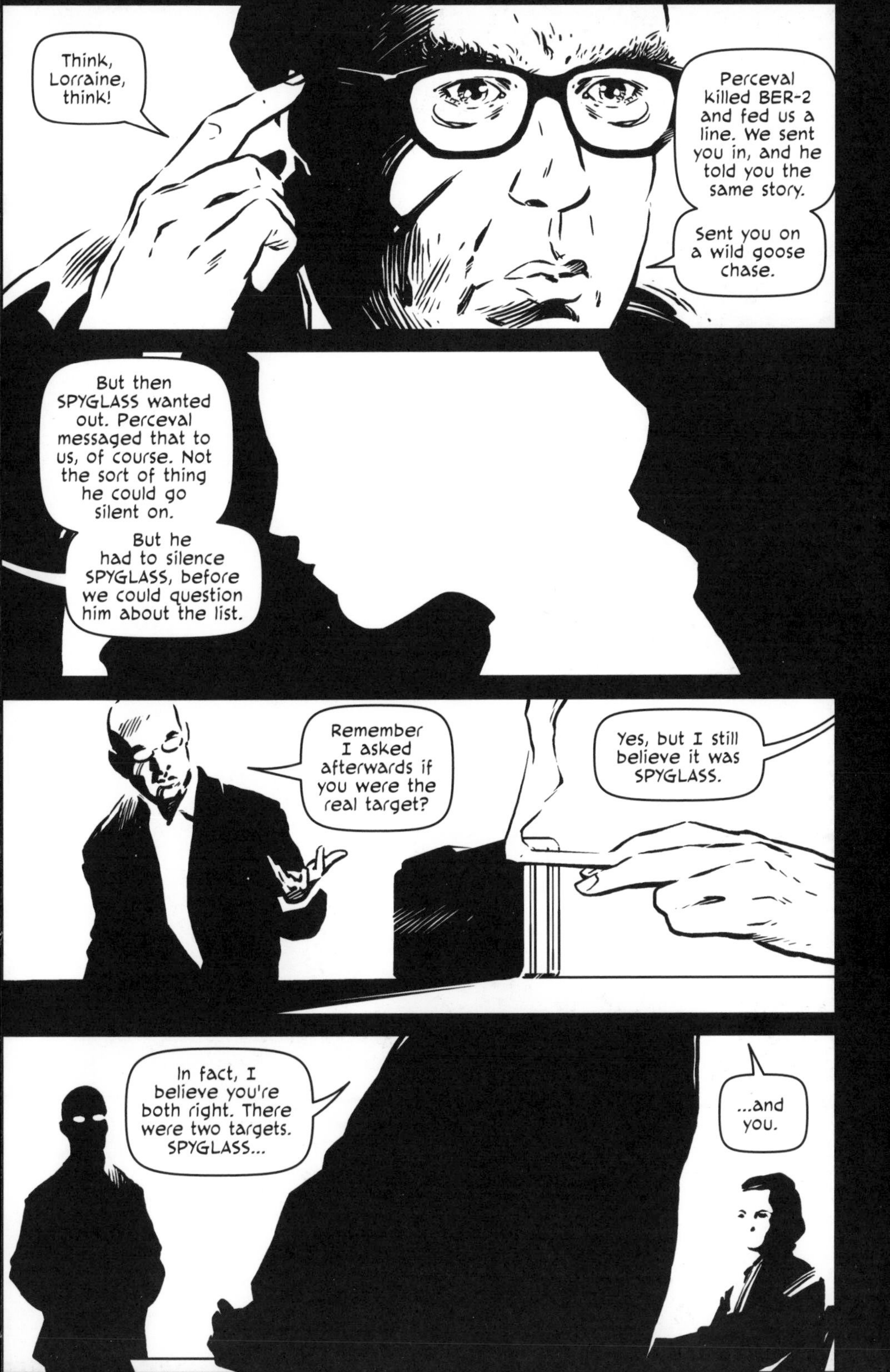
Think, Lorraine, think!
Perceval killed BER-2 and fed us a line. We sent you in, and he told you the same story.
Sent you on a wild goose chase.
But then SPYGLASS wanted out. Perceval messaged that to us, of course. Not the sort of thing he could go silent on.
But he had to silence SPYGLASS, before we could question him about the list.
Remember I asked afterwards if you were the real target?
Yes, but I still believe it was SPYGLASS.
In fact, I believe you're both right. There were two targets. SPYGLASS...
...and you.

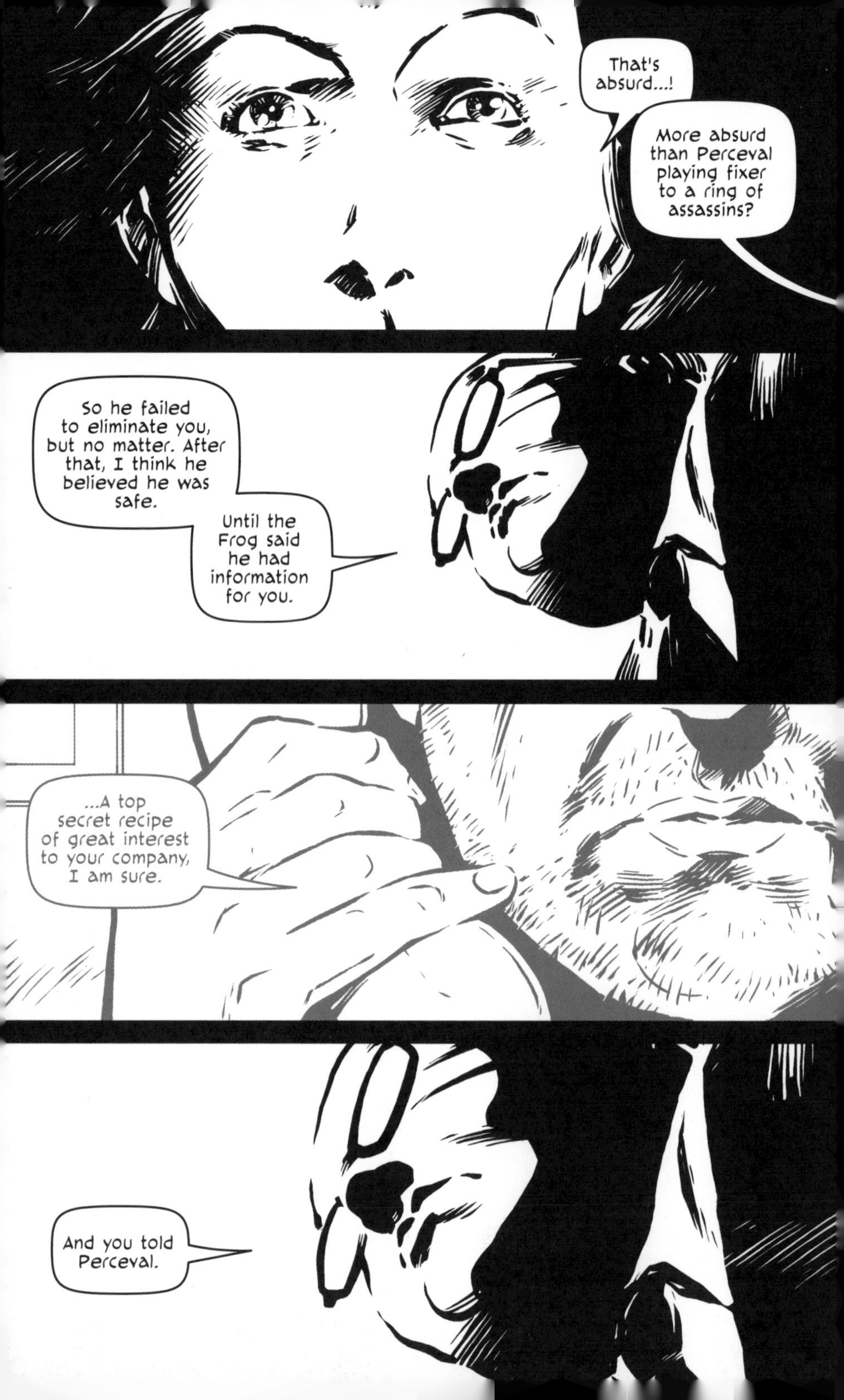
That's absurd...!
More absurd than Perceval playing fixer to a ring of assassins?
So he failed to eliminate you, but no matter. After that, I think he believed he was safe.
Until the Frog said he had information for you.
...A top secret recipe of great interest to your company, I am sure.
And you told Perceval.

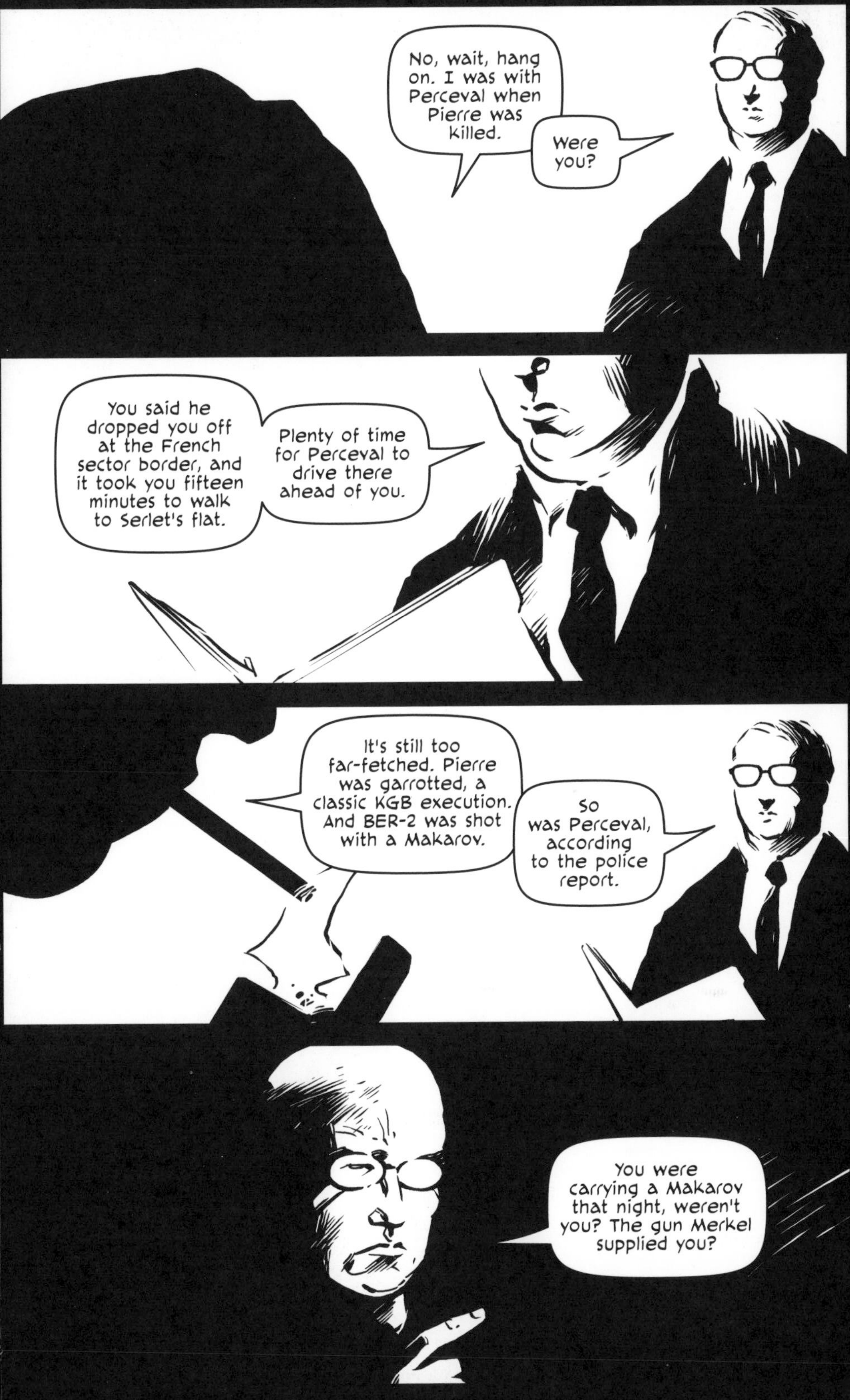
No, wait, hang on. I was with Perceval when Pierre was killed.
Were you?
You said he dropped you off at the French sector border, and it took you fifteen minutes to walk to Serlet's flat.
Plenty of time for Perceval to drive there ahead of you.
It's still too far-fetched. Pierre was garrotted, a classic KGB execution. And BER-2 was shot with a Makarov.
So was Perceval, according to the police report.
You were carrying a Makarov that night, weren't you? The gun Merkel supplied you?

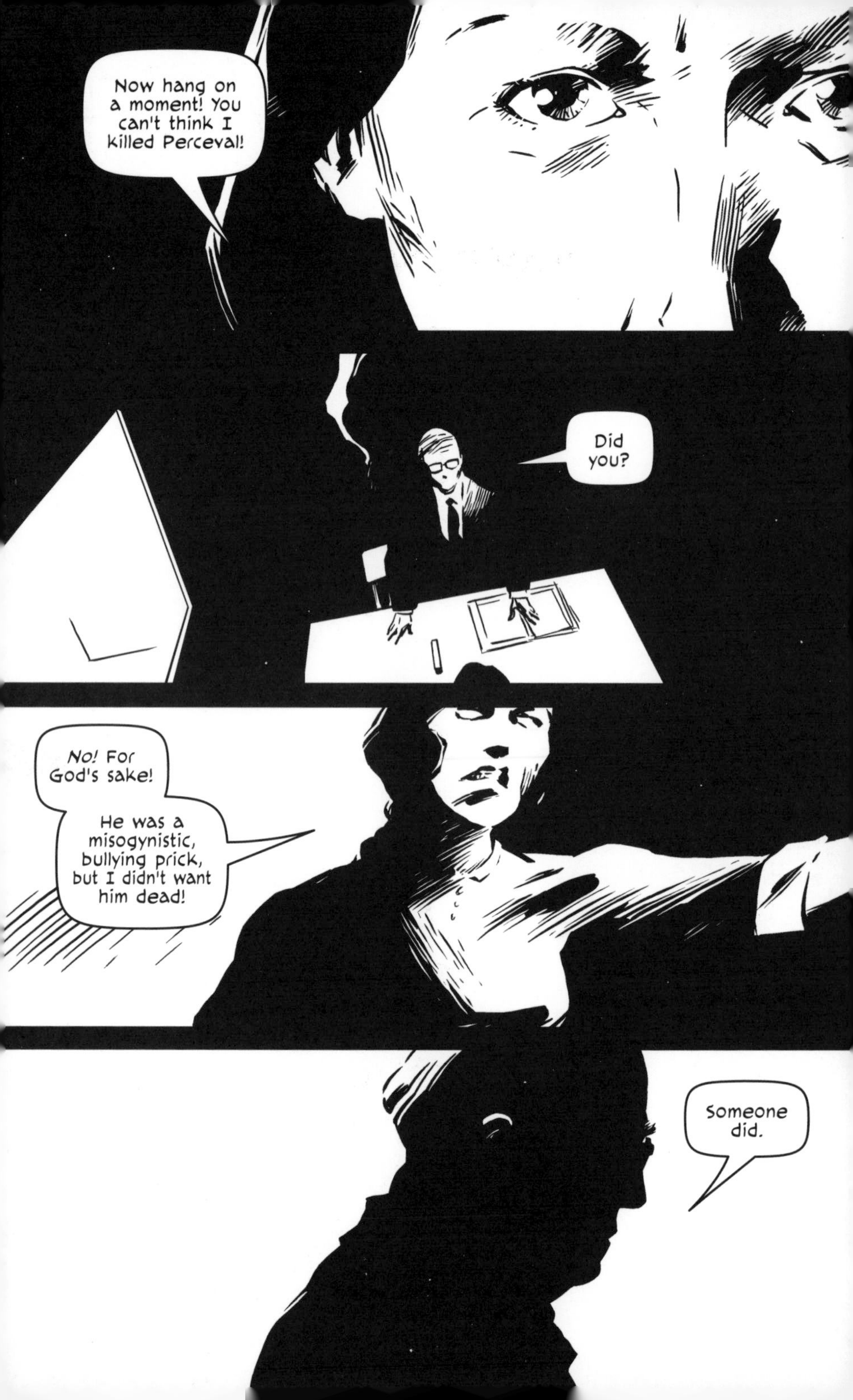
Now hang on a moment! You can't think I killed Perceval!
Did you?
No! For God's sake!
He was a misogynistic, bullying prick, but I didn't want him dead!
Someone did.

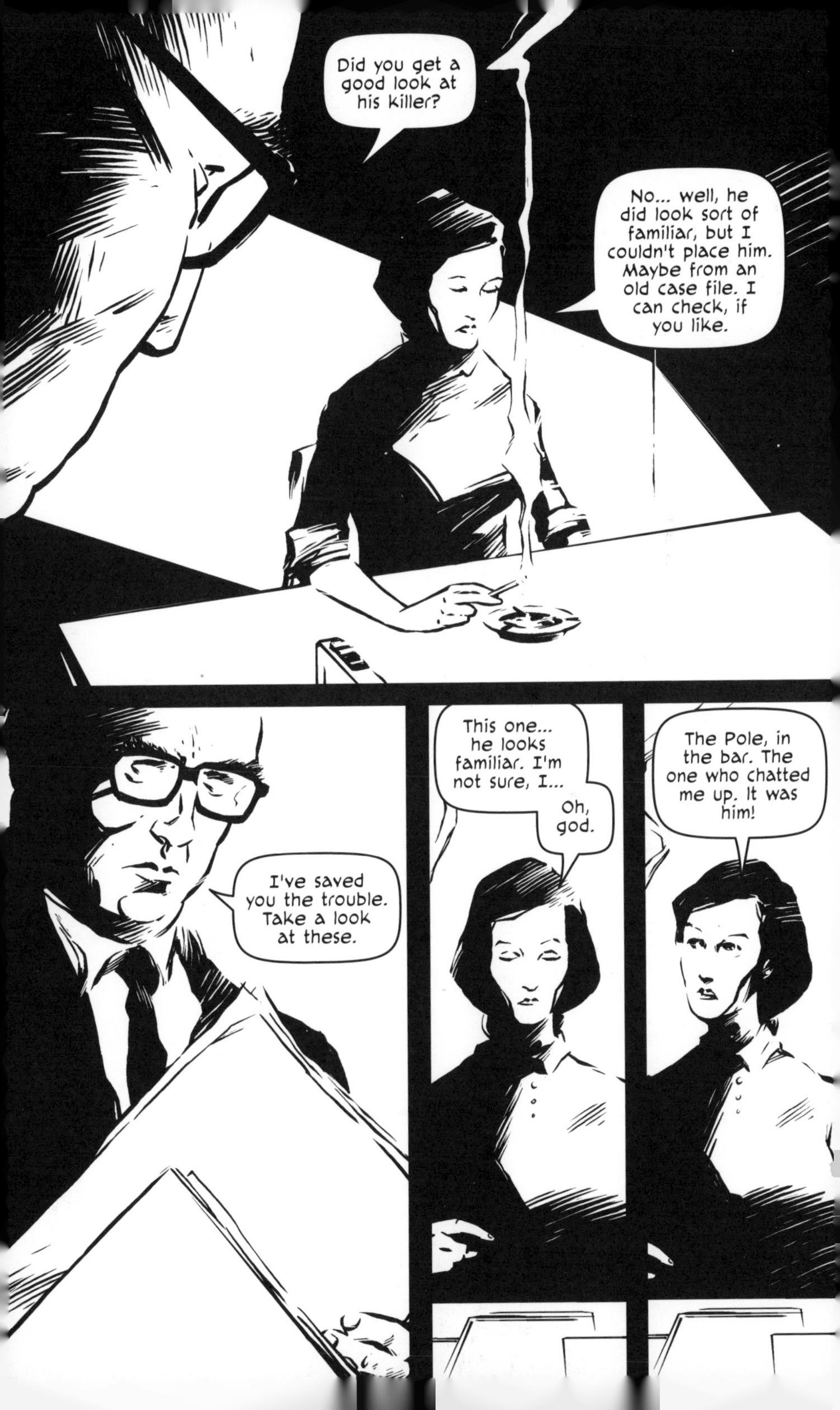
Did you get a good look at his killer?
No... well, he did look sort of familiar, but I couldn't place him. Maybe from an old case file. I can check, if you like.
I've saved you the trouble. Take a look at these.
This one... he looks familiar. I'm not sure, I...
Oh, god.
The Pole, in the bar. The one who chatted me up. It was him!

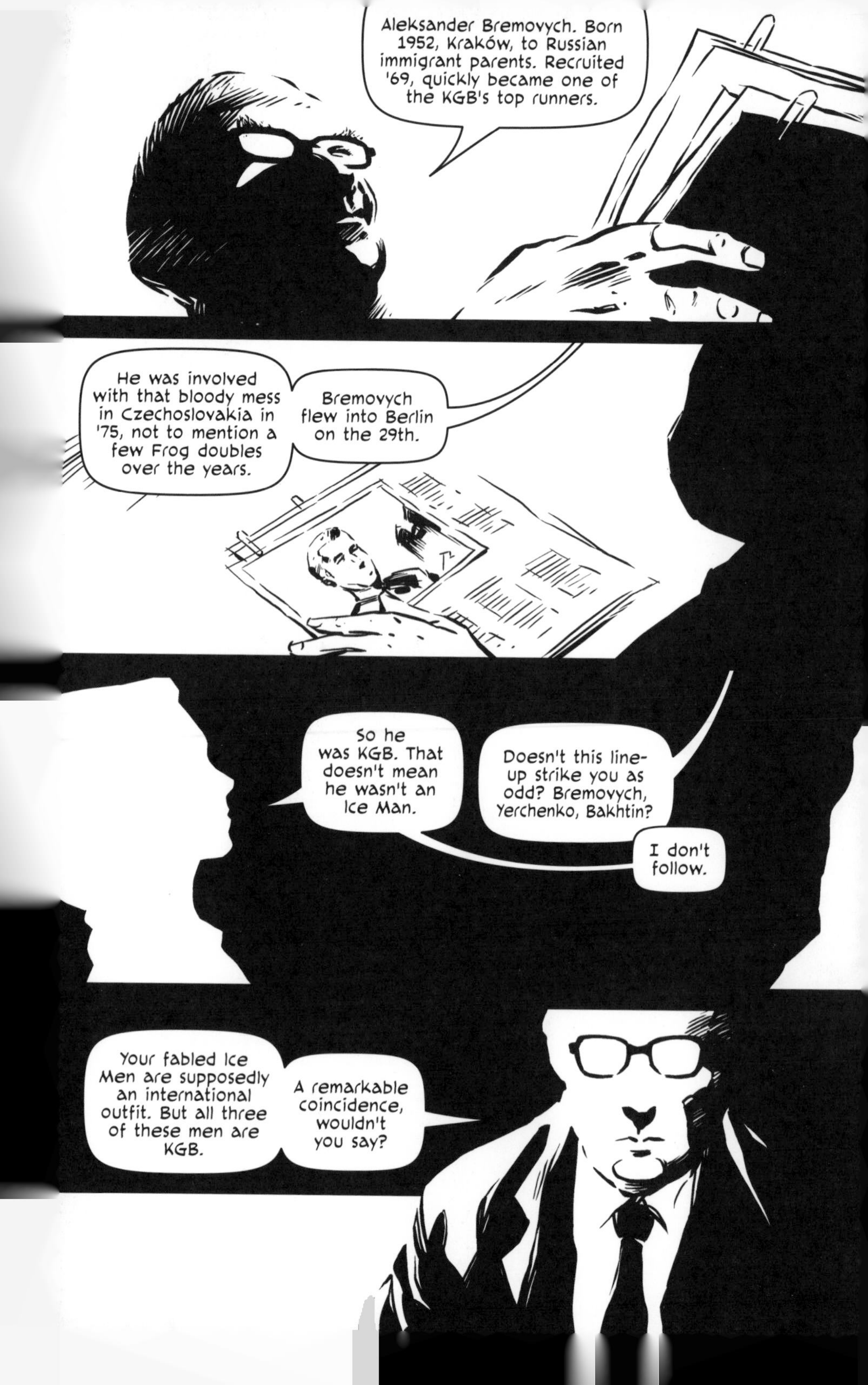

Aleksander Bremovych. Born 1952, Kraków, to Russian immigrant parents. Recruited '69, quickly became one of the KGB's top runners.
He was involved with that bloody mess in Czechoslovakia in '75, not to mention a few Frog doubles over the years.
Bremovych flew into Berlin on the 29th.
So he was KGB. That doesn't mean he wasn't an Ice Man.
Doesn't this line-up strike you as odd? Bremovych, Yerchenko, Bakhtin?
I don't follow.
Your fabled Ice Men are supposedly an international outfit. But all three of these men are KGB.
A remarkable coincidence, wouldn't you say?

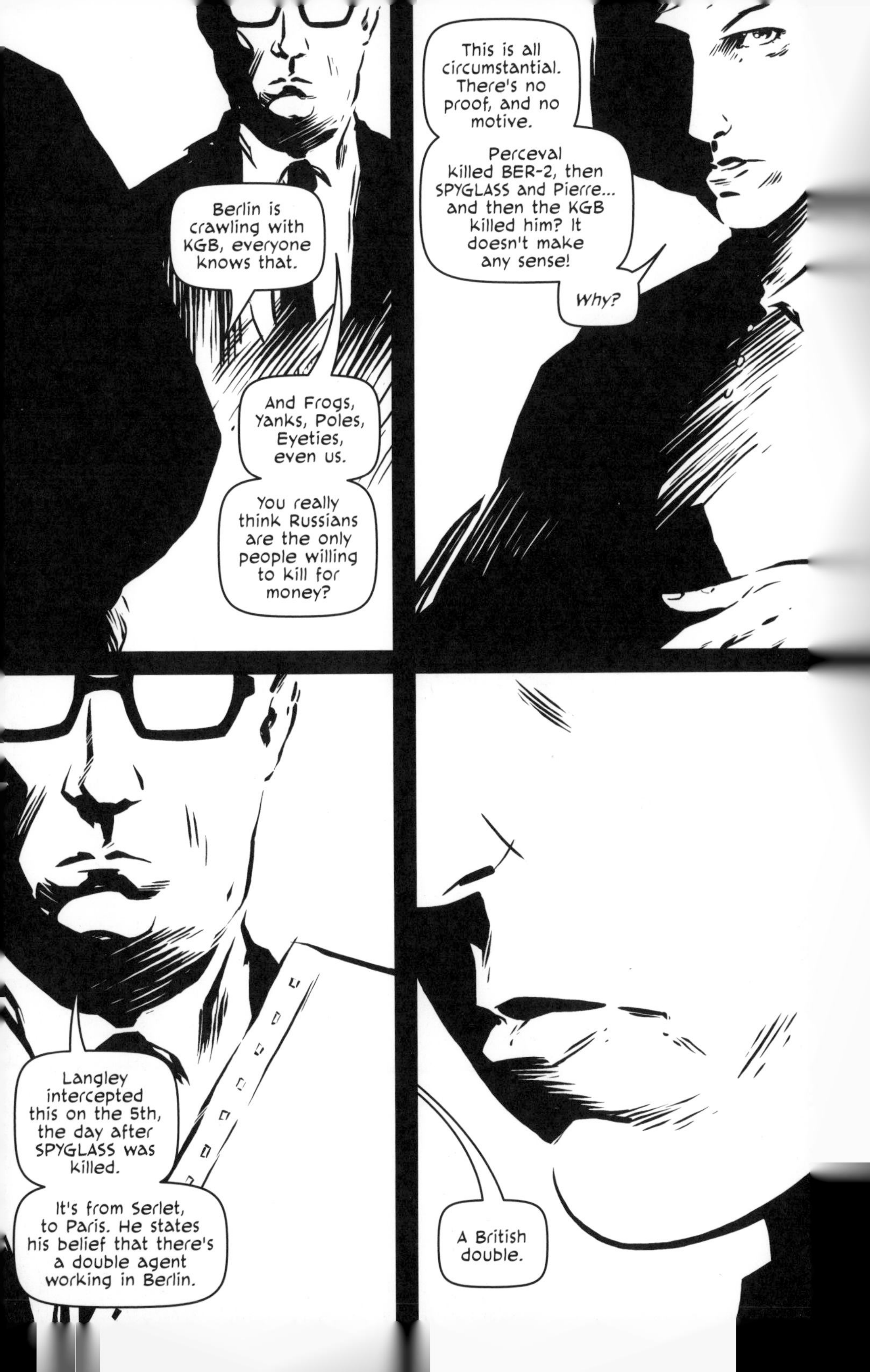
Berlin is crawling with KGB, everyone knows that.
And Frogs, Yanks, Poles, Eyeties, even us.
You really think Russians are the only people willing to kill for money?
This is all circumstantial. There's no proof, and no motive.
Perceval killed BER-2, then SPYGLASS and Pierre... and then the KGB killed him? It doesn't make any sense!
Why?
Langley intercepted this on the 5th, the day after SPYGLASS was killed.
It's from Serlet, to Paris. He states his belief that there's a double agent working in Berlin.
A British double.

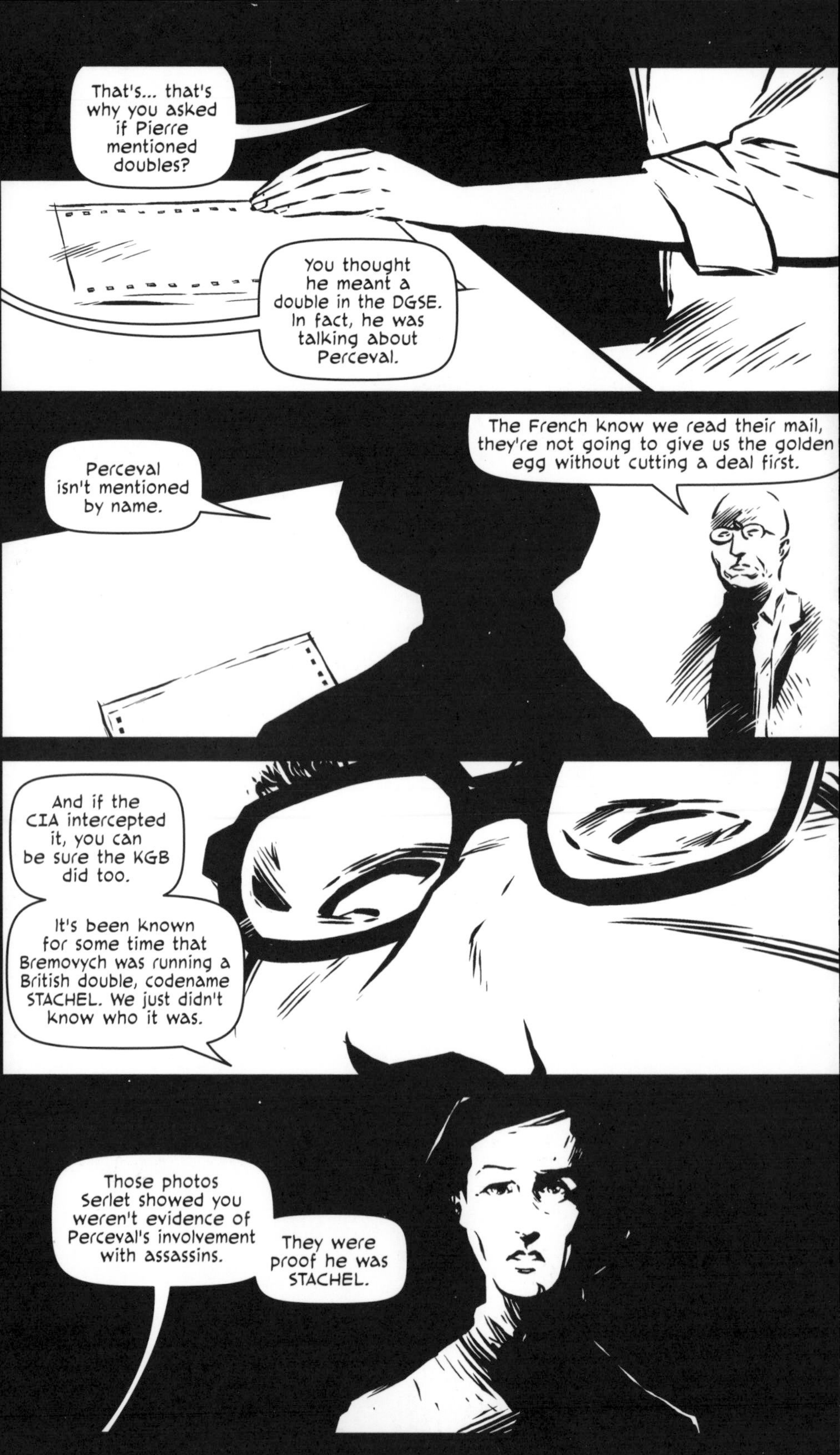
That's... that's why you asked if Pierre mentioned doubles?
You thought he meant a double in the DGSE. In fact, he was talking about Perceval.
Perceval isn't mentioned by name.
The French know we read their mail, they're not going to give us the golden egg without cutting a deal first.
And if the CIA intercepted it, you can be sure the KGB did too.
It's been known for some time that Bremovych was running a British double, codename STACHEL. We just didn't know who it was.
Those photos Serlet showed you weren't evidence of Perceval's involvement with assassins.
They were proof he was STACHEL.

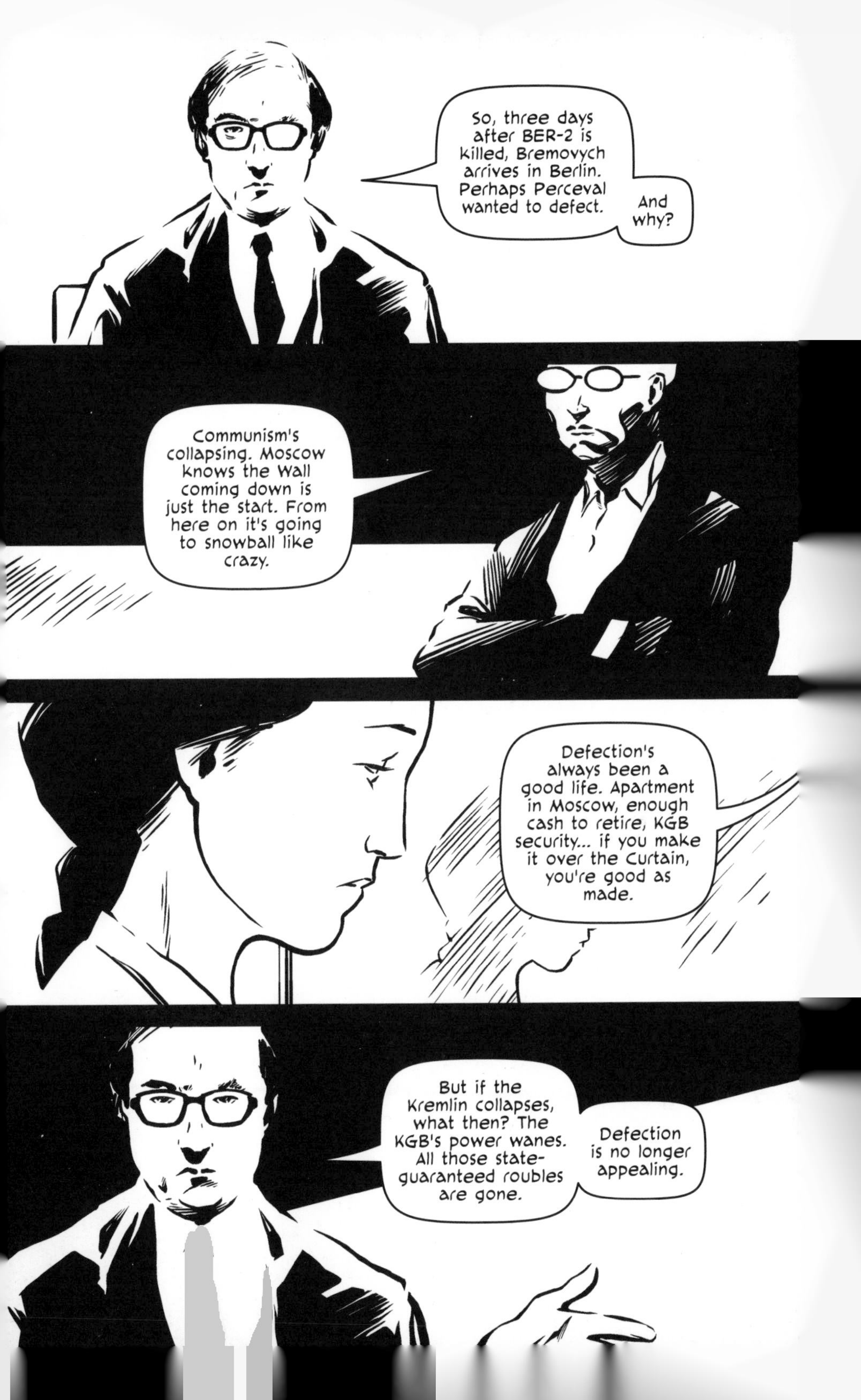
So, three days after BER-2 is killed, Bremovych arrives in Berlin. Perhaps Perceval wanted to defect.
And why?
Communism's collapsing. Moscow knows the Wall coming down is just the start. From here on it's going to snowball like crazy.
Defection's always been a good life. Apartment in Moscow, enough cash to retire, KGB security... if you make it over the Curtain, you're good as made.
But if the Kremlin collapses, what then? The KGB's power wanes. All those state-guaranteed roubles are gone.
Defection is no longer appealing.

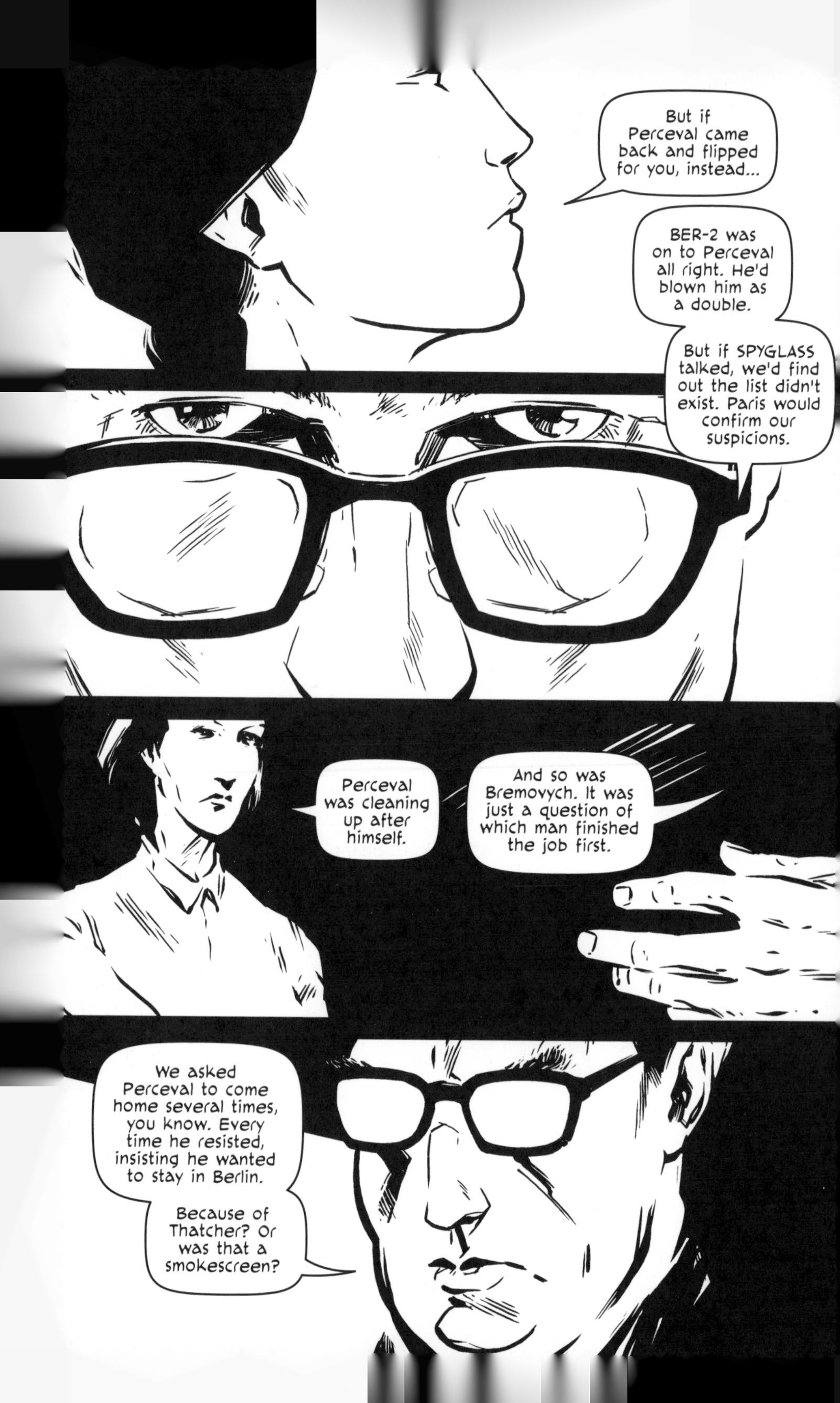

But if Perceval came back and flipped for you, instead...
BER-2 was on to Perceval all right. He'd blown him as a double.
But if SPYGLASS talked, we'd find out the list didn't exist. Paris would confirm our suspicions.
Perceval was cleaning up after himself.
And so was Bremovych. It was just a question of which man finished the job first.
We asked Perceval to come home several times, you know. Every time he resisted, insisting he wanted to stay in Berlin.
Because of Thatcher? Or was that a smokescreen?

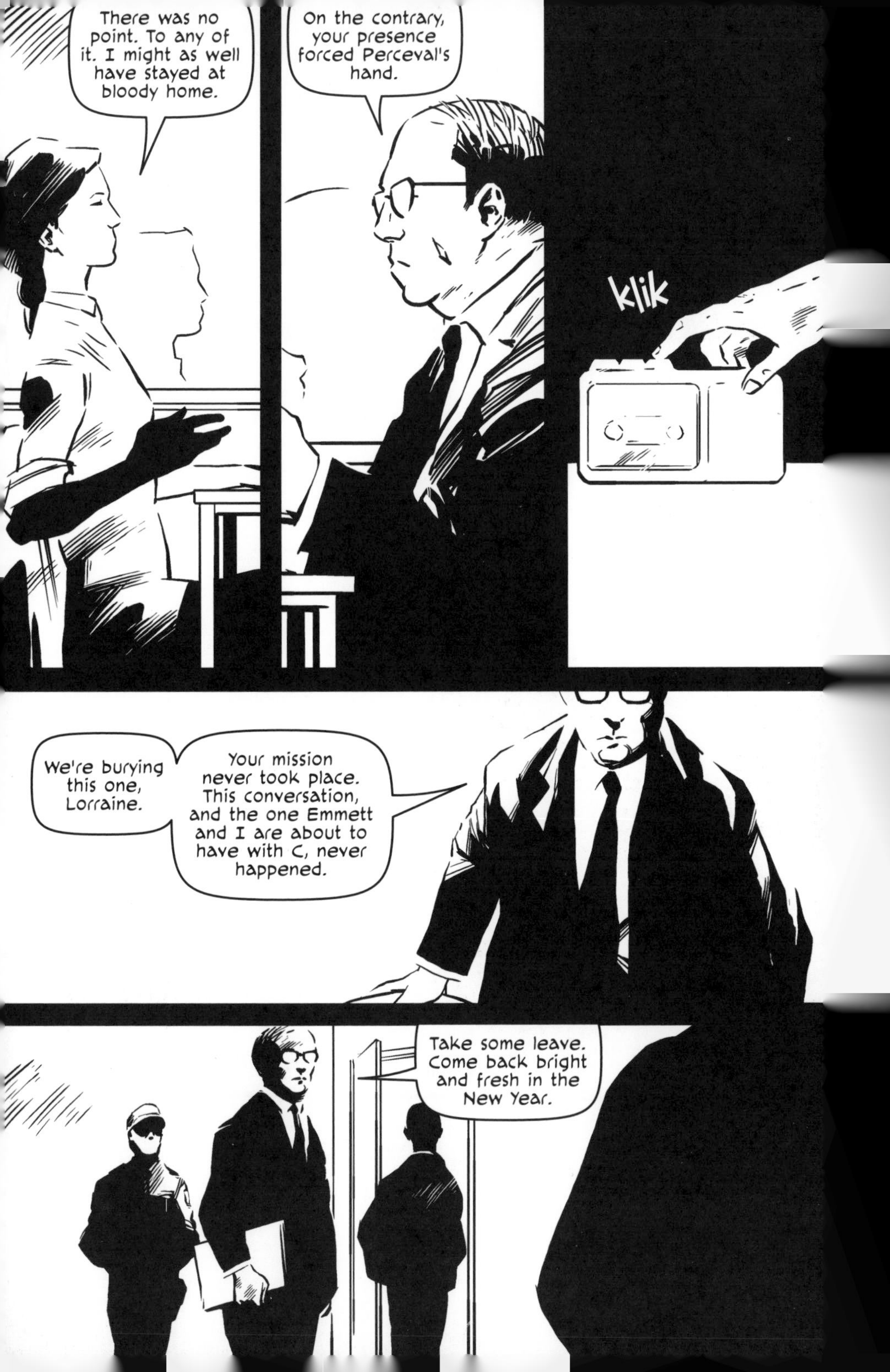
There was no point. To any of it. I might as well have stayed at bloody home.
On the contrary, your presence forced Perceval's hand.
klik
We're burying this one, Lorraine.
Your mission never took place. This conversation, and the one Emmett and I are about to have with C, never happened.
Take some leave. Come back bright and fresh in the New Year.

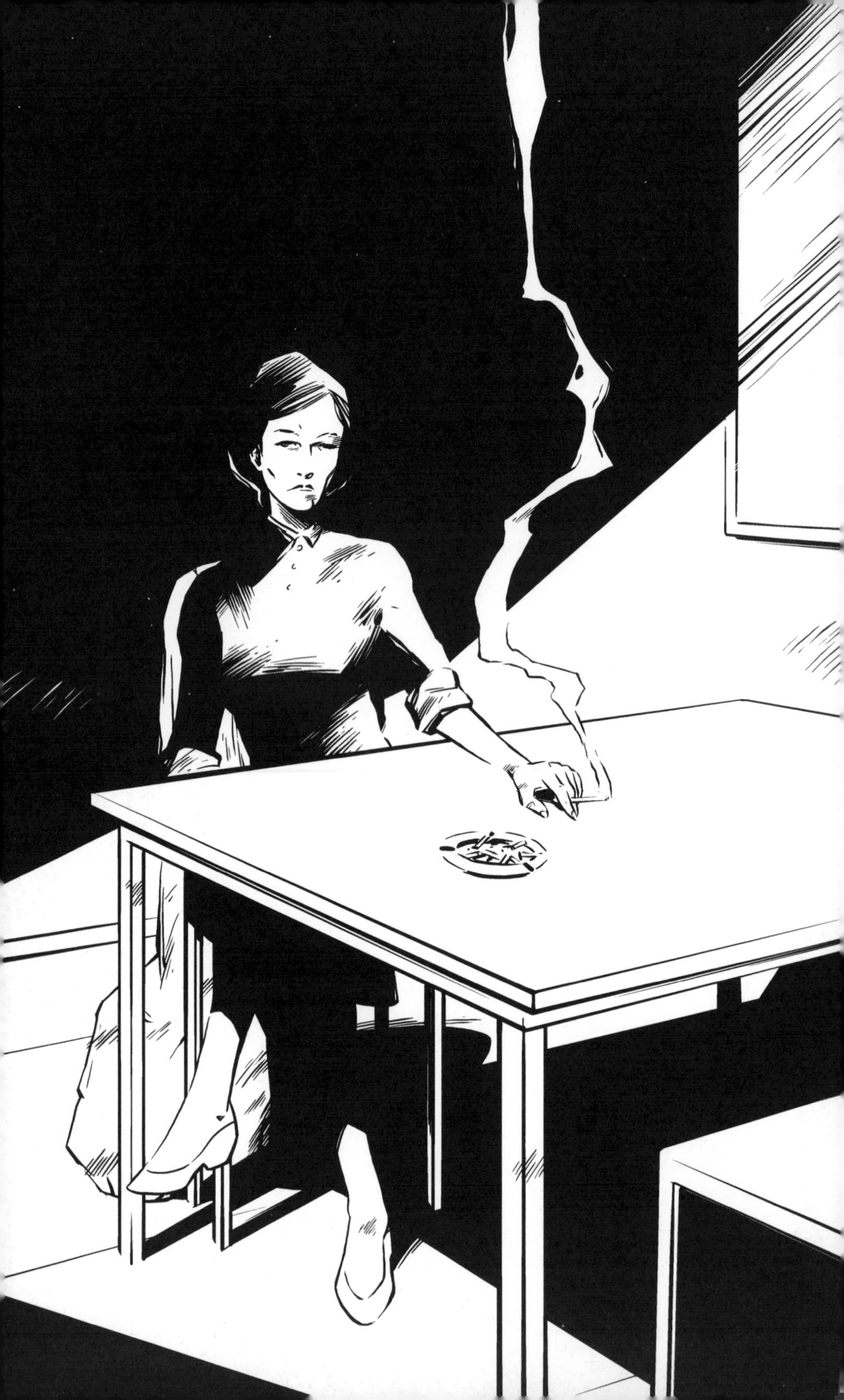

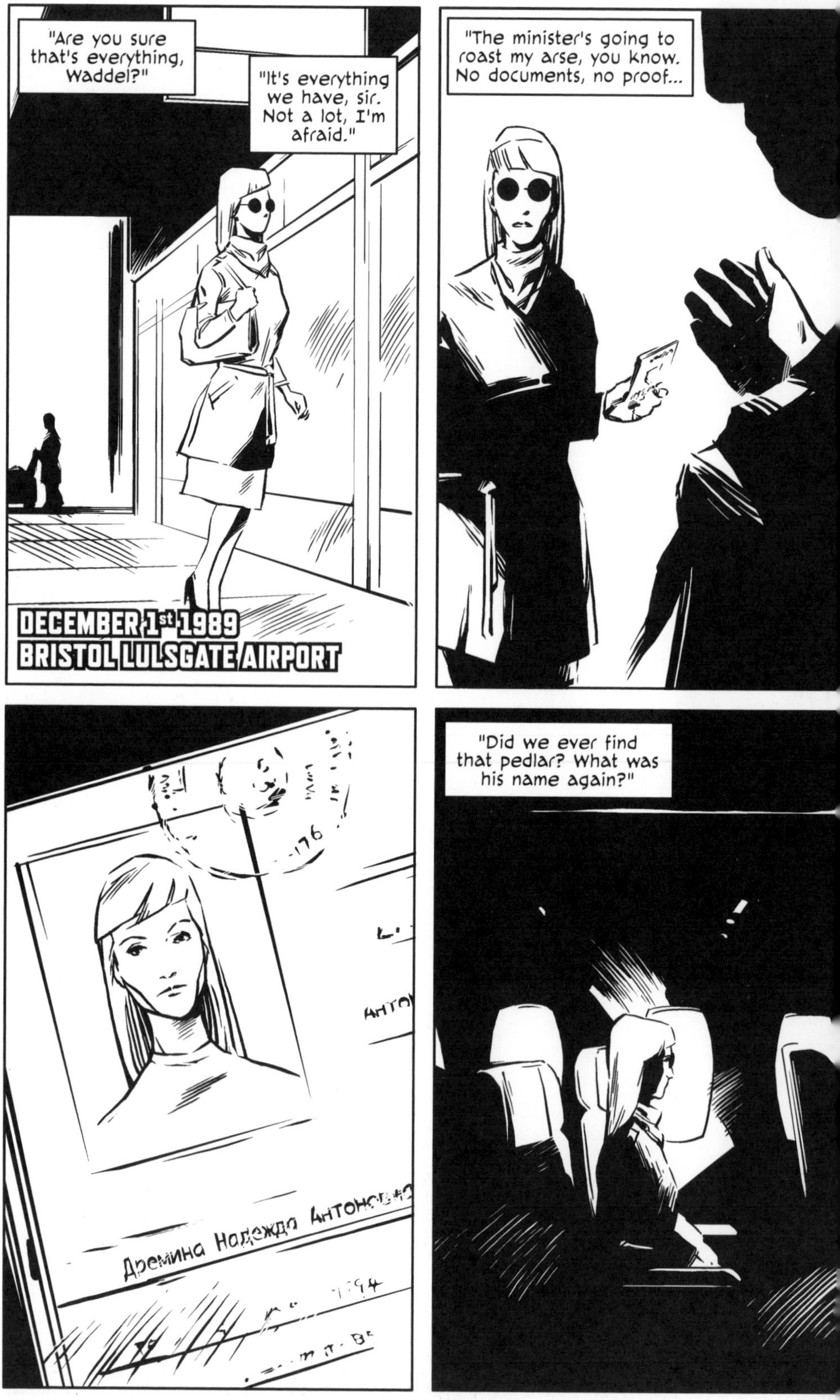
"Are you sure that's everything, Waddel?"
"It's everything we have, sir. Not a lot, I'm afraid."
DECEMBER 1st 1989
BRISTOL LULSGATE AIRPORT
"The minister's going to roast my arse, you know. No documents, no proof...
Дремина Надежда
"Did we ever find that pedlar? What was his name again?"

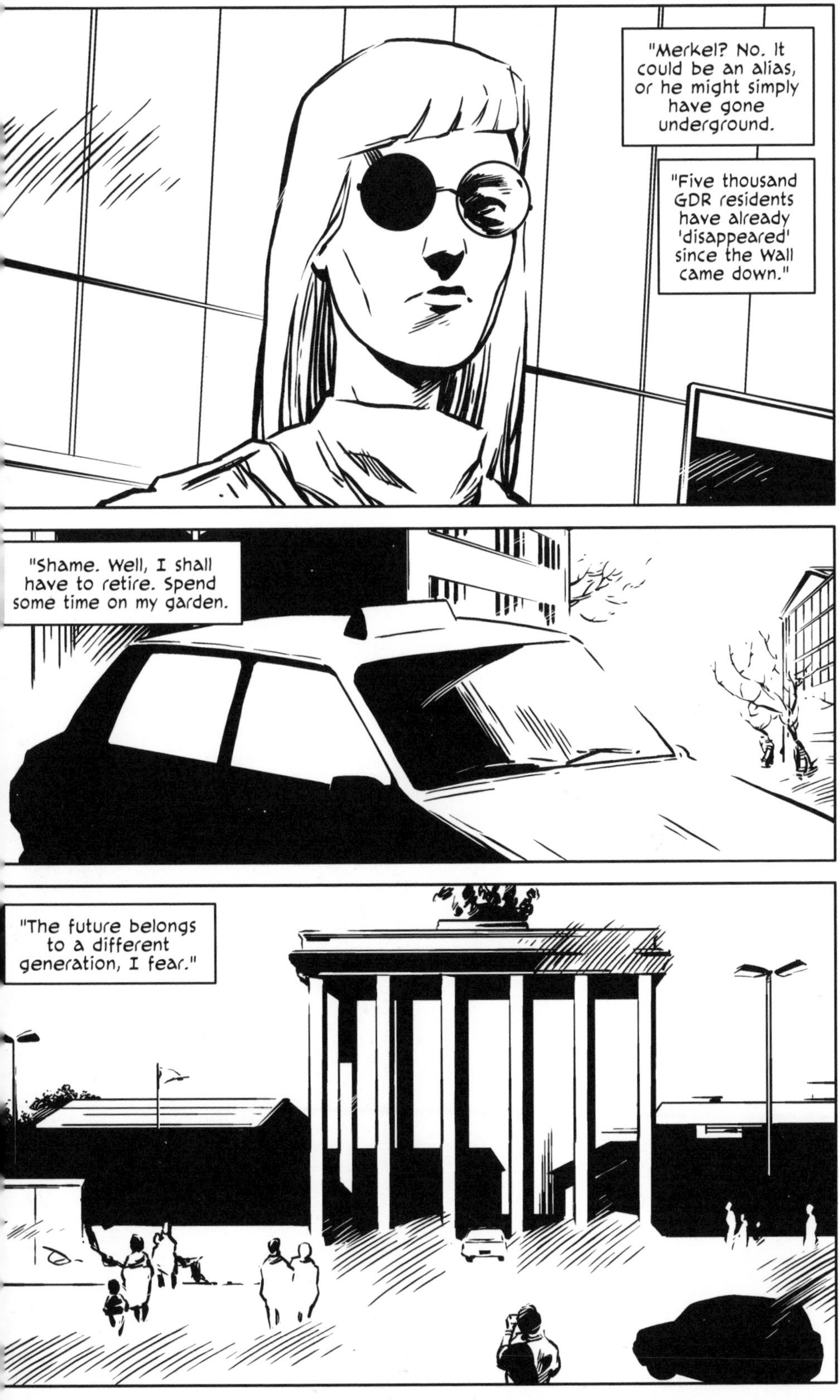
"Merkel? No. It could be an alias, or he might simply have gone underground.
"Five thousand GDR residents have already 'disappeared' since the Wall came down."
"Shame. Well, I shall have to retire. Spend some time on my garden.
"The future belongs to a different generation, I fear."

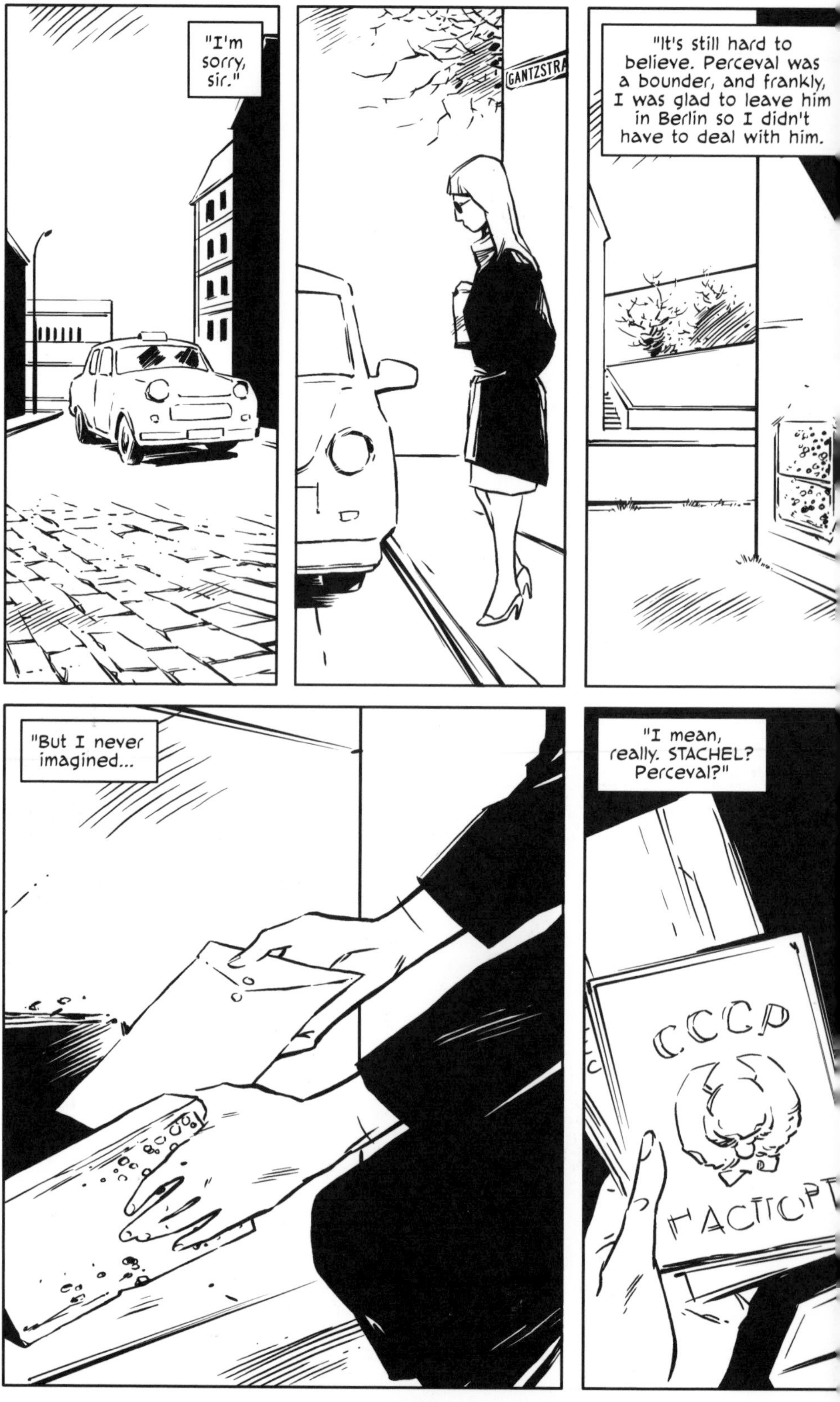
"I'm sorry, sir."
GANTZSTRA
"It's still hard to believe. Perceval was a bounder, and frankly, I was glad to leave him in Berlin so I didn't have to deal with him.
"But I never imagined...
"I mean, really. STACHEL? Perceval?"
CCCP

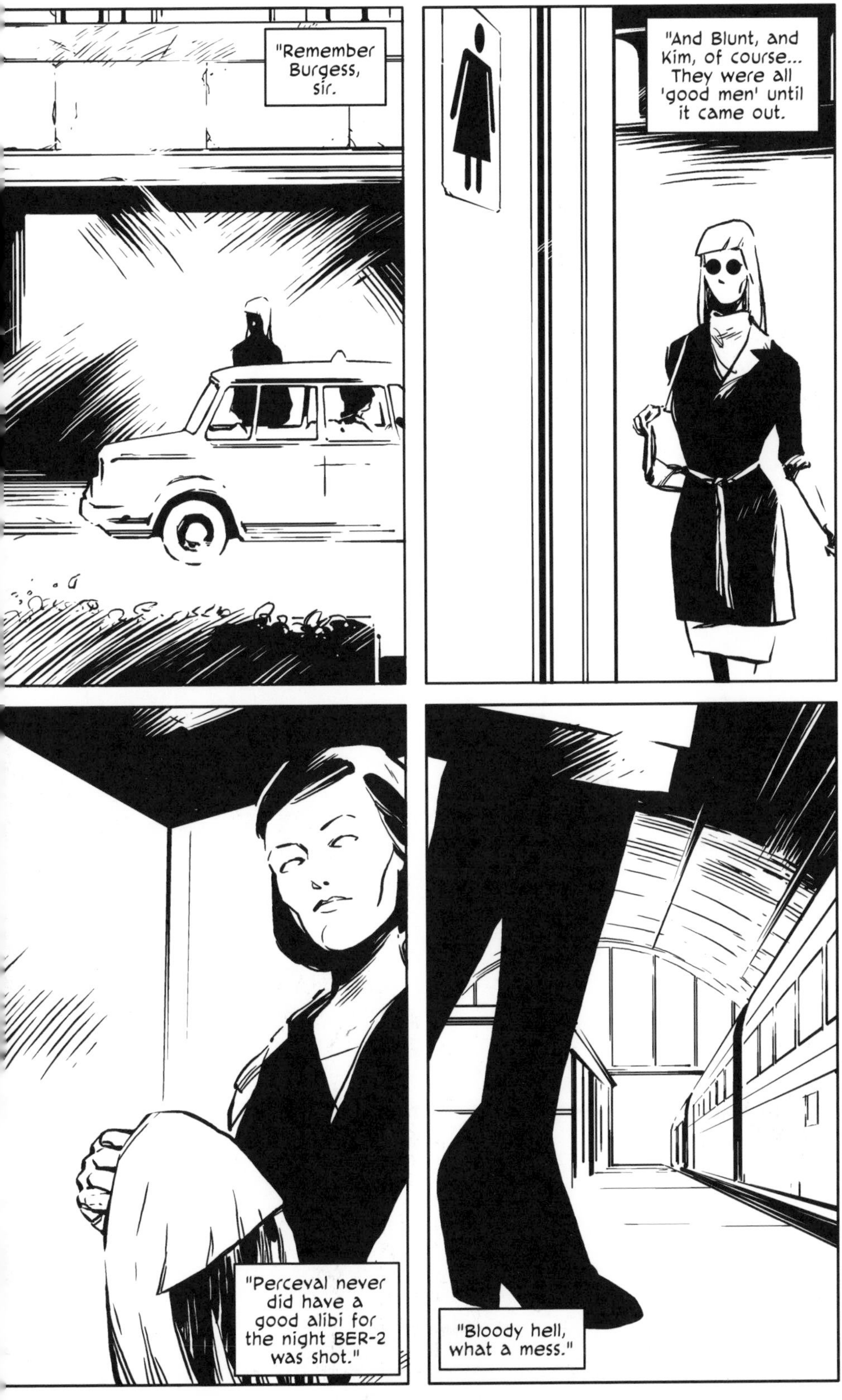
"Remember Burgess, sir.
"And Blunt, and Kim, of course... They were all 'good men' until it came out.
"Perceval never did have a good alibi for the night BER-2 was shot."
"Bloody hell, what a mess."

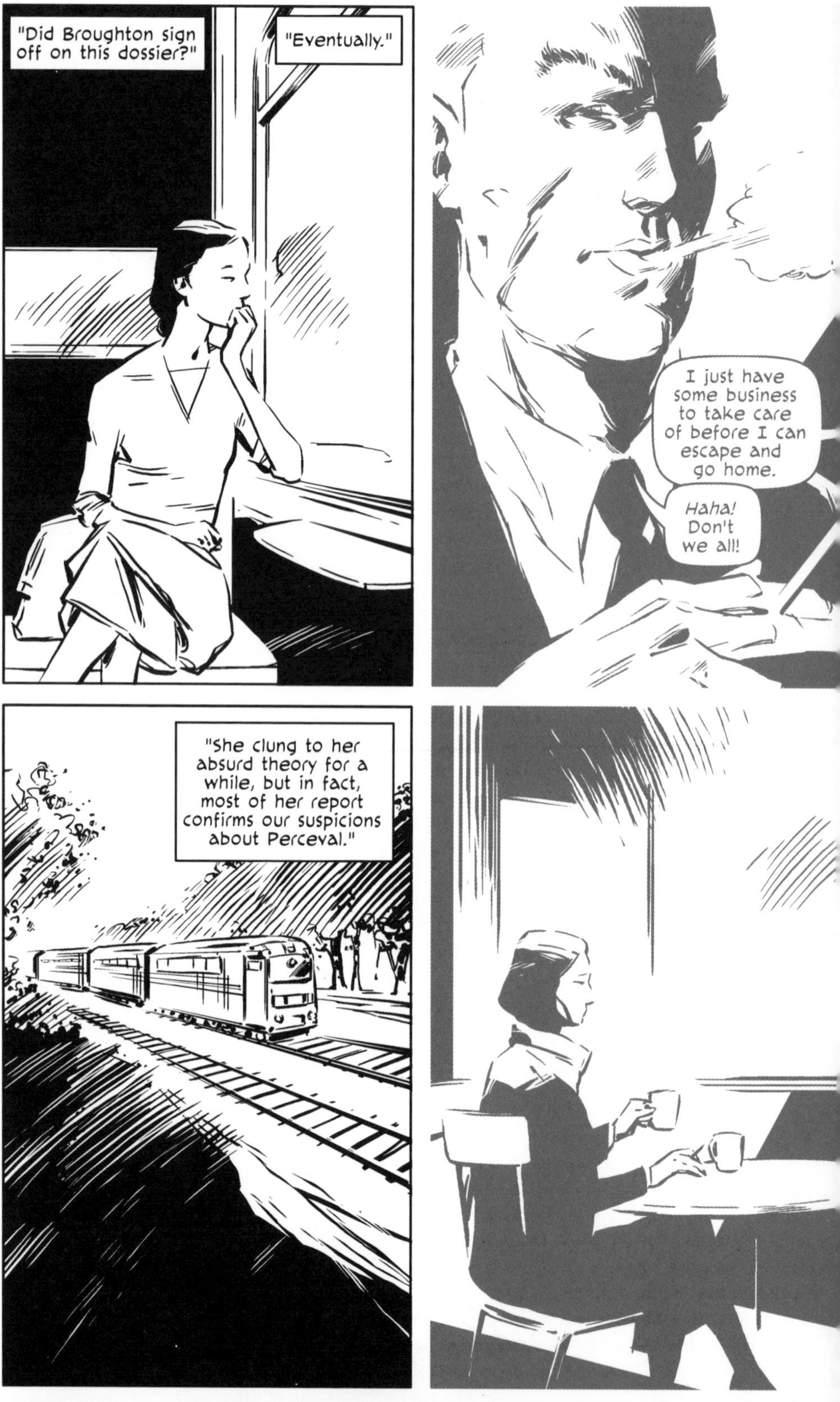
"Did Broughton sign off on this dossier?"
"Eventually."
I just have some business to take care of before I can escape and go home.
Haha! Don't we all!
"She clung to her absurd theory for a while, but in fact, most of her report confirms our suspicions about Perceval."

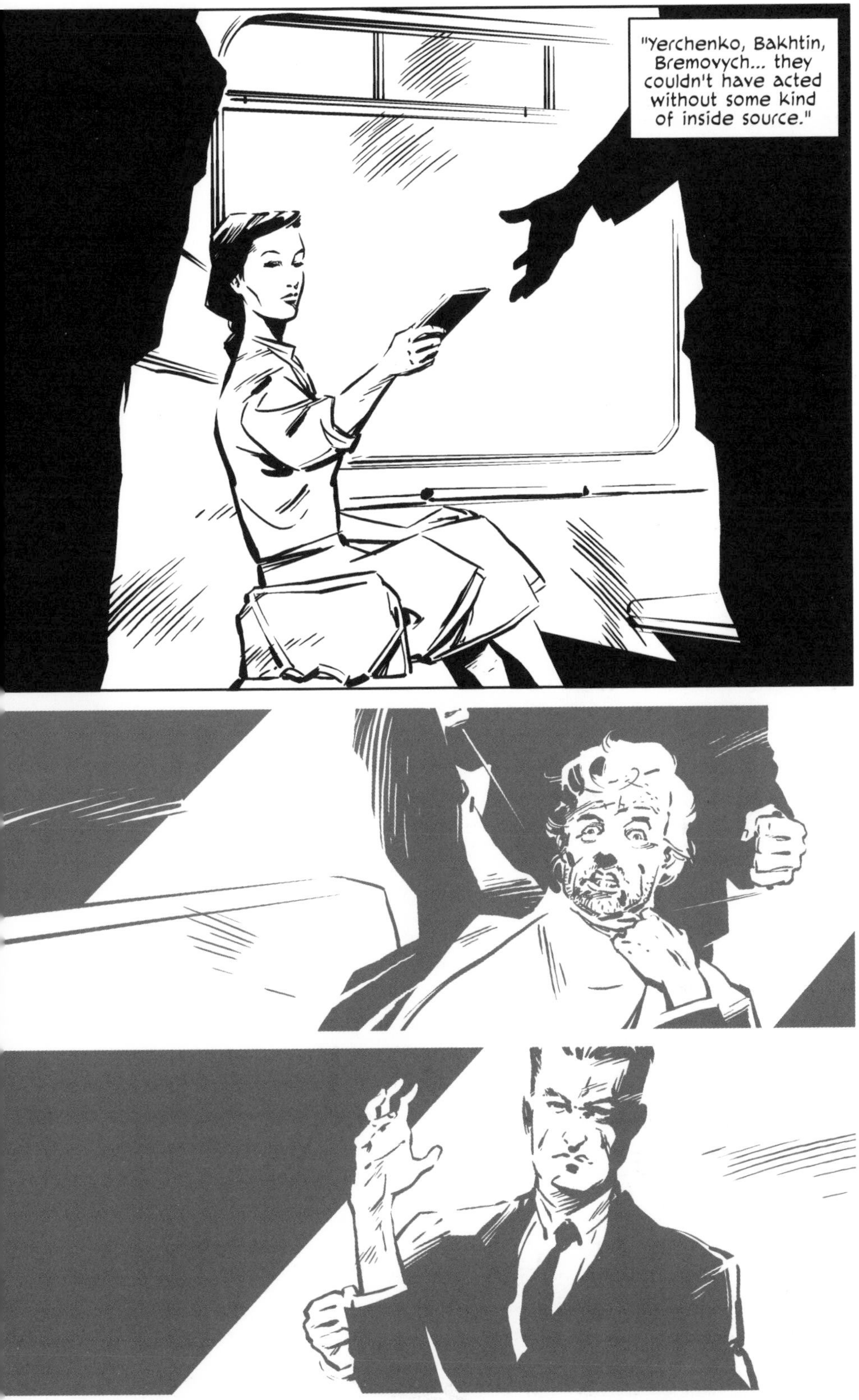
"Yerchenko, Bakhtin, Bremovych... they couldn't have acted without some kind of inside source."

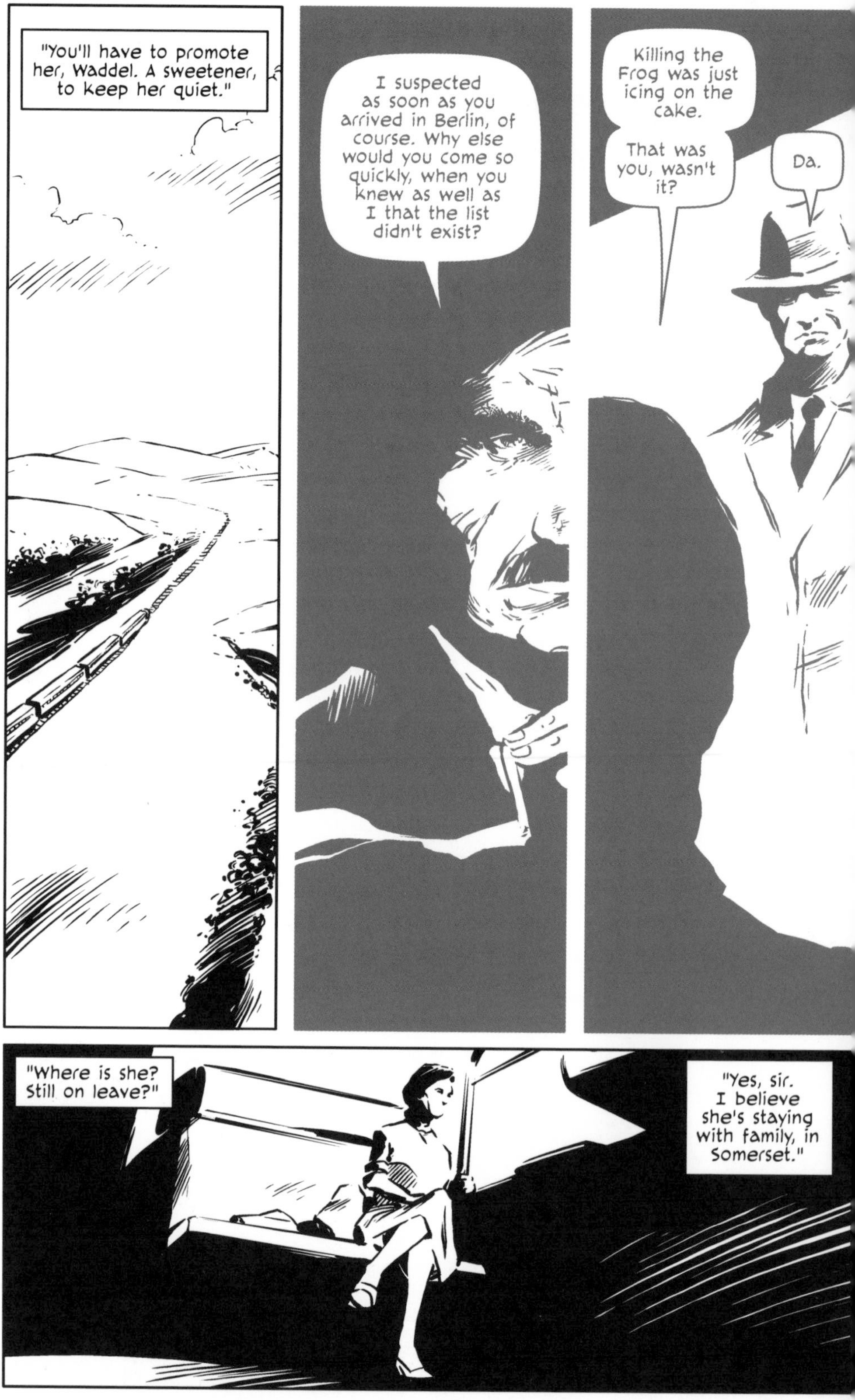
"You'll have to promote her, Waddel. A sweetener, to keep her quiet."
I suspected as soon as you arrived in Berlin, of course. Why else would you come so quickly, when you knew as well as I that the list didn't exist?
Killing the Frog was just icing on the cake.
That was you, wasn't it?
Da.
"Where is she? Still on leave?"
"Yes, sir. I believe she's staying with family, in Somerset."

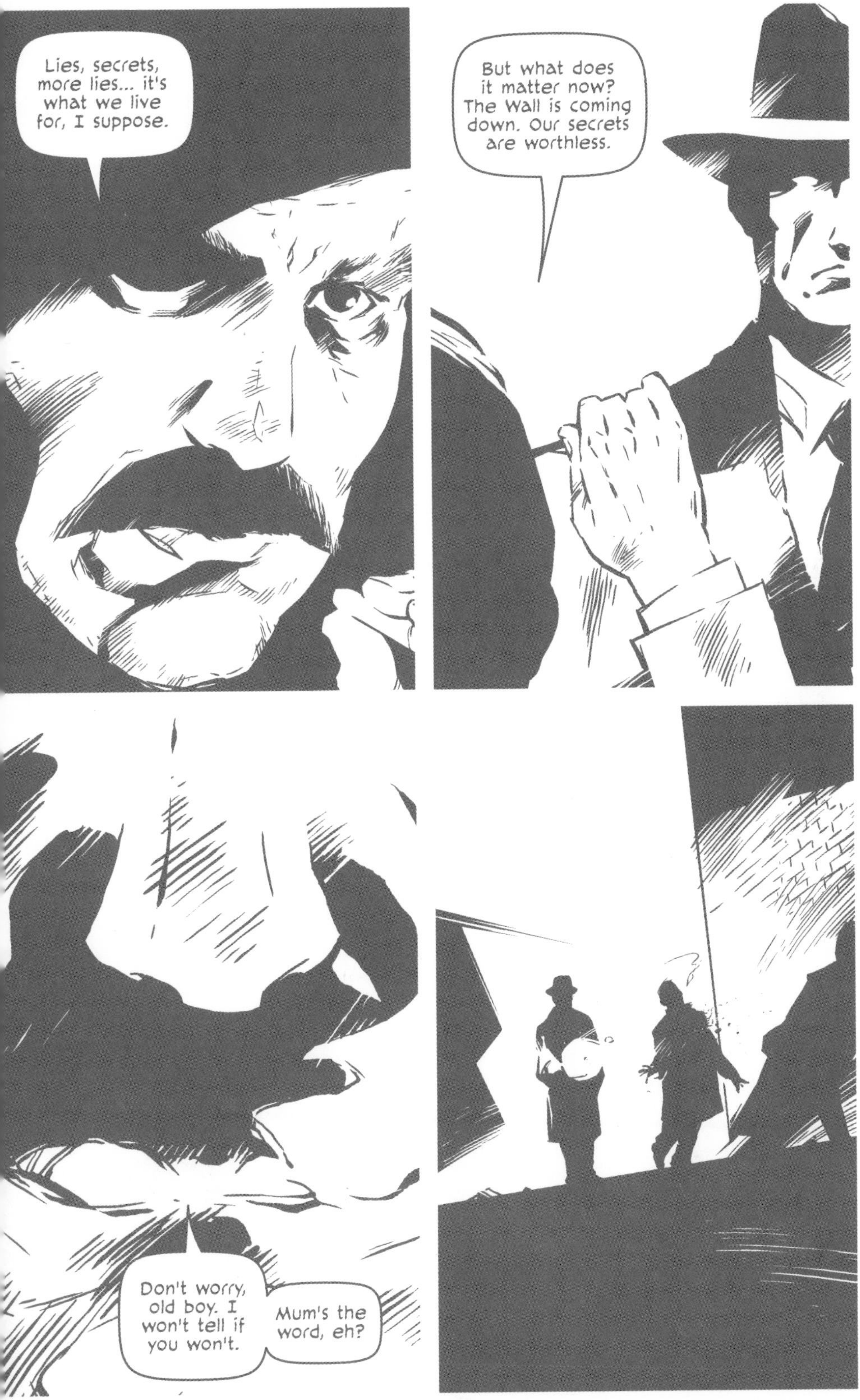
Lies, secrets, more lies... it's what we live for, I suppose.
But what does it matter now? The Wall is coming down. Our secrets are worthless.
Don't worry, old boy. I won't tell if you won't.
Mum's the word, eh?

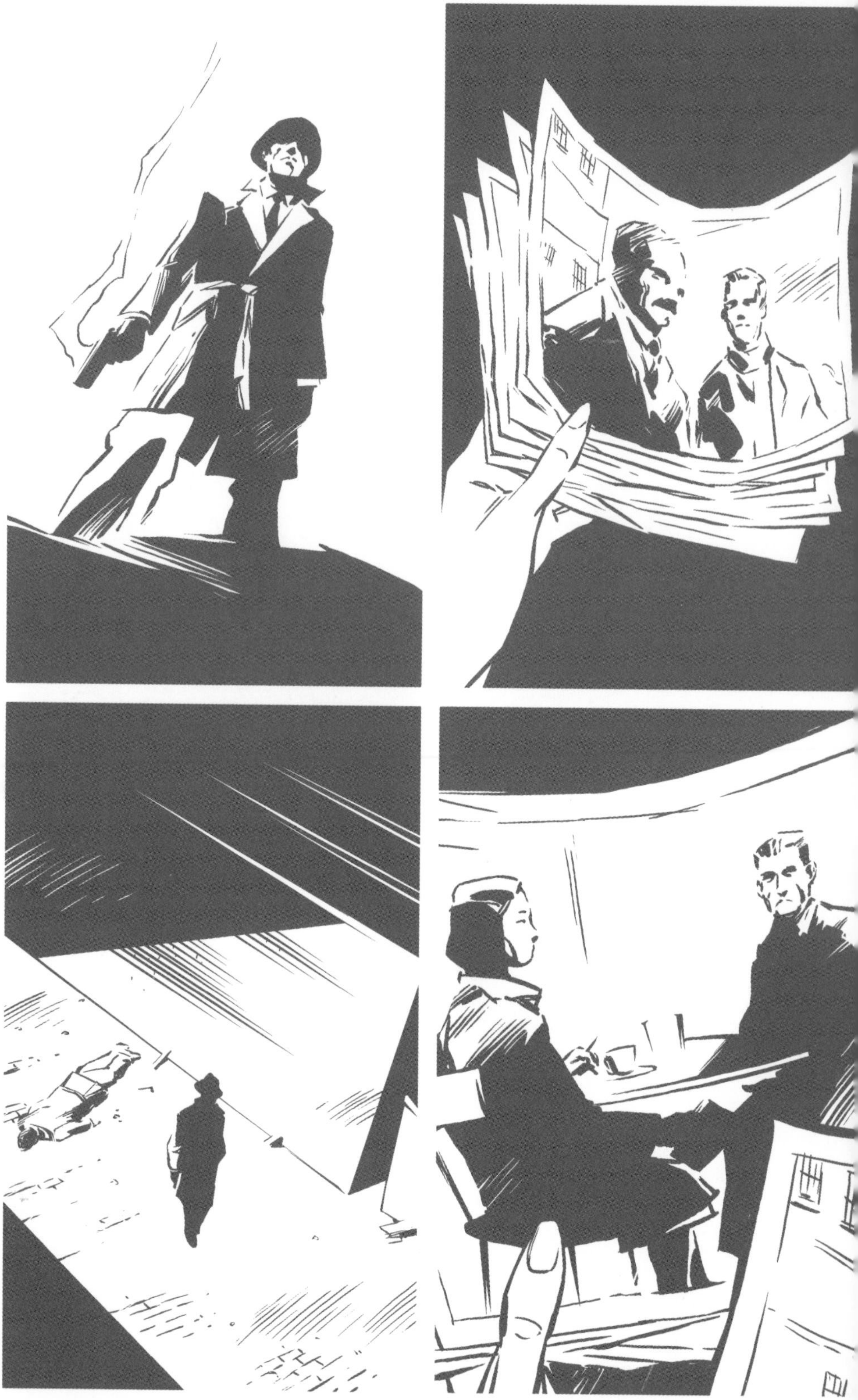

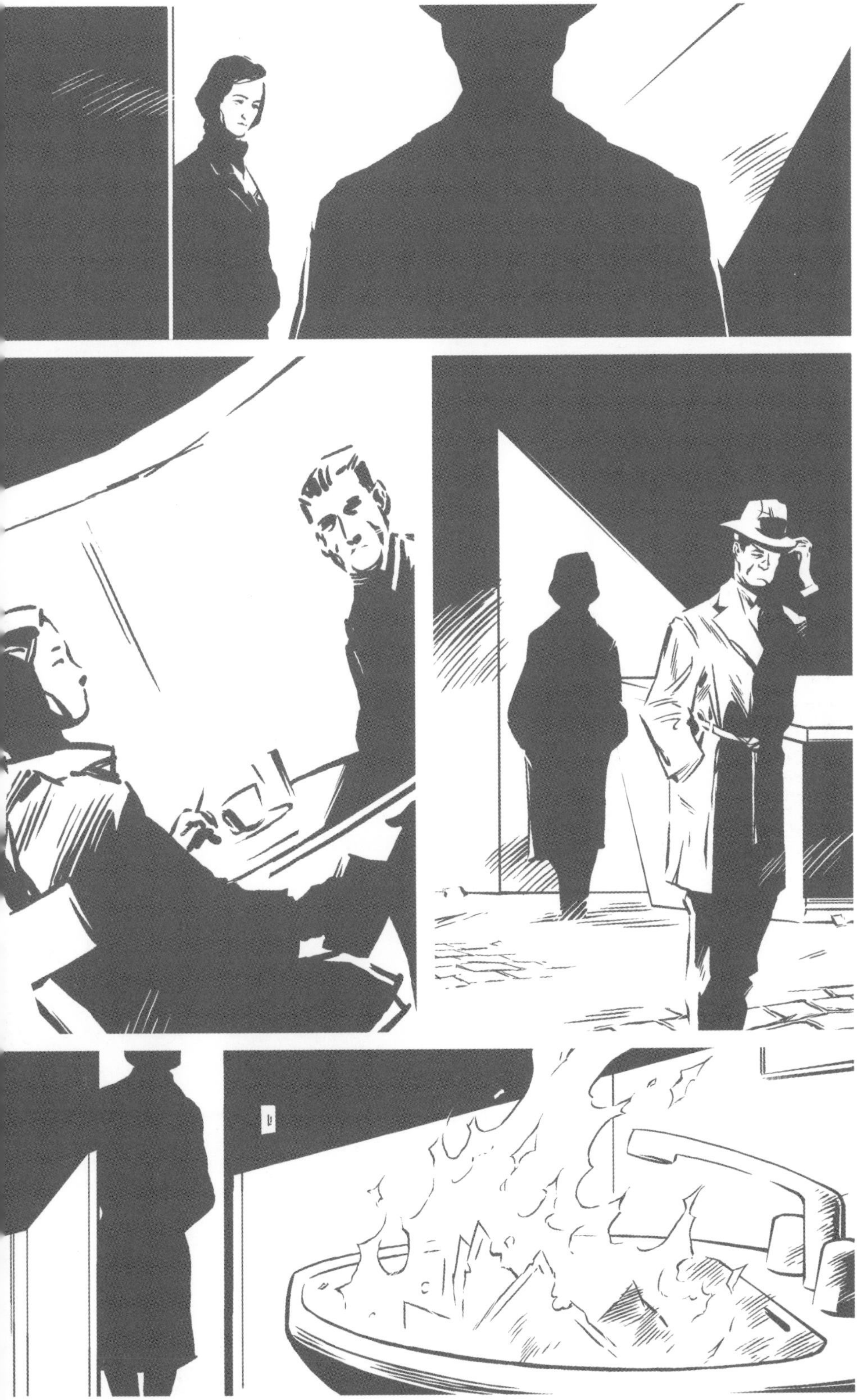

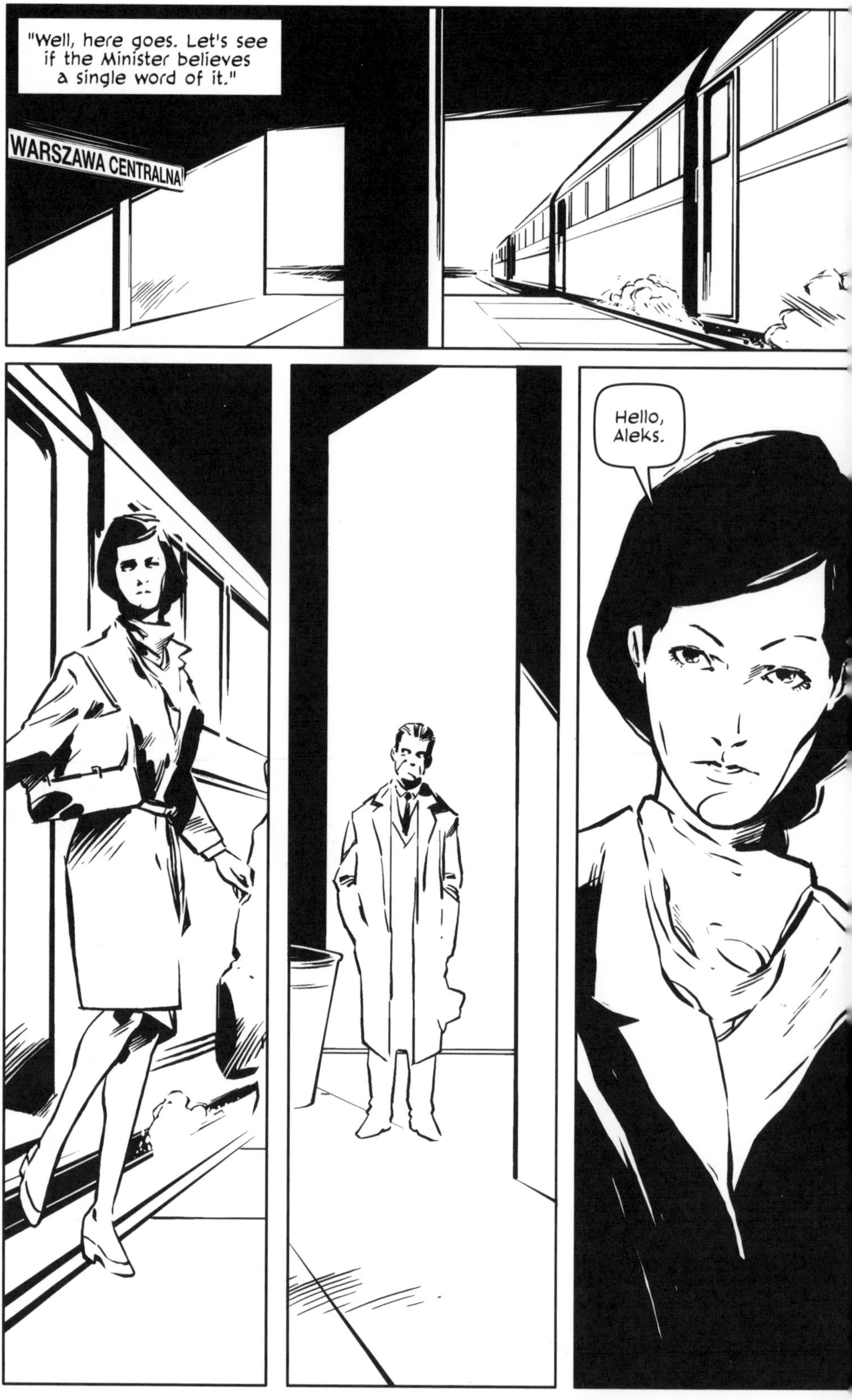
"Well, here goes. Let's see if the Minister believes a single word of it."
WARSZAWA CENTRALNA
Hello, Aleks.

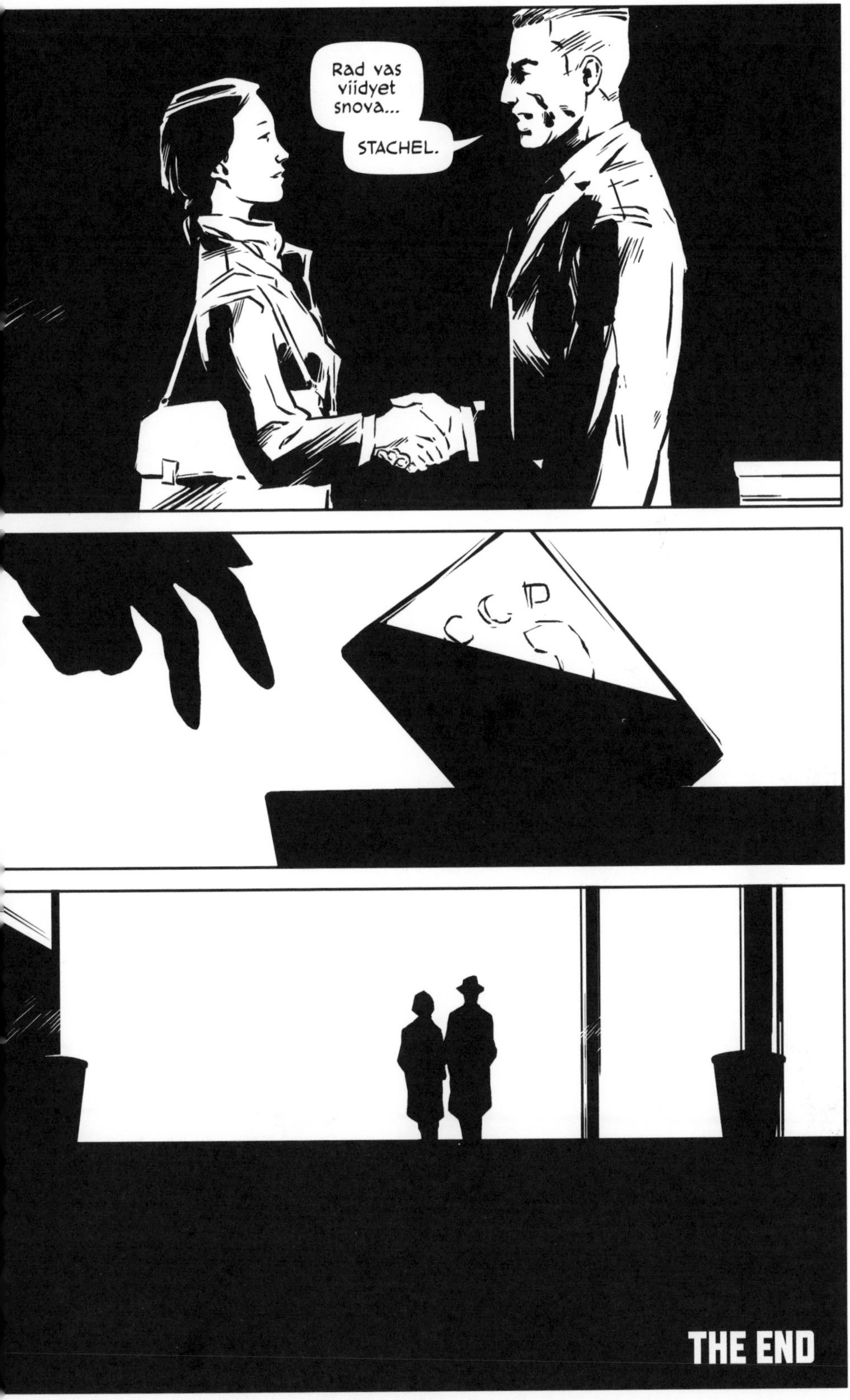
Rad vas viidyet snova...
STACHEL.
THE END

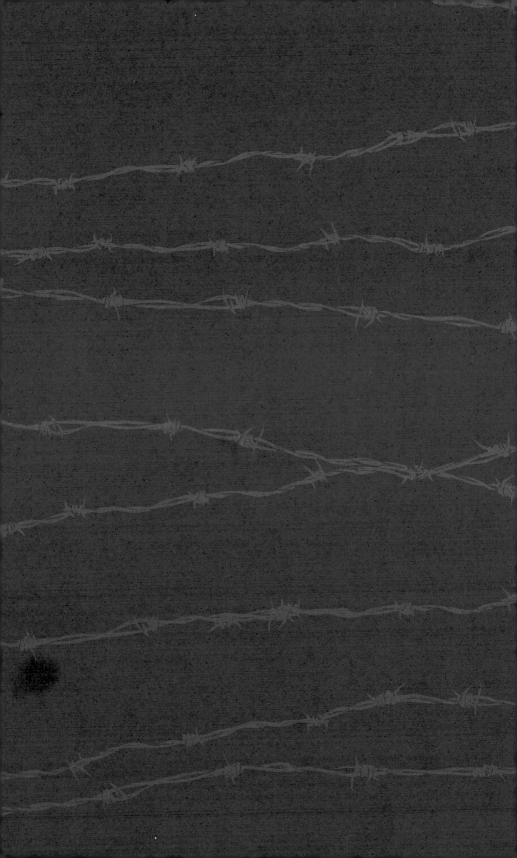

WRITTEN BY
ANTONY JOHNSTON

ILLUSTRATED BY
SAM HART

THE
COLDEST
CITY

LETTERED BY
ED BRISSON

DESIGN BY
KEITH WOOD

EDITED BY
CHARLIE CHU

Published by Oni Press, Inc.

PUBLISHER **JOE NOZEMACK**

EDITOR IN CHIEF **JAMES LUCAS JONES**

ART DIRECTOR **KEITH WOOD**

DIRECTOR OF MARKETING **CORY CASONI**

OPERATIONS DIRECTOR **GEORGE ROHAC**

EDITOR **JILL BEATON**

EDITOR **CHARLIE CHU**

DIGITAL PREPRESS **TROY LOOK**

ONI PRESS, INC.
1305 SE Martin Luther King Jr. Blvd.
Suite A
Portland, OR 97214
USA

onipress.com • thecoldestcity.com
antonyjohnston.com • samhartgraphics.com

First edition: May 2012

ISBN: 978-1-934964-53-8
Library of Congress Control Number: 2011933115

1 3 5 7 9 10 8 6 4 2

PRINTED IN CHINA

ANTONY JOHNSTON

Antony Johnston is an award-winning, *New York Times* bestselling author of comics, graphic novels, video games and books, with titles including *Wasteland*, *Daredevil*, *Dead Space*, *Julius*, and *Frightening Curves*. He has also adapted books by bestselling novelist Anthony Horowitz, collaborated with comics legend Alan Moore, and reinvented Marvel's flagship character Wolverine for manga. His titles have been translated throughout the world and optioned for film. He lives and works in England.

antonyjohnston.com

SAM HART

Sam Hart – born in the UK, lives in Brazil. Works with newspaper and magazine illustration, and advertising storyboards. Enjoys historical fiction and myths. Comic art credits include *Starship Troopers*, *Judge Dredd*, *Outlaw: The Legend of Robin Hood* and *Excalibur: The Legend of King Arthur*.

samhartgraphics.com

ALSO BY ANTONY JOHNSTON AND ONI PRESS!

WASTELAND: THE APOCALYPTIC EDITION VOLUME 1
By Antony Johnston & Christopher Mitten
384 Pages · Hardcover · B&W + A Bonus Color Section
$34.99 US · ISBN 978-1-934964-19-4

WASTELAND: THE APOCALYPTIC EDITION VOLUME 2
By Antony Johnston & Christopher Mitten
360 Pages · Hardcover · B&W + A Bonus Color Section
$34.99 US · ISBN 978-1-934964-46-0

QUEEN & COUNTRY DEFINITIVE EDITION, VOLUME 1
By Greg Rucka, Steve Rolston, Brian Hurtt &
Leandro Fernandez
366 pages · 6"x9" trade paperback · B&W
$19.99 US · ISBN 978-1-932664-87-4

QUEEN & COUNTRY DEFINITIVE EDITION, VOLUME 2
By Greg Rucka, Jason Alexander, Carla Speed McNeil &
Mike Hawthorne
344 pages · 6"x9" Trade Paperback, · B&W
$19.99 US · ISBN 978-1-932664-89-8

QUEEN & COUNTRY DEFINITIVE EDITION, VOLUME 3
By Greg Rucka, Steve Rolston, Mike Norton &
Chris Samnee
408 pages · 6"x9" Trade Paperback · B&W
$19.95 US · ISBN 978-1-932664-96-6

QUEEN & COUNTRY DEFINITIVE EDITION, VOLUME 4
By Greg Rucka, Antony Johnston, Brian Hurtt,
Rick Burchett & Christopher Mitten
296 pages · 6"x9" Trade Paperback · B&W
$19.95 US · ISBN 978-1-934964-13-2

PETROGRAD
By Philip Gelatt & Tyler Crook
264 pages · 6"x9" Hardcover · 2 color
$29.99 US · ISBN 978-1-934964-44-6

YOU HAVE KILLED ME
By Jamie S. Rich & Joëlle Jones
192 pages · Hardcover· B&W
$19.95 US · ISBN 978-1-932664-88-1

REVOLUTI**ONI**ZE COMICS
www.onipress.com

For more information on these and other fine Oni Press
comic books and graphic novels, visit www.onipress.com.

To find a comic specialty store in your area, call
1-888-COMICBOOK or visit www.comicshops.us.

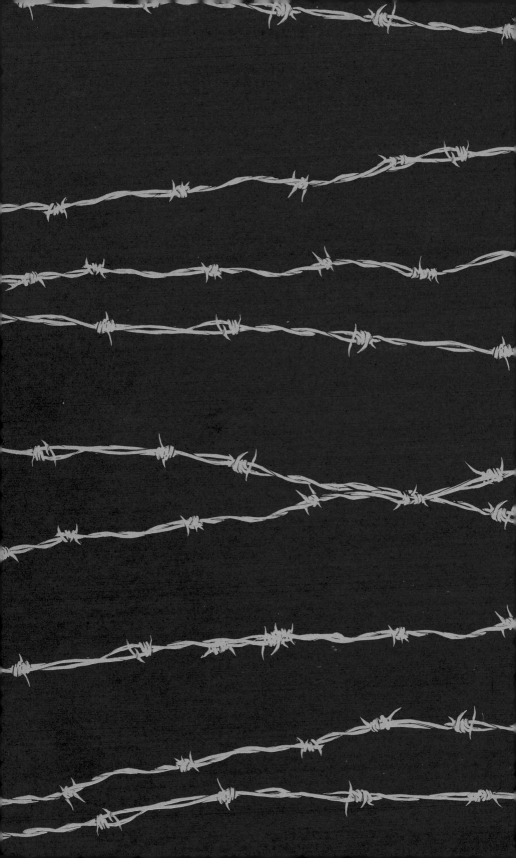